Royal Sunset

ROYAL SUNSET

The European Dynasties and the Great War

GORDON BROOK-SHEPHERD

DOUBLEDAY & COMPANY, INC.
GARDEN CITY, NEW YORK
1987

Library of Congress Cataloging-in-Publication Data

Brook-Shepherd, Gordon, 1918–
Royal sunset.

Includes index.
1. World War, 1914–1918—Causes.   2. Europe—Kings
and rulers—History—19th century.   3. Europe—Kings and
rulers—History—20th century.   I. Title.
D511.B7345 1987 940.3'112   86-19859
ISBN 0-385-19849-3

CONTENTS

Illustrations   vii
Foreword   ix

INTRODUCTION: Wedding in Berlin   xvii

PART ONE: THE POWDER KEG
1 Montenegro: King of the Black Mountains   3
2 Serbia: Many Princes, One Crown   18
3 Serbia: The Fatal Crusade   34
4 Bulgaria: The Balkan Fox   47
5 Rumania: Prussian Iron   69

PART TWO: MONARCHIES OF THE CENTRE
6 Germany: The Volcano of Europe   83
7 Germany: Imperial Fantasy   98
8 Austria: The Golden Prince   117
9 Austria: The Stone Idol   133
10 Italy: The Make-weight Kingdom   157

PART THREE: MONARCHIES ON THE WINGS
11 Russia: The Alien Giant   183
12 Russia: End of the Line   197
13 England: The Widow's Heritage   221
14 England: The Uncle of Europe   244

PART FOUR: END GAME
15 Fatal Gambits   279
16 King's Mate   306

Notes   331
Index   342

ILLUSTRATIONS

Between pages 74 and 75

Nicholas of Montenegro with his daughters and sons-in-law (Roger Viollet)

Cetinje, capital of Montenegro (BBC Hulton Picture Library)

Alexander I of Serbia (BBC Hulton Picture Library)

Queen Draga of Serbia (Roger Viollet)

Nicholas Pašić (BBC Hulton Picture Library)

Ferdinand I, King of the Bulgarians, with the four children by his first marriage (Roger Viollet)

Carol I and Queen Elisabeth of Rumania (Roger Viollet)

William II, The German Emperor, with his six sons (BBC Hulton Picture Library)

Otto von Bismarck (BBC Hulton Picture Library)

Empress Augusta Victoria of Germany with her eldest daughter, Victoria Louise (Weidenfeld & Nicolson)

Ferdinand I, King of the Bulgarians, with William II (BBC Hulton Picture Library)

Edward VII of England with William II (reproduced by gracious permission of Her Majesty The Queen)

George V of England with William II of Germany (reproduced by gracious permission of Her Majesty The Queen)

Franz Josef of Austria with the Archduke Franz Ferdinand (Austrian Nationalbibliothek)

Franz Josef of Austria (Austrian Nationalbibliothek)

Between pages 266 and 267

Archduke Franz Ferdinand with his wife Sophie (Austrian National-
  bibliothek)
Victor Emmanuel III and Queen Elena of Italy (Roger Viollet)
The Rumanian and Russian royal families (Mary Evans Picture
  Library)
Nicholas II and Alexandra of Russia at Spala (Mansell Collection)
Nicholas II and Alexandra of Russia in national dress (Mansell
  Collection)
Nicholas II of Russia with his two eldest daughters, Olga and
  Tatiana (Roger Viollet)
Queen Victoria of England and William II with some of their
  Anglo-German relations (reproduced by gracious permission of
  Her Majesty The Queen)
Edward VII of England and Franz Josef of Austria at Marienbad
  (reproduced by gracious permission of Her Majesty The Queen)
Edward VII of England at the daily morning gathering in front of
  Marienbad's mineral baths (Gordon Brook-Shepherd)
Prince George of Wales and Nicholas II of Russia (BBC Hulton
  Picture Library)
Colonel Dragutin Dimitriević with his aides (Roger Viollet)
Franz Josef of Austria with Archduke Franz Ferdinand (Austrian
  Nationalbibliothek)

Page xv
Europe: The Rival Camps

FOREWORD

This book attempts – so far as I am aware it is the first attempt – to portray the long run-up and final slide into the Great War from the standpoint of the dynasties, rather than the governments immediately involved. It has been written partly to satisfy my own curiosity. Ever since, more years ago than I care to remember, I studied the origins of that war as a special subject in my Cambridge Historical Tripos, I have been intrigued by one great puzzle which surrounds these monarchs and their courts and families. How was it that rulers, mostly related by blood or marriage and all dedicated to the preservation of kingship, allowed themselves to slip into a fratricidal bloodbath which wiped several of them out of existence and left all the survivors weakened?

At the heart of the puzzle lies the fact that, at least on the continent, they had the power to prevent the catastrophe as well as the deepest self-interest to avoid it. Each of the three monarchs whose empire was to be obliterated by that war – Franz Josef of Austria, William II of Germany and Nicholas II of Russia – was an autocratic ruler. They had constitutions and parliaments of sorts (in the Tsar's case, a very feeble thing less than ten years old) but they alone could appoint and dismiss their ministers who were responsible directly to them. The German Kaiser had given proof enough of this by removing Chancellor Bismarck, the mightiest statesman of the age, from office with little more effort than he would have brushed a troublesome bluebottle from his sleeve. Above all, as commanders in chief, they, and only they, could declare war and sanction what, in those days, was the baleful herald of war, general mobilization.

If you believe (as I think the evidence still shows, despite the old 'war guilt' accusations as well as some modern 'revisionist' theories) that none of them wanted that war, let alone actually planned it, then you must examine the follies and blunders by which they let it happen. That means looking at their circles of palace advisers, their relations with their ministers, their links or rivalries with their dynasties, their own personal strengths and weaknesses and even, in some cases, their family quarrels and scandals. Only in this maze can one hope to find what it was which rendered them either so foolish or so blind when the final challenge came.

Nor can we deal only with the four great empires (the three already mentioned, plus the British) which were involved. The war was touched off at Sarajevo in the heart of the Balkans, by the murder of the Austrian heir-presumptive, Archduke Franz Ferdinand and his morganatic wife on 28 June 1914. But that Balkan fuse had been spluttering ominously ever since the day, nearly six years before, that Austria had annexed those provinces of Bosnia and Herzegovina where the archduke was to meet his death. The annexation crisis of 1908 was the prologue to the great tragedy. Its role is so crucial that it calls for examination from the standpoint of each of the empires and kingdoms involved.

The European rulers made up an extraordinary pastiche of monarchy. The three continental emperors, for example, stood in total contrast to each other. In Vienna, the eighty-four-year-old Franz Josef was presiding with weary grandeur over the decline of his bickering, failing, multi-national realm. In Berlin, on the other hand, his ally William II was buoyed up in his bombast and stirred into restlessness by a very young and very united nationalist empire which was bursting at the seams with military and economic energy. Their fellow emperor, but in the rival camp, Tsar Nicholas in St Petersburg, stood apart from them both: a well-meaning weakling chained to a giant wheel of fate. For better or for worse – and it was in all three cases for worse – it was their wives and their family problems which had helped to make them what they were.

The kings of the Balkan powder keg itself were an even more extraordinary collection. In Serbia we have two rival dynasties who, for the best part of a century, devoted themselves to intrigue and murder in their struggle for the crown. The primitive and tiny Montenegro is dominated throughout by one figure, Nicholas, or Nikita, a bandit princeling in a comic opera mountain kingdom which he nonetheless managed, by wiles and marriage pacts, to make important. In Bulgaria, we have the preposterous self-styled Tsar Ferdinand, the most repellent monarch in all Europe, his hands flashing with feminine jewellery and his Bourbon-Coburg brain seething with conspiracy. Aloof from them all, another foreign import reigned in Bucharest, the veteran Charles of Rumania, who remained a dour and upright Hohenzollern to the end of his days.

Finally, there is the crown of England, the island empire which gets drawn, against her will, ever closer to the European maelstrom as the story unfolds. Again, it is a tale of royal contrasts. Queen Victoria, widowed at forty-two, but already on her way to becoming the grandmother of Europe, tried to run foreign affairs as though they were her own family affairs. It was an approach which was intimate yet also dangerously remote, for the millions of words she wrote over the years to her ministers at home and her many royal relatives abroad rarely ever added up to effective diplomacy. The scene changed completely when, at her death in 1901, her son at last mounted the throne as Edward VII. He, too, nicknamed 'the uncle of Europe' was linked to nearly every court on the continent. But this was a man who chose to work by personal contact rather than by correspondence, and he deliberately widened his circle to include all the leading statesmen and diplomatists of the day, as well as their rulers. He was constantly on the move, a sort of royal salesman for England, and for peace. In the process, he often strained the bounds of constitutional monarchy and, on one or two famous occasions, burst out of them altogether.

At his death in 1910 another transformation came over Buckingham Palace. With the accession of George V, personal diplomacy by the crown of England disappeared (never to resurface again) as though it had fallen down a man-hole. King George felt not the slightest itch to meddle with foreign policy and was also quite uninterested in those European affairs which had so obsessed his father. The contrast is so great that it becomes interesting to speculate what might have happened had the immensely active and prestigious Edward VII still been on the throne when the midsummer crisis of 1914 broke out.

Many such speculations – historically unprofessional but none the less fascinating – arise with the continental dynasties. How differently might it all have gone had another archduke, and not Franz Ferdinand, fallen to the assassin's bullet. The heir to the throne was the one man of iron in the imperial family and, as he had proven in earlier Balkan crises, he was also a man of peace. For that matter, might the eighty-four-year-old Austrian emperor have helped to avert the catastrophe himself had he stayed in Vienna, where he could better have controlled the 'hawks' among his ministers, instead of retreating as he had done for more than half a century, to his beloved mountain haven of Bad Ischl, and returning to his capital only when his country was at war?

Again, if the German Kaiser had returned to his capital from his Norwegian cruise only twenty-four hours earlier than he did, could his last-minute switch from provocation to panicky restraint have checked the juggernaut? And what if Tsar Nicholas, whose order for general mobilization, issued after much vacillating during the night of 31 July, had stuck to his innermost convictions and stayed his hand? It was that order, after all, which set the European, as opposed to the Balkan, juggernaut rolling. It is possible that, even if all these changes of royal moods, locations and timetables had taken place, the mighty monarchs concerned would still have been as helpless as their ministers to prevent what lay ahead. But merely to ask the questions is to probe their personal share of blame for the tragedy.

The space devoted to each dynasty corresponds roughly to the weight of each throne in the European balance. Thus, the four empires, which were ranged in pairs against each other, get two chapters apiece. Italy, the lightweight on the Anglo-Russian side (and, appropriately, ruled from 1900 onwards by the midget king, Victor Emmanuel III), merits only one. That is also the ration for each of the four Balkan kingdoms examined with the exception of Serbia, which plays a key role throughout the long pre-war crisis, and which anyway has a uniquely complicated, as well as uniquely violent, dynastic tale to tell.

The breadth of the telling again varies. The traditional starting-point for any study of the Great War's origins, 1870, is, roughly, the median year. But the dynasties make no sense if placed on a common starting-line. For the Habsburg monarchy, ruled for more than six decades by Franz Josef, we have to trace the story, however briefly, from 1848, the year of his accession, for the fall of his empire is only comprehensible in the light of everything he had tried and failed to do during his enormous reign. For Germany, 1888, the year of William II's accession is an adequate start; for Britain, the widowing of Queen Victoria in 1861. With the Serbian royal house – or rather houses – one has to begin where they do, in the early years of the nineteenth century. But the 1870s are early enough for the other Balkan kingdoms. In other words, it is the shape of the dynasties themselves and, even more, the weight of their major figures, which sets the time-scale. At the end, they all come into the picture together, for the first and last time, tumbling over each other in confusion, as their world collapses around them.

I must explain some oddities – real or apparent – of nomenclature. I refer throughout to 'England' not 'Britain' because that was the style universally used on both sides of the Channel at the time (though our empire was normally described as 'British'). On the other hand, the use of the German style for 'Franz Josef' and 'Franz Ferdinand' is a personal quirk. It is simply that, in their cases, I have got so used to reading and thinking about them in German over the years that the English form comes awkwardly to me.

The reader would not, I am sure, expect much in the way of fresh evidence to emerge after all these years. I have made some use of new documentary and eyewitness material published in recent books, including one or two of my own, and there are even some unfamiliar odds and ends in this study. These are mainly from the Royal Archives whose staff – and in particular Miss Jane Langton – I must yet again thank for their efficient help. We have, for example, a hitherto-unpublished eyewitness account of the fateful slaughter in front of the Winter Palace in January 1905, sent back to King Edward VII by his envoy in St Petersburg, Sir Charles Hardinge, as well as later despatches on the crisis. From Berlin, there are some personal telegrams on Anglo-German relations sent by the British ambassador, Sir Edward Goschen, to King George V, none of which found their way into the regular Foreign Office archives. For that matter, there is the diary of King George himself, the only European sovereign whose personal record of the 1914 drama has survived.

Abroad, I must thank Frau Annelise Schulz, who has helped my research on many previous books, for once more painstakingly digging up a good deal of obscure material; in particular, an academic study on the role of the Emperor Franz Josef in the crisis. In the peace and quiet of Upper Austria, Herr Christof Heu, a retired schoolmaster, who holds a degree from Leeds University, and who has an encyclopaedic knowledge of the courts and the genealogy of old Europe, has read the manuscript chapter by chapter. He has saved me from several slipped stitches in weaving this highly complex dynastic pattern. For any mistakes which have still escaped the two of us, I take full responsibility.

I have deliberately not burdened either the printer or the reader with another of those enormous bibliographies which can be found at the end of any serious study of the Great War's origins. I have lost count of all the volumes in all the languages I have read on the subject over the years and must have consulted close on two hundred again in preparing this present work. To save space, what I have done is to identify only the source of each quotation used. Books used purely for background are usually mentioned only when they are both recent and important.

Finally, my thanks are again due to Monica Hutchinson who, in another peaceful spot, the Yorkshire moors, typed the bulk of the manuscript. Her well-tried talent at deciphering surmounted, on this occasion, even the tightest of time-schedules.

If, at the end, I ask whether that riddle I posed myself many years ago, is completely solved, I confess that it is not. There will always remain gaps and question marks over the role which the monarchs themselves played in the tragedy of 1914. But, at least, I have brought

myself and, I hope, the reader, several steps nearer the truth about their
suicidal performance.

Hughs,
Hambleden,
Oxon.   Gordon Brook-Shepherd

ROYAL SUNSET

INTRODUCTION:
WEDDING IN BERLIN

At 5 p.m. on Saturday 24 May 1913, in the chapel of the Neues Palais in Potsdam, the German Emperor William II gave away his only daughter, Victoria Louise, in marriage to Prince Ernst August, Duke of Brunswick and Lüneburg. The bridegroom – who, as it happened, was genuinely in love with his conventionally pretty bride – would not have been overwhelmed to stand side by side at the altar with a princess of the Prussian house of Hohenzollern which, since 1871, had also ruled over Bismarck's newly-revived German empire. Prince Ernst was a Guelph, one of the most ancient families of Europe, whose lineage was studded with crowns. For more than a hundred years Guelphs had filled the throne of England with their Hanoverian monarchs.

The Hanover connection had almost prevented the wedding taking place at all, for the romance between Ernst and Victoria had threatened at times to be a replay, on German soil, of the tragic dilemma in Shakespeare's *Romeo and Juliet*. The bridegroom's father was the Duke of Cumberland, heir to the claims of the Hanoverian kings. These had lost their English realm in 1837 and, for all practical purposes, the loss had been accepted. But it was a very different story when, thirty years later, Bismarck abolished their German kingdom as well, swallowing it up in the greedy maw of Prussia and confiscating the vast private fortune of the Cumberlands. Ever since then the Duke had ostentatiously removed himself to his Austrian castle at Gmunden on Lake Traun, refusing to make formal surrender of any of his royal rights to Berlin. Indeed, for years, he had evaded all the efforts of William II to arrange a meeting even to discuss a reconciliation – so much so that he eventually earned himself the nickname of 'The Vanishing Duke'.

The feud between the houses of Hohenzollern and Cumberland thus seemed just as unbridgeable as that between the Montagus and Capulets. Happily, in this case, after months of patient negotiation, a bridge was found. Without formally abandoning his rights to the

Hanoverian throne, Prince Ernst undertook to make no move to assert them. Meanwhile, he followed the family kingdom down the throat of the Prussian military machine by becoming a captain of Hussars in the Prussian army and thus taking the oath of loyalty to its Supreme War Lord, his father-in-law. The path to the altar was open.

As befitted such a match, and such a historic reconciliation between Guelph and Hohenzollern, this was primarily a German occasion. 'The Vanishing Duke' of Cumberland himself (now decorated for the occasion with the Order of the Black Eagle) was very much in evidence, and very affable, though his stooping shoulders and crane-like neck made him look a somewhat comic sight in his Austrian uniform. Among the others who walked in stately procession through the Picture Gallery and the White Hall of the Neues Palais to the chapel were the grand dukes of Baden, Hesse and Mecklenburg-Schwerin, the dukes of Schleswig-Holstein and Trachenberg, the Crown Prince of Saxony, and a score of other princes and princelings from that straggling patchwork of courts which Bismarck had pulled together as a Hohenzollern empire less than fifty years before.

But what gave this wedding a certain political significance as well as added lustre was the presence of two foreign emperors in the procession: George v of England and Nicholas ii, Tsar of Russia. Their own German connections were, of course, strong. Both were linked by blood or marriage to the bridegroom. Both had themselves married German brides (Queen Mary, a princess of Teck, had come to Berlin with her husband, while the Tsarina, born a princess of Hesse, had excused herself on the grounds of ill health). Moreover, George v was also a cousin of the bride's father, for William ii also had Queen Victoria, dead these thirteen years past, for his grandmother.

The irony of the occasion was that, by now, these royal cousins and kinsmen stood in opposing military camps. Over the past three and a half decades a pattern of rival alliances had gradually emerged in Europe which cut clean across dynastic ties. The process had begun in 1879, when the German and Austro-Hungarian empires concluded a military pact aimed primarily against any threat from Russia, their common neighbour in the East. A massive bar of Teuton iron thus ran all the way down the centre of the European continent from the Baltic to the Adriatic seas. Four years later Italy, a young kingdom but already the instinctive opportunist in the power game, tacked herself on like some tinny appendage, turning the so-called Dual Alliance into a Triple one.

There had been a predictable, almost inevitable, reaction from the powers which stood on the flanks of this central power bloc and felt mutually threatened by it. In May 1894, after the political path to St Petersburg, the tsarist capital, had been liberally strewn with French bank loans, France and Russia finalized a defence treaty of their own, to be triggered off automatically, even by general mobilization in the rival camp. England, pragmatic still, though she had ceased to be isolationist, never joined up formally with the two wing powers but gradually became unofficially entangled through far-reaching general staff talks with the French army. The Triple Alliance was squarely faced by the Triple Entente. The two most illustrious and most fêted foreign guests at the wedding of the Kaiser's daughter were thus his potential enemies in any future European war. They all knew this and they all preferred to ignore it, hoping that war would never come, and certainly not dreaming that it was so horribly close.

It is this proximity to Armageddon – still totally obscured and out of sight, though now only a handsbreadth away – which gave the Potsdam festivities a trance-like air. True, hindsight could have pointed to several omens. Shortly before King George's arrival in Berlin, for example, his host had tactfully released three English captives. Captain Trench, Lieutenant Brandon and Mr Bertrand Stewart were no ordinary jail-birds. They were British officers imprisoned on charges of espionage against Germany. When, on the eve of the Berlin wedding, they got off the packet boat from Flushing and stepped onto British soil, they were wildly cheered by a patriotic throng which had gathered at Queenborough harbour.

The cheers, by contrast, had been noticeably subdued when King George and Queen Mary drove down the famous 'Unter den Linden' in open victorias after their arrival at Berlin's Lehrter station. According to one eyewitness (perhaps somewhat prejudiced) the loudest noises on that occasion were all made by the German armed forces – the hundred and one salvo salute from the guns in the nearby Lustgarten and the 'whizzing propellers of the Zeppelin airship "Hansa", which circled indefatigably overhead'.[1]

Yet on the day of the wedding both the omens and the political realities seemed not to exist. After the ceremony there was a banquet for 1100 guests, with the Prussian *Junkers* in the amiable (if extraordinary) role of head waiters. At one end of the vast table the food was dished out by General von Süsskind, inspector of militia, while the head of the War Academy, General von Falk, performed a similar service at the other end. Even a Berlin wedding feast had, it seemed, to be under the command of the military. But the speeches overflowed with honeyed diplomacy. The Emperor was at pains to remind his 'darling daughter' that the man she had just married was 'from an honourable German sovereign . . . stock' but equally careful to call on them both to remain 'loyal to your new House'.[2]

The company then repaired to the White Hall for the traditional 'torch dance'. First, twelve pages, holding heavy candles, lined the walls of the room. Then the bridal pair entered (she in the obligatory white satin gown with the obligatory myrtle wreath of virginity on her head; he in the obligatory uniform, on this occasion that of his new regiment, the Rathenow Hussars) to the strains of a polonaise. The bride danced first with her father; next with her father-in-law; then with the Tsar, and finally – before taking the arm of her own husband – with King George, who was dressed in the uniform of 'his' German regiment, the First Dragoon Guards. That evening many of the guests went down to the Stettin station to see the newlyweds off on their honeymoon at Hubertusstock, one of the royal shooting lodges. At the last moment Prince Eitel Friedrich, the German Emperor's second son, noticed that everyone had forgotten the rice. He rushed out to buy a bagful at a nearby grocer's shop. It was the end of a happy day, a day, moreover, when everybody had felt they belonged to one great family of monarchy which seemed indissoluble.

This feeling persisted right up to the brink of Armageddon. In May of the following year the christening took place of the couple's first child, a son. If two foreign emperors had been guests at the wedding, there were now three who stood as godfathers. King George and Tsar Nicholas were joined in the role by Franz Josef of Austria. (The venerable Habsburg ruler, by this time already eighty-four years old, had, as usual, been at work at his desk in Schönbrunn Palace at 6 a.m. when the news of the birth had reached him two months before. It had taken all the tact of his adjutant to restrain him from hurrying over to the Vienna palace of the Cumberlands there and then to offer congratulations.)

King George had sent a particularly affectionate message to the young parents on accepting 'with great pleasure'[3] to stand as godfather and, the month after the christening, the Emperor William responded with a remarkable personal gesture of his own. In 1914, as today, 6 June was commemorated as the official birthday of the British sovereign. As a special mark of honour to celebrate the occasion, William II invited the British ambassador, Sir Edward Goschen, and the entire diplomatic staff of his embassy to a state luncheon at the Potsdam palace. The band played 'God Save the King' as the Emperor, dressed in the uniform of the English 'Royals' and sporting the Grand Cross of the Victorian Order, proposed King George's health and long life.

'Nothing', the envoy reported somewhat breathlessly to Buckingham Palace, 'could exceed the gracious cordiality which he was pleased to show to Sir Edward Goschen and the other members of Your Majesty's Embassy.'[4] Part of this cordiality consisted in giving the King and his government a few tips on how to deal with their suffragette movement. The Emperor showed surprise at the 'mild treatment' hitherto meted out to these female militants and 'expressed the fervent hope that severer measures would soon be adopted'. The Kaiser, as all England called him, could never resist interfering in the most delicate domestic concerns of other nations – a habit which had often driven Edward VII, his English uncle and father of King George V, close to explosion.

There was a further, purely military, celebration to come. Another luncheon to honour the King's birthday was given for the entire British embassy by Colonel von Stolzing, commanding officer of the Regiment of Dragoon Guards of which King George V was honorary colonel. The King had greatly pleased 'his' German officers by sending them a pack of English hounds to hunt with and, partly in thanks, long and prolonged hurrahs accompanied the drinking of the royal toast. Stolzing had just returned himself from a visit to England and was full of the 'kindness and attention' which 'everyone had shown him'. How false, he told Goschen, was this 'legend of English coldness to Germans so freely circulated by the gentlemen of the German press'.

The personal report of the British ambassador to his King describing these happenings is dated 6 June 1914. Because everything the Kaiser and Colonel Stolzing had said was mocked so drastically and so soon, it makes a more ironic vignette with which to introduce the collapse of the old European order than that traditionally chosen – the funeral of Edward VII at Windsor four years before.

Its special irony was certainly not lost on King George's private secretary, Lord Stamfordham, who, later that terrible summer, filed away his master's private correspondence with the German emperor. When he came to Sir Edward Goschen's dispatch of 6 June, the words still glowing as brightly as the red wax seal on the envelope, Lord Stamfordham noted in pencil on the back the date of his reply. He then added: 'And 2 months later?!' and consigned the dispatch to the archives.

How did the monarchs of old Europe – several of them endowed with autocratic powers, most of them linked by blood, and all of them dedicated to preserving the common royal heritage – allow their crowns to slide into disaster and, in several cases, into oblivion? How much control did they exercise at home, and what influence did they have abroad? How did they personally stand in relation to that great political divide which split, and finally destroyed, the pre-1914 world? Did any of them see the juggernaut coming, or do anything to stay its course? Did any help the juggernaut along, through vanity, weakness or folly? Above all, what were they and their courts, large or small, really like?

Let us start with the Balkans where the volcano, having rumbled for years, finally erupted.

Part One

THE POWDER KEG

Chapter One

MONTENEGRO:
KING OF THE BLACK MOUNTAINS

On the evening of 30 December 1905 the curtain went up in Vienna's 'Theater an der Wien' on a new and eagerly-awaited operetta. The lavish scene showed the Paris embassy of a little Slav state called 'Pontevedro'. The hero – if that is the word for the idle and dissipated fop who played the leading role – was Count Danilo Danilowitsch, Pontevedrian secretary of legation. He declares his motive force in life as he makes his first entrance on stage. His fatherland, he complains, creates so much tiresome bother for him during his working hours that he needs his nocturnal pleasures to recover, preferably in the company of night-club ladies with easy virtue and enticing nicknames.

The words and music of 1905 are still very much with us, for the operetta in question was Franz Lehár's 'The Merry Widow'. Yet it has long since been forgotten that 'Pontevedro' was meant to be Montenegro. Moreover – what everyone in the theatre that evening fully realized – the young Pontevedrian diplomat was a parody of none other than the heir to that country's throne, Prince Danilo. (So thinly-veiled indeed was the image that the Prince was later to sue for libel.) In reality, the Montenegro of the day was a troublesome European problem rather than a music-hall joke. So what was it about the country that made a famous composer take it as the quintessence of Balkan buffoonery?

The land which the King of the Black Mountains ruled was little bigger than Yorkshire. Its greatest length, from east to west, was fifty-five miles, its greatest breadth a mere thirty-eight. Though shaped just like a leaf fallen from a plane tree, there was little that was leafy about it. An old legend conveys it best: 'God, when creating the world, carried in a sack the stones he needed to fashion its mountains and valleys. Weakened by wear, the sack burst open one day, loosing a cascade of rocks. The chaos where they fell was Montenegro.'[1]

This stony wilderness was almost landlocked. The great powers had

allotted it only a narrow thirty-mile window on the Adriatic and had
soured even that concession by forbidding it a navy. All the southern,
Albanian end of that long and much-coveted coastline was still held in
the arthritic grasp of the sultans, as part of 'Turkey-in-Europe'.
Everything to the north of Montenegro's little stretch formed the
Dalmatian littoral of the Habsburg monarchy, which policed the
shores. It was Austrian engineers, starting from their great naval base
at Kotor, who had built the main access route up into Montenegro from
the sea. This was the famous 'Scala', a winding ribbon of seventy-three
zigzags cut out of the sheer mountain face which towers over the bay.
The road, following the same trail, which leads up into the Montenegrin People's Republic of present-day Yugoslavia, still presents a
dizzy climb for vehicles. In its time of kings, Montenegro's link with the
west was little better than a precipitous bridle path, and only horses,
mules, goats and pedestrians struggled up and down it.

The same applied to communications inside the isolated country. In
an age when railway lines had been crisscrossing all the European
states since the 1850s and linking them with each other, Montenegro
did not see its first steam-engine till 1909, and this operated only on a
short narrow-gauge internal track, running inland from the tiny port of
Bar. Outside the main townships – themselves little more than villages
by any normal reckoning – even a carriage was seldom seen, let alone a
motor car. The deep Montenegrin countryside lived on, right into the
twentieth century, with hardly anything on four wheels rumbling
across it. It also existed largely without clocks. The sun told the
peasants the time, helped in some cases by an hour-glass. They needed
neither heliographs nor bonfires to keep in touch with each other in an
emergency. The air was usually so dry and clear that messages could be
shouted from ridge to ridge.

It had no industry of its own; no natural resources of interest to the
outside exploiter; and only the most primitive of handicrafts. Its
agriculture fought a long losing battle against the ungrateful mountain
soil. The country was desperately poor. It could neither feed itself nor
clothe itself nor provide for its men, a third of whom lived or worked
abroad. Only through foreign cash, in gifts or loans, could its ruler put
on even the pretence of belonging to the modern age. Its administration
was equally primitive. Throughout the nineteenth century justice was
administered according to a mountain code of honour and the 'supreme
court' was the ruler in person, adjudicating under a large carob tree on
a patch of coarse grass outside his palace. He remained to the end the
absolute chieftain over his people, despite an apology for a constitution
established in 1905 as a sop to democratic sentiments in that outside

world towards which Montenegro was inexorably being drawn.* It was abreast of its age only as regards postage stamps, and this because they were such an invaluable source of foreign currency. For this reason it had hastened to join the international postal union a few months ahead even of France. Postage stamps apart, however, Montenegro had drifted through the nineteenth century like a land trapped inside some feudal time-warp of the Middle Ages.

Yet – and here is the extraordinary contrast to all this – by the beginning of the twentieth century Cetinje, its capital, had become a miniature European metropolis. As such it remained somewhat ludicrous as well as tiny. The princely palace was no more than a glorified two-storey bungalow adorned with a balcony. The town only boasted one hotel worthy of the name (travellers in the Victorian age had put up in rough inns, carrying their inflatable rubber baths with them on horseback). Despite this, in the early 1900s all the major powers of the day – England, Russia, Germany, France, Italy and the United States – were building, or had already built, imposing legations in the streets around the palace. Though the Montenegrins were still not able to telegraph or telephone each other, their fate was the subject of constant discussion, through the diplomatic ciphers which bound the country secretly and invisibly to the outside world. How was the paradox to be explained?

The first reason was its position on the map of old Europe. The geography which had so punished it economically flattened it politically. It was wedged between the Austrian and Ottoman empires, with Serbia – the leading Slav state of the Balkans and thus the protégé of tsarist Russia – just inland across a narrow strip of Turkish territory to the east. The Montenegrin wedge was thus strategically vital. Who sat on the top of its highest peak, the 5,738-foot Mount Lovcen, could control everything below, right down to the coast, provided he had the guns. And, as Montenegro was so hard to conquer – small armies would disappear in this wilderness of stones, while large ones would simply starve – it had to be wooed instead.

The second reason for Montenegro's inflated status was the remarkable ruler who, for nearly sixty years, from his accession in 1860 to his eclipse in 1918, received this wooing, and exploited it for every rouble, franc, pound, mark, crown or lira which could be wrung out of the rival donors. King Nicholas, or 'Nikita', the First (and last) of Montenegro was more than an archetypal Balkan ruler. All the Balkan traits of his

* The Parliament, or Skupština, called into life by the constitution was dissolved two years later, as soon as it showed any pretence of independence. Ministers who showed any signs of defiance were promptly jailed.

time were exaggerated as well as lumped together in that stocky
dynamic frame of his: delusions of power, wild ambitions, an obsession
with conspiracy, material greed, slippery unreliability, credulity mixed
with cunning, martial bombast, economic ignorance and political
naïveté, the whole mixture fermented by unpredictable impulsiveness of
action. For much of this he could not be personally blamed. His reign
had been launched in bloodshed after his uncle, Prince Danilo, was
assassinated on the esplanade of Kotor bay (the assassin was said to be
avenging himself for the seduction of his wife). Throughout his own
long life on the throne, violence stood at Nikita's shoulder as well as
being implanted in his heart. Yet he was an engaging rascal and a
romantic one, at least in the eyes of outside visitors not involved in his
wars or politics.

Several of these earliest visitors were gentlewomen from Victorian
England, on horseback tours of what were then the Slavonic provinces
of Turkey-in-Europe, their well-bred flesh enduring the most daunting
challenges of endurance and bad hygiene, their minds and notebooks
ever eagerly open. One such was Lady Strangford, and she gives this
picture of the young ruler, then barely nineteen, and his little palace at
Cetinje:

He is an extraordinarily handsome man, looking much older than his age, very
tall and well-made. His forehead is wide, his hair and eyes nearly black, and
the naturally sad expression of his Southern face is animated by a very sweet
and frequent smile . . .

The Prince wore dark-blue cloth pantaloons, cut in the Syrian style, very full
and wide, gathered in at the knees with scarlet garters; a Damascus silk scarf
round the loins and, at his waist, a huge crimson leather band in which the
arms are placed; the Prince, however, is the only man who carries none at
home. The scarlet waistcoat, embroidered and buttoned with gold, is half
concealed by a closely-fitting tunic of cloth, also richly embroidered in gold.
The full court dress is the same, only that the tunic is then worn of green . . .

All the gentlemen of the court had rows of silver buttons sewn so thickly on
the fronts of the tunics as quite to conceal the cloth and to give the appearance
of armour; while some had curious shoulder-pieces of solid silver covered with
bosses, completely covering the neck and shoulders. The cap is of fur, with a
'panache' of white cloth, embroidered and tasselled, hanging down at one side;
this is in war or in travelling, or in winter; in summer or at home the
Montenegrin wears a peculiar pork-pie cap with a black silk border and a
scarlet centre. All the Montenegrins wear embroidered leggings; the Prince
alone wears high leather boots. He wore gloves, as did every one at court,
constantly.[2]

The Prince asked his distinguished guest to dinner, which she found 'well-served, and cooked in the French style, with all due accompaniments of foreign wines'. The butler, like the cuisine, was French but all the other servants in attendance were officers of the palace guard, who wore full ceremonial costume, with pistols and daggers crammed into their broad belts as closely as pins in a pincushion. Some were relatives of the nobles they were waiting upon so that services would be requested in the most deferential and patriarchal of styles: 'Bring me the wine, oh my brother.'[3]

Exchanges such as that would be made in Serb, which, with an admixture of local dialect and a smattering of Turkish words, was the tongue of all Montenegrins. Indeed, it was all that many of them spoke, even at court, and this presented protocol problems when foreigners were present. Two other English lady travellers who were entertained in the palace a few years after Lady Strangford's sojourn recorded that their host spoke French fluently; understood German, Italian and Russian; but had little or no English. 'In consideration of our ignorance of the Serb language', their chronicle goes on, 'no-one spoke at dinner who could not speak in French.'[4]

All these visitors were struck by the selection of portraits of foreign sovereigns hung in the palace reception rooms. These were life-size paintings of the Tsar and Tsarina of Russia and similarly imposing ones of the Emperor Napoleon III of the French and the Empress Eugénie. Franz Josef and Elisabeth of Austria were also represented, though on a somewhat smaller scale. It was a symbol of much that was to come.

From the first day of his reign, Nikita tried to bring into play those dynasties – and others which were to be added to his portrait gallery – to serve his own aims of enrichment and expansion. Just as Bulgaria wanted to be Greater Bulgaria and Serbia strove to be Greater Serbia, so little Montenegro, despite its pathetic size and resources, dreamt of challenging them for the leadership of the South Slav world by becoming Greater Montenegro. Nobody in the Balkans was satisfied with being what he was. In Nikita's case, at least, the frustration was understandable. Incredibly, for someone of his modest means and lineage, he was able to play the dynastic card with great effect in this contest.

His own royal house, that of Petrovich, was barely two centuries old. For centuries Montenegro, which had started life in medieval times as a province of Serbia, had been ruled by Vladikas, who were bishops elected by popular assemblies. In 1696 one Danilo Petrovich of Njegosh, just chosen as ruler, established that, henceforth, successors would be nominated from his own family. Yet for another half century there were no direct heirs of the blood, for the rulers themselves remained in holy orders and celibate. Then, in 1851, the new Vladika, also called Danilo, decided to quit the church and take to the marriage bed. Though his only child, a daughter, never succeeded, the hereditary principle was now established in the Petrovich clan – anything up to a thousand years after other ruling houses of Europe had taken that principle for granted.

It was little wonder then that the dynasty of Petrovich-Njegosh was regarded as something of a raw and outlandish freak. Nor did Nikita impress with his own choice of bride. He had married, soon after his accession, one Milena, a Montenegrin girl from the fighting tribe of the Kchevo, which may have been renowned in the Black Mountains but which was utterly unknown and unregarded anywhere beyond them. What was to matter about this undistinguished marriage, however, was its progeny. Milena bore her ardent husband ten* children over the next twenty-five years, of whom the most valuable (quite against the Montenegrin code) turned out to be the seven healthy daughters. Without exception they grew up to be tall stately young women with soft necks and full bosoms seemingly fashioned for crown jewels, and all with the bearing of queens. By dint of patient intrigue mixed with flashy showmanship, Nikita managed to secure for most of them royal partners which matched both their appearance and his own ambitions.

In 1883 he married Zorka, the eldest of them, to Peter Kara-georgević, the exiled claimant to the throne of Serbia, in the hope of fostering, long term, his dream of becoming the pan-Slav leader of the Balkans. With the same aim he even angled, on behalf of another daughter, for the hand of the Tsarevich of Russia, heir to the grand patron of all the Slavs. That hope proved too extravagant; but eventually his St Petersburg catch none the less comprised two grand dukes, close relatives of the Tsar. In 1889 his second daughter Militza married Grand Duke Peter and in 1907 her sister Anastasia joined her in the family circle of the Russian court as the bride (in her second marriage) of the Grand Duke Nicholas.

In 1896 came what was in some ways the most remarkable match of all when his fourth daughter, Elena, wedded the Crown Prince of Italy who, only four years later, was to begin his enormously long reign as King Victor Emmanuel III. The contrast between the thousand-year-old house of Savoy and the obscure eighteenth-century pedigree of the house of Petrovich was as great as the contrast in size between the kingdom of Italy and the principality of Montenegro (or, for that

* In all, twelve; one died in infancy and another in early youth.

matter, between the statuesque bride and her diminutive husband).

Nikita sought to deploy his other children as reinsurance policies in case the Russian-backed pan-Slav movement should fail to carry the day in the Balkans. Even he probably realized that there was no chance of luring an archduke or archduchess from the proud (and basically hostile) house of Habsburg to the altar. But he fished quite successfully among the lesser royalty of Austria's ally, Germany. In 1897 his fifth daughter, Anna, married Prince Franz Joseph of Battenberg and, two years later, his eldest son, the notorious Hereditary Prince Danilo, took the German link much closer when he wedded Jutta, the daughter of the Grand Duke Frederick of Mecklenburg-Strelitz. To complete the reinsurance process nearer to home, in 1902 Nikita married his second son Prince Mirko to Princess Natalie. She was linked by her paternal grandmother to the house of Obrenović, then still on the Serbian throne, though about to be cut down from it in a manner which sent a shudder across Europe.

That left Nikita with two spare daughters, Vera and Xenia, who disappointed him sadly by failing to attract Bulgarian or Greek princes for husbands; and his youngest son Peter, who married nobody during his father's lifetime, and eventually chose an English-born commoner after his father was dead and the kingdom of Montenegro had ceased to exist. But these were blots on an otherwise amazing matchmaking record. By the first decade of the twentieth century, when, as we shall see, Montenegro was approaching its brief zenith in international importance, its ruler was also enjoying his heyday as dynastic matchmaker. He was father-in-law to the King of Italy, two Russian grand dukes, one German princess, and two members of both the rival houses of Serbia.[5]

There is a picture of the entire family (without Princess Zorka who had died only seven years after her marriage) reassembled from all over Europe in the courtyard of Cetinje palace. It was probably taken in 1910, the year when Nikita, to celebrate his fiftieth year on the throne, declared himself to be king and not merely prince. The ladies are mostly in huge floppy hats trimmed with flowers or feathers. Each of the royal gentlemen is swathed in sashes and plastered with decorations and medals. Each is decked out in his own preposterous variety of the ceremonial military headgear of the day: the Russian Grand Duke with a stiff six-inch cockade jutting up from his helmet; that of the German Prince crowned with plumes; the King of Italy with a stiff black and gilt kepi higher than the face underneath is long; the three Montenegrin princes with army officers' caps flat and round like oversized dinner plates; and at the centre Nikita, still wearing the same style 'pork-pie cap' which Lady Strangford had noted nearly fifty years before as the correct daytime covering for a Montenegrin gentleman. The two unmarried daughters, Vera and Xenia, stand side by side in the middle of the back row. Each has a somewhat glum look, as though she realizes she has let the side down. But, by and large, the Petrovich family, given its obscure and relatively recent origins, is shown in that picture to have done almost as well in the European dynastic game as those legendary German marriage performers, the house's of Hesse or Coburg. Nor had Nikita collected foreign coats-of-arms as a vain indulgence. Throughout his reign the connections of the father-in-law were mobilized for all they were worth in his struggle for power as sovereign.

Even after he had won formal independence, in battle, from the Ottoman empire, that struggle continued to centre on what remained of Turkey-in-Europe. Had there been no spoils left to fight for, it would still have been hard to drive the burning hatred of all things Turkish from his subjects' hearts. Until well into the nineteenth century, the heads of Turks killed in battle were displayed in public until they rotted, stuck on rows of poles on the fortress walls of the capital. In Nikita's own childhood, schoolboys would always be forgiven for taking a day or two off from their lessons to join in border skirmishes, provided they brought back a similar trophy to the classroom with them. Fighting the Turks was not just in the geography of the Montenegrins; it was in their genes. The concept of *cojstvo*, or heroic manhood, was the national creed. At baptism, each of the ruler's new male subjects would have the butt of a pistol pressed to his tiny mouth to kiss. From six years, he would carry a dagger; from ten, a rifle.

There were three great onslaughts against the Ottoman empire during Nikita's reign. Each drew his country closer into the calculations of the European powers. In the first, Montenegro fought as a partner in the general uprisings of 1875–77 against Turkish rule, the ferment which brought Russian armies down into the Balkans to drive back the Turks and enabled the Montenegrins, by the post-war Treaty of Berlin of 1878, to double their territory and secure their precious little window on the Adriatic coast. In the second major upheaval, which came nearly thirty years later, Montenegro was reduced to the role of a furiously frustrated spectator. In 1908 the Habsburg monarchy, without even informing her own allies, formally annexed to her empire the two provinces of Bosnia and Herzegovina which the same Treaty of Berlin had allowed her to occupy and administer. Nikita played no part in the long international crisis which followed, but its resolution was none the less of great future significance for his kingdom.

As a counter-concession for her controversial move, Austria with-drew her troops from that long tongue of Turkish territory, the Sanjak of Novi Pazar, which had always separated Montenegro from Serbia. The way was thus prepared for the two Slav countries, both now vowing revenge on the Austrians for 'enslaving' their Slav brothers in the provinces, to secure a common border. For Nikita this prospect was a distinctly mixed blessing. Would Serbia, as a new and much more powerful neighbour, annex him one day? If this danger were real, ought he not to agree to a voluntary union instead? Yet these were not just Balkan concerns; they affected the balance of the great powers themselves, for Serbian expansion would mean Russian expansion. After 1908 Nikita became an even more interesting figure in European diplomacy.

But his true time, of glory and notoriety combined, came with the third and greatest explosion against Turkey-in-Europe, the Balkan Wars of 1912–13. Nikita not only touched it all off. He was ready to go fighting in defiance of all the great powers combined, well after most of his partners had given up. For months on end his name was on the lips of every European statesman.

The campaigns themselves had everything in them for which the Balkans were famous: conspiracy, intrigue, treachery, double-dealing and vengeance. Throughout 1912, four states in the region who had once stood under Ottoman rule – Serbia, Bulgaria, Greece and Montenegro – had been concocting a joint plot to seize and divide among themselves what was left of Turkey-in-Europe. Setting old enmities aside for the moment, Serbia and Bulgaria had started the alliance rolling with a bilateral pact signed in March. In May, Bulgaria made a similar agreement with Greece. Though he only formally joined the war league five months later, Nikita had been busy lighting its fuses from the late summer onwards. He did this, by agreement with his fellow conspirators, through launching repeated provocative raids against the Turkish army outposts on his borders and stirring up all the trouble he could among the Sultan's Albanian subjects.

The great powers, though ignorant of the military details of the plot, knew that something ominous was brewing and did their best to head it off. The final disintegration of the Turkish empire was deemed, in all the major European capitals, to be as dangerous as it was inevitable. The business of bringing it about could not be left to the clumsy, itching fingers of the small states of the region, who could never be relied upon to keep those fingers from each other's throats. Even Russia, therefore, which had played a major role in sponsoring this basically pan-Slav grouping, and who stood to gain most by its creation, joined the other great powers in urging Nikita not to go too far. He responded by intensifying his border raids. On 19 September the writing went up on the wall when Montenegro mobilized. 'We are committing suicide,' exclaimed Nikita.[6] It was feigned despair. The prospects, as he knew, were very different, since the combined forces of the four Balkan partners, a total of some 700,000 men, were twice the size of the Turkish opponents.

Even the attackers must, however, have been pleasantly surprised by the ease with which the obese Ottoman giant was toppled. It was on 8 October 1912 – the very day that the great powers issued their first joint warning to the Balkan states against any act of aggression – that Nikita not only declared war on Turkey but rushed to the front so that he could fire off the first cannon against the Turkish lines in person. Within a fortnight the four Balkan armies, swarming forward like columns of killer ants, had seized almost all of Turkey-in-Europe except for the narrow and strongly fortified land approach to Constantinople itself.

The ten months of fighting which followed fell into three phases. In the first the Balkan League partners secured their swift victory over the Turks. In the second they quarrelled and fought among themselves. In the third they finally had a settlement imposed upon them by the great powers whom they had driven to distraction with their greed and obstinacy. The tangle is best sorted out one thread at a time as the different countries and their rulers are treated in turn. The case of Nikita and Montenegro was fairly clear cut. Acting together with the more powerful Serbian army, his forces began by dividing between them the Sanjak of Novi Pazar which the Austrians had handed back to the Turks three years before, and thus achieved their common frontier. They then swept down together to the Adriatic coast and thrust into the northern part of Albania, whose Turkish garrison was simultaneously attacked in the south by Greek troops.

For Nikita, Albania meant above all seizing Scutari or Shkoder, the town at the far end of the great inland lake whose shores fell partly in Montenegrin and partly in Turkish hands. It had long been a dream of Montenegrin rulers to make the lake entirely theirs. Nikita decided his country would never be presented with a better opportunity than this, nor a better leader to take advantage of it. Accordingly, it was his troops which laid siege to the Turkish forts at Scutari.

He and his comrades-in-arms soon found that they had taken on not just the Turkish garrison. They were confronting the major European powers as well. These were not disposed to stand by and watch the Turkish province of Albania simply be pulled to pieces by the little Balkan states like so many lion cubs at the kill. In London, where peace talks between the belligerents had already started in December of 1912, Sir Edward Grey, the British foreign secretary, launched a parallel running conference with the ambassadors of Russia, Germany, Austria, Italy and France* to tackle, first and foremost, the Albanian problem.[7]

It was this formidable body which now strove to bring Nikita and his allies to reason. Like the two million Albanians themselves, who had raised their old national flag (the black eagle of Scanderberg on a blood-red ground), the great powers wanted Albania to be truly independent if it were to be liberated at last from Turkish rule – though ideas as to how large and how constituted that new Albania should be differed widely in the major European capitals.

First of all, however, the Serbs and Montenegrins had to be called off and, throughout the winter and spring, Nikita had resisted all pressure to abandon his siege. By March of 1913 Baron Giesl, the Austrian minister at his court, got so desperate as to implore his government 'to occupy Cetinje with Austrian troops in order to bring the king to his senses'.[8] That, clearly, was a dangerous notion, however tempting, to some of the military 'hawks' in Vienna. If Austria-Hungary struck out on her own, Russia too might be forced to intervene again in the Balkan mêlée. So there was much talk instead of a joint naval demonstration by the great powers off Montenegro's tiny strip of Adriatic coast. There was even a project for a combined land action against Montenegro, with England contributing an infantry brigade from Malta – a suggestion promptly vetoed by the British Prime Minister of the day, Mr Asquith.[9]

For months on end Nikita spat defiance. He strengthened his artillery on Mount Lovcen, which dominated the Austrian naval base of Kotor, and told the Habsburg monarchy – and with it the whole of Europe – that if they wanted to take his precious mountains from him they would 'have to chop my head off'.[10] Meanwhile he tried to use the Italian dynastic link for all it was worth, despite the fact that Italy coveted the whole of Albania for herself. None the less his son-in-law, King Victor Emmanuel, strove to get a compromise whereby Montenegro, in return for abandoning her claim to Scutari would get land near by, perhaps by diverting the waters of Lake Bojana and giving her that valley. 'My father-in-law', the Italian king declared to one diplomat at the time, 'is wrong to try and annex Scutari but his little realm does need some more cultivatable land.'[11]

* It was typical of the social system of the day that three of them – Count Benckendorff of Russia, Count Mensdorff of Austria and Prince Lichnowsky of Germany – were all cousins.

By the time, in April of 1913, that Montenegrin troops finally took the whole of Scutari, Nikita had come to accept that he would never be allowed to keep it. Prestige apart, he was none the less determined to hold the prize for a while, if only to get a better price for selling it. This, in the end, was the solution. On 17 April the ambassadors' conference in London proposed a loan of £1,200,000 to buy Nikita off, and in the first week of May he reluctantly handed Scutari over to the great powers and accepted that the future fate of Albania was in their hands.

Not the least interesting aspect of the Albanian affair was the way Nikita had mobilized his own family Mafia to the full throughout the crisis. Thus from the beginning he had used the considerable influence of his daughter Elena, Queen of Italy, to persuade King Victor Emmanuel to launch his rescue operation. The argument Elena was told by her father to employ was that his throne would be threatened unless he could show to his people some solid gains for this long and bitter fighting. In St Petersburg his well-placed daughter, Grand Duchess Militza, who had already helped him secure some extra Russian cannon, was sent the same instructions. In February 1913 she accordingly summoned the Tsar's foreign minister M. Sazanov and warned him that her father would be 'in grave danger' unless Montenegro were allowed to retain its full share of the Turkish spoils.[12] Sazanov probably took little notice of the Grand Duchess. In any case, Russia was committed to her little Slav brothers in the Balkans, however tiresome some of their monarchs could be.

By the same token Montenegro, like Serbia, was increasingly committed to the Tsar as supreme protector. For Nikita this marked the end of a balancing act which he had conducted throughout his long reign and which had begun under his predecessors. Russia appeared for the first time in the story of his people in 1711, when Tsar Peter the Great sent an envoy to Cetinje to visit Danilo Njegosh, the real founder of the Petrovich dynasty. Seventy years later the Habsburg monarchy also appeared on the scene when the Montenegrin chieftains, convulsed by internal strife, appealed to the Emperor Joseph II to help. Thus began the tussle for control between Vienna and St Petersburg which was to last right down to 1914.

Nikita exploited the contest for what mattered to him most: hard cash. Russia was his mainstay. When he came to the throne the largest single item by far in his revenue was a subsidy (variously entered in the books as 10,000 sequins or 47,000 florins or £6,000) which he received each year from the Tsar. By comparison the total he could scrape together from all the taxes on his subjects – on their dwellings, their ploughland, their fisheries, their beehives and on each and every sheep, pig or ox – only came to £25,000. The Russian subsidy by itself met Nikita's early civil lists twice over. In 1868, for example, this was fixed at 6,000 Austrian ducats or £2,820.[13] (There is no explanation why Montenegro's finances were reckoned in such a medley of currencies.) Out of this he paid for the upkeep of his modest palace; the wages for his guards and for the captains of his volunteer army, then of some 20,000 men; the salaries of his handful of schoolteachers (he had opened a boarding-school for girls soon after his accession which he maintained at his own expense); and, of course, the cost of running the state's only printing press. There was nothing else in Cetinje which could cost his treasury much money in the early days, for his capital started off with barely fifty straw-covered houses and had to wait until 1891 to be provided with a water supply and until 1910 for electricity.

The strength of the Russian connection – and with it the amount of annual subsidy – was of course increased by Militza's marriage. Indeed, on 30 May 1889, when Nikita was visiting St Petersburg to celebrate his daughter's engagement to the Grand Duke Peter, Tsar Alexander III had rather startled the outside world by declaring at the banquet toast: 'I drink to the health of the Prince of Montenegro, the only true and honest friend of Russia.'[14] It was not until 1904, however, that Russia started giving this special friend some special assistance of more significance than cash. In that year one General Potapov arrived in Cetinje, officially as 'controller of the subsidy' but in reality as military agent heading a four-man team whose task was to modernize the small terrier-like Montenegrin army along Russian lines. The general, with his colonel and two captains, had a thankless task in trying to turn the peasants of the Black Mountains into an efficient fighting force. Their performance in the Balkan Wars, despite the initial successes in northern Albania, proved the despair of their Russian mentors. Potapov was heard complaining bitterly that Nikita's soldiery had entered the campaign loaded down with new Russian war supplies, including thirty million cartridges (roughly one thousand rounds per man) and a hundred and fifty shells for each of their cannon. By the time the campaign was over, 'nothing remained but useless debris'. Any rifles left in the armouries were so rusty as to be unserviceable; the barracks empty of stores and men and the officers living at home with nothing to do, 'following the general custom of the country'.[15]

What was even more galling for the Russians, despite all their massive aid, was to see Nikita still at his old game of playing on Austria as the second main string in his diplomatic fiddle. The influence of Vienna remained genuinely strong in many ways. To the end of his reign Nikita seems to have gone on playing the old-time oriental sovereign by having his courtiers come into his rooms unannounced and gather around his bed to read him out the news. One of their main sources of information was Vienna's *Neue Freie Presse* whose articles on what went on in Europe inevitably coloured his opinions.[16] The King's legal system too was gradually coming under Austrian influence, particularly after the appointment, in February of 1912, of two judges from the Habsburg monarchy who were trying to bring Nikita's feudal code of justice into the twentieth century.

But the pull of St Petersburg finally proved decisive, especially after the end of the Balkan Wars when Nikita found his treasury empty and his personal popularity at a dangerously low ebb. The cutting off of regular subsidies of Russian roubles during the argument over the Scutari siege had left him with no ready cash to pay his army, let alone his palace staff. A stream of desperate begging letters to St Petersburg followed. Militza and Anastasia were wheeled into action again, imploring all and sundry at the Russian court to save their father's throne for him. 'We are on the brink of an abyss,' Nikita wailed to the French minister.[17]

Before the spring of 1914 came round, Tsar Nicholas II had let his Montenegrin black sheep back into the great Slav fold. It was, however, on conditions. To tie the slippery Nikita to them once and for all, the Russians proposed to launch a huge military training programme. This was designed to double the fighting strength of the Montenegrin army, drawn from a population now over 200,000, so that, in any war to come, it could put six properly equipped divisions into the field on Russia's side. Seventeen Russian officers and seventy-nine NCOs would be needed for the programme, which would cost some two million roubles a year.[18]

All this led to ever-strengthening ties between Montenegro and Serbia, Russia's principal protégé in the Balkans, with whom Nikita now had a common border and an increasingly uneasy relationship. There was renewed talk of mergers across that border. Indeed, on 26 March 1914, Nikita was reported to have written personally to King Peter of Serbia proposing a military, diplomatic and financial union (though not, of course, a dynastic one).[19] Thanks to the mighty European convulsion set off by the murder of an Austrian archduke only three months later, the Serbs and the Montenegrins were indeed to be united, though in a very different world and without old King Nikita. But by the time that convulsion came his own fate, after fifty-four years of dynastic juggling, had been cast, for good or ill, with that of the Romanovs. In the fate of the Russian royal family, Nikita's two St Petersburg daughters were, unknown to themselves, to play a deadly role.

Mustard-Seed Kingdoms in the Balkan Meadows

of the Romanov. In the fate of the Karageorgević family, then, we have to follow a human tragedy in perpetual conflict to the very end.

Chapter Two

SERBIA:
MANY PRINCES, ONE CROWN

The only other Balkan country to have a native dynasty was Serbia. It was indeed over-supplied: its curse was that it possessed not one, but two. Both were descended from warriors who became national heroes, both were born in years of violence, and both were destined to live out their time in violence, inflicting and suffering crimes of vengeance against each other. For a hundred years from the dawn of the nineteenth century, the struggle between the Karageorgević and Obrenović clans for the crown of Serbia dominated the lives of their luckless subjects. Between them they made a mockery of the supposed sanctity of royal power. Each finally managed to produce specimens of rulers who surpassed even Balkan standards of excess in their debauchery and bloodthirstiness.

There had been an era – long past, but still vivid in folk memory – when Serbia was ruled by great kings who were worthy of the name. Indeed, one of them, Stefan Dušan, had felt able to assume the title of tsar in 1346, to symbolize the fact that his little empire stretched right down to Albania and Thessaly. All that medieval splendour vanished for ever in 1459, when Serbia was finally swallowed up into the Ottoman empire. The Serbian aristocracy, like their tsars, were extinguished under the Sultan's pashas. Thus when, after nearly three hundred and fifty years of more or less passive subjection, the Serbs finally rose up, their new leaders could only come from the people.

The first and most famous of these was George Petrovich, a massively built peasant farmer from the forests of Shumadia, who made his name in history as Kara (or Black) George. When the uprising against the Turkish janissaries broke out, in February 1804, the pig-keeper, already an outlaw, proved himself an inspired guerrilla fighter. Over the next two years the guerrilla fighter grew into a formidable army commander of mountain troops who, in December 1806, captured Belgrade, put the Turkish garrison to the sword, and established a native regional government in its place. In 1811 Karageorge declared himself Prince of Serbia. One of the country's modern dynasties was born.

The new Prince was a man of almost unbelievable ruthlessness. Once, during his outlaw days, his aged father refused to cross the River Save and join the family in flight. Karageorge simply took out a pistol and shot the old man through the head. He was later, in a fit of blind fury, to hang his only brother over his door post with a bridle. Their mother barely escaped with her own life from another domestic argument. When Karageorge suspected her of cheating him out of some honey, he made short shrift by ramming the disputed beehive hard down over her head like a bonnet and walked off, leaving her shrieking with pain under the stings. It was not surprising that, once he started unleashing a temper like that on his own people, his popularity began to fade. In October 1813, when the Turks put a fresh army in the field against him, headed by the Grand Vizier in person, Karageorge's nerve suddenly failed as well, and he fled into Austria. One of his best lieutenants, a farmer's son called Miloš Obrenović, took up the standard of resistance. He put the Turks to flight after a series of savage campaigns and eventually, on 6 November 1817, declared himself to be the new Prince of Serbia. Belgrade had acquired its second dynasty. With it there began as well an eternal vendetta: that same summer, Karageorge had belatedly tried to return to the field of battle, only to have his head cut off by one of Obrenović's captains. It was forwarded to Constantinople by the new leader as a pledge of loyalty. Not for another eighty-six years did the descendants of Karageorge exact full vengeance. But when the moment came, they repaid their debt with interest.

This picture of Serbia in its cradle is needed even to follow – let alone understand – the giddy way the new state grew up. Miloš, the first Obrenović, was forced to renounce the throne in 1839, nine years after his country's independence from Turkey had been formally recognized by the European powers. His son, Michael, reigned for only three years before he too had to abdicate after another political convulsion, and Serbia now called in the son of the murdered Karageorge, who ruled from 1842 to 1858. When his turn came to be deposed, the Belgrade Skupština, or National Assembly, could think of nothing better than to summon back Miloš, the founder of the dynasty; he returned in tumultuous triumph to Belgrade, an old man of nearly eighty who died soon afterwards. He was succeeded by the same Michael who had been got rid of in 1842 and who now, like his father, had a second spell on the wobbly Serbian throne. For him it was to come to a sudden dreadful end. On 10 June 1868 he was shot dead and his body savagely mutilated while walking with members of his family in the deep forests of Topčider. Henchmen of the rival dynasty had carried out the attack in the hope of dislodging the Obrenović family once and for all. But the army, always the linchpin of Balkan power, refused to budge. The plot failed and there was a purge of the Karageorgević faction instead.

The political intrigues never ceased; but, in increasing measure, personal scandal was to prove an even greater danger to the throne. The house of Obrenović gradually reduced itself to ridicule and ruin by its own unbridled quarrels over women. The new Prince of Serbia, Milan, gave no cause for complaint to begin with. A cousin of the murdered Michael (who had died without heirs), Milan was indeed only thirteen years old when he succeeded and a triumvirate of regents (one Conservative, one Liberal and one nominee of the military) ruled in his name until he became of age on his eighteenth birthday five years later. Even before he came under their shadow, Milan was a vulnerable boy, due to the appalling circumstances of his childhood. His father had died when the child was only five years old, having not only squandered all his own money but pawned all his wife's jewels to pay for a string of mistresses. The young widow, a great beauty of the Rumanian nobility, then herself openly became the mistress of Prince Alexander Cuza, ruler of Wallachia and Moldavia (the kernel of what was to become the Rumanian kingdom). Cuza's little court in Bucharest was generally reckoned to be one of the most corrupt in all Europe. As a nursery school of morals for the future ruler of Serbia, it could only prove pernicious.

There were laurels of sorts to be won for that young ruler, however, before he began to tarnish them by his own behaviour. The hardest-fought came out of that general uprising against the Ottoman empire which was touched off in 1875 by a revolt against the greedy Turkish tax-gatherers in Bosnia and Herzegovina and which ended with the great powers intervening decisively in the Balkan mêlée. Serbia, like Montenegro, had long been trying to prod into rebellion the two Turkish provinces which ran along their borders, for both countries hoped one day to expand into these at Turkey's expense. Indeed, as far back as 1809,[1] Karageorge, the burgeoning Serbian warlord, had been dreaming of bringing the Bosnians under his control. Now that the embers of resistance in the provinces had burst into flames, there was no restraining the pan-Slavs of Serbia, whatever reservations their governments felt. The twenty-one-year-old Milan, who had hurried back from a visit to Vienna on hearing the news of the uprising, was met at the border by a band of volunteers in full battle dress who greeted him with shouts of 'To war with the Turks!' But it was only after a year of dithering on the part of his ministers (with the young Prince more than once threatening to abdicate) that, at the end of June 1876, Serbia formally declared war on the Ottoman empire and sent four separate armies out against it.

Their fate fully justified all the misgivings of the Prince's most pessimistic advisers. The four armies, named after the rivers from whose valleys they marched, totalled nearly 120,000 men. Supporting them (if that is the right word for a motley band of ne'er-do-wells) were some 5,000 Russian volunteers, recruited by the unofficial Slavic Committee in Moscow and commanded by a retired Russian general, Mikhail Cherniaev. He turned out to be a megalomaniac interested only in fame and fortune for himself. Both the Serbian soldiers and their dubious helpers were poorly led and badly equipped, many still dressed in their peasant sheepskins and with only home-made muzzle-loaded cannon for artillery. By the autumn they had been scattered like chaff in a storm and the road to Belgrade lay open to the Turks.

It was a dreadful moment for the young Prince. The four months of war had cost him 15,000 dead and wounded and rendered another 200,000 homeless in the devastated eastern areas of the country; this for a nation which only numbered some one and a quarter million. The moral shock was even greater. Serbia had not drawn the sword for her own independence (that had been established thirty-five years before) but as the champion of all Balkan Slavs who were still unfree. Now it looked as though the sacrifice had been in vain. The rebellion in Bosnia, which had touched off the turmoil, was dying down and the Bulgarians, who had also risen up in sympathy, seemed to have had the stuffing knocked out of them as well. Serbia herself could fall again under Ottoman rule. There was only one possible saviour – the Tsar of Russia. Milan appealed to Alexander II who promptly responded by ordering the Turks to halt in their tracks and seek an armistice.

This imperious ultimatum, which Alexander had dispatched without even consulting the other European powers, eventually, in April of 1877, sucked Russia herself into war against the Ottoman empire. Along with the other Balkan states, Serbia henceforth became a virtual spectator in the struggle which was to decide her fate. Unwisely, she had delayed taking to the field again against the Turks until the Russian victory was almost complete, and this was reflected in the treatment which Alexander II meted out to her when, on 3 March 1878, he concluded the Peace Treaty of San Stefano with the vanquished Turks. Montenegro, was given fat spoils by that treaty, including her long-awaited window on the Adriatic. The Bulgarians, who had risen bravely again once the Russian armies streamed in to free them, were awarded gigantic slices of Turkish territory, taking them as far east as Lake Ohrid and as far south as the shores of the Aegean itself. Serbia, which had always imagined herself to be the Tsar's chosen champion in the Balkan lists, was awarded a meagre one hundred and fifty square miles of Turkish soil, which was less than little Montenegro's share and minute compared with Bulgaria's gain. Worst of all, this redistribution of Balkan land had all been done over Serbia's head.

Fortunately for her, the other major European powers also found it unacceptable that the Tsar should carve up the Ottoman empire in this cavalier fashion. In particular, both England and Austria-Hungary were determined to oppose the creation of 'Greater Bulgaria' as a client state of Russia's. For Vienna this would erect a fresh barrier to any hopes the Habsburg monarchy had of further expansion in the Balkans. For London it signified the dreaded prospect of a Russian highway down to the Mediterranean. The outcome of their pressure was the famous Congress of Berlin, held in June and July of 1878, at which, with the German Chancellor Bismarck acting as the self-styled 'honest broker', the great powers redivided the Turkish spoils of war all over again. Bulgaria's gains were slashed by more than half, which stored up vengeful trouble on that flank of the Balkans. Far more ominously for Serbia, the Habsburg monarchy was allowed to move right up against her on the other flank. The most fateful decision of the Berlin Congress was to allow Austria-Hungary to occupy and administer the two restless Turkish provinces of Bosnia and Herzegovina which had started all the tumult three years before. Karageorge's dream of annexing them to Serbia now seemed doomed – though that did not stop his Obrenović successors from pursuing the dream with the mounting frenzy of men chasing a will-o'-the wisp.

Serbia's own award from Berlin was an extra fifty square miles of territory (which at least put her on a par with Montenegro) and the international confirmation of her status as a sovereign state. Though nowhere stated in the clauses, the Berlin treaty also confirmed something else. Like their fellow Slavs in Bulgaria and Montenegro, the Serbians had exchanged their former vassalage to the Turks only to become the puppets of the other European powers. For the rest of Milan's reign it was the Habsburg eagle which totally overshadowed Belgrade. Indeed, in order to proclaim Serbia a kingdom in 1882, Prince Milan was forced to secure Vienna's approval in advance and pay a high political price for the honour; by a secret convention with Austria, concluded by Milan behind his government's back, the king-to-be virtually signed away his country's independence in foreign policy. He committed Serbia to benevolent neutrality should Austria-Hungary go to war and to desist from all agitation against the Habsburg monarchy, even in the two provinces now occupied by Austrian troops. King he may have become, but not by regal methods.

On the domestic front the new constitution which his regents had sanctioned in 1869 (replacing the old 'Turkish' model of thirty years earlier) had given Serbia the semblance of a modern state, with a bill of rights guaranteeing personal liberty and the freedoms of religion, speech and press. But the regents were careful to retain real powers in the Prince's name, including the right to proclaim laws and to veto them over the head of the Skupština. As one modern authority put it, after 1869 'Serbia had a parliament, but not parliamentary government'.[2]

Inside this bogus outer shell of democracy the core of the nation's life remained violent and rotten. There were repeated financial scandals and in one of them – a stock exchange swindle – Milan became personally involved. He had to survive several attempts on his life, all linked with if not actually instigated by factions loyal to the exiled Karageorgević clan. In November 1883 there was a mass peasant uprising against the Crown, the so-called Timok rebellion, which was crushed by the army with savage reprisals. Two years after that came military humiliation when, egged on by Vienna, Milan declared war on a still expansionist Bulgaria which had already offended by harbouring some of the Turkish rebels. It was all over in a fortnight. In true *opéra bouffe* fashion both commanders fled the field after the decisive clash at Slivnitsa, each convinced that he had lost the day. It soon transpired that the Serbs were the ones who had got it right. There was even panic that the Bulgarians, like the Turks seven years before, could take Belgrade. Milan was only rescued by Austria-Hungary, who threatened the Bulgarians with force unless they halted hostilities. On 3 March 1886 what was probably the shortest treaty of modern times was signed between the belligerents. It consisted of just one article which declared that peace was restored.

This shaming disaster was compounded by the scandal which had now erupted over Milan's family life.[3] This had originally got off to a rousingly romantic start. Though his ministers had been angling for the hand of a Russian princess on his behalf, Milan astounded them all by announcing, in May of 1874, in an open telegram from Vienna, that he had become engaged to a Mademoiselle Nathalie Kechko. Who on earth *are* the Kechkos, everyone asked in Belgrade? This particular Kechko turned out to be the daughter of a Russian cavalry colonel, now deceased, but said to have left vast estates in Bessarabia. Milan was not interested in the estates, if indeed they existed. What had captivated him was the beauty of this sixteen-year-old girl: huge dark eyes, a brilliant complexion, a supple young body and some special magic about her – perhaps from an Armenian ancestor – which suggested the beauty of the Orient combined with that of Europe. At all events, the thirty-year-old Prince, no stranger as a bachelor to feminine charms, fell head over heels in love with her. So did the people of Belgrade the moment they saw the engaged couple, radiating happiness, drive through the streets of the capital in an open carriage.

The bliss of the newlyweds did not last for long. Milan took to a string of mistresses and ended up with an elderly charmer who enslaved him so much that he started to parade her in public. This was a Madame Artemisia Hristić, the Greek-born wife of an official in the Serbian foreign ministry whom the King made his personal secretary to ensure easier access to the lady in question. Things reached a head at the midnight Easter service of 1888 in Belgrade Cathedral. According to Orthodox custom, the dignitaries in the congregation filed up to the King and Queen to receive the kiss of peace. There was a gasp in the church when a smirking Madame Hristić suddenly planted herself in front of Nathalie. The Queen ignored her. The King shouted loudly at his wife to kiss his mistress. The Queen still icily refused. At this, Milan rushed at her in fury and had to be dragged off by his officers. The congregation dispersed into the night in confusion after this most un-Christian of paschal occasions. Milan crowned his outrageous behaviour by leaving the cathedral with Madame Hristić firmly tacked onto his arm.

Thus far, it was a Belgrade scandal. The affair went on to shock Europe, however, through the blazing row which now erupted between the publicly estranged couple over the custody of their twelve-year-old son Alexander, heir to the throne. After the cathedral insult, the Queen decided she could no longer live in the same city as her husband, nor did she consider it a fit place for their son. She left for Wiesbaden in Germany, taking Alexander with her. From now on, the sordid drama was played out in the columns of the European press.

Milan needed little persuading by Madame Hristić that the only course open to him was to divorce his wife. He dispatched his minister of war, General Protić, to Wiesbaden to try and talk the Queen into an official separation on the promise that Alexander could be allowed to finish his education under her wing in Germany. When she refused, Milan persuaded Germany's 'Iron Chancellor' Bismarck to order the police in Wiesbaden to remove the boy from his mother's arms by force and return him, in July 1888, to Belgrade. Three months later, on 12

October, a decree dissolving the marriage was published in the official Serbian gazette. Milan had been unable to produce a shred of guilt to cast against his wife in the matter and he could hardly cite his own adultery as grounds. So, instead, he talked the Metropolitan Theodosius into giving him a divorce by simple edict, allegedly following Orthodox Church precedents in the history of the tsars of Russia.

Though a free man, he was also a shunned one. By his combination of self-inflicted military and domestic humiliations, he had turned the crown of Serbia into an obscene jester's cap. Ever since the disaster of the Bulgarian war he had anyway been tired of wearing it. Abdication was now the logical next step. But before quitting the political stage of Belgrade, Milan decided to instal new scenery.

Prompted partly by the need to give his scandalized capital something else to think about, and partly perhaps by a quirky desire to improve his historical image, only three days after the divorce decree, he launched a committee under his own chairmanship to draft a new constitution for Serbia. The draft, which was duly approved in its entirety by the National Assembly at Christmas of 1888 was, on paper, a great advance on the model of 1869. Civil liberties, such as the freedom of the press, were now spelt out in legislative detail; power was shared out more equally between King and Assembly; the right to secret ballot was proclaimed; and a new system of semi-autonomous local government devised. It all looked splendid, too preposterously so by Serbian standards to last. The cynically weary King was well aware of this; but he reasoned that it might well buy off the critics of the Crown in general (and the Obrenović dynasty in particular) long enough for his son to achieve his majority as heir. Not that Milan himself was prepared to wait around for that to happen.

His last act for posterity completed, he bowed out in characteristically dramatic style. On 6 March 1889 Belgrade's officialdom and society were summoned to court for a reception to mark the country's seventh anniversary as a kingdom. When all were gathered, Serbia's first king had his abdication read out to a dumbfounded audience (only a handful of ministers and advisers were already in the know). At thirty-five years of age (twenty-one of which had been spent on the throne) he now embarked on a new life with a new identity. Calling himself the Count of Takovo, he departed for the fleshpots of Paris, taking with him all the cash and jewels he could get together. Forty-eight hours later his hapless son, the twelve-and-a-half-year-old Crown Prince Alexander, was proclaimed King. However, neither he nor his kingdom were finished with the Count of Takovo yet.

In the spring of 1889 everything looked so hopeful because it all looked so new. The government was now dominated by the so-called Radicals (who had won five-sixths of the seats in the 1888 assembly), a party only formalized seven years before. Its label became increasingly misleading as time went on, for the professors and merchants who came to control it were a far cry from the idealistic socialist students who had founded the movement in the 1860s. Equally misleading was the title of the main opposition party, the Liberals, for these were, in fact, the king's men and, as such, the conservative force in the country. Indeed, their leader, Jovan Ristić, had been named by King Milan as one of the three regents (the other two being a brace of army generals devoted to the Obrenović cause). None the less, this loyalist trio allowed the neo-Socialist government to proceed unhindered with further democratic reforms and, for a while, it looked as though a fresh era of peace and toleration had indeed dawned.

Not for long. Within six months Serbia was again rocked by the feud between father and mother for control over their son. Not without reason did the boy king once exclaim: 'I am an orphan whose parents are still alive!'[4] Milan had arranged that he should be joint guardian, with the regents, of his son's upbringing. As for Queen Nathalie, she was eventually allowed to come to Belgrade to see her precious 'Sasha' for brief prearranged visits up to twice a year. Resenting these restrictions, the Queen Mother simply turned up unannounced from abroad, only to find that the palace gates were barred to her by guards who had conspicuously failed to salute her carriage. But the people of Belgrade had welcomed her and the house she took in the Terazia, Belgrade's main street, during that winter, became a political salon, especially favoured by the opposition Liberals.

Then, on 16 May 1890, the Count of Takovo turned up again. He had by now tired of the brothels and gaming tables of Paris, where he was anyway a nobody. He was also out of money and did not even have his Artemisia to console him. (She was in Istanbul trying to divorce her own husband.) But though no one in Belgrade was exactly surprised to see Milan again, nobody, apart from a few old cronies, welcomed it. Indeed, with mother and father back in the capital wrangling over the boy king, scandal turned into farce. After Nathalie finally lost a drawn-out battle to have her divorce decree made invalid (a wrangle which preoccupied both government and Assembly for months) Milan literally cashed in on his victory. He demanded the huge sum of six million dinars (some seventeen times his fixed apparage) as his price for leaving the country in peace again. In April of 1891 he was finally bought off with three, for two millions of which his estates were pledged as collateral. So desperate was he for the ready cash that he agreed to renounce not only all royal rights but his citizenship as well, and promised never to set foot in his former kingdom again. Needless to say, he had not the slightest intention of honouring the pledges.

Queen Nathalie gave both the Radical government and the royalist regency just as much trouble, though in her own honourable way. She refused to follow her husband into exile, so stubbornly that, in May of 1891, the government resorted to two attempts to expel her by force. The first failed ignominiously when her coach, heading under escort for the waiting Danube steamer *Deligrad*, was surrounded by cheering supporters who unhitched the horses and dragged the carriage back to her house themselves, despite a charge of cavalry and infantry to restore order. The next day the police returned before dawn, climbed over her back garden wall with ladders and took her unprotestingly to the railway station to board a train for Austria-Hungary.

The farce, which made Serbia the laughing-stock of Europe dragged on for the rest of the century. Though both Milan and Nathalie were formally banned from re-entering Serbia, he was back, at his son's invitation, in 1894,* and she returned a year later.

A Russian diplomat who served briefly in Belgrade at this time found a court and a capital divided between the Queen and her weakling son. The young King, whom he once ran into walking down the main street of the city 'dressed in a deplorable suit of some checkered material with a very loud green necktie and a bowler hat' made a pathetic impression – awkwardly built, awkward in all his movements, vulnerable and friendless. Belgrade itself struck the diplomat as being 'rather like . . . a Russian provincial town such as Kursk or Orel'.[5] It seemed to him to be without a middle class as well as without an aristocracy. The hierarchy was composed mainly of army officers and officials, most of the latter placemen of the three parties – the Radicals, whose backbone was the peasantry; the Progressives, largely the party of the intelligentsia, and the misnamed royalist Liberals.

These were the men who filled the salons of the two royal palaces: the more modern building where Queen Nathalie held a cultural court (Molière's *Malade Imaginaire* being performed, for example, in the ballroom) and the smaller, older Konak where Alexander held more modest fortnightly dances. Getting to and from these functions presented something of a problem. As the class known in England as 'carriage people' was almost non-existent, so were the carriages, and the court had to place conveyances at the guests' disposal.

* By now, the teenaged Alexander had deposed the regency council and had assumed power, backed by the army, in a *coup détat*.

Despite the love which bound mother and son, the two palaces inevitably became the focus of rival political camps, so that their personal vendetta grew into a constitutional tussle. However, Queen Nathalie's most fateful act for her son, her dynasty and her country had taken place not in Belgrade but in Biarritz. In January of 1895 she managed to persuade Alexander into spending a month's holiday with her in the villa which she had named 'Sashino' after him. Employed in the household (some said as a glorified maid, others said as a companion and lady-in-waiting) was a twenty-eight-year-old widow named Draga Mashin. Of modest peasant stock herself – from a poor fishing village on the Danube called Milanovats – she had a father who had died in a lunatic asylum and a mother who was an alcoholic. She had not done much better with her own marriage. Her husband, a Bohemian mining engineer of sorts, was a hopeless drunkard and gambler who died of *delirium tremens* soon after she divorced him for ill-treatment. Since then she had been living in Belgrade on a pauper's pension – supplemented, her many enemies claimed, by the hire of her body to selected lovers. Some of the gossip was almost certainly founded on fact, but, given Queen Nathalie's own reputation for decency, it seems strange that she would have taken a notorious society harlot under her wing.

Draga's background mattered not a scrap to the young Alexander one way or the other. Like his father seven years before, he too became first physically captivated and then completely enslaved sexually by an older woman – attractive, companionable, but above all experienced in the ways of the world. The boy King's headlong plunge into bondage is explicable only in terms of his upbringing. He had grown up as a political shuttlecock batted about between his parents and, as a result, was an immature love-starved youth full of complexes and frustrations. The voluptuous Madame Mashin, with her understanding manner, and her huge velvety brown eyes, was the first woman he had met who could satisfy all his yearnings, emotional and sexual. He never looked at another. After nearly five years of living openly with her as his mistress (a situation which became so much of a fact of Belgrade life that the minister of war would ring Draga's house to make quite sure that the proposed dates for army manœuvres would not clash with any personal travel plans of the King's) Alexander announced, on 19 July 1900, that he was resolved to marry her.[6]

Everyone was stunned. Even his father and mother were, for once, united in horrified opposition. As for his ministers (who had been hoping, like the parents, for a royal match with a German, Greek, Russian or even Montenegrin bride), they first tried unsuccessfully to spirit Draga out of the country; then attempted to put the King off his lady by telling him that one or two of their number, plus several army generals, had themselves slept with her for money; and finally, when even these resorts failed to have the slightest effect, they resigned from office *en bloc*. Alexander had to dredge around to find eight officials who, with an undistinguished judge as Prime Minister at their head, were prepared to serve as a 'wedding cabinet' to endorse this marriage. The nuptials were duly solemnized in Belgrade Cathedral on 21 July 1900. There were the usual artillery salutes, peals of bells, firework displays, open-air dancing and free wine for the populace. But the rejoicing had a hollow sound. It was indeed a fateful moment in Serbia's history. King Milan's turbulent love-life had merely speeded up his abdication, shaking the dynasty but leaving it in place. His son's infatuation for Draga Mashin not only signed both their own death warrants: it was to wipe out the Obrenović dynasty for good.

The main cause of the disaster was undoubtedly the almost insane personal ambitions which Madame Mashin developed from the moment she became Queen Draga. Not content with wearing a consort's crown, she became determined to found her own dynasty by replacing the Obrenović on the throne of Serbia with some offspring of her own obscure Lunyevitsa family. It would have mattered relatively little that their pedigree consisted, at the best, of pig-dealers and local officialdom. Neither of Serbia's royal dynasties had sprung from anything more. What counted more in this context was her parents' history of alcoholism and lunacy.

Many rumours swirled around Belgrade as to how Queen Draga proposed to achieve her ends. According to one version, she planned, after making sure that she bore Alexander no heir, to arrange the succession in favour of her own brother Nikodem. (As the latest Serbian constitution excluded collateral branches of the Obrenović family, this was legally feasible.) According to another account, she was scheming to bring off the time-honoured palace trick of the baby switch in the royal bed of labour: she would first feign a pregnancy and then, after careful time-planning with her married sister Kristina, would substitute her new-born infant for the child the Queen was supposed to be conceiving. If this was indeed the plot, it went sadly wrong. Within a month or two of the wedding the news was spread about that the royal couple were expecting a happy event by midsummer of 1901. A distinguished French gynaecologist, Professor Chaulet, who had been summoned to examine the Queen, even issued a bulletin confirming the reports. At this the Tsar and Tsarina of Russia (who, in the cause of pan-Slavdom, had been represented by proxy at the wedding) sent gifts and offered to be godparents to the unborn child. Then came consternation as it was put about that there had been a mistake. To clear the matter up, in April of 1901, the Tsar sent two of his own physicians to examine the lady and they confirmed that she was not, after all, pregnant. Why had the French professor got it so wrong? Was it, as stated, that what he had diagnosed was merely a tumour? What was the answer to the mystery? It is given in a document which has lain unpublished for more than eighty years.

Such was the diplomatic importance of the royal marriage question and such the horrified fascination with which King Edward VII (no stranger himself to scandal of a very different, more decorous nature) was following it that the Foreign Office in London brought together the key papers in one bound volume.[7] Among these is a dispatch sent by the British minister in Belgrade, Sir George Bonham, to the foreign secretary of the day, Lord Lansdowne. It was written on 18 June 1903, after the scandal had turned to tragedy but relates to the summer of 1901.

The envoy clearly found it hard to put pen to paper. Indeed, he began thus to his lordship, 'It is with great reluctance that I revert to circumstances connected with the Queen's false hopes of an heir.' But his new information left him no choice. The Queen, he had been told by 'a source which I cannot disregard', had already had an operation to have her ovaries removed when Professor Chaulet came to examine her. Indeed, he had performed the operation himself. By announcing that she was with child therefore he 'must have planned a fraud which could only have been brought about by the substitution of a suppositious child'. The King, the ambassador surmised, probably knew nothing and was simply 'a dupe'.

Draga's fatal mistake was not, however, causing confusion over her false pregnancies so much as antagonizing the army with her byzantine bed-chamber plots. Alexander – this nervous, shortsighted, spineless young man who had become the helot of his queen – was prepared to equate any opposition to her or her family with treason to the state. Cabinet ministers were dismissed or imprisoned on such charges; the Skupština packed with docile nominees; court officials sacked wholesale; and even his own parents threatened with arrest should they return to the country. (Draga had stoked up her husband's suspicions about his father by reviving worries that the exiled king was himself plotting to put one of his bastards by a Greek mistress on the throne, having first consigned Alexander to a mental home.) All these repressive measures created social and political turmoil, but it was an unrest which the throne could just control. It was when the purge was extended to the army that things got out of control.

The officers had found it humiliating enough to see their élite regiments renamed after Queen Draga. They found it was harder to swallow the behaviour of her young brother Nikodem, himself an army officer notorious for his drunken orgies, who was now going around being addressed as 'Your Highness' by a band of his hopeful cronies. (At court Nikodem, like his brothers and sisters, was already being placed, contrary to all protocol, next to the King and Queen, though Draga had not yet managed to get them declared officially as members of the royal family.) But then Draga started along the fatal path of interfering with army appointments. Any officer suspected of opposing her was either denied promotion or pensioned off altogether. The staff college was up in arms because many of the best candidates selected for courses were blocked as they had provoked the Queen's displeasure. She retorted by persuading her pathetic husband to move the college lock stock and barrel to a new location. To top everything else, pay was often in arrears for months at a time. The Queen was not merely inviting trouble; she was, unwittingly, down on her knees praying for it.

It was the junior army officers who led the way. A group among them had long been in agreement that the weakling King and his vixen of a wife would have to be eliminated if Serbia was to preserve any shred of honour or dignity in the world. The earliest of their assassination plots was prepared, by seven young officers, to take place at the Queen's birthday ball in the first September of her reign. It had to be postponed because the royal couple failed to appear. Throughout 1902, as unrest also flared up among the student and peasant populations, the conspirators gradually increased their numbers to over one hundred and fifty. The driving force, in both recruitment and planning, was a certain Captain Dragutin Dimitriević, nicknamed 'Apis' for his bull-like stature. It was the same Apis, who as a colonel and the head of Serbian army intelligence, was to help shift the course of world history in June of 1914. Now, at the dawn of the century, he was concerned only with shifting the course of Serbian history by eliminating the current occupants of the palace. At their final meeting, on 8 June 1903, the conspirators fixed the night of 10-11 June, the anniversary of Prince Michael's murder in Topčider Park, for the deed. It was to be the bloodiest ever recorded, even in that long chronicle of violence which stained the Serbian crown.

Shortly before 2 a.m. soldiers of the 6th Infantry Regiment – the key army unit in the conspiracy – marched out of their Belgrade barracks and sealed off all approaches to the palace. The soldiers stayed where they were and the final attack itself was carried out entirely by officers, some forty of them in all, who had spent most of the night getting as drunk as lords in various clubs and cafés of the town. People wondered why they had raucously sung, again and again, the newly-composed 'Draga March'. Their leader was one George Genchich, a former minister of the interior under King Milan who had been exiled after Draga's marriage. The man in overall charge of the military operation hated Draga even more. He was her own brother-in-law by her first marriage, Colonel Alexander Mashin, described as 'a squat, villainous-looking little man with a bald head and an oily luxuriant grey beard'.[8]

The palace guards had been strengthened, for the air of Belgrade had been thick with conspiracy rumours, but the plotters had won over one of their officers who admitted the raiders through the back entrance to the grounds. The stout oak door to the palace itself should also have been opened, but the fellow conspirator allotted that task was asleep, dead drunk, and it had to be dynamited instead. That explosion, added to the noise of revolver fire as shots were exchanged with some loyal guards, roused Alexander and Draga from their beds in terror. King Milan had prepared for just such an emergency by having a grating built under the carpet which led to a secret staircase and so to an escape route via the palace cellars. Alexander, rashly, had sealed this up.

The best that the hunted couple could do now was to squeeze themselves into a small clothes closet of the Queen's whose iron door fitted flush into the bright pink wallpaper and was thus difficult to detect. The conspirators only noticed it themselves on their second visit to what seemed an empty bed-chamber, having spent some ninety minutes in the meantime in a furious search of all the other palace rooms. (The electric light had been put out of action by the explosion so they had to operate only with candles, procured from the terrified servants.) They had taken captive the King's aide-de-camp, General Petrovich, who had remained stubbornly loyal, and it was he who, seeing the officers' axes about to smash down the closet door, called out to the royal couple to give themselves up. Lured out by a false promise of safe-conduct, they emerged. The King was clad in trousers and shirt. Draga, flamboyant female to the last, was in her white silk stays and wearing one canary yellow stocking which she had somehow managed to pull on in the darkness. The whimpering pair hardly had time to shout out their appeals for mercy. The leading officers emptied their revolvers into them, thirty-six bullets into the King's body and fourteen into the Queen's. They then hacked the corpses to pieces with their sabres, chopping off the King's fingers and, in a deliberately obscene act of defilement, slitting the Queen's stomach up. The mangled corpses were then hurled through the window into the gardens below. Also murdered in Belgrade that night were the Prime Minister, the minister of war and both the Queen's brothers. The minister of the interior was left for dead but survived. In all, fifty-four people had been killed or seriously wounded.

The legation building of the Russian minister, Charikov, was dead opposite the palace on the road that was still called King Milan Street. The envoy, who appears to have been watching events through his fingers during the night, stirred himself as dawn broke and went across to try and secure a decent burial for the murdered couple. Their remains had simply been left on the grass in a pool of their own congealing blood. The conspirators agreed to release the corpses, but only after holding a post-mortem, conducted by their own military surgeons. These duly produced the required bulletin, intended to mangle the King's name as his body had already been mangled. His skull, they claimed to have discovered (among other physical deficiencies), was abnormally thick and the brain exceptionally small.

After dark a cart – the one normally used for carrying the corpses of suicides and murderers – arrived to take the bodies to the old cemetery of St Mark, where some of the King's obscurer ancestors lay buried. The soldiers detailed to accompany the burial party started to grumble, as midnight passed, about the length of the religious service. 'You have finished your work thoroughly,' the priest replied, 'leave me to mine.'[9] When he had finished, two rough crosses in the ground marked the end of the Obrenović dynasty. Nobody, inside or outside Serbia, was in much doubt as to what would follow.

Chapter Three

SERBIA:
THE FATAL CRUSADE

It will be recalled that one of the political 'reinsurance' marriages concluded by Nikita of Montenegro was to wed his daughter Zorka to Peter, head of the exiled Serbian house of Karageorgević, just in case the fortunes of the reigning dynasty in Belgrade should change. It was an even money bet, as the massacre of 1903 showed. 'Long live Peter Karageorgević' was the shout the officers had raised in the Konak as they hurled the bodies of their victims out of the window. It had been the cry raised by every conspirator over the years, but it could now be taken in earnest. There is no evidence that Peter had actively connived at the brutal events of June 1903. But there is plenty of evidence that he had kept in constant touch, not only with his own supporters in Serbia but also with St Petersburg and Vienna, to ensure himself of Russian and Austrian goodwill should the road to Belgrade be free for a Karageorgević once again. These contacts intensified after Alexander's disastrous marriage, which seemed to open up that road.

According to an Austrian intelligence source (quoted in a dispatch sent to London by the British military attaché in Vienna)[1] Prince Peter had been approached in Geneva, his Swiss town of exile, during the winter of 1902–3, and asked outright whether he would accept the throne of Serbia. He is said to have agreed, on three conditions, namely:

1 That the throne should actually be vacant and that, before any formal offer was made, he should already have been 'duly elected king by the nation';
2 That both Austria-Hungary and Russia should approve; and
3 That no blood should be shed in the process.

The second condition Prince Peter had more or less secured for himself in advance. The Obrenović had always leant towards Austria (however resentfully at times); the Karageorgević were held, on the other hand, to be pro-Russian. But what concerned both the Austrian and Russian Emperors more than the leanings of the rival factions was that, with so much republicanism in the air, Serbia should remain a monarchy in the first place.

How seriously the exile's third condition about the shedding of blood was meant is uncertain. After the slaughter in the palace and the political murders all over the capital, it had already been violated in the grossest possible fashion. The assassins could have argued that coups cost broken heads just as omelettes cost broken eggs. But even they seemed, to begin with, nervous about public reaction. They instantly conjured up a 'plotters' cabinet' on the morning of 11 June which broke the news very gently to the nation that, during the previous night, King Alexander and Queen Draga had 'lost their lives'.[2] No mention of assassinations, let alone mutilations and shabby midnight burials. But then, as the people of Belgrade, seemingly indifferent to the fate of the unpopular couple, joined with gusto in all the festivities arranged for them – bunting was draped from street flagpoles and military bands performed in every square – the junta moved swiftly and confidently to secure Prince Peter's first and prime requirement. On 15 June at a joint session of both houses of the Skupština, 119 deputies and 39 senators voted unanimously, with only one abstention, to elect Peter Karageorgević as the new King of Serbia. How much of a *fait accompli* it was may be judged by the deliberations preceding the vote, which lasted a mere forty-five minutes. A telegram was immediately dispatched to the Prince in Geneva and a reply with his acceptance was received in Belgrade that same day. A deputation of twenty-four members of the Skupština was accordingly sent to Switzerland to escort him home. They were an odd lot. Some were conspirators, including one of the murderers; others men of irreproachable record. Some travelled to Geneva in frock coats; three of the party were peasants in astrakhan caps.[3]

The Prince who now brought the house of Karageorgević back to the throne was fifty-nine years old. He was lean, with thin hair greying at the sides, and a bristly handlebar moustache which topped a weak mouth and a soft, round chin. Only the piercing dark eyes and thick eyebrows reminded one of his famous grandfather who had founded the dynasty a century before in the battles against the Turk. The grandson was described by one contemporary diplomat as being 'of unpretending appearance and chiefly inclined to a comfortable and quiet way of living'.[4] This was a little bland, given some of the things Prince Peter had been up to in his life. After an early upbringing in Hungary he had moved to France, joined the French army and completed the officers' course at St Cyr. He then fought for France in her disastrous war of 1870–71 against Germany and was decorated for his services with the

Cross of the Legion of Honour. After four post-war years, which appear to have been passed mainly in the fleshpots of Paris, he joined the revolutionaries in Bosnia in the great uprising of 1875 and fought with them under the assumed name of Peter Mrkonjić. Though he never became an inspiring leader, like 'Black George' of old, by the mere act of volunteering he had extended the family legend. He also proved a true Karageorgević in his life-style after returning to Paris. Expensive mistresses and uncooperative roulette wheels gradually soaked up his entire fortune as well as that of his father, who was compelled to sell up most of the family estates in Hungary to keep his profligate son supplied with cash. All in vain; by 1883 Prince Peter was bankrupt and saddled with debts amounting to the then huge sum of a quarter of a million French francs.

It was at this point that the wily Nikita of Montenegro stepped in to snap up a dynastic bargain on his own terms. He offered his eldest daughter in marriage on the condition that the spendthrift Prince came to live in Cetinje, where both his behaviour and his household expenses could be more carefully controlled. There Peter passed the next ten years, growing increasingly bitter against his father-in-law and his own wife. Indeed, the miscarriage of their third child, which led to her death in 1890, aged only twenty-six, was widely held to have been brought about by his physical violence towards her. This did not, of course, prevent Nikita from exuding delighted congratulations when his one-time son-in-law returned from Geneva (where he had moved after finally quitting Montenegro) as King of Serbia. For Nikita the match had been a political investment which, after lying fallow for twenty years, now promised a fat yield. His daughter, the Princess Zorka, had not wed and suffered in vain.

The news of King Peter's accession reached Cetinje on the afternoon of 15 June and national rejoicing was ordered. According to the British envoy's account,[5] the great bell of the cathedral was sounded, salvoes of artillery were fired and Nikita, surrounded by all the members of his family, appeared in front of his modest palace to call for three cheers from the crowd. That evening the town was illuminated and patriotic ballads, recounting the ancient brotherhood of the Serbian and Montenegrin peoples, were sung until the small hours.

Nikita's reaction was far from universal. Indeed, apart from the monarch of the Black Mountains, only the Tsar of Russia and the Emperor of Austria-Hungary gave instant recognition to Peter Karageorgević. Their telegrams to Geneva differed somewhat in tone. Those from Cetinje and St Petersburg avoided all mention of the dreadful acts which were about to place the crown on Peter's head. The seventy-three-year-old Franz Josef could not, on the other hand, refrain from adding to Vienna's formal good wishes the hope that the new king of Serbia would succeed in 'raising up his country from the state of deep ruin into which it has fallen as a result of the particularly repugnant crime which has provoked the deepest displeasure in the eyes of the civilized world'.[6]

Though the Emperor was already, in 1903, the patriarchal *grand seigneur* of European monarchy (and must, therefore, have gritted his teeth at the need, for political reasons, to give such swift recognition at all) it was King Edward VII of England who was universally acknowledged as the leader of European society. He was also the supreme guardian of its protocol, which he strove to apply even to his own meticulously-conducted love affairs. For him, the massacre in their palace bedroom of a reigning couple – even if the King was a sickly nonentity, the Queen a bourgeois harridan, and both the dynasties involved the mere progeny of nineteenth-century Balkan pig-farmers – was unpardonable sacrilege against the sanctity of anointed monarchy.

His own telegram of good wishes, sent only on 30 June 1903, four days after King Peter's return to Belgrade, avoided all mention of official recognition, merely offering instead 'the assurance of my personal goodwill'. It pointedly echoed the Austrian emperor's sense of shock by expressing the hope that 'the good name of your country, on which recent events have left such a deplorable stain' might now eventually be restored.[7] But in his outrage King Edward had gone further than delay a cool telegram of good wishes. He had declined both to hold court mourning in London for the slaughtered Obrenović couple or to have his own minister in Belgrade, Sir George Bonham, present in the capital when the Karageorgević exile returned in triumph. It was a question of 'a plague on both your houses'.

Bonham had been recalled already on 19 June and a junior Foreign Office official, Mr Wilfred Thesiger, dispatched to take charge of the legation in his place as second secretary and head of archives. 'The King entirely approves', is the annotation on the telegram of recall.[8] The luckless Thesiger had barely arrived in Belgrade when Britain, on 23 June, actually suspended diplomatic relations with Serbia, thus stranding him in a ludicrous limbo between official and unofficial status. 'The King considers Mr Thesiger's position is a very difficult one,' Edward VII had the grace to minute on one of the first telegrams sent home by the second secretary. His dispatch showed the breadth of the European diplomatic boycott which King Edward had led. On the day Britain suspended relations, Thesiger reported, the ministers of France, Turkey, the United States and Holland had all left Belgrade;

while, of those remaining, the envoys of Germany, Bulgaria, Italy, Belgium, Greece and Rumania had all been ordered to stay away from the new monarch's arrival ceremonies. Thus, when he stepped onto the platform at Belgrade station, only the Russian and Austrian ministers, those established rivals for the control of Serbia, were standing with the welcoming party to greet him. The Austrian envoy, Herr von Dumba, had agonized as to whether he ought to wear his gold-laced diplomatic uniform for the occasion. He only put it on at the last minute when he heard that his Russian colleague was doing the same.[9]

It was largely due to the unbending attitude of England and her sovereign that the dynastic boycott of 1903 was prolonged for three years. Throughout this period the Foreign Office and the Court of St James insisted that, if King Peter wished to be accepted, he would first have to remove the 'regicide officers' from all office and influence. King Peter dithered and dallied. This was not least because, of the other great powers, Russia had laid down no preconditions of any sort, whereas Austria-Hungary (backed by her German ally) was actually encouraging him to resist London's demands, in order to exclude Serbia from British influence.[10] But Peter knew that, though he had been duly crowned in Belgrade Cathedral on 8 September 1903 as King of Serbia, he could never get the Karageorgević dynasty re-established in Europe until he was acknowledged by Edward VII and the mighty British empire.

There was a long haggle over who, precisely, the 'regicide officers' were. In the end Sir Edward Grey, the British foreign secretary of the day, identified seven in a memorandum to his sovereign. Pašić, the indestructible Serbian Prime Minister, got Grey to drop one of the names. One of the remaining six jumped before he was pushed by offering his resignation. That left five: Colonel Popović, commander of the Danube Division: the awful Colonel Mashin, Queen Draga's brother-in-law who had now risen to become acting chief of staff; Colonel Mišić, tutor to the future Crown Prince Alexander; Colonel Lazarević, commandant of the Belgrade garrison, and Major Kostić, commander of the palace guard. As can be seen, between them they held military control over the capital – and thus over the palace – in their hands. Even when their hour had come, the regicides thus needed to be withdrawn very gently, like so many time-fuses from a live bomb.

It was finally arranged, through intermediaries in Vienna and Rome, that, on 11 June 1906, three years to the day after the assassinations, normal relations between Great Britain and Serbia would be resumed. After an agreed delay of one day (which saved the faces of all concerned in Belgrade, including that of the King), the five officers resigned their military and court positions. In true Balkan style they retained all their honours and received their full pensions. Though the prim and proper Queen Wilhelmina of the Netherlands did not end her boycott until 19 November of that year, the return of a British minister to Belgrade signified the return of the house of Karageorgević to the European drawing-room.[11]

At home, King Peter not only felt the unsavoury hands of these murderers on his shoulders; he had also inherited an almost bankrupt economy. (Exactly how close to bankruptcy was hard to establish, for such was the disarray in the finance ministry that the authorities did not even possess a proper balance sheet for the year 1901!)[12] The new reign of a new dynasty seemed to provide the psychological impetus for the government to put its fiscal house in order at last. Within three years, Pašić's Radical administration had produced a healthy budget surplus, thanks to increased taxes and tariffs, a huge expansion of the domestic banking system and a steadily increasing flow of foreign loans.

France (by now the chief banker as well as the close ally of Russia) was also in the forefront of aid to Serbia. Culturally, French influence on the transformation which now took place in King Peter's capital was even stronger. His new palace (the old Konak had been promptly torn down in an attempt to obliterate the memory of a crime as well as that of the victims) resembled nothing so much as a stolid nineteenth-century French provincial château. It was a Frenchman, Léger, who reconstructed the centre of Belgrade around the Terazije Square; it was another Frenchman, the famous architect Cambon, who was called in to rebuild the entire street plan of the city, sweeping away more of the narrow, cobblestoned Turkish alleyways and replacing them with the wide boulevards of his native Paris.

The Serbs looked to France to help them rejuvenate their minds as well as their economy and their capital. It was above all to Paris that, in the early 1900s, Serbian students went for their university courses abroad; and they brought a strong dash of French culture back with them. Thus, both the founder and the editor of the *Serbian Literary Herald*, the leading journal of the day, were Paris-educated.[13] This did not mean that native writing or, for that matter, music and painting, languished. Indeed, King Peter's reign saw a brilliant flowering of Serbian art of all forms, a development which consolidated Belgrade's position as the focus of Slavdom in the Balkans. The city itself gradually became, in the decade before the Great War, an established if still unusual stopping-place on the European tourist route, as opposed to the goal of the occasional intrepid Victorian traveller. A Baedeker of

1905 gave a somewhat rosier account than that of the Russian diplomat quoted in the previous chapter.* It pointed out that Belgrade's Grand Hotel was not only larger, with its forty rooms, than its namesake in the Bulgarian capital of Sofia, but also had 'a lift and electric light'. (The capital had in fact had electric street lighting since 1892, and an electric tramway since 1894.) As its contacts with Western life-style expanded (Belgrade's first motion-picture 'theatre' appeared to wild acclaim, only in a tent at first, in 1906) the capital grew in size. In 1900 it had numbered less than 70,000 inhabitants; ten years later the figure was close to 90,000. It was, in short, King Peter's good fortune to preside, in a benevolent and well-intentioned fashion, over an eleven-year spell of increasing national prosperity and pride. Fatefully, however, this burgeoning Serbian self-confidence took on, more and more, the strident tones of pan-Slav fanaticism.

The danger was inherent in the circumstances of his accession. Though, as an exile, Peter had been careful to keep a line open to Austria-Hungary as well as to Russia, his basic affinities, as with most of the Karageorgević family, lay always with the latter. It was significant that, at the time he unexpectedly came to the throne, both his sons were being educated in St Petersburg: the sixteen-year-old Prince George at the Imperial Cadets academy and the fifteen-year-old Prince Alexander at the Duke of Oldenburg's preparatory school, which was also situated in the Russian capital. But the decisive swing came after his coronation. To consolidate his position after such a murky start, King Peter, or rather his 'regicide' advisers, had to play the pan-Slav 'Greater Serbia' card for all it was worth. Nationalism alone could give to the Karageorgević dynasty the impetus and respectability it sorely needed when mounting that blood-stained throne. It was not for nothing that, in the very year of the 1903 'putsch', a movement known as the 'Slovenski Jug' (or 'Slav South') was founded in Belgrade. It grouped together army officers, government and court officials and parliamentary deputies in a chauvinistic organization that spawned some terrible offspring.[14]

This violent chauvinism fed in the popular mind on ancient legend, inasmuch as it aspired to restore the medieval empire of the 'Tsars' of Serbia who ruled in that golden age before the darkness of the three-and-a-half centuries of Ottoman rule. But the political upheavals of the early twentieth century gave it an even stronger impulse; and the most far-reaching in this respect was the crisis of 1908, when the Habsburg monarchy decided, off its own bat, to convert its military

* See supra, p. 27

occupation of Bosnia and Herzegovina into formal annexation. If the tiny Slav kingdom of Montenegro had been greatly agitated by Austria's move, Serbia, now more than ever the fount of pan-Slavism, was shattered by it. Not only had her dream of 'Greater Serbia' been dissolved overnight by the proclamation from Vienna of 6 October; the kingdom in its existing boundaries was now totally outflanked. The reaction in Belgrade was commensurate. The Skupština met in emergency session to vote credits for war; mobilization was set in train; Serbian envoys were dispatched to all points of the European compass on rescue missions. Those sent to the Western capitals sought only diplomatic support; but the veteran Radical Prime Minister Pašić, who set off in person for St Petersburg, pleaded outright with the Tsar, great brother of all Slavs, for armed help.

In 1908 Russia was still licking the deep wounds inflicted on her only three years before in the disastrous conflict with Japan. Nicholas II, no bellicose figure at the best of times, had no option but to tell his little Slav brothers that Russia was not yet ready to help them. (A heavy emphasis was placed on that 'yet', a hostage to fortune which everybody in Europe except the Serbs managed to ignore or forget in the years immediately ahead.) Pašić got even less comfort from the Tsar's overambitious and over-clever foreign minister, Alexander Izvolski. There was good reason for this. As we shall see when looking at the annexation problem from the standpoint of the great powers, Izvolski, by having struck a secret bargain with Vienna which went disastrously wrong, was himself one of the chief architects of the crisis.

Denied 'active' Russian help, Serbia could only hiss and spit in meaningless defiance. Her own army, no match when at its best for the vastly superior forces of the Habsburg monarchy, was just in the throes of refitting, and Serbia had no Balkan partners on whom she could rely. None the less, Pašić fought a dogged diplomatic delaying action throughout the winter, demanding an autonomous status for the two provinces and territorial compensation for Serbia elsewhere. Not for the first or last time, all the European powers had to struggle to prevent a sudden flare-up in the Balkans igniting those longer fuses of war which could so easily run to their own capitals.

The turning-point came early in the new year when Turkey (who was still the nominal suzerain of the disputed provinces) was bought off for 2½ million Turkish pounds. That left Russia and Serbia isolated: either they too would have to accept the *fait accompli* or go to war. In March 1909, after some anxious sabre-rattling moments, it was all over. On the 22nd of that month Germany, powerfully supporting her Austrian ally, persuaded Russia to back down officially. Encouraged by this, Austria flung a military ultimatum at Belgrade, threatening invasion unless the Serbs also gave way. Pašić had no choice. On 31 March Serbia was forced not merely to recognize Austria's annexation. The bitter pill of acceptance was covered with a coating which made it even harder to swallow. Serbia further undertook to cease all agitation in the matter and 'to change the direction of her present policy towards Austria-Hungary in order to live henceforth on terms of good neighbourliness'.[15]

That was one promise which nobody in Serbia, from King Peter and Prime Minister Pašić downwards, was prepared in his heart to honour. The 1908 crisis was the true prelude to Armageddon in that it drove the pan-Slav crusade down the slippery slope from chauvinism to outright terrorism. Even the relatively moderate Narodna Odbrana (or National Defence), formed in the wake of the annexation in order to fight for 'Greater Serbia' proceeded to set up its own network of agents in the provinces once the crisis was over. The more famous and more fanatical 'Crna Ruka'* or 'Black Hand', which was formed in 1911, proclaimed, in the first two of its thirty-seven secret articles, the goal of unifying all Serbs 'by revolutionary rather than cultural action'.

The 'Black Hand' seemed, to anyone unfamiliar with Balkan mumbo-jumbo, to be something straight off the stage of a Grand Guignol theatre. Its seal was engraved with a skull and crossbones, a bomb, a dagger and a bottle of poison, thus encompassing most of the working tools of any good anarchist. Recruits were initiated in a darkened room lit only by a single candle on a black-draped table, which bore a real dagger, accompanied this time by a revolver and a cross. The cross was intended to give a whiff of sanctity to the primeval oath of allegiance whereby the novice swore his readiness to make any sacrifice 'by the Sun that warms me, by the Earth that nourishes me, by the blood of my ancestors, on my honour and on my life'. After the oath had been administered by (it is almost superfluous to add) a hooded and masked figure also garbed in black, the new member was given his personal pseudonym and allotted to a secret cell which, he was warned, would punish him by death for any abuse.

The 'Black Hand' not only looks forward to 1914, for it armed and trained the Sarajevo assassins. It also takes us straight back to 1903 and King Peter's accession. There were many civilians among its ranks – government officials, lawyers, university professors and the like. But the hard core of the organization wore uniform – policemen and, above all, regular army officers, led by the very savages who had master-

---

* Its real title was 'Ujedinjenje Ili Smrt', meaning 'Unification or Death'.

minded or actually carried out the Obrenović murders. Dragutin Dimitrievć, or 'Apis', now a full colonel and widely regarded as the real power behind the minister of war, was a prominent example. These men had soon wearied of the non-violent tactics of the 'National Union' and were gradually coming to despair of Peter Karageorgević, who seemed to them to be just as supine in the 'Greater Serbia' cause as his slaughtered predecessor had been.[16] Moreover, they had caught the palace firmly in their toils by winning over Prince Alexander, who had replaced his elder brother George as heir apparent in 1909.*

The Balkan Wars against Turkey inflamed these unruly spirits further. There came, first, the headiness of the initial victories of October 1912 when, as already described, the Serbs swept across the Macedonian frontier, routing the Turkish garrison on the way, and joined up with King Nikita's Montenegrin forces for a further push towards Turkish-held Albania and the sea. Then, after the crippled Ottoman empire signed an armistice with the four Balkan allies on 3 December, came months of haggling at the peace conference, held in London under the watchful eyes of the great powers. When the Treaty of London was finally signed on 30 May 1913, the exclusion of Turkey from all but a small patch of her European territories was confirmed; but, thanks to the opposition of both Austria-Hungary and Italy (each of whom had designs of its own on the southern Adriatic) Serbia was barred from Albania and denied its coveted corridor to the coast. This ban remained in force even after the Second Balkan War of June–July 1913 when Bulgaria was crushed by her neighbours and former allies in the squabble for the Turkish spoils. The final result (enshrined in the Treaty of Bucharest of 10 August) left Serbia vastly increased in size, thanks mainly to her acquisitions in Macedonia. King Peter's kingdom had grown from 48,300 to 87,300 square kilometres and the number of his subjects had also nearly doubled, up from about 2,900,000 to nearly 4½ million.[17] There were no Serbs left under Ottoman rule; a common border had been achieved at last with Montenegro; Serbia was the unchallenged champion of Slavdom in the Balkans.

Yet these laurels, which had been won at a heavy cost in lives and treasure, were still tarnished. Serbia had lost at the conference table what she had struck out most of all for on the battlefield – the blue waters of the Adriatic. And quite apart from launching a bitter tariff war (the so-called 'pig war') against Serbia, Austria was entrenched, more firmly than ever, in the Slav provinces of Bosnia-Herzegovina.

---

* This riotous prince had been the cause of many scandals. He got into unpardonable public disgrace after kicking his own manservant to death.

'Greater Serbia' had been given a huge new impulse, yet still denied its principal goals. Triumph was mixed with frustration. It was a dangerous blend of emotions, especially for the radical spirits in the Serbian army who presented a growing challenge to both king and government.

By the time 1914 dawned, two things were clear, both to King Peter and to the powers, small and large, who surrounded his kingdom. The first was the inevitability of a showdown between the military extremists, led by Colonel Dimitriević and the moderate civilian forces, led by the aged Radical Prime Minister Pašić. The second was that if, in any emergency, outside help were needed, it could only come from Russia.

This dependence was symbolized, in the first month of the year, by a baptism in St Petersburg. The mother of the baby boy was Princess Hélène, a daughter of King Peter, who had married a son of the Russian Grand Duke Constantine. Peter decided to go himself to the ceremony and took with him not only Crown Prince Alexander, but his Prime Minister as well. It was thought to be all too much just for a christening[18] and indeed more serious dynastic and political business was afoot. King Peter was striving to bind the small upstart Slav dynasty of Karageorgević once and for all to the mighty Romanovs by marrying his heir to one of the Tsar's daughters. Pašić and the Crown Prince stayed behind after the christening in the hope of forging this brilliant family link there and then. In a report dated 20 January 1914,[19] sent back to his monarch in Belgrade, the veteran Serbian statesman describes how his one hour's audience with Tsar Nicholas II had gone.

There was much preliminary political talk of how best to counter the Austrian thrust, backed by Germany, into the Balkans. Pašić noted that these two mighty allies were arming Bulgaria – with whom Serbia had remained on uneasy terms since the Second Balkan War – with large consignments of rifles, ammunition and howitzers. Could Russia, who had been rearming so vigorously herself since the 1908 crisis, give similar help to Serbia? The Tsar promised to look benevolently at a shopping list already handed over to his minister of war, Sukhomlinov. There was a long political *tour d'horizon* which included Albania (about to become independent under a German princeling); Montenegro (whose absorption into Serbia, it was agreed, was 'only a matter of time'); and the promising progress made by Serbia in winning over the Slav subjects of Austria-Hungary to her cause. Then King Peter's 'special delegate' came to the real point:

If only it could be granted to us to have as our queen a daughter of the Emperor of Russia, she would not only have the feelings of the whole Serbian people behind her. She could become, if God and the situation permitted it, Tsarina of the whole South Slav and Serbo-Croatian peoples. Her influence and her glory would stretch over the entire Balkan peninsula.

Pašić was offering the Tsar, through the proposed marriage bond, nothing less than a second empire for his daughter, part of it at the expense of the Habsburg monarchy. The weak and gullible Nicholas heard these words, according to Pašić, 'with visible joy'. On the subject of the marriage he said neither yes nor no in advance, but indicated that it was up to the Crown Prince – who, he agreed, should stay on in St Petersburg – to do his wooing for himself. Pašić withdrew from the presence convinced that he had succeeded in his matchmaking mission. As for the political and military bonds between the two countries, the audience left no doubt that these were tighter than ever. The Tsar's last words to Pašić were: 'Tell your king that, for Serbia, we will do everything.'[20] Neither man can have dreamt how soon that pledge would be called in.

At home, the tussle between Pašić and Apis reached its climax that spring over the issue of whether the territories recently annexed in Macedonia should be under civilian or military control. A typical example of the new-found arrogance of the Serbian army, and its contempt for the government, took place in May 1914, when General Popović, commander of the Vardar Division in Skoplje, refused to salute the minister of culture on an official visit to the Macedonian region.[21]

In this struggle, the monarch seemed a helpless spectator, still too much the prisoner of the uniformed fanatics who had put the crown on his head to fight resolutely for his constitution and elected government. 'The royal family remains without prestige; the King non-existent', was the withering verdict passed by the French minister in Belgrade, M. Descos, on 26 May.[22]

The following month King Peter, who had mounted the throne in high and bloody drama, bowed out in buffoon-like farce. On 2 June 1914 the military applied such pressure over the Macedonian issue through King Peter and the 'Greater Serbia' faction in the National Assembly that Pašić resigned. But Serbia without Pašić was like a ship without a rudder. Little more than a week later the King had to plead with him to return. Pašić agreed but only on the condition that the obstreperous National Assembly was dissolved.

For the exhausted and discredited monarch and his almost invisible court (there had only been one court ball, on 31 December 1913, during the entire winter season)[23] this was the final humiliation. On 24 June, the day King Peter departed for his annual sojourn at the spa of Vranska-Banya, he announced in the Serbian official gazette *Srpske Novine* that, as illness would prevent him for some time from carrying out his duties, Crown Prince Alexander 'will govern in my name as long as my cure lasts'.[24] As he also took the opportunity of 'commending my dear fatherland to the protection of the Almighty', it sounded ominously like an abdication.

Yet nobody knew for sure, and the country buzzed with speculations. Would it be a long regency? Would King Peter live partly in Switzerland, his old place of exile? Was this all a coup engineered by Baron Hartwig, the very powerful Russian minister in Belgrade?

Just four days later, on 28 June 1914, these, and other matters of somewhat greater moment, were decided when in Sarajevo, capital of the Bosnian province so coveted by the Serbian militants, the heir to the Austrian throne was murdered by an assassin they had trained.

Chapter Four

BULGARIA:
THE BALKAN FOX

To the east of Serbia and Montenegro it was foreign princelings – above all Germans – who were called in to rule over those other provinces of Turkey-in-Europe to break loose from Constantinople. On the face of things, this seemed a reasonable arrangement. The Bulgarians, for example, found themselves without even an aristocracy, let alone a native dynasty, after they finally shook off the Turkish yoke, with powerful Russian military help, in 1877.* So when, in July of 1878, the Congress of Berlin established Bulgaria (much reduced in size from the large satellite country the Russians had tried to set up) as an autonomous principality under the nominal sovereignty of the Turks, some prince had to be produced from outside to sit on its throne. As the smaller courts of Germany swarmed with unemployed second and third sons, and even natural sons, there was no shortage of candidates.

Yet, however sensible it appeared on the surface, the bargain sometimes turned out to be a rough one underneath. The first choice of the Bulgarian National Assembly was Prince Alexander Battenberg, a morganatic offspring of the grand-ducal house of Hesse, who was elected to the Bulgarian throne on 29 April 1879. 'Sandro' was a handsome and charming young bachelor who could claim to be a protégé of Queen Victoria of England. (So, of course, could many another European princeling; but he was one of her especial favourites.) More importantly for a newly constituted state which owed its existence largely to the armies of the Tsar, Alexander was also a nephew of his powerful namesake, Alexander II of Russia.

The twenty-two-year-old Sandro was popular with his subjects, energetic and ambitious; too ambitious for his very limited political

---

* The brutality with which the Turks put down the original uprising went down in history – thanks partly to the indignant oratory of the Liberal British Prime Minister, Mr Gladstone – as the 'Bulgarian atrocities'.

talents. Reluctantly at first, he began to play with the idea of restoring that 'Greater Bulgaria' – stretching westwards to the Albanian border and southwards right down to the Aegean – which had existed for a few heady months in 1878. When the inhabitants of Eastern Rumelia, part of that dream kingdom which the Congress of Berlin had broken up, rebelled in September 1885 and drove out their Turkish garrison, Sandro marched in to support them. From Philippopolis (Plovdiv), capital of the liberated province, he was duly proclaimed the ruler of Bulgaria, north and south.

The court at St Petersburg, instead of being delighted at this further victory of pan-Slavism against the Turks, was furious. Sandro was supposed to act on Russian advice and orders and not on his own initiative. What made matters far worse for him was that his great friend and protector, Alexander II, was by now dead and gone, blown to pieces by a terrorist's bomb on 13 March 1881. The next Tsar, Alexander III, detested all Germans. In particular he hated all his Battenberg cousins and the hapless Prince of Bulgaria most of all. In sulky displeasure the Tsar now recalled all the Russian advisers who were training the raw Bulgarian army and, as a gratuitous personal affront, made public in an order of the day, struck Sandro's name off the list of honorary Russian officers.*

The rift with St Petersburg deepened two months later. The Serbs who had attacked Bulgaria, were thrashed in the field by an enthusiastic young army led, with great dash and courage, by Sandro himself. His triumph in the field made him a hero with his people. It also marked him down politically as a dead man at Russia's hands. Indeed he was lucky to escape physically from attempts made by the Tsar's agents to poison him. Eventually, in August of 1886, they lured him on his own yacht onto the Russian bank of the Danube and held him there while a coup against his throne was mounted in Sofia. As can be seen, the Soviet KGB of today has a long, authentic lineage.

Brave as he was in battle, Sandro had neither the subtlety of mind nor the moral stamina to cope with such pressures. He managed to regain his capital amid wild acclaim a fortnight later but then inexplicably ruined everything by dispatching a servile telegram of submission to the Tsar (who promptly had it published). Sandro's own subjects were shattered by this self-inflicted humiliation, and the cheers turned to head-shaking. Queen Victoria was appalled at the *naïveté*

---

* Sandro's father, Prince Alexander of Hesse, had, if anything, suffered a worse humiliation earlier on. He had been reduced by the Tsar to the rank of sergeant in the Russian army, for his *mésalliance* with Countess Julia Hauke, Sandro's mother.

displayed by her protégé: 'I am speechless,' she informed him. . . . 'You are blamed for having telegraphed the Tsar instead of asking advice here first.'[1]

What followed, with a man of Sandro's unstable temperament, was unavoidable. Having thrown away by a moment's foolishness everything he had gained by his valour in months of war, Bulgaria's first prince of modern times abdicated on 7 September 1886, and promptly left the country. After his reign of barely seven years, Sandro faded out of history on that day. Calling himself henceforth Count of Hartenau, he married, three years later, a pretty singer called Joanna Loisinger. She bore him two children before his death as an obscure exile at the early age of thirty-six.

The problem of the Bulgarian throne, however, could not disappear with him. Sandro's abdication had left a power vacuum which, at first, the Russians attempted to fill. Theirs was a clumsy bid, for the Tsar dispatched to Sofia a ham-fisted megalomaniac, General Nikolai Kaulbars,* who tried to browbeat the country into becoming a Russian protectorate over the heads of its ministers and the three regents they had appointed. It was soon clear to all concerned that the only way to meet the very real threat of Russian occupation which this madman represented in caricature was to find a new foreign prince. Europe, which had looked aghast at General Kaulbars' antics, agreed. But who would take on such a primitive and vulnerable throne? For the next three months, Europe was scoured. Royal dukes, operetta princelings, a Croatian count and, of all things, a Turk (who would have symbolized a return to Ottoman suzerainty) were considered, and either discarded or dropped out by themselves. The search even extended across the Atlantic: the name of an American officer, General Sherman, was mentioned at one point. On the evening of 13 December 1886 the three-man Bulgarian mission which was touring the major capitals in search of the answer found at last their suitable volunteer in – of all places – the Vienna opera house. If the setting was ludicrous, the candidate himself seemed even more so.

Prince Ferdinand-Maximilian-Charles-Leopold-Marie of Saxe-Coburg-Gotha (who had invited one of the delegates, Konstantin Kalcheff, to his box, indicating there and then his interest in their quest)[2] certainly had all the lineage required and more to rule over a poor Balkan principality. Through his father, Prince Augustus, he belonged to that prestigious Coburg clan (dubbed 'the stud-farm of

---

* Tsarist Russia appears to have had a regular supply of these military eccentrics at its disposal. The parallel case of General Cherniaev in Serbia will be recalled.

Europe' by Bismarck) which had managed to place its members, as rulers or consorts, on several major or minor thrones, including that of England. His grandmother on the Coburg side had been Princess Antonia Koháry, one of the richest landowners in Hungary; all her six castles and estates there had passed to Ferdinand, thus making him one of the great magnates of the Habsburg monarchy. (Still closer links with the Austrian court were to follow.)

Even more illustrious, romantic, and formative of his own character was his mother's lineage. Princess Clementine was a daughter of King Louis Philippe, which made Ferdinand half a Bourbon. Moreover, when, on 26 February 1861, at the advanced age of forty-four, Clementine gave birth to Ferdinand in the Coburg Palace in Vienna, she became obsessed with grooming this, her last-born child, for a destiny worthy of her Bourbon blood. As his two brothers were much too old to be his playmates,* the mother was able to focus her energy, like some loving burning-glass, on Ferdinand's education. His intelligence matched her resolve. He learnt to speak five languages – French, German, English, Italian and Hungarian – either perfectly or fluently. He developed, from an early age, a passion for history and the natural sciences which eventually assumed respectable academic proportions. Finally, thanks to the brilliant 'salon' which his mother ran in her Vienna palace, and his own extensive travels, he met almost everyone worth knowing in Europe. Why then, one may well ask, was that Europe so appalled when word got around that he might become the next prince of Bulgaria?

Queen Victoria spoke succinctly for the European royal establishment when, on 16 December 1886, only three days after that first contact in the Vienna opera box, the rumour spread to London. She promptly telegraphed her Prime Minister, Lord Salisbury, from Windsor: 'Hope no truth in respect of Prince Ferdinand of Coburg as candidate. He is totally unfit – delicate, eccentric and effeminate. Only seen it in "Times". Should be stopped at once.'[3]

The Queen may still have been smarting under the fate of her brave and handsome Sandro; yet there was no disputing the adjectives she had flung at his would-be successor. Ferdinand was about the least-manly figure to be seen anywhere on the European royal horizon. He could not even ride a horse properly, let alone cut a credible figure in battle. His body was as soft as his wit was sharply sarcastic. Neither

---

* They duly augmented Ferdinand's royal links. The elder brother Philip married Louise, daughter of King Leopold II of the Belgians, herself of course a Coburg. The other brother, Augustus, married Leopoldine, daughter of Pedro II, Emperor of Brazil, thus establishing an exotic South American tie.

quality commended him for Balkan kingship.

The face, soon to become renowned throughout Europe, was a mixture of the chilling and the comic, a blend of Byzantium and Cyrano de Bergerac. The daughter of a British minister to Sofia, recording her impressions after being presented to him, captures this sense of meeting, not so much a live human being, as a bizarre encapsulation of history:

I think my first reaction was one of fear, combined with a curious feeling that somehow his face was familiar, that at some time those small, amazingly brilliant eyes had peered out at one from an old picture. . . . The fair moustache and pointed beard, the high dome-like forehead, the fierce arrogant nose, the long artistic fingers heavily loaded with superb rings, all these I felt I had seen before . . .[4]

His horror of dirt (all the carriages he used had to be washed daily with strong disinfectant and sometimes the horses as well, which caused the poor beasts to lose their coats) was complemented by his passion for gleaming jewels. He carried pocketfuls around with him – rubies, sapphires, pearls, diamonds and emeralds – and he was for ever slipping them through his fingers, like an Arab with his prayer beads, as though their touch brought him both solace and ecstasy.[5] Dominating all was that grotesquely huge nose which he nicknamed 'the sufferer' and which he would pick and poke around in (despite his normally fastidious manners) like a sweep in a chimney-piece. He was acutely sensitive of 'the sufferer', aware that it would always prevent his striking features from ever being handsome; conscious that, surmounted by his tiny eyes, it made him look rather like an elephant. As he would point out, with a sigh, at least he possessed the sagacity, as well as the appearance, of that beast.

Such was the figure who, on 14 August 1887 (it had taken fully eight months before he dared to brave Russia's opposition and take up the Vienna opera house offer), was sworn in as Prince of Bulgaria at Tirnovo, the medieval capital of his new realm. It was the peasant leader Stefan Stamboloff, in his capacity as Regent, who had talked Ferdinand into taking the plunge and so confront all the great powers with a *fait accompli*. It had not been a question of luring Ferdinand to take up the crown – which he had yearned for from the moment he heard it was vacant – so much as overcoming his sheer funk over seizing it. Scared both of Austrian police agents and the Tsar's assassins, Ferdinand had approached his kingdom disguised as an ordinary passenger in a second-class railway carriage (repeatedly locking himself, for extra safety, in the toilet). Even here, his foppishness was at odds with his caution. He destroyed any pretence at anonymous discretion by travelling in a long, brilliant yellow coat.

Nervous or not and unrecognized or not, he was now Bulgaria's elected prince, 'by the Grace of God and the wish of the people', as his proclamation declared. He next had to set about creating his own court and founding his own dynasty.[6] His indefatigable mother had already been at work on the first task by importing impoverished French noblemen such as the Comte de Grenaud to serve as his principal palace officers. As for the palace itself, this was soon transformed, thanks to Ferdinand's own refined tastes and personal wealth, from the cramped and insanitary 'Konak' (or former Turkish governor's residence) of Alexander's day into a handsome yellow-washed building which combined French elegance with Germanic solidity. Gradually it accumulated its appropriate tally of marshals, chamberlains, commandants, chancellors of noble orders, dames and maids of honour, attachés, aides-de-camp, physicians, masters of ceremonies and all the other human paraphernalia which any self-respecting court of the day demanded.

Ferdinand's contrasting ancestry came out in the way his palace was run. The discipline and etiquette were punctilious, almost to Prussian standards. The cuisine, which became renowned, was Parisian. Everything was permeated, like the scent of some heavy perfume, by the presence of this opulent, feline princeling. Apart from adding Bulgarian to his collection of languages, Ferdinand also now took to enlarging an already preposterous wardrobe with medieval Bulgarian raiments. One of the few colourful sights of Sandro's court to survive was kept on precisely because of its theatrical appearance. This was the royal bodyguard of twelve strapping young soldiers, dressed in baggy scarlet drawers, on top of which came an embroidered tunic girdled by a rainbow-coloured cummerbund holding the ceremonial dagger. It was no wonder that Bulgaria, like Montenegro, became the setting for a Viennese operetta: in Sofia's case, Oscar Strauss's *Der tapfere Soldat*, or, to give it its English title, *The Chocolate Soldier*.

Ferdinand's next priority – or rather, that of his mother – was much more difficult to solve. Finding a suitable wife was to prove a herculean task compared with that of finding suitable accommodation. Indeed, there were even problems finding suitable mistresses. According to Ferdinand's latest biographer,[7] until his early middle age the prince's desire for women still overshadowed his homosexual impulse. But how could this desire be met? As, thanks to the Russian veto (followed, with varying degrees of enthusiasm, by the other great powers), his crown had not been recognized, he could not travel freely abroad and sample the discreet but voluptuous pleasures available in cities like Paris and Vienna. His own capital was like a provincial village where almost every woman was in bed, either alone or with her husband, by ten. What passed for society in Sofia was imbued with a strong streak of patriarchal puritanism.

None the less, thanks partly to his anxious mother's efforts as a go-between, he managed to conduct a series of affairs inside this social prison. One concerned a certain Madame Belcheff, who was beautiful as well as being a poetess, thus satisfying the prince's physical and spiritual needs. For convenient access right inside the palace, Princess Clementine appointed her one of her ladies-in-waiting. Another of Ferdinand's homespun mistresses in these first years was Madame Petroff, a buxom brunette who was the wife of the Bulgarian chief of staff. Needless to say, Colonel Petroff's future was assured. Both these ladies appeared in an ornate *tableau vivant* which Princess Clementine staged for her son in the ballroom of the Sofia palace on 26 February 1888, his twenty-seventh birthday and his first as Prince of Bulgaria. Madame Petroff was one of three beauties on the podium, all arranged in the national colours of red, white and green. Madame Belcheff, attired in angel white, held a victor's laurel wreath aloft over a bust of Ferdinand. To make clear the sort of victory his mother had in mind, the marshal of the court, dressed in Byzantine robes and wearing an imperial crown, pointed straight at Ferdinand's marble head. Mistresses, mother and courtiers alike were inviting him to restore the Bulgarian empire of pre-Turkish days.

Quite apart from throwing a screen of decency around Ferdinand's private life, the right marriage was also a key to these ambitions. Moreover, as the Russians were constantly conspiring to depose or even murder him (the most flagrant attempt, led by a fire-eating Bulgarian from Macedonia, Major Panitza, was uncovered in January 1890 at the last minute), the Crown badly needed an heir. So in 1891, the year after that abortive *coup d'état*, Ferdinand set out in earnest in search of a bride, despite the fact that the crown he could offer the unknown lady was still not formally recognized anywhere outside his own principality. It proved a long and humiliating process. For all his wealth the Prince was not exactly an appetizing choice for a husband, and his obscure little realm positively reeked with the fumes of assassins' gunpowder. (Ferdinand himself had taken to wearing a light chain-mail vest under his elegant costumes to protect himself from direct attack.) In the days when bombs were commonly hurled at sovereigns and marriages were anyway arranged not in heaven but in dynastic conclaves, these considerations could have been easily brushed aside by the parents of any prospective bride were it not for the political clouds which hung over the bridegroom's crown. As things stood, any family accepting Ferdinand as a son-in-law would meet with the constant hostility of the Tsar of Russia, without gaining any friends from the other major courts.

Louisa, the eldest daughter of the Grand Duke of Tuscany, a lateral branch of the Habsburgs, was the first target. In the account she gives in her own memoirs[8] of Ferdinand's wooing, she portrays herself as the haughty Austrian archduchess mockingly rebuffing an effeminate, overdressed and overvoluble suitor who, in support of his pleas, constantly waved well-manicured hands which glittered with those costly rings. Whether that version be accurate or not, Ferdinand was perhaps lucky that she rejected him, for Louisa turned out to be one of the darkest female blots on the Habsburg escutcheon. She eventually married Crown Prince Frederick Augustus of Saxony and bore him five children but then, in 1902, turned her back on the court of Dresden by eloping with their Belgian tutor, a Monsieur Giron, whom she in turn abandoned for Enrico Toselli, the Italian composer. The scandal shook everyone except her phlegmatic Saxon husband. Ferdinand would have felt enraged and humiliated almost unto death.

His 1891 tour of western capitals, in search not only of a wife but of any crumb of official recognition tossed to him, ended in frustration all round. Things went rather better when he set out again the following year. In June of 1892, he was received with courtesy by Lord Salisbury, the Prime Minister, in London, and even with some warmth by the old Queen Victoria in Balmoral.[9] But she made it clear that she had no intention of giving him one of her own granddaughters in marriage – if only for fear of offending the Tsar. Ferdinand met the same reaction when he toured the German courts on the way home.

His mother decided that there was nothing for it but to lower their sights a little. Negotiations were accordingly intensified with Duke Robert of Bourbon-Parma for the hand of Marie-Louise, the eldest of his daughters. The Duke had lost his small realm thirty-two years before and, from his two marriages, had several daughters to settle. However, he was a full Bourbon to Ferdinand's half-Bourbon, and a devoted Catholic. As such, he insisted that Article 38 of the Bulgarian constitution, which laid down that the heir to the throne must be baptized in the Orthodox faith, should be amended to a Catholic upbringing for any children of the proposed marriage. Stamboloff, still Ferdinand's Prime Minister despite growing personal friction between the two men, agreed to try to push the change through the National Assembly on his personal authority. He triumphed, one of his last services to his country, on 19 December 1892. In February of the following year Ferdinand travelled to Schwarzau, Duke Robert's Austrian seat south of Vienna, for the engagement party.

The occasion has been well described as a royal 'blind date'.[10] There is no record of Ferdinand ever having clapped eyes on his bride-to-be before greeting her already as his fiancée. Perhaps just as well, for he cannot have been entranced by what he saw. She was a slight, plain girl with a long, lemon-like face and protruding ears. However, she had a nice singing voice; was intelligent (like her husband, fluent in five languages); kindly and conscientious. Indeed, though she was only to live for another six years, she more than fulfilled anyone's expectations by producing, in that short spell, four children, two sons and two daughters. It was the arrival of the first child, Prince Boris, on 30 January 1894, nine months after the wedding, which was to transform Ferdinand's fortunes.

The tiny heir to the throne created problems, literally from the first. Stamboloff had insisted on his constitutional right as Prime Minister to witness the birth, which was a long and difficult one. The shock at being exposed to this indignity may well have been one reason why the mother needed such a long convalescence before showing herself in public again. But arguments over the birth were as nothing compared with those which now arose over the infant's upbringing. The death, in November 1894, of Ferdinand's most formidable enemy, Alexander III, seemed to open the road to reconciliation with St Petersburg; the new Tsar, the weak and kindly Nicholas II, had none of his predecessor's fierce prejudices. But even he had a price for his blessing: the baby Prince, who had been christened as a Catholic, must first change his religion and embrace the Orthodox faith. Ferdinand's father-in-law, Duke Robert of Bourbon-Parma, to whom the marriage pledge over Catholicism had been given, was a dispossessed ruler of negligible political weight. The Tsar of Russia was the Slav colossus who alone stood between Ferdinand and European recognition. Ferdinand tried to bargain (using the genial Prince Edward of Wales, heir to Queen Victoria, at one point); but in the end the scales of advantage could only come down one way.

Despite the anguish of the Bourbon family (and especially his own wife and mother); the anger of the Austrian emperor Franz Josef (who had helped arrange the match), and the steely hostility of Pope Leo XIII (who, without fully excommunicating Ferdinand, declared him anathema)*, the Bulgarian Fox could not resist the prize. On this

* The punishment, which allowed Ferdinand to attend Mass, was rescinded by Leo XIII's second successor, Benedict XV.

matter his own personal ambitions anyway coincided with the feelings of his people. They had never understood why the heir to their throne, with its ancient Orthodox lineage, should have been baptized a Catholic in the first place. So, on 15 February 1896, in an elaborate ceremony in Sofia Cathedral, the two-year-old Prince Boris of Tirnovo was transferred (no re-baptism was required) to the Orthodox faith. The Tsar had sent a chrism with holy oil for the ceremony and also a general, bearing the most famous of all Russian military names – Kutuzov – to act for him as proxy godfather. Within a week all those European powers who, in 1878, had signed the Berlin Treaty establishing the new Bulgaria, had followed Russia's lead and formally recognized Ferdinand as its rightful ruler. He was part of Europe's dynastic patchwork at last. His wretched wife could not bear to share in his triumph. She left his kingdom for a while, taking with her Kyrill, Prince of Preslav, the second son she had borne him two months before. Ferdinand was well able to bear the pain of temporary separation.

The path of opportunity, now open to him abroad, had already been cleared of potential rivals at home. In November of 1893, on the eighth anniversary of his famous victory against the Serbs, Sandro had died. The exiled ruler had never shown any inclination to try to regain his throne; none the less, for Ferdinand it was a relief to see him drop out of the reckoning for good. Sandro returned to his lost capital in his coffin and was given an elaborate state funeral.

There had been much more anguish and controversy in 1895 over the removal from the scene of Ferdinand's only real challenger for power, Stefan Stamboloff, the granite-hard peasant leader who had brought him to the throne and guided his first years there. Stamboloff was no longer the popular hero he had once been. The people laboured under the repressive police regime he had introduced after the Macedonian Panitza conspiracy, and there were widespread grumbles about corruption. None the less, as a dedicated patriot and the nearest thing to a statesman his country possessed, Stamboloff deserved a dignified exit. Instead, his downfall lived up to the worst traditions of Balkan intrigue and violence.

Ferdinand, always jealous of Stamboloff, had only waited until his own position was strong enough to topple his mentor – just as four years before, in Germany, the Emperor William II had disposed of his political tutor, the 'Iron Chancellor', Bismarck. The lever used to unseat Stamboloff – and one fully exploited by Ferdinand even if he did not set it in motion – was a Sofia sex scandal. Madame Savoff, the wife of the Bulgarian minister of war, was notorious for her loose morals. Knowing that the husband's jealousy matched her infidelity, the opposition press hit on the diabolical idea of parading Stamboloff as one of her lovers. Colonel Savoff was duly goaded into challenging his own Prime Minister to a duel. Instead of a duel, a muddled government crisis ensued. On 29 May, Stamboloff offered his resignation (as he had often done before, only to be reinstated). This time the offer was accepted and Constantin Stoiloff – one of the three emissaries whom Ferdinand had received in that Vienna opera box nearly ten years before – became the new Prime Minister.

If all this ruffled the susceptibilities of other European courts, what followed revolted their conscience. Stamboloff embarked on a public slanging match against both Stoiloff and the Prince, whose policies he once castigated as 'hermaphrodite', a particularly stinging insult. The ex-Prime Minister's enemies countered by bringing a clutch of Sofia prostitutes into court to accuse him of having raped them (a somewhat bizarre charge, given their profession). Then terror entered this sordid scene as Stamboloff's Macedonian enemies, sworn to avenge Panitza's execution, began to close in on him. Even Stamboloff's iron nerve cracked. Twice in that summer of 1895 he demanded his passport (which had been impounded) so that he could join his Prince at the Bohemian spa of Karlsbad. Twice the request was refused, on the second occasion with Ferdinand's approval.[11]

That second refusal was Stamboloff's death warrant. On the evening of 15 July 1895 he was attacked on the streets of Sofia and hacked to pieces by three Macedonian fanatics. The then British minister to Sofia, the distinguished diplomat Sir Arthur Nicolson,* had been talking to Stamboloff only minutes before at the Union Club. A week later, (Stamboloff lived on with his terrible injuries for three days) the envoy attended the funeral as Queen Victoria's personal representative. The coffin lid mercifully spared the mourners a gruesome sight. Stamboloff's head, which had taken twelve of the twenty-three sabre wounds, was barely recognizable. His hands had to be put in separately, alongside the body. A surgeon had amputated them in the struggle to keep him alive, and when the corpse was being laid out for burial, they had floated in a bowl of alcohol 'like a pair of gloves'.[12]

Though Ferdinand had not conspired in the murder, for which he bore only very indirect responsibility, the assassination made a dark backdrop to his formal entry on the European stage six months later. None the less, it did mean that Ferdinand could now appear on that stage recognized not merely as a sovereign abroad but as the

---

* Later ambassador to St Petersburg and ennobled as Lord Carnock.

undisputed master of his own country at home. The royal dandy had become also the royal despot.

He lost no time in savouring his hard-won legitimacy. In the spring of 1896, he set out on a tour of European capitals, beginning with a three-week visit to Constantinople. Sultan Abdul Hamid – still nominally the suzerain – welcomed him to the florid decaying metropolis of the Ottoman empire as though he were already a fully independent sovereign. He was given a palace to himself; the highest Turkish order was pressed on his breast; the dream of ruling this doomed Byzantium mounted in his head. Why else would he have insisted on walking quite alone in the great mosque of St Sophia to stand on the spot where, four and a half centuries before, Turkish janissaries had stopped the Mass?

Next came St Petersburg, where Nicholas II welcomed him warmly back to the Slavic fold; then Paris, where President Faure and the crowds lining the boulevards honoured him as the grandson of Louis Philippe, their 'bourgeois king'. Berlin was not quite so flattering. There was, for example, no guard of honour at the railway station. William II did not want to irritate his Austrian ally unduly, and the doors of the Habsburg palace in Vienna remained, for the time being, firmly closed in front of Ferdinand's long nose. Yet, ironically, it was Ferdinand's new friend, the Tsar of Russia, and not the offended Emperor of Austria, who administered the most wounding snub of the year. The Tsar's master of ceremonies had no choice in the matter when Ferdinand turned up in Russia again to attend the coronation of Nicholas II. The Prince of Bulgaria could now be received as a legitimate ruler, yet he remained, in law and therefore in protocol, a vassal of the Sultan. To his acute displeasure, therefore, Ferdinand found himself wedged between two fellow-vassals, the Emir of Bokhara and the Khan of Khiva, at the Moscow ceremony. Kings and princes from all the royal houses of Europe were present to witness his humiliation. We may be sure that most of them positively enjoyed it.

As with Peter Karageorgević, craving European acceptance after the terrible Belgrade bloodbath of 1903, so with Prince Ferdinand now: socially even more than politically, England was the key, especially after Edward VII mounted the throne in 1901. Edward simply loathed Ferdinand, and for so many reasons. For all his illustrious lineage and their blood links through the Coburg clan, he struck the King of England as being somewhat vulgar; of having unfathomable and unsavoury sexual habits; and, above all, of being far too clever and quick off the mark. The King could never forgive Ferdinand when they met – unavoidably – at great European spas such as Marienbad for so often being the first to inform him on the latest news from the outside world.[13] But Ferdinand possessed a curious skin which was as hard as an armadillo's as well as being delicate as a baby's. He pressed on regardless to win the King's favour, his ultimate aim being a state visit to England.

A document in the Royal Archives at Windsor shows Ferdinand at work on this in the autumn of 1907, the zenith of Edward VII's reign. Sir George Buchanan, then British minister to Sofia, writes to the King's secretary, Lord Knollys, saying that he has made it clear to Ferdinand that only a *private* visit to London would come into question that October, and even then the King could only find time to see him between the 24th and the 27th. At hearing this Ferdinand had gone cold on the whole idea and had complained instead (to Edward VII of all people) on a point of royal manners. Why, on the recent death of Ferdinand's brother, the sixty-two-year-old Prince Augustus, had the King of England not followed the example of the emperors of Russia, Austria and Germany and 'most of the other European sovereigns' and sent him a personal message of condolence? The envoy was able to reply that his royal master had, as usual, not been caught napping over protocol. A telegram of condolence *had* been sent to Prince Philip of Saxe-Coburg and, as he was the head of that multi-branched house, it was surely his business to pass the message on.[14] Ferdinand appears to have been stumped by this, though he realized full well that he had been neatly, and deliberately, bypassed.

Though there was an enormous measure of preening and prickly self-obsession in episodes like this, Ferdinand's ambitions and tantrums were not all vanity. The security of his country, as well as that of his own crown, depended on a higher degree of recognition, and this, he had by now decided, could only be secured through a higher degree of sovereignty. In August of that same year, 1907, he had managed a visit (again only private) to the Emperor Franz Josef at the latter's beloved summer villa at Bad Ischl. A communiqué issued after the meeting described as 'malicious invention' reports that the visitor was about to proclaim the complete independence of his country from Turkey. Ferdinand had made it clear to his host that he 'did not occupy himself with vain questions of formality or titles or other personal satisfactions'.[15] In fact, of course, Ferdinand was obsessed with such questions. As to the future, he was already scheming to proclaim for himself something more than mere independence – and this with the active connivance of the Emperor's ministers.

The annexation by Austria of the twin provinces of Bosnia and Herzegovina which she had occupied and administered since 1878 was, of course, a grievous blow to Serbia; moreover, after a long European crisis, it finally brought diplomatic humiliation for Russia as a great power patron of the Slav cause. But for Ferdinand it spelled nothing but triumph. By secret agreement with Austria – who felt that any Balkan support or distraction would be invaluable once she had decided on her own *coup* – Bulgaria unilaterally declared full independence from Turkey on 5 October 1908, the eve of the Austrian action. For good measure, as he had now declared his country to be a proper kingdom, he also assumed the title of tsar as Bulgarian King. Whatever historical precedents could be advanced for this (and there had been so-called tsars of tenth-century Bulgaria, long before they appeared in Russia) every court in Europe regarded Ferdinand's self-proclaimed glory as just another example of insatiable vanity and of a growing leaning towards oriental pomp and despotism. So much, they sniffed, for that declaration made the year before from the lakes of the Salzkammergut that the Prince of Bulgaria 'did not occupy himself with vain questions of formality or titles or other personal satisfactions'.

Not that one of those powers, the Habsburg monarchy, could feel either traduced or surprised. The tacit bargain between Vienna and Sofia for linked action against Turkey went back to March of 1908 when Franz Josef's ambitious new foreign minister, Baron von Aehrenthal, had given Ferdinand private assurances that, if it were decided to abandon the politics of status quo *vis-à-vis* Turkish suzerainty in the Balkans, 'there would be no clash of interests between the Monarchy and the Principality'.[16] Broader hints followed from Aehrenthal and also – more precious as well as more positive for Ferdinand – august dynastic backing. Less than a fortnight before both Monarchy and Principality pounced to pull up such straggly roots as the Ottoman empire still possessed in south-east Europe, Ferdinand had been fêted in Buda Castle by Franz Josef. The Emperor had made a point of sponsoring 'the development of young Bulgaria'.

But complications remained, quite apart from the sabre-rattling of Serbia. To begin with, the great powers who had signed the 1878 settlement could not swallow Austria's action nor accept Ferdinand's claims until Turkey had agreed compensation terms for the loss of her dignity and faded historic claims, thus enabling the Congress of Berlin to be forgotten. Ferdinand had a special problem. Like Sandro in 1885, he had offended St Petersburg by independent action, in this case by conspiring to put himself on equal terms with the only 'real' Tsar, who dismissed his self-promotion as 'the act of a megalomaniac'. So, for the second time in his reign, once as elected prince and now as self-styled tsar, Ferdinand found himself looking to Nicholas II to set the example of acceptance. As it became clear, early in 1909, that Turkey would settle for cash, all that Ferdinand needed to solve his personal problem was a fitting pretext. As if on cue, the Grand Duke Vladimir, uncle of Nicholas II, died in February 1909 at the age of sixty-two. Ferdinand immediately asked whether he might come to St Petersburg to attend the funeral, if need be only as a private mourner. The comedy which ensued is described in the telegrams which the British and German ambassadors to Russia sent home over the next few days. Ferdinand was obviously craving for guards of honour, twenty-one-gun salutes and all the other trimmings of royal reception abroad. But as Turkey had not yet signed on the dotted line, could any or all of this be accorded without formal recognition?[17]

The kindly Nicholas decided that, on political grounds, it could. The 'megalomaniac' must have guessed that he was home and dry the moment he was advised to appear in the uniform of the Russian regiment of which he was honorary colonel. But even he must have been delightedly surprised by the fulsomeness of his reception. There to greet him at St Petersburg station on 21 February was the Grand Duke Constantine, plus three generals and three aides-de-camp. The guard of honour was indeed drawn up for him and when he gave it the customary Slavic greeting of 'Your health, my brothers' they thundered back 'Good health to Your Majesty, the Tsar'.[18]

Ferdinand had none the less to dine by himself that evening and the next day he was instructed to go behind all the other court mourners into the cathedral. It was the sort of challenge he excelled in, and he proceeded both to follow his orders and to flout them. He duly appeared last of all but then, wandering about agitatedly as though he had arrived late and forgotten his placing, he made for the front row and planted himself down on a seat right next to the principal mourner, Nicholas II.[19] That 'brio' performance was, in fact, an apt symbol of his triumph. He had got the most out of the 1908–9 crisis and it had all cost him nothing. He even had the effrontery before leaving St Petersburg to assure both Nicholas and his foreign minister, Izvolski, that there had been no question of any complicity between Sofia and Vienna in the whole affair. Izvolski, a schemer himself, could only reply: 'If you say so I am bound to believe you, but I feel obliged to add that many people feel otherwise.'[20]

Of course, Ferdinand being Ferdinand, he was still not satisfied. To begin with, the mere sight of his modest little capital after all these truly imperial splendours was depressing proof of the gap between his reach and his grasp. 'Merde, merde, merde,' he was heard to mutter as he acknowledged the salutations of his courtiers on returning to his palace.

Moreover, he knew that, whatever he called himself, the established
dynasties would always regard him as a parvenu. A year later, for
example, he was so snubbed by his fellow sovereigns at the London
funeral of Edward VII that he snarled to the young King Emmanuel II of
Portugal: '*Riez, riez, mon cher cousin. Je suis, en effet, un roi d'hier, mais êtes-
vous bien sûr d'être un roi de demain?*' It was both a barb and a prophesy.
Emmanuel had only reached the throne two years before on the
assassination of both his father Charles I and his elder brother Louis
Philippe. He himself was soon to be forced by a revolution to flee his
country, to die in England and to bring an end to the reigning house of
Braganza.

When he proclaimed himself to be Europe's new 'Tsar' (and in the
minds of all his royal cousins, those inverted commas would never be
removed), Ferdinand was forty-seven years old. The brown, carefully
waved hair of his youth had shrunk to two greying strips low on the
sides of his face, and the bald dome which now rose above them made
the large nose look even more prominent. He was now well into the
mainly homosexual phase of his life and the blond blue-eyed chauffeurs
chosen to drive his limousines caused as much stir as did this unheard-
of fleet of motor cars itself (electric and petrol-driven from half a dozen
countries). If anything, his passion for trains – he loved driving them
himself and was proud of his membership of the German Railwaymen's
Union – was surpassed by this growing fascination for automobiles.
The latter also provided more privacy. Often, when his ministers were
looking for him he would have disappeared on a car trip to the
mountains, sharing champagne and caviar with his current favourite
among the chauffeurs.[21]

It was not surprising therefore that when he decided it was time to
remarry (to find a good stepmother for his four orphaned children and
to have a stately consort to appear by his side at ceremonial occasions)
sentiment scarcely entered into it, let alone love. The lady selected for
him by one of his elderly admirers, the Grand Duchess Marie Paulovna
(an aunt of Nicholas II), was Princess Eleonore of Reuss. She was a
plain square-faced German spinster, full of the solid German values of
efficiency, uprightness and dedication to duty. She had distinguished
herself as a Red Cross nurse in the Russo-Japanese war of 1904–5 and
Bulgaria probably appealed to her primarily as a mound of under-
privileged mortality crying out for good works. Being a year older than
Ferdinand, she must have abandoned all thoughts of marriage, let
alone of the marriage bed. That was just as well, for Ferdinand was
determined to take her no further than the altar. He was furious when,
on their return trip from the emotionless marriage services in Germany

(a Catholic one in Coburg followed by a Lutheran one in her native Reuss) the newlyweds were given a suite with only a double bedroom in the royal palace at Bucharest, where they were paying an official visit. He ejected his wretched wife from the suite, which he insisted on occupying alone, and told her to go and sit with their hostess, the enchanting Queen Elisabeth of Rumania, until separate rooms could be provided for her.[22]

It was this type of appalling behaviour – brash, intemperate, inconsiderate and, above all, vulgar – which, on the public stage, was making Ferdinand the most detested monarch in all Europe. His fellow-royals, as that exchange of messages with King Edward VII indicates, would groan at the mere prospect of having to receive him at their courts. They would, if possible, walk the other way when encountering this byzantine apparition at those weddings, christenings or funerals which intermittently brought the European dynasties together. It was an age when good form and good manners made up the surface mould of society. Ferdinand was born a prince and had become a sovereign. But he had clearly never been a gentleman; and that, quite simply, was that.

This verdict also applied to his politics. He became known in his day – and indeed has gone down in history – as 'Foxy Ferdy', the very personification of duplicity. His apologists have rightly insisted that throughout his reign he was obliged to weave his way between the two great empires which surrounded him, the Russian and the Austrian, and play both these mighty sides against the modest Bulgarian middle. But it is too much to claim that even this delicate and fragile situation justifies everything he got up to. All that we know about Ferdinand's private life shows that he was both devious and unscrupulous by nature and eaten up by vanity. He would have been a consummate liar had he never set foot outside his Vienna Coburg palace and his six Hungarian Koháry castles. When such innate moral dishonesty was applied to the tricky business of diplomacy, the results had to be seen to be believed. Fortunately they still can be seen, scattered among the various official archives of his time.

His grand aim, one of his own ministers was quoted as saying, was 'to sow dissension between Austria-Hungary and Russia and finally to side with whichever of the two would pay the higher price for his co-operation'.[23] This meant, in the Europe of rival alliances, sowing dissension everywhere. Thus, in Vienna he would seek to curry favour by branding the Serbs as 'a gang of criminals', even going so far, in 1908, as to suggest that the kingdom of Serbia ought to be absorbed into the Habsburg monarchy. But on his frequent stays in St Petersburg and on his one visit (25 November 1909) to Belgrade itself, he indulged in crude personal abuse against the Emperor of Austria.[24] When, however, that aged monarchy wearily gave way at last to Ferdinand's years of lobbying to be awarded the Golden Fleece and, in 1911, conferred this most prestigious of all Catholic honours on the Bulgarian ruler, Ferdinand gushed for weeks with joy and devotion. He was lost for words, he told Franz Josef's envoy in Sofia, to express his 'unquenchable gratitude' and he saw happy political omens in the fact that 'the highest order of Christianity should shine for the first time in lands this side of the Balkans'.[25] Within months, however, he was back at his anti-Austrian games.

It was no wonder that he had become the most distrusted ruler in Europe. At that family wedding gathering in Berlin with which this book opened, the one point on which all three sovereigns present (King George of England, Tsar Nicholas II of Russia and Emperor William of Germany) had 'most heartily' agreed was that 'King Ferdinand must be called to order and kept in order'.[26] But the sensitive position he occupied, as well as his own constant intrigues, made him difficult to pin down. As he once put it, with characteristic wit, 'I'm like a flea in a place where nobody dares to scratch.'[27]

Despite his personal wealth he enjoyed no financial security. Throughout his reign he used his crown as a jewelled begging-bowl. At times there seems to have been an almost desperate shortage of ready cash. In 1911, for example, soon after getting his Golden Fleece from Vienna, he squeezed a personal loan of two million francs out of Tsar Nicholas, putting up one of his properties as security. He later persuaded France to join with her ally Russia in providing a substantial loan (the Franco-Russian interest being to prevent Bulgaria falling too deeply into the rival Austro-German camp). The terms were still being negotiated when Ferdinand demanded an immediate advance of eighty to ninety million from the French banks.[28]

Ferdinand certainly needed money to build up his army and to develop the infrastructure of his country. Progress here had been considerable. Sofia had grown during his reign from the squalid Turkish town of Sandro's day, with its paltry 15,000 inhabitants, to a city with a fair-sized population of 75,000 and amenities which – by Balkan standards – were equally respectable. The extension of the Orient Express network to Sofia – which enchanted Ferdinand the engine-driver – had indeed forced his capital to try to match the standards of the European continent to which it was now joined. Timetables for 1905 show the famous train taking 94½ hours to reach Sofia from Paris via Munich, Vienna and Budapest. Travellers from

Berlin could join the Orient at the Hungarian capital for the journey southward and there was another service three times a week from Belgrade.[29] Ferdinand's Sofia was as firmly on the European railway map as it was on the political one.

Yet when all allowances are made for necessary development, it was Ferdinand's excessive personal expenditure which landed him in trouble. Fortunes were spent not only on the Sofia palace but on country residences such as Vrana, south-east of the capital, and Euxinograd on the Black Sea. (The park of the former contained three free-roaming elephants with whom, as already explained, Ferdinand felt a doleful affinity.) The extravagance of their ruler even damped popular enthusiasm over his proclamation of the independent tsardom in 1908. His subjects, it was said, feared that Ferdinand's added vainglory would cost them too much money.[30] Three years later, the British minister to his court, in a personal report to King George v, describes how Ferdinand's demand to have his civil list income doubled at a stroke from £80,000 to £160,000 (a considerable sum in 1911) was considered excessive 'even by his well-wishers'.[31]

Now, however, Ferdinand needed funds for something more than his palaces, his trains, his private zoos, botanical gardens and fleets of limousines. By the end of 1911 Ferdinand was in negotiation with his old rival Serbia as well as with Greece and Montenegro for the creation of a Balkan alliance. The aim of this alliance, which duly crystallized in the spring and summer of 1912 as a package of bilateral agreements, was a joint offensive against Turkey. After years of dreaming about Byzantium, dressing himself in the robes of a Byzantine emperor, and gazing soulfully across to Constantinople from the Black Sea shore at Euxinograd, Ferdinand. had finally resolved to bring to life that imperial tableau which his mother had staged for him nearly twenty-five years before in the palace at Sofia. It had been at his suggestion that, on 8 October 1912, King Nikita of Montenegro set the fireball rolling.

For Ferdinand, and for Bulgaria, who had both come so well out of the 1908 crisis, these Balkan Wars of 1912–13 were to spell disaster – a disaster doubly hard to bear since it followed such glorious initial triumphs. The Bulgarian army, whose line of march, by agreement, was towards the Ottoman capital itself, had a tougher task than its Balkan allies, but did even better. Within a fortnight the Turks had been driven right out of Thrace (with the exception of the fortress of Adrianople) and Ferdinand's troops had pressed the enemy back to the heavily fortified Chatalja line which guarded the narrow·isthmus only twenty miles in front of Constantinople. Ferdinand, an incongruous figure in uniform, kept well away from the front, preferring to follow developments from his comfortable headquarters at Stara Zagora, nearly one hundred and fifty miles away from the forward battlefield. An eyewitness who saw him there at this time described him as bounding in the air with delight 'like an india-rubber ball'.[32]

It was soon clear however that his dream of riding as the Christian conqueror into Constantinople (in his Mercedes rather than on a white horse) would not be fulfilled. It became a military impossibility, for any hope of dislodging the Turks from their almost impregnable defensive ridge disappeared when cholera ravaged the Bulgarian assault force. It was also, as Ferdinand in his sober moments must have realized deep down, always a political impossibility. Russia was just as opposed to little Bulgaria controlling the Sea of Marmara as Austria-Hungary was opposed to little Serbia establishing herself on the Adriatic. Both vetos lay almost like open cards on the conference table when, in December of 1912, the Balkan allies started peace negotiations with Turkey in London, under the auspices of the European great powers.

None the less, Ferdinand could reasonably expect that he might now regain those frontiers of 'Greater Bulgaria' which had been taken away from his country more than twenty years before at the Congress of Berlin. His hopes were only strengthened when, in another sudden flare-up of the fighting in March of 1913, the Bulgarians, after a fierce hand-to-hand engagement, stormed the great inland fortress of Adrianople. Even the uncomely sight of real battle, the fear of physical injury and his own dread of cholera could not hold Ferdinand back from a quick trip in mufti to the captured city. Unknown to all but a handful of people, he entered it by car on 27 March along roads lined with Turkish prisoners of war. But that was to prove the pinnacle of his success.

As though it were an omen of the future, a black cat was seen prowling across the marble courtyard of Adrianople's famous Sultan Selim mosque just as Ferdinand's car was driving away. All his life he had felt a superstitious dread of cats, especially one like this, which appeared on his left. He ordered his manservant to jump out and break its back with his cane. The wretched animal was then finished off by policemen's boots. But Ferdinand's unease remained. 'I shall lose Adrianople,' he told himself with a shudder.[33] In fact, he was soon to lose far more than that, largely by his own amazing folly.

Macedonia, that ethnic punchbag of the Balkans coveted by Bulgaria, Serbia and Greece alike, was the root cause of his downfall. This, even more than Thrace, was what Ferdinand needed to restore the old kingdom of 1878, and his alliance partners knew it. No sooner had Adrianople been taken by Ferdinand's troops than 'much jealousy and ill feeling' was being reported as coming from both Serbia and Greece, whose troops were occupying Macedonia. By April of 1913 there were already rumours of secret pacts between them 'to guard against Bulgarian aggression',[34] and by the summer the rumours had become reality. The Balkans were smoking yet again and on 8 June Nicholas II felt constrained to send personal appeals for restraint both to Ferdinand and King Peter of Serbia. The chances of Ferdinand complying were lessened when his government learned – and his people sensed – that Serbia and Greece had in fact agreed to carve up Macedonia, the supreme prize in the Balkan game, between them. None the less, his best hope of satisfaction still lay in having great power pressure for peace exerted on his behalf and that meant, above all, not putting himself in the wrong.

Instead, during the night of 29–30 June, on the direct orders of Ferdinand issued behind the backs of his ministers, Bulgarian troops attacked both Greek and Serbian forces in Macedonia. It was not so much a case of Ferdinand throwing caution to the winds as fondly deluding himself that those winds of war would always go on blowing as they had done in Adrianople. The odds were hopeless, as anyone with an inkling of what war was really like would have realized. The decimated Bulgarian troops were too weak to take on even the two garrison armies occupying Macedonia. Greece and Serbia soon had the better of the fighting. The defeat in the south became a disaster all round when Rumania, who had stayed neutral in the 1912 war (being left with hands which were clean but also empty) now joined in against Bulgaria in this second round. Sofia itself was under threat and, to add indignity to catastrophe, Turkey, the common enemy of the year before, bestirred itself to recapture Adrianople. The black cat in the mosque was both vindicated and avenged.

Desperately, throughout July, Ferdinand struggled to regain on the political table what he had thrown away on the ground. His attempts to mobilize dynastic supports abroad even included a personal appeal, sent on 24 July, to King George V for England to 'take the leading part' in halting the advance of his enemies.[35] All, of course, to no avail. As we have seen, no fellow-monarch had anything but hearty dislike for the Tsar of Bulgaria, and, as the aggressor, Ferdinand had anyway put his country beyond the pale. The bill for his blunder was presented – and had to be met – at Bucharest in the peace treaty signed there on 10 August 1913. Almost all that Bulgaria came away with for her enormous sacrifices in blood (she had lost 140,000 men killed and wounded) was a grubby little window on the Aegean with the third-rate port of Dedeagach. Turkey regained most of the territory of Thrace (including Adrianople) for which so much of that Bulgarian blood had been shed. As a reward for her military promenade, Rumania was allotted a fat slice of northern Bulgaria. Worst of all, the Greeks and the detested Serbs were confirmed as joint occupiers of Macedonia. As George v commented to his kinsman and friend Count Mensdorff, the Austrian ambassador to London: 'Your friend Ferdinand, with all his cleverness and intrigues, has made a fine mess of it.'[36] The would-be emperor of Byzantium had been shrunk to a Balkan buffoon.

It was Ferdinand's determination to gain revenge on Serbia which led him, in the last twelve months that the old Europe now had to live, to move closer and closer to the Habsburg monarchy. When the heir of that monarchy was assassinated at Sarajevo, Ferdinand was overjoyed, not only that one of his most disdainful and dangerous opponents had been removed from the scene, but also that the stage now seemed set for the humiliation of the Serbs. He sat out the first year of the conflagration which followed before deciding, on 6 September 1915, that the central powers were the people to back and that an alliance with the Austro-German bloc offered him the best chance of one day regaining Macedonia. It was Foxy Ferdinand's last blunder, and his biggest. Being on the losing side of the Balkan Wars had cost him prestige and border territory. Picking the wrong side in the Great War was to cost him his throne.

Chapter Five

RUMANIA: PRUSSIAN IRON

Rumania was the most stable of the powder-keg kingdoms and Bucharest, with one eccentric exception, the most stolid of the Balkan courts. Both the stability and the stolidity were imparted by Charles of Hohenzollern-Sigmaringen, the German prince who was chosen as ruler of Rumania on 20 April 1866 and who then sat on that throne for the best part of fifty years. To his task he applied all the qualities of his race and house. These included a discipline which was steely and a dedication which was leaden. Though both qualities sat uneasily on a people which, uniquely in the Balkans, had a Latin language and a Latin personality (this had once been the Dacia of the Roman empire) they were needed to keep the patchwork of his country together.

His realm was essentially the two Danubian principalities of Wallachia, which lay north of the great river and south of the Carpathian mountains; and Moldavia, which lay east of those mountains. They had emerged as such as far back as the thirteenth century and had fought side by side in the long struggles which followed, first against Turkish invasion, and then against Turkish rule. In the late sixteenth century they were for the first time united under the Wallachian prince, Mihai the Brave, and though the union was short-lived, it left behind an indelible memory. It was out of the stuff of such legends from ancient times, as we have seen with the Serbs, that modern Balkan history was spun.

But the Danubian principalities had more than the Turks to cope with. Indeed, when the Ottoman empire started to roll back out of Europe, two new threats – each from a more formidable source – appeared on the horizon. To the west lay Austria-Hungary, which had emerged during the eighteenth century as a great power, incorporating among its other possessions the province of Transylvania with its large Rumanian-speaking population. From the north in the following century Russia came driving down into the Balkans in its quest for a gateway into the Mediterranean. Three times (1828–34, 1848–51 and 1853–54) Wallachia and Moldavia fell under Russian occupation. Finally, in the aftermath of the Crimean War, the great powers agreed on the union of the two principalities under the name of Rumania, and a native leader, Alexander Cuza, was chosen as ruler. He soon fell foul both of the clergy and the landlords, however, by launching over-ambitious liberal reforms and when, in 1866, he was forced to abdicate, the Rumanians looked to the courts of Germany for salvation.

Carol 1 of Rumania (as he now became known) was the second son – and therefore available for exportation – of Charles Anthony, head of the senior South German and Catholic branch of the Hohenzollern family. He was thus closely related to those kings of Prussia who were soon to become German emperors and the mightiest military monarchs on the European continent, a kinship which was to mould his political leanings. As one would expect from anyone with his name, Carol was a good military man. He had served as an officer in the Prussian army in the first of Bismarck's lightning wars, the campaign of 1864 against Denmark. In the upheavals of the Russo-Turkish war of 1877–78 he personally led his own Rumanian forces, supported by a Russian contingent, to a great victory against the Turks at Plevna. As a result Rumania won complete and formal independence from Turkey in 1878 and, three years later, was proclaimed a kingdom.

Plevna became, quite literally, the strength of Carol's new crown. He ordered this to be fashioned for his coronation not out of gold and jewels but from the plain steel of Turkish cannon captured on that battlefield. Few kings of modern times can have launched themselves on such a high Wagnerian note. Yet for Carol this was almost the end of heroics. Henceforth, with the exception of his brief incursion into the second of the Balkan Wars, Rumania remained a pool of relative tranquillity amid all the Balkan turbulence of the times. The Rumanians were not Slavs so they were not caught up like the Serbs in the great Slav-versus-Teuton confrontation of the 1908 annexation crisis. But nor were they Germanic, though it seemed inconceivable that when the grand demarcation lines began to be drawn between the rival European alliances, Carol, as a Hohenzollern prince, could choose anything but the Austro-German camp. As early as October 1883 he signed his highly secret (known only to himself and a handful of ministers) defence treaty with the central powers, and it was renewed at intervals right down to 1914 – with neither the Rumanian parliament being consulted nor the Rumanian people being informed. It was an amazing feat to sustain such security over more than thirty years. Carol had stiffened the traditionally sloppy Balkan autocracy with his Prussian efficiency.

Efficiency was also the keynote to his domestic policy. He developed his kingdom as though it were a well-run business and, like any shrewd and conscientious proprietor, he took a personal and often a financial interest in everything that went on. Towards the end of his long reign Rumania had taken the first steps into becoming a modern industrial society with the exploitation, for example, of the oil in the Ploeştl region. But the country remained rooted in the soil. Even at the beginning of the twentieth century, agriculture still accounted for more than three-quarters of Rumanian exports.

However, if the peasants were the King's main source of wealth, they were also his main source of worry. Indeed, they produced the only really strong domestic earth tremor he was ever to feel under his throne. In 1907 resentment over exploitation by state and private landlords alike erupted into violent rebellion. The violence started in Moldavia, from where it ran like a gunpowder fuse throughout the land. Grain stores and even manor houses were put to the torch and the local police were overwhelmed. An English governess in Bucharest at the time[1] describes how the capital shuddered under the news from the countryside:

Every day dreadful stories were in circulation as to the doings of the peasantry. We were told the most harrowing tales of how houses were being wrecked, costly furniture burned and even life-stock destroyed. Travellers from the interior ... related how they saw flames rising to a great height in all directions, as one splendid country house after another was burnt to the ground. Woe betide any unpopular land agent who was found near the scene! In very many cases he was thrown into the flames.

What the good governess did not mention was that many of the 'land agents' were Jewish and, as such, unpopular anyway. By the time of the rebellion, the number of Jews in Rumania had shot up, after waves of immigration from Russia and Austria-Hungary, to nearly 300,000. It was not only a large minority in a nation of only six million; it was a very destabilizing one. Forbidden to buy rural property, those Jews who lived in the countryside took to managing estates for absentee landlords or else practised their traditional trade as moneylenders. Neither occupation exactly endeared them to the peasants.

Whatever the mixture of fuel which was feeding the conflagration, it had to be put down. Carol had no option but to call in his regular army. It was a tricky decision, for the majority of the soldiers came from the same peasant stock they were being asked to march against. But despite one or two instances where the troops sided with the insurgents, the army did its job, thanks largely to the energy of its commander, General Alexander Averescu. His became a name that peasant mothers would threaten their naughty children with for years to come. Entire villages were razed to the ground and an estimated ten thousand people were killed before order was restored. Bucharest escaped, thanks to a careful display of force. The governess recorded approvingly:

A full regiment of infantry, fully equipped with all the impedimenta of war, including some cannon and a few ambulance wagons, was paraded through the streets at regular intervals in order to strike awe into the hearts of the people. The cabarets were closed at an early hour, and suspected quarters were patrolled all night. These measures proved effectual . . .[2]

Not a single shot was fired in Bucharest. More remarkable still, this sudden dangerous surge of violence ebbed away as though it had never arisen and the capital returned to its accustomed calm, almost as though nothing of grave consequence had happened. Such underlying tranquillity was partly due to the fact that the peasantry had no political influence; even after the franchise was extended in 1884 the system of voting by electoral colleges was maintained, and that shut off the common people from power, whether in the towns or the countryside. Another major factor in Rumania's domestic calm (which, by Balkan standards, was almost trance-like) was the moderation of the two main political parties, the Liberals and Conservatives. Each formed the government three times between 1900 and 1914, alternating almost as if by gentleman's agreement to share out equitably the fruits of office. Under either label the King's ministers were, for the most part, the King's men, for he could dismiss them and call for new elections whenever he chose. Each party represented the established order, whether of the landowners (in the case of the Conservatives) or of the professional and burgeoning business classes (as with the Liberals). And as, in happy contrast to Serbia, there were no rival claimants to the throne, the political factions were never split along dynastic lines.

There was a radical nationalist fringe to the political spectrum who reproached Carol for the one thing he could not deny, namely, that he was a foreigner. Their journals would occasionally appear with black-bordered edges when some event linked with ex-Prince Cuza arose; on one occasion a fanatic fired two shots through the window of King Carol's study in the royal palace. But, like the peasant revolt of 1907, such tremors left no permanent damage behind. If there was one contrast, above all else, which set Bucharest apart from a typically ruthless Balkan capital such as Sofia, it was the fate of the strong men who stood beside the imported rulers of these courts. The grisly end of Stamboloff, 'Foxy' Ferdinand's champion, has already been related. King Carol too had his Stamboloff, in the person of Ion Bratianu, the Liberal party leader who helped him to the throne and guided his early years upon it. Bratianu left office with honour in 1888 and died peacefully in his bed in 1891.

Such differences as did develop under the surface were of taste, rather than loyalty. Even more than Belgrade, twentieth-century Bucharest was French in spirit. Its boast of being 'the Paris of the East' was not without substance, whatever ironic amusement the claim may have caused among the real Parisians of the day. French was the language of the educated classes who also took, as their intellectual matrix, French literature, drama and opera. Physically, too, King Carol's new capital (based on the old seat of Wallachian princes) had a pseudo-French stamp. The broad new boulevards and the beautifully landscaped parks were constructed on the Paris model and even the 'amusement places' of Bucharest (to quote the phrase in a contemporary Baedeker) were Rumanian copies of Paris cabarets.

Yet the court, which presided over all this, was essentially Germanic. Despite the fact that Carol had a maternal grandmother, the Princess Antoinette Murat, who was French, he was a Teuton to the core and, in 1869, had chosen for his bride a German princess from the Rhenish house of Wied. She however turned out to be that eccentric exception, mentioned at the beginning of this chapter, to the general stuffiness of Bucharest palace life. Carol could only have fallen in love with her in the first place through the attraction of opposites, for it would be hard to imagine a greater contrast between man and wife. He was humourless; pedantic; a slave to duty; a fanatic about regular routine and habit (one of his standing instructions in the palace, for example, was that no chair should ever be moved from one room to another); but, despite this dreariness, as solid and dependable as granite. She, on the other hand, seemed permanently suspended in a glistening cobweb of whims and fantasies. She ignored all timetables (more than once, even at state banquets, the gongs would sound in vain for the Queen to take her place); she despised the practical and seemed obsessed only with developing the creative spark in herself and others. She was, in short, the royal apotheosis of those talented and slightly dotty ladies who presided over their intellectual 'salons' in the great capitals of the continent. Again, Paris was the closest model.[3]

Writing as 'Carmen Sylva' – prose and verse, in English, French, German and Rumanian – Elisabeth displayed literary gifts of her own.

But in all her outpourings she never came within a mile of writing a masterpiece, and the contemporary fame of her best-known works (*The Bard of the Dumbovitza, Deficit, Letters from the Battlefield*) rested largely on the fact that their author was a queen. More important than anything she achieved herself was what she helped others to achieve. Georges Ernescu (who became a composer and violinist of world stature) was one of her particularly rewarding protégés. Unfortunately, when such real geniuses, either homegrown or imported, were not available, she collected around her pretentious fakes whose cause she would promote with equal relish. Her niece has left us this vivid picture of the poetess-Queen in her drawing-room, a circle of 'ecstatic young girls, their eyes glued on her face' at her feet:

There were generally also a few men in the room, mostly long-haired and pale-faced – waiters, musicians, a stray architect, a sleepy general, and a few nondescript youths who would discreetly lean about in shadowy corners, whether amused or bored it is difficult to say. The air was always vibrant with tense excitement over some topic, some new hobby, some bit of music, of embroidery, some painting or the marvellous discovery of some new book. Nothing was ever taken calmly; everything had to be rapturous, tragic, excessive or extravagantly comic. . . . She could not admit those around her to be ordinary, so she saw wonderful talents in quite commonplace people, beauty where there was none, and wits in many who were often absurd. She saw everything and everyone through the prism of her desires. . . . She needed a continual audience and this audience was trained to hang on to her every word, to follow her every mood, to laugh, weep, praise or deplore according to the keynote given.[4]

Had 'Carmen Sylva' not been by nature a kindly soul (she was as indefatigable in her care for her country's poor and sick as she was in the promotion of its arts) she would, clearly, have been a crushing ego-maniac.

Part of this other-worldliness may have been rooted in her native Rhineland, the home of those sagas and legends out of which Richard Wagner was busily weaving his rich operatic tapestries. But there seems little doubt that it was a personal tragedy which drove Queen Elisabeth to such permanent refuge in this other self of 'Carmen Sylva'. In 1874 the only child of the marriage, a daughter, died of scarlet fever. Once it was clear that she would bear no more children, Carol's nephew Ferdinand,* or 'Nando' as he was known in the family, was proclaimed heir to the throne. Though still Queen, Elisabeth now

---

* Born in 1865, the year before his uncle had been called to the Rumanian throne, Ferdinand was the second son of Prince Leopold, the head of the Catholic branch of the Hohenzollerns.

Nicholas of Montenegro, the political matchmaker with his daughters and sons-in-law.
Back row, *from left to right*, Grand Duke Peter Nicolaievich of Russia, Prince Franz
Joseph of Battenberg, Princesses Vera and Xenia, Crown Prince Danilo, Princes Mirko
and Peter. Seated, Crown Princess Militza, Grand Duchess Militza Nicolaievna of
Russia, Queen Elena of Italy, Queen Milena, King Nicholas, Prince Anna of Battenberg,
King Victor Emauel III of Italy and Princess Natalia. Seated in foreground, Princess
Helen of Serbia, Grand Duchess Anastasia Nicolaievna of Russia and Crown Prince
Alexander of Serbia.

Cetinje: primitive capital of the Black Mountains.

The impressionable King Alexander I of Serbia and his unsuitable bride – a mésalliance resulting in their brutal murder which shocked Europe.

Nicholas Pašić, the veteran statesman who strove for decades to steady the turbulent Serbian state.

Ferdinand I of Bulgaria, Europe's most disliked sovereign, with the four children by his first marriage to Marie-Louise of Bourbon-Parma.

Carol I, Rumania's stolid German-born ruler with Elisabeth, his highly eccentric and artistic wife, in the grounds of their country castle at Sinaia.

(*Above*): William II with his six sons striding down the streets of Berlin on New Year's Day 1912, all, as usual, in uniform.

(*Right*): Otto von Bismarck, Chancellor of Germany 1871–90, and the greatest statesman of his age.

The German Empress Augusta, whose fanatical Protestantism and remorseless domesticity dominated Potsdam family life, pictured here with her eldest daughter, Victoria Louise.

'Foxy Ferdinand' of Bulgaria and the German Kaiser – each looking uncomfortable in the other's uniform.

The 'Uncle of Europe' with his imperial nephew in Berlin, 9 February 1909. 'There was always electricity in the air when they were together.'

(*Above*): George V and William II with officers, on the occasion of Victoria Louise's wedding to the Duke of Brunswick, May 1913 – a deceptive bonhomie.

(*Left*): Franz Josef and his impatient and strong-willed heir, the ill-fated Archduke Franz Ferdinand.

Franz Josef, Austrian Emperor 1848–1916, the 'grand seigneur' of European royalty and supreme bureaucrat of his own eleven-nation monarchy.

became a semi-dowager as far as the dynasty was concerned. To Nando and his English bride Mary (eldest daughter of Alfred, Duke of Edinburgh, and therefore granddaughter of Queen Victoria) the poet-Queen was 'Aunty'; and one gets the feeling that, by the end of the nineteenth century, the whole court regarded her less as a reigning consort than as some odd and unpredictable royal aunt who had carved out her own niche in the palace. The change in her physical appearance matched the transformation inside. The flaxen hair of the twenty-six-year-old Rhenish princess Carol had married turned, first prematurely grey, then almost snow-white, and this, with the burning blue eyes and the resonant voice, made 'Carmen Sylva' seem perfectly cast for her chosen role.

The more she became absorbed in that role, the further she drifted apart from her down-to-earth martinet of a husband. For one thing, the gap between their ages, which was in fact only four years, yawned even wider in spirit as time passed. Carol had never been young at heart; indeed he once commented tartly that 'only the frivolous consider youth the best years of life'.[5] By middle age he had the set habits of an old man and, when an old one, the rigid habits of a patriarch. But as 'Carmen Sylva', living in her timeless fantasy-world of the spirit, his Queen became ageless, despite her poor health. If he, to the end of his days, preserved all his iron resolve, she maintained an almost childlike vivacity.

There was only one occasion when their two temperaments clashed over a serious affair of state. It concerned the infatuation of a weak-willed princeling for a strong-willed and ambitious lady-in-waiting and provides us with a rare parallel between the nineteenth-century courts of Belgrade and Bucharest.[6] Before Nando became safely and satis-factorily betrothed in June of 1892 to his English princess, he had fallen hopelessly in the toils of a certain Helen Vacarescu, a great palace favourite of the Queen. Helen and Elisabeth were *amies de coeur*, for each wrote poetry which they declaimed and praised to each other. For Nando, however, who was an impressionable youth, Mademoiselle Vacarescu became a raging passion, despite – or perhaps because of – her rather coarse appearance and manners.

More, he resolved to marry her. Worse still, 'Aunty', always on the track of exotic romance, decided to support the match. The wily Helen helped to win her over by organizing a spiritualist séance at which the voice of the Queen's father, Prince Hermann of Wied, was conjured up for advice. When asked to prophesy Mademoiselle Vacarescu's future, the voice thundered out in French (it was probably that of the Queen's secretary, who came from Alsace): 'Hélène-Reine'.

Assured by this sign from heaven, the Queen tackled her husband on the subject. Carol was predictably horrified and predictably adamant. To his wife he made the plausible objection that no Rumanian lady would allow one of her country women – and not a very distinguished one at that – to command obeisance from the throne. To Nando the King was much more abrupt. Neither he nor his ministers, the wretched young man was informed, would ever countenance such a match. His nephew must choose on the spot between the plump lady-in-waiting and the Rumanian crown. Nando tearfully chose the crown and was sent packing for a few months to his father's home in Sigmaringen, to get Helen out of his system.

This was a rare intrusion of 'Carmen Sylva's' into the serious business of kingship. For the most part she hovered over Rumania's royal palaces like the bogus ectoplasm at that seance – illuminating everything and touching nothing.

By far the most famous of these palaces was Peleş, which Carol had constructed out of an old shooting-lodge in the mountainous forests of Sinaia. It was completed and formally consecrated on 7 October 1883, a date appropriate to its origins, for this was the height of the stag-hunting season. The castle itself was sombre and overornate, even for the tastes of the King's English niece Marie, inured as she was to the suffocating drawing-rooms of Queen Victoria. She wrote of it:

Castel Peles . . . was a grand abode, but too overpowering for the country; like the Bucharest palace, it had about it the quality of a cage. In his love for 'Altdeutsche' (the old German style) King Carol had over-decorated his royal residence; had put in gloomy stained-glass windows which shut Nature out; everything was heavily carved, heavily draped, heavily carpeted. There were some splendid old pictures, but the rooms and corridors were so dark that one could hardly see them. . . . Everything seemed to have been planned to shut out the sky, the sun.[7]

If Peleş was indeed in some ways a cage, its creator and owner appeared quite contented in it. Though he rode in the surrounding forests, he had no great desire for the open air and no great feeling for nature. Perhaps it was altogether too profligate and untidy for his strictly disciplined soul. During late summer and autumn, when the royal family moved to Sinaia, he continued with the same routine of audiences, formal meals and social *cercles* which dominated palace life down in Bucharest. His principal distraction seems to have been billiards. Nephew Nando paid penance for the Vacarescu escapade by being summoned, evening after evening, to play with his uncle.

It was Nando's English bride who, after years of smouldering rebellion against the stuffy regime of Peleş, liberated her husband and their steadily growing family by persuading the King to build for them close at hand their own smaller residence, Peleşor. This Princess Marie decorated to her own taste, and constructed nearby something which epitomized English eccentricity as well as the English passion for the open air. This was 'Juniperus', a three-roomed hut built high up in the crown of a clump of huge fir-trees. It included a kitchen where full meals could be prepared, though the meal that every visitor wanted to take at the tree-house was tea. Even the King found it a welcome diversion for guests he found difficult to entertain. So this English 'folly' set in the heart of the Rumanian mountains gradually achieved its modest fame among many of the courts and chancelleries of Europe. (The King was less inclined to take people to the retreat which his own wife had built for herself in Sinaia. This was in the style of a mock-Swiss dairy where 'Carmen Sylva' wrote endless poems and conducted endless rustically spiritual gatherings. What cannot have escaped any visitor was that the whole family seemed to want to get away from Peleş and its killjoy of a master.)

Over the years, these visitors included a broad spectrum of foreign royalty, ranging from the heir to the Austrian throne, the prickly Archduke Franz Ferdinand and his morganatic wife Sophie, to the homely Dowager-Queen Emma of the Netherlands. The Archduke's visit in July 1909 (the first formal excursion he and his beloved Sophie had been allowed to make outside the confines of the Habsburg monarchy) was a tremendous personal success inasmuch as King Carol shrewdly showered attention equally on man and wife, treating Sophie in every respect as though she were a royal personage.

Coming so soon after the annexation crisis of 1908 had subsided, it had a certain political significance. King Carol had always made it very plain in Berlin that Rumania had only secretly joined the central powers' camp, and would only remain in it, on the condition that Germany, not Austria-Hungary, played the dominant role. With Germany, Rumania had not a single political quarrel and was bound by the strongest of dynastic links. With the Habsburg monarchy there was always the problem of the suppressed Rumanian population of Transylvania. Moreover, especially after her seizure of Bosnia-Herzegovina, Austria-Hungary had emerged more sharply than ever as Russia's great challenger in the Balkans and both geography and history had convinced Carol that he must on all accounts try to remain on friendly terms with his mighty neighbour, the Tsar. Franz Ferdinand had done all in his power to damp down the 1908 crisis. More important for Carol, the Archduke's anti-Magyar views were

already notorious; under his sceptre there might one day be hope for
Hungary's Rumanian subjects (who daily sent delegates with loyal
addresses to the royal guest at Peleş). But could this strangely
compelling Archduke really subdue the Hungarian half of the
Monarchy, once given the chance? Could he steer that Monarchy off a
collision course with Russia, which would force Rumania into the
agonizing choice between loyalty to an old alliance and sheer self-
preservation? This was the grand dilemma which intensified, also for
Rumania, during the final years of King Carol's reign.

The short and sharp Second Balkan War in midsummer of 1913
epitomized the problem. Carol had joined in this round of fighting to
crush Bulgaria because his policy of aloof neutrality in the first round
had left him with hands which were as empty as they were clean. But
there was more to it than that: when the Balkan victors over Turkey
started squabbling among themselves, public opinion in Rumania
demanded that the country should stand with Serbia in any clash with
Bulgaria. As Rumania's only realistic hope of grabbing some extra
territory for herself was at Bulgaria's expense, sentiment and self-
interest marched together.

Already on 9 June 1913, when the first signs of conflict between her
neighbours emerged, Carol warned all the great powers that 'as of
today, any eventual aggravation of the situation could not leave
Rumania indifferent'.[8] Ten days later he was using much blunter
language to the French envoy in Bucharest, M. Blondel: 'Cost what it
may, we will not allow Serbia to be crushed.'[9] A week after that
Bulgaria was told in no uncertain language that Rumania would enter
the scene 'at the first cannon shot exchanged between Bulgaria and
Serbia'.[10]

When, despite these warnings, Ferdinand rashly started firing his
cannon in Macedonia, Carol led his troops on what was to prove a
military promenade towards Sofia. Before that promenade had ended,
Carol was already hinting that Bucharest, rather than London, ought
to be the venue to wind up this Second Balkan war. And so it proved.
After the briefest of campaigns to crush an overweening Bulgaria on the
battlefield, there followed, in the first week of August, the briefest of
peace conferences in the Rumanian capital to seal Bulgaria's humiliation at the negotiating table. King Carol not only secured for his
country a satisfactory slice of the Dobrudja region from the Bulgarian
spoils. He had also thrust Rumania into what seemed a central position
on the Balkan stage. His intervention had been decisive in bringing
Bulgaria so rapidly to her knees. His capital had played host to the
peace delegations. The rival alliances of the great powers both

redoubled their efforts to secure his favour. Did his declaration of all-out support for Serbia mean that he was slipping into the Franco-Russian camp which backed the Serbian cause?

The German Emperor sensed the danger. The day after the Treaty of Bucharest was signed, William II sent a telegram congratulating his fellow-Hohenzollern on his 'fine success', adding the prayer, 'May Almighty God preserve you for a long time to come for the welfare of your country.' Carol sent a message back thanking the German ruler for his 'warm interest and effective sympathy in the crisis'.[11] This was no empty praise. Unlike her Austrian ally, who had given Bulgaria all the diplomatic backing she could against Serbia, Germany had remained evenhanded.

It was the Habsburg monarchy which now led the drive to keep Rumania firmly in the Austro-German camp. In January of 1914, Count Ottokar Czernin – a brilliant but unstable amateur diplomatist who was later to become Austrian foreign minister – arrived in Bucharest as Franz Josef's new envoy to the Rumanian court. He was accompanied by a counsellor, three political secretaries and two attachés, which constituted a veritable general staff by the modest personnel levels of the day. Moreover, as his English colleague noted: 'All are rich and ready to spread their money to preach the good gospel'.[12]

The Entente powers were quick to retaliate: France with loans and Russia with high-level visits. On 14 June 1914, Tsar Nicholas himself sailed down with his family from Livadia in the Crimea to call on King Carol at Constantza. Polite hopes were exchanged of closer ties in the future and there was even talk of a dynastic match between Nando's eldest son (a prospective Crown Prince of Rumania) and one of the Tsar's daughters. The ill-fated young grand duchesses were said to have 'preserved an enigmatic air' over all this and to have held themselves somewhat aloof from their potential suitor.[13] Yet the mere fact that such a subject could be aired showed how finely King Carol's calculations between the two power blocs were balanced.

A fortnight after this peaceful family gathering in Constantza, Gavrilo Princip's bullets at Sarajevo put paid to all thoughts of such old-style royal romance – along with much else and much more in the old order of things. King Carol was now faced with that agonizing choice he had hoped to avoid throughout the last thirty years of his reign. He was as appalled as any other European monarch by the act of assassination, more particularly as it had removed from the scene Rumania's best Habsburg hope for the future. Moreover, in the event of a general conflagration, Rumania's formal commitments to the central powers were clear: the secret treaty of 1883 which bound her to Germany and Austria-Hungary had been renewed again only four months previously, on 26 February 1914. Yet, when the final crisis came, pro-Serb and pro-French feeling among his government and people proved too strong for Carol to ignore. He opted for neutrality. The anguish of that decision, taken against all the feelings of his Hohenzollern heart, seemed to have broken that heart. On 10 October 1914, when the Great War was barely two months old, he died in his palace at Sinaia. He must have spun in his vault when, two years later, Ferdinand I, his nephew and successor, decided to take Rumania into the war against Germany. He was disowned by the Hohenzollern family accordingly.

Part Two

MONARCHIES OF THE CENTRE

Chapter Six

GERMANY:
THE VOLCANO OF EUROPE

The most powerful ruler on the continent of old Europe was William II
of Germany, whom the English-speaking world has always called 'the
Kaiser', almost as though his ally, the King-Emperor* of Austria-
Hungary, had never existed. William was also the most controversial of
European sovereigns. Scores of historians, German and non-German,
have tried for more than half a century to plumb the mystery of his
character. None has completely succeeded and probably none ever
will. He was one of the most complex mixtures of good and bad,
intelligent and naïve, brave and cowardly, far-seeing and shortsighted,
brash and shy ever to sit upon a throne. Since, however, he occupied
that throne from 15 June 1888 to his abdication more than thirty years
later, this royal enigma and his court are all that we need examine in
considering dynastic power as exercised from Berlin.

One hardy legend ought to be disposed of once again at the start –
that, as both man and ruler, he acted as he did mainly because he was
what we would nowadays call 'a handicapped person'. Not that his
physical defect was unimportant, especially for a prince and future
ruler of the Prussian house of Hohenzollern, for whom soldiering was
not so much a way of life as life itself. Perhaps because of this, there was
at first a stubborn refusal all round to recognize his defect. The day
after a terrible thirty-six-hour labour, when his English-born mother
Princess 'Vicky' (eldest daughter of Queen Victoria) had given birth to
him in Berlin on 27 January 1859, the English midwife pointed out that
there seemed to be something strange about the infant's left arm, which
hung loose and was discoloured. Both the princess and her husband,
the admirable, upright, Crown Prince Frederick shrugged off the
blemish in their joy at producing, for themselves and the dynasty, a son
for a first-born. The arm would surely come right with treatment.

* Emperor of the Dual Monarchy, and crowned King of Hungary.

Treatment, much of it painful and all of it humiliating, was what the young prince had to endure throughout his nursery and boyhood days. When massage failed to do anything but soothe, the doctors tried electric shocks to galvanize the shrivelled muscles into life. And when those failed, they resorted to mechanical devices, some of which might have come straight out of a medieval torture chamber. His mother described one in a letter to Queen Victoria:

The machine consists of a belt round the waist to which is affixed an iron rod or bar which passes up the back to which a thing looking very much like the bridle of a horse is attached. The head is strapped into this and then turned as required with a screw which moves the iron. When the head is firm in the leather strap it is made to turn towards the left so as to stretch the muscles of the right side of the neck.[1]

The arm was never cured and remained, for all practical purposes, a withered stump. This meant that the young boy had to endure long hours of special training (and countless falls) before he could adjust his grip and balance to sit a horse properly, a prerequisite for a Hohenzollern. It also meant that, to the end of his days, the Kaiser could never eat normally with knife and fork, but usually tackled his food one-handed with a contraption which was a mixture of both. All this inevitably left a mark on his soul and spirit, producing a complex of physical inadequacy which bred, in turn, the need to overcompensate.

Yet, by a combination of will-power and patience, the fact is that he did largely overcome the handicap. He sat firmly and proudly on a horse to the end of his reign. By using specially-made weapons (his shotguns, for example, were single-barrelled and small gauge) he did not disgrace himself, even in the demanding company of the day, as a sportsman. The ornate military uniforms and cloaks which he wore incessantly concealed the poor left arm, whereas the good right arm developed over the years into a limb of steel. Indeed, he took great pleasure, whenever shaking hands with someone he disliked or wished to impress, in crunching his victim's fingers in a vice, the grip being made all the more painful by the heavy rings he habitually wore. In other words, by the time he came to the throne, he had accepted and learned to live with his disability. Other rulers of our time have serenely overcome equal or greater handicaps. King George VI mastered his dreadful speech impediment sufficiently well to inspire wartime England as a soldier-monarch. During those same years President Franklin D. Roosevelt was ruling America as a paralysed man in an armchair.

To probe deeper into the human volcano which became the Kaiser, we must look closer at the volcanic landscape around him: the speed at which his new realm had been created; the suddenness with which he himself had been catapulted into his throne; and, above all, the boundless, restless dynamism of the nation underneath him. As for the first, it had taken Bismarck precisely seven years to transform the 'Brandenburg sandbox' of the Prussian kingdom into the German empire of forty-nine millions which dominated the centre of Europe. Three savagely convincing military campaigns had achieved the transformation: against Denmark in 1864, to dispose of the quarrel over the border provinces of Schleswig-Holstein; against Austria and her allies in 1866, to settle once and for all who was master in the German-speaking world; and finally, against France in 1870, to secure yet more territory (Alsace-Lorraine) but also to prepare for the proclamation, at Versailles on 18 January 1871, of a new German 'Kaiserreich' and William I, the then King of Prussia, as its first emperor. All the pumpernickel principalities and minor kingdoms which had stood across Bismarck's path had been absorbed into this new empire or subjected to it. A military colossus now lay across the heart of the continent, the like of which had not been seen since the prime of Napoleon Bonaparte. The man we call the Kaiser was only twelve years old when this empire was created. William I was his grandfather and his model of Prussian diligence and virtue.

The boy can never have imagined how abruptly he would fill his grandfather's place. On 9 March 1888 the modest old soldier King, still wearing his white military tunic, died in his camp bed (no four-poster with imperial eagles for him). The man to whom the succession passed, Crown Prince Frederick, was, however, already mortally ill with cancer of the throat. He and his English-born 'Vicky' reigned for exactly ninety days, three months of exhausting political as well as family tensions in which the new Crown Prince came to hate his mother for – as he saw it – keeping him from his dying father. On 15 June the surgical automaton with tubes sticking from his throat who had ruled briefly as Frederick III was released from his suffering. Aged only twenty-nine, William II became the last of Bismarck's emperors. Within the space of six months the crown had sat on three heads.

The nature of his inheritance was to prove even more unsettling than the speed at which he had come into it. Politically the new empire was the oddest of patchworks including four kingdoms, six grand duchies, five duchies and the three ancient free cities of Hamburg, Bremen and Lübeck. The potential strains were obvious from the start. For the first time, for example, Germany's baroque Catholic south was linked to her austere Protestant north. Yet it was not just Prussian wiry thread which succeeded in holding the seams together. Every layer and every corner of what was to go down in history as Wilhelminian Germany began to pulsate with an economic energy which made the easy-going Bavarian as profit-conscious as the Berliner. Bismarck's 'Reich' thrived not least because the common pursuit of money, power and status soon made imperialists of them all.

Not since the steam-engine, the cotton mill and the iron foundry (plus, of course, the raw material riches of the colonies) had transformed the frame of Victorian England had Europe witnessed such an economic explosion within one state. The surge in population was both cause and effect of the phenomenon. The empire the young Kaiser had inherited numbered less than fifty million; the one he eventually took into war sixty-seven million. Their achievements exceeded their fertility. Over this same quarter of a century, iron and steel production increased eightfold (passing that of Britain by the turn of the century); coal output leapt threefold and exports (again partly at Britain's expense) more than trebled. There was a parallel growth in food production. The new empire became the industrial as well as the military giant of the continent. It was a very different proposition from that cosy collection of chocolate-soldier kingdoms which Queen Victoria, thinking always of her husband's native Coburg, used to call her 'dear little Germany'.

This empire had to have a fitting capital. The pickaxe and the hammer got to work accordingly on the old Berlin of the Brandenburg Mark. The five milliard gold francs of French reparations paid after the 1870–71 war provided the first infusion of capital. Afterwards the wealth largely generated itself, as the bankers joined hands with the new breed of entrepreneur. The German, from north or south, has always favoured the bulky in everything from his food to his women. It was not surprising, therefore, that massiveness should be the hallmark of his new metropolis. The old Prussian Berlin had had some hefty buildings. Imperial Berlin went right over the top. Its symbol was the 'Siegesallee' or Victory Avenue running through the Tiergarten park, lined with thirty-two statues of Prussian monarchs and warriors, and crowned by the huge red granite 'Victory Column' which towered up over the whole city.

Everything followed, and in turn fed, the official taste for the monumental. Wertheim's became the largest department store in Europe, with a novel façade, designed by Alfred Messel, in which great expanses of glass gleamed between the sandstone columns. The huge villas, and even palaces, of the new tycoons sprouted up everywhere as the capital expanded to the west. The wealthy who were not yet tycoons contented themselves with apartments numbering up to sixteen rooms. Inside, dark oak and mahogany replaced the lighter and slighter peach, pear and beechwood of the Biedermeier era. As the most recent chronicler of the city's history wrote: 'High ceilings, more columns, paintings of mythological scenes, plush, marble – the 'haute bourgeoisie' had imposed its own taste of neo-renaissance on the classical modesty of old Berlin.'[2]

The new Berlin also needed a new culture. Considered as a whole, this was by no means subservient to the conservative Prussian ethos of the day. In 1889, the year after William II came to the throne, Otto Brahm founded his famous 'Freie Bühne', an avant-garde theatre which experimented with everybody and was afraid of nobody. German artists like Corinth imitated the great French impressionists of the 1890s. An art nouveau movement sprang up, though it soon transferred itself to the more congenial pastures of Munich. In dramas such as *The Weavers* Gerhart Hauptmann probed the social problems created by the new materialist ethic. In his novels Thomas Mann depicted the inner decay of the very class which imagined itself in growing ascendancy – the bourgeoisie. In journalism the left-wing weekly *Simplicissimus* led the whole continent, not merely Germany, in its brilliant and sustained *tour de force* of political satire. On a more conventional plane there was *Die Zukunft*, a review founded by Maximilian Harden soon after William's accession, and one which was to give him the worst personal shock of his entire reign.[3]

Yet all these examples of dissent and questioning remained exceptions which tested the general rule without overthrowing it. It was in the opera and the concert hall that this new Germany dominated, and the musical symbol of this was Richard Wagner. Wagner's *Ring* was as gloomy and over ornate as a Berlin dining-room, which, like his masterpiece, was illuminated by hues borrowed from the past, heraldic stained glass panels through which colour and mystery were filtered. For all the revolution he created in the art of opera – and all the convulsions his own outrageous behaviour produced on the social scene – his spirit was a perfect match with the new age. There was the same strident vigour, the same excessive heroics and self-indulgence, the same worship of élitism, the same search back into legend to find those roots so lacking in a brash present. Bayreuth mesmerized Berlin, and not merely in the opera house.

This then was the empire which William II inherited. It would have pushed him into histrionics had that left arm of his been as strong as an oak tree. He was anyway a play-actor by inclination, and all his life went for effect rather than reality. Yet, on a stage with an audience which clamoured for drama, he would have needed remarkable wisdom, modesty and restraint (and he was born with none of these) to have behaved otherwise. The tragedy was that the audience, which started out by being a captive one, ended up by shouting the lines for him. Before coming to that, we must look at William the monarch and at his court.

First, the family man. A passionate youthful attachment to his cousin Princess Elisabeth of Hesse had come to nothing, not least because the lady in question, who went on to marry the Russian Grand Duke Serge, could find no flame in her heart for him. William's eye then fell on Augusta Victoria, eldest daughter of the Duke who bore the amplest name in all Germany, Frederick of Schleswig-Holstein-Sonderburg-Augustenburg. Despite that drumroll of a title, there were delays because the family were not considered in Potsdam to be quite royal enough. Eventually William's wish was granted and, in Berlin on 27 February 1881, he married his 'Dona', as she was nicknamed.

The bride, a blue-eyed blonde princess (plumpish: her double chin is very much in evidence even in the betrothal portrait) was to give William almost everything he could have wished from a wife and future empress. To begin with, she presented him, over the next eleven years, with no fewer than six sons before rounding off her fertile labours, in 1892, by producing their only daughter. If 'Kinder, Küche, Kirche' ('Children, kitchen and church') was the ideal of contemporary German womanhood, Dona had set a shining royal example as regards the first. She would doubtless have proved an excellent cook had the need arisen, while her devotion to the Protestant church was intense to the point of fanaticism. She was the embodiment of duty, chastity and charity. She developed into a dignified imperial consort and she never ceased to dote on her husband. None the less, when that husband was William, whether as Prince, Crown Prince, or Emperor, Dona had her drawbacks.

To begin with, that placidly ample exterior of hers was built round a bundle of nerves; she could drive herself, and everyone around her, to distraction by worries over her children's health and education. Also, though she acquired over the years an air of stateliness and a certain homely wisdom, her mental horizons never matched the imperial sceptre. As one of her husband's chancellors, the witty and slippery Bernhard von Bülow, put it: 'She would have made an admirable "Commandeuse", as we used to say in the army – that is to say, she would have gained universal respect as the wife of a General, or Provincial Governor, or Minister of State.'[4]

Her xenophobia and narrow Lutheran conservatism pandered to all that was negative in the Prussian ethos – indirectly, for she rarely mixed in politics. Worst of all, she was a woman totally without natural charm (to one royal observer her smile seemed 'permanently glued on')[5] and without either cosmopolitan wit for the drawing-room or an earthy feeling for the hunter's forests. For someone like William, who craved distraction, dabbled in all the arts and sciences, and loved the chase, these were grievous defects. While staying deeply attached to his wife, he soon found her both boring and exhausting, a lethal combination. The question that was often asked during his lifetime was whether he ever sought and found distractions from his Dona in affairs with other women.

One can disregard the sensationalized 'disclosures' about the Kaiser's private life brought out in the Entente capitals during the war, as much for political propaganda purposes as for private profit.[6] None the less, there are occasional hints of amorous adventures which come from very reputable quarters. One such source is Count Heinrich von Lützow, Austro-Hungarian ambassador to Rome from 1904 to 1910 and the very model of the punctilious old-style diplomat. He recalls being in Venice at the end of April 1905 to meet his foreign minister, Count Goluchowski, when Kaiser William's yacht dropped anchor in the lagoon. The main purpose of the brief royal visit was to take lunch with the beautiful and witty Countess Morosini. She was a good friend of the ambassador's and indeed had asked him to call later that day when her exalted guest would have departed. Lützow accordingly turned up at her palazzo at around three in the afternoon but was obliged to carry straight on without stopping: two German marines from the yacht's company were standing guard at the gates, indicating that their Emperor was inside. The guards were still there hours later. They eventually informed the ambassador, who could no longer control his curiosity, that though the Kaiser had already left, nobody had ordered them to stand down. By this time Venice was buzzing with the tale of Countess Morosini's very extended private luncheon.[7]

The truth, so far as one can ever ascertain it, about the Kaiser's extra-marital interests seems to be that he could luxuriate in the company of that rarest of creatures – a woman possessed of good looks, charm, intelligence, high birth and discretion. Being a compulsive showman, he would doubtless play the gallant on such occasions; but that is probably where it stopped. When his uncle (by the time of the Venice visit, King Edward VII of England) found, in Alice Keppel, a lady who combined all the above qualities, she promptly became his mistress and, eventually, the *grand amour* of his life. It is in some ways a pity that the nephew, because of that Lutheran Prussian straitjacket which always enclosed him, could never do the same. If he had copied 'Uncle Bertie', Berlin would have been far more scandal-ridden as a capital, but also far more relaxed.

As it was, William sought his distractions, from Dona and everything else that was boring about life in his Potsdam palace, in travel; in the company of a few selected courtiers who accompanied him on some of those travels; and in the officers' messes of his crack regiments. Each tunnel of escape was bad for him, and bad for Germany.

His passion for scurrying about all the corners of his empire, and of the European continent which enclosed it, soon earned him the nickname of 'Reisekaiser', or 'Travel Emperor'. (The saying had it that he had come after the 'Weisekaiser' or 'Wise Emperor' who had been his father and the 'Greisekaiser' or 'Aged Emperor', who had been his grandfather.) It meant that from 1894 onwards he spent less than half of the year (the average was put at forty-seven per cent) in his capital.[8] He was usually in Berlin – or Potsdam which was a brief train ride distant – from New Year's Day until mid-March. As in most continental capitals, these were the months of the official season, of court balls, presentations, diplomatic receptions and so on. But William's *Wanderlust* took over with the approach of spring.

In April he headed south for the sun, as did generations of North Europeans before and after him. But, being William, he operated in grand, even theatrical, style. Not content with the royal yacht *Hohenzollern* as a floating palace, in 1907 he bought himself an imposing residence on the eastern confines of that ocean. This was the Villa Achilleion on Corfu, complete with a ruined Greek temple to excavate. It had once belonged to the beautiful, half-deranged Empress Elisabeth of Austria, another restless creature whose perpetual wanderings had come to a tragic end ten years earlier. Corfu provided an elegant platform from which to dabble in a little Mediterranean diplomacy; but its principal attraction for the Kaiser was that he could display himself in his non-martial role as one of the *cognoscenti* of the ancient world, a lover and patron of European culture. The cost of renovating and running the place (one hundred servants were shipped there or hired locally) was so enormous that the comptroller of William's household, Baron von Wedel-Piesdorf, resigned in protest and despair. Nor was it all worth it, to anyone except the host. The crushing boredom of being invited to Corfu – and it was nearly always the same faces which appeared, year after year – was summed up by one guest who finally gave up even keeping a diary: 'There was no point in making any entries at all. Life was too deadening. The Kaiser's ruthlessness and egotism lay across everyone like an alpine mountain.'[9]

The Villa Achilleion at least had the domestic merit that William visited it as a family man: his wife, his fourth son, August Wilhelm, and his only daughter Victoria Louise were among the regulars. From then until Christmas, Dona only saw her husband at intervals. In May he was usually off on visits all over Germany, ending up at some hunting-lodge for the roebuck. After a short stay at Potsdam for the spring parade, June and July were spent in the northern waters. First came the Kiel yachting week, the only part of their master's annual programme of which the conservative courtiers disapproved, mainly because the masts in Kiel harbour were festooned with *nouveaux riches* social climbers. Then William set sail on the *Hohenzollern* for his month-long cruise along the Norwegian fjords. Again, the regulars were basically the same and, regular or casual, they were all male. These 'Nordland-reisen', as they were known, were even more of a strain on the guests than the descents upon Corfu. They also offered the Kaiser much more ambitious temptations in the way of instant personal diplomacy, of which more later.

The next event in the calendar, until 1895, was the royal regatta at Cowes, where rivalry between English and German racing yachts became a symbol of something far deadlier. After 1895 Cowes was dropped (William found it very easy to be seasick and rather hard to win) and August was henceforth spent with the family at the Wilhelmshöhe estate instead. He had to be on parade for most of September for the Berlin military review and the army and navy manoeuvres, but from then until Christmas, hunting took over. Dona was sometimes invited but never seems to have felt comfortable in these surroundings (she once appalled her husband by dressing for the forest in dazzling white). Nor did he feel entirely at ease when she was around. The long autumn of hunting – partridge, pheasant, duck, deer, boar and, above all, stag – was, for him, like July in the fjords, a time for men.

What sort of people were his closest 'confidants', official or otherwise? The three most important were: a career army officer; a politically-minded cicerone; and a sporting bon vivant. All three were aristocrats and the second, who was closest to the Emperor, had been elevated by William to the topmost rank of prince. The third did not need such promotion; he had been born one anyway. The career soldier was Count Alfred von Waldersee, born in Potsdam itself on 8 April 1832 while his father was serving there as a major in the élite 'Garde du Corps' Regiment. But Alfred, though in many ways a Prussian officer down to his marrowbone, could also raise his eyes to broader horizons. He came closest to William during the three years (1888–91) when he served as the Kaiser's chief of staff, in succession to von Moltke. As an entry in his diary shows, his master expected more than military advice from this general who was almost twenty-seven years his senior and already a good friend. The new chief of staff noted on 27 January 1889: 'The Kaiser wants me to take a look at things outside the military sphere and might want to count on me as a counsellor for both domestic and foreign policy.'[10]

His advice on the home front was blunt and predictable: the monarch should take the offensive against the Socialist leaders, who had been fomenting damaging strikes, before these demagogues could capture the soul of the German workers and lead them away from the path of upright piety which the nation must always follow. But it is unjust to dismiss Waldersee as being simply 'a thoroughly unashamed and bumptious reactionary'.[11] He could feel both shame and humility, as the following extract from his diary for 9 November 1890 (not quoted by his critics) shows:

What is completely unhealthy about our situation is the glaring contrast between rich and poor. That cannot go on in the long run because we are human beings. . . . The only force which could be put to work to soothe and conciliate is religion, and that is not being used. . . . The state contents itself with trying to improve the material conditions of the working class, but has so far only succeeded in heightening their demands. Because it has become possible, through speculation, to gain large sums of money quickly, a leaning towards luxury and indulgence has developed, affecting wide circles of society. German family life is being visibly destroyed. . . . Unhappy marriages, infidelity, the premature corruption of the young, the desire to appear richer than one is are all increasing at a terrible rate. . . . The uneven division of money with all its consequences must, in the end, lead to catastrophe.[12]

That was the Kaiser's chief of staff communing honestly with himself. It is more than likely, however, that what the monarch got to his face was a proud if fearful *Junker* preaching the doctrine of no change against a new economic order which the old Prussia could neither comprehend nor contain.

It will be noticed that Waldersee's private musings have a strong religious lining to them. That was, in large measure, due to the influence of his wife. Marie Esther, born Miss Lee in College Place, New York, in 1837, was one of that remarkable tribe of wealthy young American women who had bought, flirted and married their way to the topmost rungs of nineteenth-century European society. The already widowed Marie Esther, whom Waldersee had met and married in 1874, when he was commanding the 13th Uhlans at Hanover, was a woman of remorseless and all-consuming Presbyterian piety. When he first took her with him to Berlin in 1881, as general 'à la suite' to the Emperor and then as chief of staff, his wife automatically entered court life and soon found there her spiritual twin, the Empress Dona. The two women became close friends and fellow labourers in the spiritual vineyard. For nine years they strove together to get all Germany down on both knees, one of them for God and the other for the Hohenzollerns. So another clamp was added to the Kaiser's Protestant straitjacket. His other two boon companions provided, among other things, relief and escape.

The more remarkable of the two – and indeed the Kaiser's only true *ami de coeur* – was Count Philipp zu Eulenburg. It was a friendship with political dimensions, for the Count, because of his remarkable intimacy with the monarch, became the real power behind the scenes in the Potsdam palace during the 1890s. The fact that his cousin August was court chamberlain while another cousin, Botho, was Prime Minister of Prussia, certainly helped; yet the extraordinary chemistry of Philipp's personality, when mixed together with the complexes of the Kaiser, would have sufficed by itself. Philipp was a *Junker* who had served in the same élite 'Garde du Corps' as Waldersee but had then turned his back on army life and eventually drifted into diplomacy. A gifted amateur musician and poet, a hedonist and would-be philosopher, a man of immense charm and even deeper culture, but, with it all, a great conversationalist and a 'good fellow', Philipp was everything that both the palace and the officers' messes at Potsdam were not. More important, he was everything that one side of the Kaiser, the face that peeped out, straw-hatted, between the columns of the Villa Achilleion, yearned to be. From the moment the two men met, at a hunting party in East Prussia in May 1886 – when William was a twenty-seven-year-old prince still two lives away from the throne – a bond, well described as 'heliotrope-scented',[13] sprang up between them. That it had homo-erotic undertones was undeniable; (Philipp would always refer to the Kaiser in private as his 'Liebchen' or 'Darling'). That there was a physical homosexual relationship between the two men is, on the other hand, improbable. It is more likely that, in the dream world in which he lived, William merely played at this masculine eroticism as he played at every other role he assumed – alcove gallant, warrior, scientist, aesthete or statesman. The play-acting in this case was just as well, in view of the public scandal that was to bring Eulenburg crashing down from his pedestal.

The third of the Kaiser's boon companions was the least complicated of men, especially when contrasted with Eulenburg. Maximilian Egon

Fürst zu Fürstenberg* was an exceptionally handsome Austrian aristocrat with velvety dark eyes, a strong nose and chin and a theatrical handlebar moustache which, for once, looked right on such a face. His riches far surpassed even his looks. He had already inherited his father's vast estates in Bohemia when, in 1896, Karl Egon IV, the head of the German branch of the family, died without issue and great properties in Baden and Württemberg fell to him as well. By birth a subject of the Austrian emperor, Maximilian thus became also a subject of the German emperor, and a hereditary member of the Upper House in both Vienna and Berlin. The fact that he sought neither titles nor posts nor lands from either monarch automatically put him on an easier footing with William than, for example, Waldersee, whom the Kaiser appointed and later removed as head of his army. But what bowled the Kaiser over was Fürstenberg's Austrian charm and *joie de vivre*. His wife Irma (born the very Austrian Countess Schönborn) made them into a couple who, as guests or hosts, could relax and entrance not only William but also the wooden and basically insecure Dona. The Fürstenbergs could entertain on a scale unsurpassed in either empire. His principal castle, at Donaueschingen, not only had one of the finest shoots in Europe. It was, above all, a place which soothed, the sort of haven which, in differing degrees of grandeur, everyone in every walk of life yearns for when under stress. Indeed, it was to Donaueschingen that William was to flee during the worst crisis of his reign. Fürstenberg was no avuncular model of unbending uprightness like Waldersee. He was no softly gleaming jewel of the intellect, like Eulenburg. He was, quite simply, a man's best friend.

None of these intimates could exercise a decisive influence on the Kaiser so long as Otto von Bismarck remained in office as Germany's 'Iron Chancellor'. But Bismarck was only to survive the first two years of William's reign. From the start, the impetuous new ruler had chafed at having to stand under the shadow of this political giant who had created his empire for him. Gratitude is difficult for ordinary mortals to feel; for monarchs it is intolerable. William wanted the limelight for himself, and that meant asserting the power of the throne against the office of the chancellery which Bismarck had made so formidable. It was over this constitutional issue that, on 17 March 1890, the inevitable showdown came. To keep himself in power after the elections in February of that year (at which the Social Democrats had emerged as the largest party) Bismarck put private feelers out to the Catholic

---

* The title of Fürst is untranslatable, for it was carried only in the German-speaking lands and only by the chief of a princely family, all the other male members of which were usually princes.

Centre Party. When challenged by William that he had no right, as chancellor responsible to the Emperor, to negotiate directly with party leaders, Bismarck cited an old Prussian statute of pre-imperial days in his support. William angrily ordered the statute to be revoked by decree. Bismarck refused and offered his resignation, never dreaming that it would be accepted on the spot. But it was.

Within the week, the toppled giant had to leave the Berlin he had dominated for so long and, with it, leave the centre of the European stage. Three hundred packing cases, filled with personal and state papers intended for his memoirs, went with him, as did a cellar which included the staggering total of 13,000 bottles of champagne. The honours which the exultant Emperor now bestowed on him (he was promoted to colonel-general and made Duke of Lauenburg, which had precious little meaning for anyone famed as Prince Bismarck) only added insult to injury. What the episode had revealed was that even the greatest of chancellors really did have an imperial master. William had inherited enormous powers. Unhappily for himself and his people, he mostly displayed them at the wrong moments in the wrong causes and failed utterly to exercise them when his empire faced a world crisis. Bismarck's successor was Leo von Caprivi, a *Junker* general who, despite his ungermanic name, looked the epitome of a Prussian officer: forehead domed like a helmet, fierce eyes, a splendid white walrus moustache and a strong cleft chin. The appointment was a surprise, not least to his fellow *Junker*, General von Waldersee, who had hopes of the job himself (in fact Waldersee's removal from his own post as chief of staff lay less than a year ahead). Caprivi was an able and conscientious man, like his successor, the seventy-five-year-old Prince Chlodwig of Hohenlohe-Schillingfürst (called 'uncle' by the Kaiser on the grounds that Dona's mother had been a Hohenlohe). But from now until the end, Germany's chancellors were a string of amateur *ad hoc* politicians, called in from the army, the ranks of high society or the diplomatic corps as the whim of the Kaiser, fashioned by the strongest currents of persuasion around him, dictated. With the possible, heavily qualified, exception of Bernhard von Bülow, who served from 1900 to 1909, there was not a statesman among them.

Tenniel's *Punch* cartoon on the Iron Chancellor's fall, 'Dropping the Pilot', was thus the most apt as well as most graphic comment. If we stay with the nautical parallel, the engine-room of the *Germania* down below worked harder and harder in the post-Bismarckian era, producing an ever greater head of steam to drive the great ship forward. But there was now nobody up on the bridge with any clear idea about the course. Above all, there was no one at the wheel who could recapture the old master's touch, which had been deft as well as firm. An example of this – significant, even though its importance has often been exaggerated – was the failure to extend Bismarck's 'Re-insurance Treaty' with Russia when it came up for renewal only three months after his fall.

With this secret pact of 1887, Bismarck had succeeded, short-term, in doing what, over the long term, was to prove impossible – namely, ally Berlin both with St Petersburg and Vienna. Only thus might the Tsar perhaps be preserved from the all-out embrace of France, and Russia and Austria be kept from war over their rival ambitions in the Balkans. One of Bismarck's last acts in office had been to urge that the 'wire to Russia' be kept up. To do him justice, the Kaiser, only four days after Bismarck's dismissal, when Berlin was a city of numbed uncertainty, came out personally for a treaty renewal.[14] But then the leaders of the German Foreign Office got busy with their memoranda and audiences, urging that Germany should do nothing which might prejudice her pivotal alliance with Austria and Italy. The most quietly persuasive of these voices was that of Frederick von Holstein, who had been appointed counsellor at the Foreign Office back in 1878, when the Austro-German alliance was being first prepared and who survived as Berlin's *éminence grise* right down to 1906. But it was not just the diplomats who were at William's ear over this. All three of his bosom friends, in different tones and for different reasons, were also giving him the same advice.

Waldersee, from the start, had never ceased to bombard the Kaiser with statistics about Russia's steadily increasing military strength: for him, as for most East Prussian *Junkers*, the Slav colossus was the real menace which must be toppled, not courted. For his part, Fürstenberg, born an Austrian magnate and always an Austrian at heart, used his unique position with William throughout to act as a private sword-bearer protecting the sacred alliance of the German-speaking empires; indeed, he achieved quasi-ambassadorial status between the two capitals. Finally, Philipp Eulenburg too urged conservatism in foreign affairs on the Kaiser just as he urged it at home; and conservatism abroad meant that nothing should be allowed to weaken the bond with Vienna. The Kaiser, unchecked by his new chancellor whose feet were still lost in Bismarck's seven-league boots, allowed himself to be overruled. The wire to Russia, which might at least have delayed Europe's rigid division into rival power blocs, was now pulled down from the Berlin end. From his northern estates at Friedrichsruh, Bismarck, in morose and bitter exile from power, fulminated against the error, chiefly through the columns of the influential *Hamburger*

Nachrichten. At least one of his dire predictions came true: 'By following the path on which she has entered, Germany is in danger of becoming gradually dependent upon Austria, and in the end she may have to pay with her blood and treasure for the Balkan policy of Vienna.'[15]

The old demi-god, aged eighty-three, died at last on 30 July 1898, crippled with physical pain and mental frustration. It is pleasing to think that, whatever or whoever let him down, those 13,000 bottles of champagne lasted him out faithfully. Almost his last conscious act had been to gulp down one final glass of it when a relative at the bedside timorously offered a spoonful.

What of the imperial captain left in charge of the Iron Chancellor's bridge?

Chapter Seven

GERMANY:
IMPERIAL FANTASY

The chameleon always stalked the Kaiser in his private life. The same animal was at his side whenever he was on political show. Bernhard von Bülow, the best known of his chancellors, has left this description of his master seemingly transforming his whole character, like Alcibiades of old, according to the different roles he was summoned to play on the world stage:

In Russia, he felt like some worthy Adjutant-General of the old stamp or a prince who had emigrated from Oldenburg, Altenburg or Strelitz; in England he felt like the Queen's grandson and the 'Admiral of the Fleet'; in Vienna, he thought in terms of Hapsburg black and yellow, and in Budapest like a Magyar. In Italy he shone in various colours. In the royal Quirinal Palace, he was completely 'Casa Savoia'; in the Vatican he saw himself as protector of the Papacy as the Roman emperors of the German race had been, or had sought to be. In Sicily, he followed in the tracks of the Hohenstaufen.[1]

Throughout, the Kaiser had a terrible habit of overplaying these roles, usually with lines written by himself, and often topping off the rhetoric with actions which scarified all Europe, let alone his own ministers. He was adept at turning out vivid phrases; but more than one of them, when rashly used, would haunt both him and the German empire right down to the end. A classic example was produced at a banquet in Kiel in December 1897. The setting, a farewell speech to his brother Prince Henry, who was about to leave for the Far East, could hardly have been more innocuous. Yet as the Kaiser warmed to his impromptu toast, a vision of German medieval knights rose up in his brain and he ended by conjuring the prince to strike back with a 'mailed fist' (*Gepanzerte Faust*) at anyone who sought to damage the nation's interests. The phrase, totally out of place and out of context, was to be quoted as a synonym for German foreign policy for the next twenty years.

Worse was to come three years later. On 18 June 1900 the German minister to China, Baron von Ketteler, had been assassinated in broad daylight on the streets of Peking as the so-called 'Boxer Rebellion' – directed as much against 'foreign devils' as against the imperial dynasty – raged, seemingly unstoppable. A European military expedition was hurriedly raised to rescue the international community in Peking and, without clearing the announcement in advance with the other powers involved, William brought his old friend Waldersee back into the limelight and appointed him overall commander of the force. On the strength of the appointment the count was raised on the spot in military rank from general to field marshal. This spectacular promotion showed that more steamy visions of Teutonic glory were swirling before the Kaiser's eyes. Nobody, inside or outside Germany, can, however, have been prepared for the blood-curdling harangue which he delivered to his embarking troops from an improvised wooden tribune on the quayside at Bremerhaven on 27 June 1900:

There will be no quarter, no prisoners taken! As, a thousand years ago, the Huns under Attila gained for themselves a name that still stands for terror in tradition and fable, so may you imprint the name of a German for a thousand years on China, and so deeply that never again shall a Chinese dare so much as look askance at a German.

Bernhard von Bülow (then still state secretary in the Foreign Office) was so horrified by what he was hearing that, before the oration had even ended, he had already busied himself trying to commit all the journalists present to reproducing only a doctored version. But the original duly leaked out – much to the delight of the irrepressible monarch, who was complaining that the watered-down text had 'missed out all my best bits.' For Bülow, those 'best bits' amounted to 'perhaps the most harmful speech that William II ever made'.[2] Certainly the epithet of 'the Huns', used by the Western allies as a strong propaganda punch throughout the conflict to come, was born on that Bremerhaven quayside. What so appalled the rest of the continent was how alien, as well as chilling, this sort of language sounded. The fact that Waldersee never got the chance to rival Attila (he reached China six weeks too late) was beside the point. No other European ruler would have uttered the Kaiser's words and no other European nation would have swallowed them. This new Germany was becoming a frightening stranger in their midst.

Over the years to come, William did indeed emerge as that most dangerous of phenomena – an intelligent man who lived in, even revelled in, a fool's paradise. The political illusion that the new Germany was not just powerful, but all-powerful, rested ultimately on a feeling of insecurity. So did the Kaiser's private illusion – that, as the personification of this omnipotence, he only had to speak or make his presence felt to impose the German will on others. His vanity, and yearning for what the Italians call *bella figura* made it easy for his advisers to manipulate him into such situations. The classic case was his descent on Tangier on 31 March 1905.

The year before, London and Paris had buried their colonial hatchets by agreeing that, as regards the Mediterranean, England would enjoy primacy in Egypt in return for acknowledging French interests in Morocco. But what, they asked themselves in Berlin, about Germany's established economic rights in North Africa? Egypt, the lifeline of the British empire, was too deadly a matter to meddle in; Morocco was a softer target. Baron Holstein, now approaching the end of his twenty-eight years' reign at the German Foreign Office, urged Chancellor Bülow to make some sort of demonstration. Bülow talked the Kaiser, who was anyway embarking on a spring cruise in those waters, into doing the demonstrating in person.

For once, William was reluctant. Morocco was a long way from the Brandenburg Mark. Moreover, he was sailing there not on the royal yacht but on a chartered German cruise liner, the *Hamburg*. There was neither the clink of Prussian breastplates nor the familiar surroundings of the *Hohenzollern*, which was Potsdam afloat, to reassure him. Typically, it was only when the dashing young German consul-general in Tangier, Herr von Kühlmann,* swarmed up the *Hamburg*'s rope ladder to make his obeisance dressed in his Bavarian Lancers uniform, complete with tchapka helmet on his head, that his imperial master took heart. The heroic spark had been kindled.

Later that morning, with the Bavarian lancer at his side and a company of mounted Moroccan troops as escort, the Kaiser rode up on an over-frisky Barbary stallion to the German legation. Arab bedlam engulfed the building, with a military band blaring away and rifle shots being fired off in greeting. The Kaiser's restraint went, as well as his nerves. Shouting above the din, he assured the assembled handful of German officials and merchants that Morocco was independent, that all powers had equal rights there and that his own presence was a pledge of Germany's 'great and growing interests'. Then, sweating profusely, he remounted the Sultan's steed and somehow, with his one good arm, made his way safely down to the harbour again.

---

* He was eventually to become state secretary at the Foreign Office.

The fatal thing about this episode was that, for all the Kaiser's misgivings and grumbling, his Tangier escapade did in the end lead to an illusory diplomatic triumph. France and England at once recognized the challenge that Berlin had thrown down to their freshly-concluded Entente (which Bülow had characterized as a 'continental dagger' pointed at the heart of Germany). For two months there was much diplomatic growling between all three capitals and some excitable talk of war in Paris. Then Bülow both defused the crisis and capitalized on it by persuading the Sultan of Morocco to call an international conference of all powers represented at his court. The French war party had the ground cut from under its feet, and the foreign minister, Delcassé, who had led the agitation, was forced out of office. A delighted Kaiser made his chancellor a prince. That was on 6 June. It was not surprising that, with this unexpected triumph under his belt,* William should have promptly pressed ahead to secure a much greater quarry than an Arab Sultan. The following month, in what was perhaps his most extraordinary venture in personal diplomacy, the Kaiser attempted to bypass all chancelleries and embassies, and ensnare the Tsar of Russia single-handed.

The setting could hardly have been in greater contrast. Instead of the steamy harbour of Tangier, it was now the ice-clear waters of Björkö on the Gulf of Finland where the Kaiser had invited cousin Nicholas II to meet him, ostensibly to nothing more than an exchange of family gossip and a look at the midnight sun. But the 'simple tourist' (as William had announced himself) had with him, on board the *Hohenzollern*, not only the then state secretary at his Foreign Office, Heinrich von Tschirschky, but also, in his pocket, the draft of a Russo-German treaty of alliance. There had been talk of this the previous autumn and the idea had certain attractions for both sides. Russia, reeling from her defeat at Japanese hands in the Far East war, was seeking fresh support in Europe, while Germany had an obvious interest in preventing Russia from sliding into the newly-formed Anglo-French camp. But Bülow was determined to do all the negotiating himself and had urged his imperial master to do nothing more than a dynastic reconnaissance.

Undeterred, on 25 July 1905, William II tried all by himself to retrieve the blunder he had allowed to happen fifteen years earlier, when Bismarck's 'line to Russia' had been cut. For years, in the

---

* It was to prove a temporary one. The Sultan's international conference duly convened at the little Spanish port of Algeciras, close to Gibraltar, on 16 January 1906. When it ended, three and a half months later, French predominance in Morocco was left unchallenged, despite face-saving declarations about independence and the freedom of commerce.

so-called 'Willy–Nicky' correspondence, the Kaiser had been bomb-
arding the Tsar with advice on all matters, foreign and domestic,
always playing the role of the wiser and older mentor. Now, having
softened up the weak and impressionable Nicholas with much anti-
English talk on the *Hohenzollern* the evening before, the Kaiser, on his
return visit to the Russian yacht *Standart*, played what he hoped would
be remembered by posterity as his diplomatic master-stroke. His
chancellor, unsuspectingly enjoying a peaceful summer holiday at the
Baltic resort of Norderney, was shattered two days later to read what
had been going on behind his back at Björkö, set out in a glowing
personal telegram from his sovereign:

I drew the envelope out of my pocket and unfolded the paper on the writing
desk of Alexander III, in front of the portrait of the Tsar's mother. . . . I prayed
to God that He would be with us now and influence the young ruler. He was as
still as death. There was no sound but that of the sea. . . . Right before me,
glistening white, lay the 'Hohenzollern', the imperial flag fluttering aloft in the
breeze. I was just reading the letters 'Gott mit uns' on its black cross when I
heard the Tsar saying at my side: 'That's quite splendid. I entirely agree.'[3]

When the Tsar had signed, the beads of nervous perspiration
dripping from the Kaiser's brow were joined (in his own words) by
'tears of joy'. This was, he declared to Bülow, surely 'a turning point in
European history'.

In fact, nothing turned an inch. The 'Treaty' of Björkö (which would
have bound Germany and Russia to come to each other's aid if either
were attacked by any European power) never got beyond that writing-
desk of the Tsar's father. When Nicholas sheepishly revealed the secret
to his foreign minister, Count Lamsdorff, back in St Petersburg, he was
told that it was a flagrant and unacceptable breach of the various
treaties which Alexander III had concluded with France more than ten
years before, and which had given Russia prosperity as well as security.
The Prime Minister, Count Witte, agreed. After much embarrassment
and head-scratching, it was finally agreed that Nicholas should write to
the Kaiser suggesting that their private pact be put on one side 'until we
know how the French will look upon it'.[4]

Compared with the ructions which awaited the Kaiser back home,
his cousin in St Petersburg had been let off lightly. On 3 August, von
Bülow wrote his master a long dissertation which tore the pact to shreds
(mainly on the grounds that it was confined to Europe and thus
excluded Russia from any action against England in Persia or Jordan).
He ended by begging William 'in deepest devotion, to place the
leadership of our foreign policy in other hands'.[5]

He snapped like a dry twig in Bülow's hand and wrote back what must be one of the most servile letters ever penned by an emperor to his head of government. He pleaded with Bülow, almost on his knees, to withdraw his resignation: 'You cannot and must not repudiate me. . . . This I cannot survive . . .' He even dredged up the Tangier escapade as a moral debt which his chancellor owed him:

I landed because you wanted me to, in the interests of the Fatherland, mounted a strange horse in spite of the impediment which my crippled left arm brought to my riding, and the horse was within an inch of costing me my life. . . . I had to ride between Spanish anarchists because you wished it and your policy was to profit by it . . .[6]

Bülow somewhat unctuously claims in his memoirs that it was the reference to the 'crippled left arm' which softened his heart. It is much more likely that, having read such a pathetic outburst, he had high hopes of ruling supreme over Germany's affairs from now on. At any rate, he promptly withdrew his resignation, though his high hopes were not to be fulfilled.

The Björkö incident is of interest not merely because it marked the most ambitious, as well as the most dismal, of the Kaiser's ventures in personal diplomacy. Much more significant, it revealed how the emperors of Germany and Russia, the one an autocrat and the other a near-absolute ruler, could buckle under like the weakest of constitutional monarchs when faced with a ministerial showdown. It was not power which either the Kaiser or the Tsar lacked, but backbone. This was to be demonstrated again, and this time lethally, when Europe faced its supreme test nine summers later.

It will be recalled that William had tried to soften the Tsar up at Björkö by a little anti-English propaganda. To be precise, he had been trying to poison his cousin's mind against King Edward VII. Here we come to the Kaiser's central and overwhelming obsession in foreign affairs.

There seems to have been never a moment in his life when William, whether as Prince, Crown Prince or Emperor, did not envy and resent his English kinsman. Indeed, the first manifestation of this came when he was only four years old and in attendance, as an insignificant little guest, at his uncle's marriage to the Danish princess, Alexandra, in St George's Chapel, Windsor, on 10 March 1863. The infant William had been dolled up for the occasion in Highland dress, and that pleased him mightily. (He was to preserve a sentimental affection for everything Scottish, from kilts to scones, throughout his life.) But what infuriated him was that, despite his finery, as the ceremony unfolded nobody in the glittering company was taking the slightest notice of him. After trying vainly to attract attention by brandishing his tiny dirk, he settled for the bare legs of two other kilt-clad figures who flanked him, Prince Arthur, Duke of Connaught, and Prince Leopold, Duke of Albany. They stoically sat out their brother's wedding while the future German Kaiser busied himself by digging his nails and teeth into their vulnerable calves. William the child was demonstrating two traits of William the man: a complex over his British links and a frustrated sulkiness whenever he was upstaged. The uncle at the altar was to give him problems on both counts.

Even as Prince of Wales, the polished, assured and pleasure-loving Edward always outshone his nephew socially as they matured into middle age and manhood respectively. William's only moments of triumph were the cheaply won victories of protocol after he had succeeded to the German throne while his uncle was still waiting impotently on the steps of the English one. With indecent haste and characteristic insensitivity, he rubbed in this difference in rank only four months after becoming emperor. Having discovered that the Prince of Wales was proposing to end a tour of Central Europe by calling in at Vienna on 3 October 1888, the brand-new Kaiser, who was himself arriving in the Austrian capital that same day, made it plain to his hosts that he wanted the Vienna stage to himself. As William II was a crowned head paying an official visit, an embarrassed Emperor Franz Josef had no option but to comply. The Prince of Wales departed in a fury that he managed to communicate to his mother on reaching England. Apart from the family snub, she also felt the political dangers which the outrageous behaviour of her German grandson presaged. 'The Queen much *fears*', she wrote, 'that with such a hot-headed, conceited and wrong-headed young man, devoid of all feeling, this may, at *any* moment, become *impossible*.'[7]

Her Prime Minister, Lord Salisbury, was more succinct in his verdict. For him the Vienna incident was simply proof that the new German emperor 'was not quite all there'. The lofty undertone of that appraisal would have sent William through the roof. If there was one thing he resented even more than English criticism it was English condescension. For all the menace that he symbolized, they never really took him seriously as a person.

On 22 January 1901, with the death of Queen Victoria, one of the many things which changed for ever on the new dynastic scene was the Kaiser's ability to score protocol points off his uncle. At the relatively advanced age of fifty-nine years and two months (still four years less than his mother's enormous reign) the Prince of Wales was now King-

Emperor, ruler over the greatest empire history had seen. The Kaiser, who had hurried from Germany to be in time at his grandmother's death-bed, was under no illusions about the inheritance she had handed on. He wrote, at the end of that year, when exchanging greetings with King Edward: 'What a magnificent realm she has left you, and what a fine position in the world. . .'

This particular letter from nephew to uncle, which was an unusually warm one, revealed the Kaiser's rather touching, if gushing, senti-mental side. Memories of those childhood days at Balmoral with the revered Grandmama had been revived in a flood of affection by the Christmas present which King Edward had sent to Potsdam – a Highland suit, unearthed at Windsor, which had once been worn by William's father, the ill-starred Frederick III. After reminiscing fondly about the last time he had worn Highland dress at Balmoral twenty-three years before, and the deer-stalking there with a 'gigantic old "Jaeger" ', William ended with an emotional plea for the partnership of these two peoples: 'They are of the same blood and they have the same faith and they belong to the great Teutonic race which Heaven has entrusted with the culture [sic] of the world.'[8]

As we shall see, this appeal had ironically arrived in London just as the British government, with the new King's approval, was preparing to step away from any closer ties with Germany. It was not the sort of message which might have encouraged second thoughts. As usual, the Kaiser had grossly over-egged the pudding for the English palate.

The new year brought ample evidence of the increasingly ambivalent relationship between the two monarchs, and their two countries. On 5 July 1902, when King Edward was officially declared to be 'out of danger' from the acute appendicitis which had caused the postpone-ment of his coronation, the Kaiser interrupted a regatta dinner at Travemünde to call for three cheers at the news. His delight was spontaneous and, no doubt, quite sincere. Yet within a few days he was telling the passengers on an American-owned yacht (which happened to anchor in the same harbour as the *Hohenzollern*, then on its annual Norwegian cruise) that the elderly Prime Minister of England was 'just a protoplasm', while the permissive life-style of England's king was a scandal. If he carried on the way his 'Uncle Bertie' did, he assured the astounded tourists from the New World, the German people would soon get rid of him. This onslaught, too, was spontaneous and sincere. Edward VII was family; but he was enviable and, above all, dangerous family.

The Kaiser's lecture to the Americans had reached London because, unbeknown to William, one of the listeners had been an ex-British diplomat. This could be shrugged off as a private irritant. Soon afterwards, however, an official row was brewing between Potsdam and Windsor. The Kaiser had infuriated London often enough while England's exhausting war against the Boers was raging.* He was continuing to give offence now, after peace had been concluded, by threatening to receive three Boer generals who were on a triumphal tour of Europe. It would have been an intolerable gesture, especially as the Kaiser was about to leave for England himself on a private visit to his uncle. Edward VII let this be known, in crisp language, and the Boers left Berlin without the audience.

Reporting to London on the end of the affair, the ambassador in Berlin, Sir Frank Lascelles, went on to discuss details of the forthcoming visit, which had been arranged to emphasize its family character, around the King's sixty-first birthday celebration at Sandringham on 9 November. 'I have told Eulenburg', Sir Frank wrote, 'that in any case the King hopes that the Emperor will arrive at Sandringham in plain clothes.'[9]

That simple sentence showed something of the gulf that always stretched between the two rulers and their peoples. For William – and increasingly also, for his nation – life was one unbroken military parade. Informality was always a stranger to them both, and so, therefore, was relaxation. The Kaiser's idea of the latter may be judged by the fact that he duly appeared at Sandringham in what amounted to a special uniform he had designed himself for shooting: high leather boots, dark green *loden* breeches and cape, and a stiff hat, usually adorned with the brush of a chamois or the feather of a capercailzie. The omnipresent military face of Germany was also reflected in his large suite of army officers who scandalized the King by pulling service revolvers out of their holsters to take pot shots at Sandringham hares when the pheasants were not streaming overhead.

For the Kaiser, that visit came to mark something of a watershed. He had plugged away with the Prime Minister and two of his Cabinet colleagues (who had been invited for part of the time so that the imperial guest might indulge in politics) urging them to strengthen ties with Berlin and understand Germany's need to build a large fleet alongside her formidable army. He had got nowhere and, only six months later, he watched helplessly as his uncle set a highly personal seal of favour on the other European camp. From now on the Kaiser's obsession with Edward VII as the architect of all Germany's troubles

---

* Notably by sending a telegram of congratulations to President Kruger on the occasion of his capturing a force of English irregulars from the Transvaal on 2 January 1896.

knew no bounds. Whatever happened anywhere in Europe which might threaten Germany's interests was, ultimately, the work of his uncle – ceaselessly at work spinning his anti-German web, and using every dynastic, diplomatic and personal thread he could get his plump hands on. The Kaiser's famous marginal comments on the German diplomatic documents of the period show the scope of this fixation.

Thus when, on 9 March 1906, King Alfonso XIII of Spain announced his betrothal to Edward VII's niece, Princess Victoria Eugenie, the Kaiser, who had been trying hard to make the Spanish ruler his nephew by marriage, took it as far more than a family defeat. He scribbled on a report from his Madrid embassy about the affair: 'The whole of these pathetic and corrupt Latin peoples are becoming instruments in England's hands, in order to hamper German commerce in the Mediterranean.'[10]

When it came to Anglo-French relations and the historic Entente of 1904, the Kaiser was, as we shall see, quite right in attributing much of this to the direct influence of Edward VII. But the Kaiser far overshot the mark in gauging how far this influence went. Commenting on an assurance given to the Germans by the British foreign secretary Lord Lansdowne that no thought of a formal alliance had even been discussed in Cabinet, the Kaiser snorted with his busy pen: 'That I well believe! H[is] M[ajesty] has raised the matter *all by himself* on his two Paris visits!'[11]

He saw the King as always trying to weaken the ties between Germany and her Triple Alliance partners. On a report from Vienna that both England and France were hard at work trying to improve relations between Austria and Russia (and thus weaken those between Austria and Germany), the Kaiser wrote simply: 'King Edward VII'.[12]

When his embassy in Rome described how anglophile Italian leaders were, 'including the best of their diplomats, the Marquis San Giuliano', the Kaiser commented: 'Because of that he won't even be posted to Berlin but kept on Edward VII's strings.'[13]

As for Anglo-German relations themselves, the King was to blame for everything that was sour about them. Some of the Kaiser's outbursts showed how much, for all his close links with England, he remained in ignorance as to how democracy in that country operated. When he read that King Edward had been quoted as saying how he regretted the anti-German tone of the English press, the Kaiser wrote: 'Then he should prevent it. He has the means of doing so.'[14]

His uncle was the reason why society in England was so anti-German (in contrast, the Germans fondly believed, to the working, middle and merchant classes) and when his ambassador in London, Count

Metternich, suggested that 'English society would be won over if the two sovereigns could come closer', the Kaiser made another of his dream-world comments: 'I don't believe it. Meetings with E VII are of no lasting value because he is so envious.'[15]

Envy was just about the last thing the King of England could be accused of: he enjoyed life far too much for that. Periodically he attempted to assuage the envy and suspicion which his nephew undoubtedly felt by almost blatant appeals to the emotions. Thus in a letter sent on the occasion of the Kaiser's forty-seventh birthday, Edward VII wrote:

We are, my dear William, such old friends and near relations that I am sure the affectionate feelings which have always existed may invariably continue. Be assured that this country has never had any aggressive feelings towards you and the idle gossip and silly tittle-tattle on the subject emanates from mischief-makers and ought never to be listened to.[16]

This message, signed by his 'very affectionate uncle' did push politics aside and revive, for a moment, memories of Balmoral and Grand-mama Victoria. But the image was always as quick to dissolve as it was to form in William's mind. For him, the present and the future were what counted and the dreaded 'encirclement' of Germany was, quite simply, 'all my uncle's fault'.[17]

This 'encirclement' was completed in German eyes when an Anglo-Russian convention followed on the Anglo-French entente and the three great powers on the flanks of Europe became loosely bonded together against the monarchies in the centre. Once again, it had been Edward VII who had set his personal seal on English diplomacy by embarking on a particularly harmonious 'family visit' to his new ally. The fact that this took place in Russian waters on the royal yachts of the two sovereigns must have been particularly irksome to the Kaiser, who was still ruing his illusory mayfly triumph over the Tsar on board the same *Standart* in 1905.

The Reval meeting between Edward VII and Nicholas II fell in June of 1908, a year that was to prove one of the grimmest of the Kaiser's reign, on both the personal and the political fronts. The autumn, in particular, was sown like a minefield with tensions. There was, to begin with, Germany's involvement in the European crisis touched off by Austria's annexation of Bosnia-Herzegovina, which has already been looked at from the receiving end.

Suggestions that it was Germany who had put her ally up to the move, in order to strengthen the Teutonic grip on the Balkans and humiliate the Russians, were very wide of the mark. Bülow is on record as to how concerned he was when, on 5 October, he heard of the Austrian move. He immediately sent a message to the Kaiser (who was shooting on his Rominten estate): 'In view of the present situation in Europe, we cannot oppose Austria's wishes. Our position would become really grave if Austria-Hungary lost faith in us and turned away from us . . .' But he went on to hope that Austria 'will so proceed as not to offend Turkish self-respect too deeply . . . and not encourage the Balkan states to take aggressive action against the Ottoman empire'.[18]

As for the Kaiser, he was livid that he had been given no advance warning but had merely received, along with other major European sovereigns and heads of state, a personal letter from the Emperor Franz Josef on the eve of the Austrian move which, in the circumstances, amounted to the declaration of a *fait accompli*.

William wrote under his chancellor's message:

That we will not oppose the annexation is obvious, but I am wounded to the quick in my feelings as an ally that I was not taken in the slightest into H.M.'s confidence. . . . The first I heard of the impending annexation was last night in a message from Turkish sources in Stamboul. . . . So I am the last of all in Europe to learn anything at all! That's a nice thanks for our help . . .

As so often, the Kaiser then went over the top in his exasperation by almost volunteering to fight for Turkey in the confrontation: 'If the Sultan, in desperation, takes to arms and unrolls the green flag of holy war in Stamboul, I wouldn't particularly blame him and it would be a healthy lesson for those treacherous gallows vultures – the Christians of the Balkans!'[19]

In fact, Germany's role in the affair was the precise prescription set out in Bülow's first reaction: strong support for her ally over the annexation as such, coupled with intense activity behind the scenes to stop the political crisis developing into armed conflict. The Kaiser put himself behind the conciliation efforts. On 5 January 1909 when, after three months, a solution seemed as far away as ever, he wrote, from the shooting-lodge at Hubertusstock, a personal letter (in English) to his 'dear Nicky' in St Petersburg stoutly denying all rumours that Germany had 'pushed Austria to take this step'. 'These small states', he went on loftily, (meaning Serbia) 'are an awful nuisance. The slightest encouragement from any quarter makes them frantic. . . .' (A clear hint to 'Nicky' not to do any encouraging.) 'I do hope with all my heart that . . . a peaceful solution will be arrived at. Anything I can do in that direction I certainly will do.'[20]

In the end it was a German diplomatic formula aimed at securing

Austria's annexation while also saving Russia's face which broke the international deadlock. The combination worked that time. The mistake was to think it would work again.

Though the Kaiser had emerged without discredit from the annexation crisis, the year brought two other blows, one of them self-inflicted, which reduced him to a nervous wreck ready, at one moment of hysteria, to give up his throne. Between them they drained both his confidence in himself and his prestige among his people in a measure that was never to be made good.

The first disaster, which shook William to the marrow, was a personal one. On 21 April 1908, as the climax to a long and complex series of libel actions, a Munich court declared Philipp Eulenburg to be a practising homosexual on the sworn evidence of two Bavarian locals, a fisherman and a labourer. So far all the accusations, counter-accusations and lawsuits which had been swirling around Eulenburg's head for eighteen months past had generated only a legal fog – albeit a fog nasty enough for William to have demanded Eulenburg's resignation from the diplomatic service while he set about clearing his name. Now that name, the name of the Kaiser's own *ami de coeur*, was not cleared but damned.

Bülow (presumably acting on the authority of his royal master) had Eulenburg arrested for perjury, and his castle searched. His trial commenced in Berlin on 29 June 1908, only to be suspended after eighteen harrowing days when the defendant collapsed in court and was declared by the doctors unfit to plead. (It was resumed a year later with the same result and from then, right down to 1919, in war and peace, Philipp Eulenburg was examined, once every six months, by court doctors, who continued to pronounce him too ill to stand trial.)

Though the doctors had saved the Kaiser's closest friend from the dire threat of imprisonment, the disgrace could not be wiped out, and its stain touched William himself. Homosexuality was linked in the public mind with decadence, a vice seemingly emanating from the highest order of society to threaten all those stout middle-class tenets of religion and family life on which the moral foundations of the new Germany were supposed to be built. 'The fish', as a proverb went, 'always starts to stink from the head.' The shock and damage which the Eulenburg scandal had inflicted on the Kaiser explain the exaggerated effects of the other *cause célèbre* of the year, his famous *Daily Telegraph* interview.

On 28 October 1908 the readers of that sober and patriotic journal were astounded to learn that, in the opinion of the German Emperor, they and all their fellow-countrymen were 'mad, mad as March hares'.

As proof of his own goodwill, the Kaiser informed the ungrateful British public that, at their blackest hour in the Boer War, he had personally worked out the proper military strategy for them and sent it to Queen Victoria at Windsor. As further reassurance he told his anonymous interviewer* that German fleet expansion was directed, not against England, but against 'eventualities in the Far East', i.e. Japan.

Through the incompetence at several levels inside the German Foreign Office and, ultimately, through the negligence of Bülow in not even reading the text when it was sent to him, this farrago of abuse and nonsense had been released and reproduced, uncensored, throughout the world. England and, for that matter, Japan, had every reason to be offended, and were. But the significant thing was the disproportionate clamour which arose in Germany itself. The anti-English majority were up in arms because of the sympathy their Emperor seemed to show for his Anglo-Saxon cousins; the pro-English minority offended at the damage he had done to their cause. Those with no strong views either way were aware that the Kaiser had made a laughing-stock both of himself and of his country. These resentments surged to form a tide of opposition against the person of the ruler and the Potsdam/Berlin clique through which he ruled.

William bent before the storm by asking Bülow (whose resignation had been offered and duly rejected) to bale him out before the Reichstag. He then fled the political storm as well as his tearful wife and reproachful courtiers, by taking himself off to the country. Even the luxurious asylum of Donaueschingen, where he ended his visit, did not bring its usual relief, despite all the energetic efforts of the Fürstenbergs to distract him. Indeed, their entertainment only served to darken the drama further with an episode of the blackest farce.

On board the *Hohenzollern* or in the smoking-rooms of shooting-lodges, someone always had to play the clown when the Kaiser sought relaxation among his friends. On the final evening of the Donaue-schingen stay, the ill-starred volunteer was one of his principal military aides, Count Hülsen-Haeseler, who had the picaresque idea of entertaining the after-dinner company by pirouetting before them in a ballerina's tutu. Unfortunately the elderly gentleman had under-estimated the exertions demanded by the terpsichorean art. After a few spins he collapsed on the spot and died of apoplexy before the house-doctors could revive him. The corpse was then extracted from its tutu, reclothed in full military uniform, and laid out in state in the grand

---

* Rapidly identified as Colonel Montagu-Stuart-Wortley, from whom the Kaiser had rented Highcliffe Castle in Hampshire during his visit to England the previous autumn.

salon of the castle for burial the next day. The general may not exactly
have died for his fatherland, but he had certainly died for his emperor.
Ironically, the sacrifice had been counter-productive. The tragedy was
another brand-mark on the Kaiser's whole way of life.

He returned to Berlin in worse shape than he had fled his capital.
When Bülow, moving in for the kill, forced him to sign a declaration
which virtually gave his chancellor a blank cheque for future policy the
Kaiser took to his sick-bed, sent for the Crown Prince and told the court
chamberlain to inform Bülow that he was abdicating. Nobody, except
perhaps Crown Prince 'Willy', could take the offer seriously. With all
his glaring faults, the Kaiser was still a far better advertisement for
monarchy than his chinless, dissolute and very unpopular eldest son.*
Nor was there any lasting weight about the offer itself. The Kaiser had
only been indulging in a spectacular exercise in histrionics and self-
pity. After a long and soothing talk with Dona, he abruptly changed his
mind. It was a doleful Christmas at Potsdam; but by the time the Berlin
season began on New Year's Day the Kaiser, outwardly at any rate,
was his old bouncing self again. Yet his reputation never quite bounced
back, inside Germany or outside. On that score, his English uncle,
shortly to visit Berlin, was right when he wrote: 'Of all the political
gaffes which H.I.M. has made, this is the greatest.'[21]

The year 1908 brought about something far graver for Anglo-
German relations, and for Europe, than an intemperate newspaper
article. It was also the year when the naval rivalry between the two
countries passed the point of no return and thus sharpened the latent
hostility between the rival power blocs to which they belonged. The
English were willing, if not happy, to accept that the Germans, with the
strongest army in the world, were the military masters on the continent.
But when, in the 1890s, the Kaiser started also to construct a powerful
fleet whose warships were clearly designed for long-range operations,
that army became capable of swimming – a prospect which the British
empire would not accept.

The third German Naval Act of 1908, which provided for a further
increase of twenty per cent in German expenditure on the fleet,
whipped up this old storm at sea into a new fury. At the dynastic level

---

* It was significant that when William II was forced into abdication, after Germany's military
collapse in the autumn of 1918, even the monarchists, before yielding to the republic, passed
over the Crown Prince and tried to transfer the regency instead to his brother, Prince Eitel
Friedrich.

the Kaiser had infuriated his uncle by writing direct, on 16 February, to Lord Tweedmouth, the First Lord of the Admiralty, on the subject. At the diplomatic level, the British foreign secretary, Sir Edward Grey, had made it clear, in July, that Anglo-German relations would never improve until Germany abandoned the naval race. The following month the Kaiser made it equally clear, when his uncle visited him at Cronberg, that he had no intention of limiting his fleet. By November of 1908, while the Kaiser was trying to recuperate from his own problems at Donaueschingen, Grey was declaring bluntly to his ambassador in London that there was now no half way for England between complete safety and absolute ruin. At the popular level, the streets of London and the lobbies of Westminster were echoing with the cry of 'We want eight (Dreadnought battleships) and we won't wait'. The whole quarrel had slipped anchor and had begun dangerously to drift.

Despite repeated efforts by official missions and private mediators alike to contain it, the quarrel was still out of control in the summer of 1914, when the talking stopped for good and the two navies were put on action stations for war. Though not a direct cause of that war, it had by then become one of several European inflammations which made hostilities so hard to avoid. It was very typical that one of the sharpest pre-war confrontations between Germany and the Entente powers should have been touched off by a German warship – the gunboat *Panther* which, on 1 July 1911, dropped anchor in Agadir as a demonstration of Germany's continual determination to maintain her position in Morocco. Typically, too, it was the Kaiser who had personally authorized the operation. He must have felt it a distinct advance over his earlier precarious Moroccan adventure on a barbary stallion.

The *Panther* affair (which, like the Tangier crisis six years before, only served to strengthen rather than weaken the Anglo-French entente) highlights the central question about the Kaiser's reign: had he, by the end, become the tool of that military establishment over which, in theory, he held absolute mastery as Germany's Supreme War Lord? The general line of control was clear enough. Prussia dominated Germany and the *Junker* officer in turn dominated Prussia. With every year that passed, agriculture, the financial prop of the *Junker* class, became less and less important in relation to industry, which took over as the mainstay of the economy as a whole. Yet, to the end, this narrow conservative élite kept its archaic disproportionate hold on power. One reason, of course, was that worship of uniform, which most Germans had inherited in their genes. The swindling feats of the bogus 'Captain of Köpenick'* could only have been accomplished with such ease in the German capital. Only in Berlin would a Cabinet minister who happened, at one time or another, to have held even junior rank in a fashionable regiment, turn up on formal occasions in the dress uniform of that regiment, as opposed to his black morning suit, in which every Prussian somehow felt quite naked.

But as the *Junkers* well knew, the ground was shifting all the time under them, and the only way they could keep their foothold was through their influence on the Kaiser and their presence at his court. If the influence was mainly social and ethical, the presence was institutionalized. William had inherited the so-called military and civilian cabinets at Potsdam, and to them he added, in due course, a naval cabinet. These bodies, responsible solely and directly to the emperor, not only controlled appointments to the armed forces and civil service; their chiefs also selected which official reports, from any source, the ruler would have presented to him in private audiences held almost daily. Thus, apart from his vast personal entourage of uniformed adjutants and aides, William also had, in his palaces, a government within a government, in which uniforms predominated, and *Junker* uniforms at that. With the exception of the navy (which had expanded so quickly that commissions had to be broader-based) the officers surrounding the Kaiser remained overwhelmingly hereditary noblemen or persons ennobled by him. Even Dona was surrounded by aristocratic generals alongside her ladies-in-waiting. All this despite the fact that, by the outbreak of war, nearly three-quarters of the German officer corps as a whole were of bourgeois stock. It was not surprising that the Kaiser should often be so out of touch with reality when his personal entourage remained so isolated from the social and economic changes within the nation.

It is in this context that the disgrace and fall of Philipp Eulenburg in 1908 had a political impact even wider than that caused by the scandal itself. Bülow (who had been helped into office by Eulenburg) was himself dropped by the Kaiser the following summer. Both had been non-military, and in some ways anti-military, figures, and each had exercised great influence over the ruler. Thus, within the space of twelve months, the two most powerful chocks pushed under the wheels

---

* An ex-convict, William Voigt, hired a captain's uniform in Berlin and with it commandeered a squad of men from the nearest barracks. He took his detachment by train on a so-called 'official inspection visit' to the town hall of Köpenick suburb and made off with 4,000 marks which, he claimed, had been improperly accounted for. The mayor and councillors stood by like sheep, hypnotized by the mere sight of an imperial epaulette. The episode was made into a famous play by the dramatist Carl Zuckmayer.

of the German war machine had been removed, at a time when that machine was revving up, louder and louder, for action.

And so we come to the much-debated gathering of military chiefs convened by the Kaiser on Sunday 8 December 1912 and later dubbed a 'war council'. This, it will be recalled, was at the height of the attack being waged by the allied Balkan states against the Ottoman empire, a war which threatened to produce a direct confrontation between Austria and Russia and so escalate into a European conflict. As during the annexation crisis four years before, the broad objectives of both the Kaiser and his chancellor (now Theobald von Bethmann-Hollweg)* were the same: to show firm support for their Austrian allies without allowing them to get too imprudent. But the partial mobilization of the two great Balkan rivals called for a military appreciation of the situation in Berlin, hence the war council, to which, as usual, no civilians were admitted. General Helmuth von Moltke, who had been the Kaiser's chief of staff since 1906, had long been of the opinion that war (by which the Germans always meant war with England) was inevitable and he hammered home the point even harder at this meeting by insisting 'The earlier, the better'. The only participant who made a first-hand record of the proceedings was the head of the naval cabinet, Admiral von Müller. He states in his diary that while the Kaiser 'quite agreed' with Moltke, he also 'reluctantly accepted' the point made by his navy commander, Admiral von Tirpitz, that the German fleet would require another eighteen months to be ready.[22]

While it is true that the following year, 1913, saw large increases in German military expenditure, it would be too simplistic to deduce that in December of 1912 the Kaiser and four of his senior officers (an Admiral von Heeringen was also present) had picked the summer of 1914 as the firm date on which to unleash a European war. All the general staffs of all the major powers were constantly juggling with the calendar on the one hand and their armament and recruitment programmes on the other to see when they would be best placed to take to the field and the high seas. The English and German naval staffs did little else but plot their graphs of battleship construction so as to provide themselves with what this nuclear age calls a 'window of opportunity'. As for the confrontation on land, the Tsar, as we have seen, had assured the humiliated Serbs in 1908 that the Russian army

---

* Bethmann-Hollweg, even as chancellor, loved to wear his Prussian regimental uniform, which set off his giant stature and close-cropped hair to perfection. In fact he was cautious, polite and ambivalent, reflecting the long years he had spent in the civil service, before becoming Prussian minister of the interior.

would be strong enough to help them in a few years' time. The generals were only doing their job in preparing for war. There is another point to remember. On all sides, the generals talked so loudly of war because, until the 1914 holocaust, they had no concept of what this could mean. But to prove that this Potsdam meeting had plotted the war to break out roughly when it did, we also need to prove that, when the political crisis of the Sarajevo murders erupted, the Kaiser then steered ruthlessly and relentlessly for Armageddon. The truth was very different.

What the so-called war council of 8 December 1912 did show was how totally cocooned the Kaiser was by his military entourage, to a point where life-and-death questions of the nation's future could be debated without even the chancellor or any civilian minister being in the room. It was this exclusive omnipresence of the German military, as much as their pressure, which counted fatally in the final crisis. As Edward VII had said to his greatest 'confidant', the Portuguese Marquis de Soveral after the Algeciras conference of 1906:

The Kaiser is even more cowardly than vain and, because of this, he will tremble before all these sycophants when, urged on by the General Staff, they call on him to draw the sword in earnest. . . . It is not by his will that he will start a war, but by his weakness.[23]

That was not a bad forecast of Potsdam in December of 1912, or in August of 1914.

Chapter Eight

AUSTRIA: THE GOLDEN PRINCE

For nearly seven decades the eleven nations and fifty million souls who made up the Habsburg monarchy moved to the wand of one man, their emperor, Franz Josef I. His reign, launched in the aftermath of the great revolution of the nineteenth century, only ended in the middle of the Great War of the twentieth. By then he had reigned for longer than most of his subjects had lived. Time itself became a dimension of his power.

The beat of this imperial metronome grew heavy and leaden as the years went by. But at the beginning it had seemed brisk and bright enough, as befitted the circumstances of his accession, aged only eighteen, on 2 December 1848. The Habsburg monarchy, like most of continental Europe, was then looking back on a year which had seen the absolutist old order shaken to its foundations by liberal-nationalist insurrections. In April the veteran Chancellor Prince Metternich, pillar of that absolutism in the Austrian empire, had resigned and sought asylum in England. (The bank-house Rothschild, hovering, as ever, in the political wings, advanced him one thousand ducats travel expenses.) In May the imperial family followed the deposed statesman in fleeing the Viennese mob, though, in their case, the move went only as far as Innsbruck, capital of the ultra-conservative mountain province of Tyrol.

By August, with the situation seemingly stabilizing, the family were back in the Vienna Hofburg again; but not for long. On 6 October the body of the war minister, Count Baillet-Latour, was found hanging from a lamppost outside his offices, the skull crushed from the back by a workman's hammer and the face and chest lacerated with stab wounds. It was the signal for a new round of violence and for another outbreak of understandable panic at the palace. This time the imperial family, with a miniature army of seven thousand troops as escort, headed north, not west, and a week later set up court in the castle of the Prince-

Archbishop of Olmütz in Moravia. It was from here that Prince Alfred Windisch-Graetz, the military governor of the neighbouring province of Bohemia, set out as field marshal and commander-in-chief of the loyalist forces to put an end to the nonsense once and for all, and restored the dynasty to its rightful capital. There was little that the outnumbered and disorganized rebels could do before a combined imperial army numbering over seventy thousand men. By the beginning of November the black-yellow Habsburg flag was flying again over the inner city. The imperial family remained for the time being in Olmütz. It had problems of its own to sort out before returning home.

Order had been restored, at least in Vienna, but what was to be done with it? The nine months of almost non-stop violence and upheaval had demonstrated clearly enough that the Habsburg empire was not, and did not wish to become, a second France which could switch between republic and monarchy as the mood of the mob dictated. Despite the temporary impact, the revolution in Austria was as unreal as a Grand Guignol carnival. Vienna was still a capital inconceivable without its double-headed eagle. Yet the ruling house none the less had to think hard and act boldly, for it was not only in the Austrian provinces that rebellion had flared. Peace had only just been restored in the North Italian territories of the empire thanks to the campaigns of the legendary Marshal Radetzky; a more serious revolt still remained to be put down in Hungary. How could the dynasty appear to change while staying the same; bend a little with the tempest, while remaining firmly anchored in its roots?

There was general agreement that a better anchor had to be found than the reigning monarch, Ferdinand I. He was a dim-witted epileptic who could neither walk nor talk properly, a living damnation of dynastic inbreeding whose concept of the crown was summed up in his immortal command: 'I am the emperor and I want dumplings.' As Ferdinand was without issue, his younger brother Franz Karl was heir-presumptive. Yet he too was far from ideal as a ruler to present as an inspiring symbol to a frightened and strife-torn empire. He was unimpressive physically, with a long thin face out of all proportion to his slight body, and very slow on the uptake, if well-meaning, mentally. His own mother-in-law, Queen Caroline of Bavaria, summed him up thus, the original being a mixture of German and French typical of the court language of the day: 'He is a good fellow and wants to do well. He asks everyone for advice, but he's really terrible. . . . He would bore me to death. Every now and then I would want to hit him.'[1]

Sophie, her intelligent and fiercely energetic daughter, had been persuaded, with eyes fixed only on the Habsburg crown, to marry

Franz Karl back in 1824. It was she who now stepped in to dominate the confused picture. The idea that the succession might pass straight over her husband's head to their son, the Archduke Franz Josef, dated, in fact, from the pre-revolution era. But Sophie began to press for it to be carried out in earnest the moment the 1848 troubles began, first with Metternich and, then, with Windisch-Graetz. It was agreed, at all events, to wait for the youthful Archduke's eighteenth birthday, which fell on 18 August 1848. After that the pitiful Ferdinand had to be persuaded to abdicate, and Franz Karl talked into renouncing his rights. It was Sophie who secured her husband's agreement, though it meant that she would never be empress herself, only the mother of an emperor. She fully intended to make out of that the next best thing.

The accession, which was in fact a transfer act from Habsburg old to Habsburg new-old, was solemnized in the throne-room of the archbishop's residence at Olmütz. Ferdinand managed one of the best performances of his sorry reign in its dying moments. He stroked the hair of the young Archduke, about to become his successor, as he knelt at his feet. Then, raising the boy up, he said to him simply: 'God bless you. Be always good and God will protect you.' The nephew's mumbled thanks he brushed aside: 'No need. I didn't mind.' One could truly say of his time on the throne, as of Shakespeare's Macduff, that 'nothing in his life became him like the leaving it'. Ferdinand's own life continued, in tranquil retirement in Prague, for another twenty-seven years. That gave him plenty of opportunities to mumble, whenever crises or confusions were reported from Vienna: 'I could have done as well as that myself.'

These abundant troubles of his nephew's lay well in the future. For the time being the eighteen-year-old Archduke, proclaimed Emperor at Olmütz (and duly presented in turn to Vienna and all the great cities of his empire) seemed the best as well as the last hope of the Habsburgs. To begin with he looked every inch the radiant unblemished princeling, a role for which he might almost have been sculpted: tall and slender; nimble on his feet; a good horseman, which pleased the men; an excellent and enthusiastic dancer, which enchanted the ladies; fair-haired, with wide-set blue eyes, a straight nose and a generous mouth almost unblemished by the congenital Habsburg distortion of a pendulous lower lip and over-heavy jowl. The symbolism of the succession matched the promise of his person. There had never been a Franz Josef on the throne before, and while the first half of the double name was solid Habsburg, the other half recalled Joseph II, the 'enlightened despot' who had ruled over Mozart's Vienna, and striven to work for the happiness of his peoples. 'Viribus unitis' ('With united strength'), the motto which his young successor now took as his own, sounded like a pledge that the work of the great reforming emperor of the eighteenth century would be carried forward in the nineteenth.

Disillusionment came swiftly, at least to those liberals who had provided the intellectual spark of the 1848 uprisings. When, in the summer of 1849, the revolt in Hungary was finally squashed (thanks largely to the services of Russian troops) it was answered by repressions so savage as to bury any hopes of reconciliation with the Magyar nationalists. Five hundred death sentences were pronounced, of which more than a hundred were carried out. Nearly 2,000 rebels were thrown into prison and 4,000 more only escaped by fleeing with their leader, Lajos Kossuth, to Turkey. (On the way, he buried the ancient crown of St Stephen, symbol of Hungary's separate nationhood, under a mulberry tree near Orsova and it took the Austrians three years to find it.)[2] Well might Field Marshal Windisch-Graetz remark that his young sovereign had not ascended his throne by the grace of God so much as by the grace of cannon.

Cannon: the military. It is impossible to overestimate the bond which existed, throughout his long life and reign, between Franz Josef and his army. It is, however, easy to forget that the grip was exerted both ways. The army was his prize possession and he was its supreme commander. He was also, in some ways, its captive. Its psychological hold on him began in infancy. He was drilling before he could read or write. At two he had his tiny sword and rifle; at five his first complete uniform. 'The army is what I like best,' he declared that same year. The verdict never changed.

In the terrible months of revolution he came to realize that his passion as a boy was also his salvation as a prince. A few weeks before the court fled Vienna for the first time, the young Franz Josef had been sent to Verona, to spend a few weeks at the headquarters of Marshal Radetzky. It looked to be the safest as well as the most suitable place for an archduke, who was already seen as the dynasty's best prospect, to ride out the storm. For the young Franz Josef (who on 6 May got close enough to the front to see a cannon-ball land near him) this military bastion of the empire was a paradise of loyal, disciplined calm after the outrageous mayhem of the imperial capital. When, at Custozza on 25 July, the emperor's troops inflicted their decisive defeat on the Piedmontese rebel army, the Radetzky cult, which had already captured Franz Josef's heart, went on to fire the pride of every loyalist in the monarchy. In keeping with the mood (and deepening it in the process) Johann Strauss the elder produced his 'Radetzky March', which remains to this day among the finest half-dozen military marches ever written for any army. Grillparzer, that most Austrian of poets, penned his famous hymn of praise to the grizzled war lord in Lombardy, verses which included the line: 'In your camp stands Austria.'

Franz Josef never forgot the message of those words. It was not until, after his time, at the end of a world war seventy years later, when that great multinational military camp began to fragment, that the fate of the Habsburg monarchy itself was sealed for ever. Until then the army was not only the inanimate cement which held the imperial edifice together. The living spirit of the empire could always best be found – and sometimes only be found – on its parade-grounds and battlefields.

That the monarchy, therefore, should put down armed rebellion in 1848–49 was understandable enough. What turned self-defence into counter-revolution was when the attack moved over to the political front. The young Emperor had acquired, as chief minister, Prince Felix Schwarzenberg, a brother-in-law of Windisch-Graetz, who had sponsored him for the job. Schwarzenberg had, until then, done little but amuse himself, and cause considerable commotion in the process, as a handsome bachelor in the diplomatic service. (His liaison, while serving in London, with Lady Ellenborough, the wife of the English Lord Privy Seal, led, for example, to a divorce scandal and the flight of the loving couple to Paris, where an illegitimate daughter was born.) But, given the unexpected chance to play the statesman, the flighty diplomat seized on his new role with full heart and mind.

He had two ambitions. The first, in which he failed, was to establish the enduring supremacy of the Habsburg monarchy among the company of German monarchs – which, in effect, meant lording it over the Hohenzollerns of Prussia. The second aim, which ran parallel to the first, was to restore the absolute and centralized power of the crown inside Austria-Hungary by dismantling the concessions made to reformist demands in 1848. Here he triumphantly succeeded. In March 1849, exactly twelve months after the revolution, he persuaded the young Emperor to issue, by decree, a constitution of his own (resting, of course, on unity under the crown), thus bypassing completely the somewhat farcical 'parliament' set up the year before. Two years later, on 31 December 1851, in his so-called 'Sylvester Patent' or 'New Year's Decree', Franz Josef formally abrogated the 1848 constitution altogether as well as cancelling most of the 'fundamental rights' which he had granted to his subjects in 1849. Ministerial responsibility had already been abolished in August of 1851. Now, at the close of the year, everything which smacked of popular representation or popular control was snuffed out. Henceforth the Emperor was in full and sole charge of all political affairs. (He was already, since 1849, commander-in-chief.) Franz Josef had not been pushed into donning his absolutist purple mantle. He could not wait to get it round his shoulders. Indeed, he shrugged off the pleas of even his revered mentor, Schwarzenberg, to wait a little longer.

So the young Emperor, whose accession had supposedly signified no return to absolutism, had, in three years, restored the old order of a paternal police state in all its vigour. Metternich, now seventy-eight years old, returned from exile in time to enjoy the spectacle. He was too shaky to play any further role, and when, in April of 1852, Schwarzenberg died suddenly of a heart attack (aged only as old as the century) it was Franz Josef who mopped up this last reservoir of personal power outside the Crown. He announced that, from now on, he would assume the responsibilities of minister-president himself. That meant that, as his own name would be at the bottom of every ordinance, criticism of any aspect of the administration was tantamount to treason. He was now the supreme bureaucrat as well as the supreme ruler. The long decades at the treadmill of state documents had begun. His desk chair had become his real throne.

Though the Viennese, with characteristic perversion, had greeted the once-detested Metternich with cheers, this did not mean that the trampling underfoot of all the hard-won constitutional reforms was popular. That strange gunpowder mixture of students, professors, workers, disgruntled bourgeois, progressive aristocrats, fanatical Magyars and Italian nationalists which had combined to bring about the great explosion of 1848, all felt betrayed. The populace at large was, at best, cowed. Something was needed to restore the Emperor's human 'image'. This duly happened at midday on 18 February 1853 when the Emperor, strolling with an aide on the Vienna ramparts, was fallen upon and stabbed in the neck by a Hungarian tailor's apprentice called Janos Libenyi. There could be no doubt about the grudge he bore his sovereign. The would-be assassin repeatedly shouted 'Éljen Kossuth' ('Long live Kossuth') as he was overpowered and led away. In a very real sense the military had saved Franz Josef once again. He was, as always, in uniform, and this time, ironically, had chosen that of a Hungarian Hussar regiment. The stiff collar blunted the thrust which could easily have been mortal. Even so he was a month convalescing and there was anxiety for a while that his sight might be damaged.

One result of the attack was an upsurge of monarchist feeling. When, after thirty daily medical bulletins, the imperial invalid reappeared in an open carriage, the crowd cheered as though he had been crowned. (A church, the so-called 'Votivkirche', was eventually erected, out of voluntary subscriptions, just off Vienna's Ringstrasse as a monument of thanks for the deliverance.) Another, and for Franz Josef more important result, was the realization that it was time to think of marriage and an heir. To be sure, Pope Pius IX had sent him as a blessing no less a talisman than a tooth of St Peter's. But even that most precious of relics would not ensure the perpetuation of the dynasty.

It was, of course, his mother, Archduchess Sophie, she who had groomed him for the throne and helped him ascend it so young, who now set about the urgent business of selecting his wife. Finding a suitable bride for a reigning emperor who was an Apostolic Majesty to boot was no easy matter. Saxony, which had provided the Habsburgs with several royal matches, was one obvious hunting-ground. However, the candidate in Dresden on whom Sophie alighted, Princess Sidonie, was rejected by Franz Josef as being altogether too plain. (She was also, as it turned out, much too frail, and died nine years later.) The Berlin court of King Frederick William IV, which Franz Josef visited in 1852, had young princesses enough and one of them, Anna, the twenty-one-year-old niece of the King, was undeniably pretty. She was also undeniably Protestant and though Sophie saw no insuperable obstacle in this (her own sister Elise, by marrying the Prussian king, had, after all, crossed the faith barrier in the opposite direction) the Hohenzollerns proved harder to persuade and the idea was dropped. This, too, proved just as well, though for very different reasons than in the Dresden affair. Protestant Prussia was destined to fight and conquer Catholic Austria in the struggle for mastery over German Europe. A Habsburg empress born a Hohenzollern would have been in a desperate situation, faced with such a conflict and all its consequences.

But then, out of the blue (or rather, out of the blue and white colours of Bavaria) came the surprise ending which, following on the assassination attempt, established Franz Josef as the romantic hero of the empire. In the summer of 1853 he did something rare enough for any archduke and quite unheard of for an emperor. He fell at first sight head over heels in love, like some princeling in an operetta, and brought home to Vienna a bride who was not only eminently suitable as regards lineage, politics and faith, but who was also the most beautiful empress the capital had ever known. Both the setting of the betrothal and its circumstances had much of the operetta about them.

His mother, very put out by the failure in Berlin, had turned to Munich and her own Bavarian family of the Wittelsbach. Her sister, Ludowika, had a slim and elegant daughter of nineteen, Duchess Helena, who seemed altogether admirable as a future empress and who was surely attractive enough to win Franz Josef's approval. Accordingly, mother and daughter were invited to Ischl (set amid Salzburg's lovely chain of lakes, and already established as the summer residence of the Austrian court) to attend the celebration of the Emperor's twenty-third birthday on 18 August 1853. Almost as an afterthought, and in order not to make the visit appear too blatant a matchmaking expedition, Helena's sixteen-year-old sister Elisabeth was included in the family party. But from the moment Franz Josef clapped eyes on his two Bavarian cousins again (the first time he had seen them since their childhood) it was the afterthought who swamped his feelings. It was not just the striking looks of this raven-haired little beauty which attracted him; he was captivated just as much by her bubbling spontaneity which was like fresh spring water amid all the turgid tides of protocol which engulfed him. He confessed his passion straightaway to his mother who, for once, was helpless. At the ball on the evening of the 18th, his preference was made public when he chose Sisi, as she was nicknamed, to partner him in the closing *cotillon*, even handing her the entire collection of bouquets he had accumulated at earlier dances.

The next day it was made official. Ischl exploded with pride and delight and, as darkness fell, instead of just 'FJ' with a crown being picked out in flares from the top of the nearby Siriuskogel as an anniversary greeting, the letter E shone out as well, with a bridal wreath surrounding it in pinpoints of light. Perhaps the worthy mayor, sniffing romance of some sort from the visit, had originally prepared an 'H' for the mountainside; we shall never know. What seems certain is that, just as Helena was understandably put out, 'Sisi' was just as understandably overwhelmed. She had arrived in Ischl on 16 August as a happily prattling little companion for her important elder sister. Three days later, thanks to a *coup de foudre* of the All-Highest, she was pledged in marriage to a mighty sovereign. Without returning his instant infatuation for her, she seems to have liked her betrothed well enough. For her, he only had one obvious drawback. 'If only he was not an emperor,' she is said to have sighed. Their marriage, which was solemnized on the evening of 24 April 1854 in Vienna's Augustine Church was to bear out all her fears.

For a few years, however, it gave Franz Josef something of a political honeymoon with his subjects. There was another surge of loyalty when, after the birth of two daughters, an heir to the throne, the ill-starred Crown Prince Rudolph, was produced at last on 21 August 1858. But the popular idyll came to an end with the decade. It was buried, the year after Rudolph's birth, on that familiar graveyard of Habsburg hopes, the Lombardy battlefield.

By now the groundswell towards the unification of all the Italian states – which necessarily meant the expulsion of the Habsburg monarchy and the lesser rulers of Parma, Tuscany and Modena, from the northern regions – had found a new and powerful foreign sponsor. The parvenu French emperor, Napoleon III, himself elected by plebiscite, had seen his chance to strengthen his populist grip at home by embracing the liberal-nationalist movement south of the Alps. Already in July of 1858 he had met at Plombières with the political architect of that movement, the Piedmontese Prime Minister Cavour, and agreed to come to his aid against any Austrian attack. Piedmont, who had fought so fiercely in the campaigns against Radetzky ten years before, was itching to renew the battle on better terms.* But the trap could only be sprung if Austria herself released it and exposed herself before all Europe as the aggressor. With almost unbelievable *naïveté*, Franz Josef and his advisers performed this service for their enemies. On 19 April 1859 the Emperor himself dispatched an ultimatum to the joint kingdom of Piedmont-Sardinia to demobilize the armies they had been mustering, or face the consequences. Cavour, Napoleon III, and Piedmont's ambitious house of Savoy were only too delighted to meet a challenge they had conspired to bring about.

The Monarchy's military punch proved to be as abysmal as its clumsy diplomatic touch. Radetzky's successor as commander-in-chief in Lombardy (the old warrior himself had died, aged ninety-two, the year before) was a vain, idle and incompetent Hungarian general, Count Gyulai. Some idea of his sense of priorities can be judged by one of the first orders he issued from his Verona headquarters. The decree stated that every soldier in the army, officers and men alike, must henceforth sport a black moustache when on parade. This meant that every fair-haired moustache would have to be dyed, whereas upper lips with no moustaches at all would have to simulate the effect with black boot-polish. Gyulai proved just as slovenly in the field as he was eccentric on the drill ground. After a month-long desultory pursuit of the Piedmontese he drew back, in June of 1859, to the great Austrian defence quadrilateral,† having achieved nothing except obligingly giving Napoleon III time to bring up his supporting forces.

The critical clash came on the 24th of that month at Solferino, in the

---

* In the Crimean War of 1854 tiny Piedmont had joined Britain and France in coming to the aid of Turkey in her war against Russia. It was a shrewd political investment, as events were now showing. The Habsburg monarchy, on the other hand, which had remained virtually neutral in that conflict, had broken her bridges to Russia, her saviour in 1849, without gaining any sympathy with the two western powers.

† The fortresses of Verona, Mantua, Legnago and Peschiera.

rice fields of the Po valley, south of Lake Garda. After a terrible slaughter which cost the Austrians over 22,000 men against 12,000 losses for the French and 5,500 thousand for the Piedmontese, Franz Josef had to accept defeat. The damaging thing was that he had to accept it on the spot and in person. He had taken over the supreme command himself, perhaps with visions of repeating those victory scenes of 1848. The direct responsibility was therefore his and so, now, the shame.

Two days later, having retreated with his vanquished army through roads turned into quagmires by torrential rain, he re-entered the Austrian quadrilateral. In Verona, there was time at last to write to his beloved Sisi:

So I was forced to give the order, to retreat. I rode through a terrible thunderstorm to Vallegio and so on to Villafranca. There I spent a dreadful evening amidst the confusion of the wounded and the refugees, waggons and horses. . . . Such is the sad tale of an appalling day on which we strove hard but were not smiled on by fortune. I have gained much in experience and I know what it feels like to be a vanquished general. The heavy consequences of our defeat are still to come . . .[3]

As he wrote those last lines even the chastened Emperor could not have realized how far-reaching the consequences would be. At first he cherished vain hopes that someone would come to his rescue against the French. But who? Russia, whom he had failed in the Crimea conflict, held severely aloof. England was too remote and, anyway, too liberally-inclined to intervene on his side. Prussia felt it was none of her business, for the fighting was outside the confines of the German lands. There was nothing but to talk peace with Napoleon III.

The two sovereigns met at Villafranca on 12 July and provisional terms were drawn up. Austria was to cede all of Lombardy except the fortress quadrilateral but allowed to retain her other north Italian provinces of Venetia. As for the minor dynasties, Napoleon agreed not to oppose the return of the expelled rulers of Tuscany, and Modena, provided this was not achieved by force. This, in the climate of the day, was tantamount to abandoning the two princelings, as was duly confirmed when the definitive peace treaty, much severer for Austria, was signed at Zürich on 10 November. Their little states were united with Sardinia 'according to the wishes of the people'. The young Emperor had performed no better at the round table of international diplomacy than he had done on the battlefield.*

---

* Franz Josef had been more than willing, however, to agree to Parma being tacked on to Piedmont-Sardinia, for the duchy had stayed neutral during his struggle.

The greatest impact was dynastic. An absolute ruler must command absolute respect. A romantic hero must return as the shining victor to his awaiting bride. When, on 12 September, Franz Josef and Sisi appeared in public in Vienna for the first time since the Lombardy débâcle, their reception was icy. Some of the men ostentatiously abstained from removing their hats, thus remaining covered in front of their sovereign, a heinous protocol offence. When, a few days later, the royal couple entered their box at the opera, the audience almost ignored them. There was even wild talk of abdication. Death had mercifully spared Metternich (as it had spared Radetzky before him) from witnessing this humiliation. The one-time prince of absolutism had succumbed to a stroke a fortnight before Solferino.

Abdication never entered Franz Josef's head, then or at any time; but clearly things had to change, or be made to appear to change, around him. The first concessions to the liberalism which had triumphed in the Italian provinces and was flexing its muscles again in Vienna were purely governmental. The post of minister-president, abolished since Schwarzenberg's days, was now revived. Some of the unpopular 'hard men' in the Cabinet were removed; the minister of the interior, Alexander von Bach, the architect of Franz Josef's bureaucratic centralism, was, for example, packed off to Rome as ambassador.

But more was needed than a change of cast. The stage set itself had to be transformed if the audience were to be kept happy. That meant, over the next eight years, a succession of governmental and constitutional changes, all designed to damp down disenchantment and what, for the Monarchy, was its fatal concomitant, nationalist unrest. Thus, in May of 1860, a so-called 'National Assembly' ('Reichsrat') was called into life, supposedly to represent all of the Monarchy's different provinces and sectional interests. But every single delegate had been approved, if not personally chosen, by the Emperor. Not surprisingly, therefore, though the nominees included some Austrian bourgeois (a class that had only properly developed among this German-speaking core of the empire) it remained, essentially, an assembly of landowning nobles, headed by three archdukes from the royal family.

On 21 October, a painfully conceived New Order was promulgated to go with the revived Reichsrat. Under this so-called 'October Diploma' the Crown relinquished some of its rights but again only to the autocratic, conservative forces as represented in Diets of selected nations. The single concession to real reform was that henceforth taxation required the consent of the Reichsrat (in all other matters it was called upon merely to 'co-operate'). This arrangement satisfied nobody. To the Liberals it was not enough; to the Conservatives too much. The Austrian Centralists feared that, through the Diet system, their control over the Hungarians, their only serious challengers, had been dangerously weakened. The Hungarians themselves, who had been sniffing Viennese blood ever since the Emperor's Lombardy fiasco, resented the control of even this bogus federal 'Parliament' (whose six Hungarian nominees attended only in their personal capacity). Clearly, Franz Josef and his advisers would have to think again.

The result of the re-think appeared four months later in a series of enactments known as the 'February Patent'. This certainly looked different. For one thing, the Reichsrat was reconstructed into two separate chambers: an upper house composed of aristocrats and other life members, all of them nominated by the Emperor, and a House of Deputies consisting of 343 delegates elected to it from the various provincial Diets. Henceforth, its consent was to be required for all legislation and not simply for fiscal measures – a concession wrung very grudgingly out of the Emperor. To balance this, however, Franz Josef resuscitated his 1849 powers of emergency legislation while retaining the sole and unimpeded right to appoint and dismiss governments and ministers as he chose. The new arrangement proved, once again, too little for the Liberals and, too much for the Hungarian Nationalists who saw the bi-cameral 'Parliament' sitting in Vienna as an even greater threat to their separatist ambitions.

So far, Franz Josef had resembled a devious and desperate bridge-player reshuffling and redealing the pack in such a way as to keep the court cards in his own hand, and calling 'no-trumps' every time. Then, in 1866, as in 1859, defeat in war forced him to change the game. This time the defeat was crucial for the standing of the empire abroad and equally crucial for the future of the empire at home.

The arrival of Bismarck to power in Berlin in 1862 had thrown down the Prussian glove to challenge the Habsburg monarchy for supremacy in the German-speaking world. When, in 1866, the inevitable duel took place, Austria was again outmanoeuvred both in diplomacy and in battle. The real signal for war came when, on 8 April of that year, Bismarck concluded an offensive and defensive alliance with an Italy which was, by now, almost completely united under the house of Savoy. The best political retort that Austria could produce was to sign, on 12 June, a treaty with her old enemy Napoleon III in which she bought French neutrality in the coming conflict for the promise, win or lose, to cede her last remaining Italian province of Venetia.

In fact, in the war which Bismarck promptly declared, Austria lost, and lost swiftly. Successes in the south against the relatively weaker

Italians on both land and sea were nullified by the crushing defeat inflicted by the Prussian army in the north at Königgrätz on 3 July. Though the armies were roughly matched numerically (221,000 Prussians facing 215,000 Austrians) the Austrians proved on the day to be inferior to their opponents in everything except their artillery and their courage. The instrument of victory was the new breech-loading Prussian rifle which could fire at five times the pace of the old muzzle-loading Lorenz gun still used by the Austrians. The Prussians were also better equipped, better supplied and, above all, better led. Ludwig von Benedek, who commanded the Monarchy's northern army, was a sound general who had acquitted himself well in the Italian campaigns of 1848 and 1859. But he was a spent force after that, and also something of a nervous wreck. Already in 1863 he had applied in vain to be allowed to retire as chief of staff giving, as one of his health reasons, the thousands of laxatives he had been obliged to swallow over the years. In 1866 he had pleaded, again in vain, to escape command of the unfamiliar northern front, bluntly declaring himself 'a donkey' so far as the German battlefield was concerned.

Something of a donkey he turned out to be on the crucial day, placing his troops across and not behind the line of the river Elbe, for example, thus cutting off his own retreat. The casualty lists of the two armies when fighting was broken off gave the measure of Benedek's defeat: 359 officers and 8,794 men lost on the Prussian side compared with 1,313 officers and 41,499 men from the Austrian forces. In an attempt to protect the Crown, Benedek was publicly disgraced, having first been persuaded to give his word of honour that he would say nothing in his own defence. It was a shabby end to a disastrous episode.

Military responsibility Franz Josef could dodge; but there was no escaping the political consequences of Königgrätz. The first of these was the abandonment – as it turned out, for ever – of Prince Schwarzenberg's dream of a 'Greater Austria' of seventy or eighty million Germans under Vienna's sway. Prussia had begun the war by marching into Hanover, Saxony and Hesse, three of the German states which had backed Austria in the struggle for mastery. Now it was Berlin who wielded their sceptres. One of them, King John of Saxony, had managed to join the Austrian forces at Königgrätz with a small supporting army, which lost 15 officers and 120 men in the battle. At nearly 3 a.m. on 4 July – some eight hours after Benedek's telegram announcing the disaster reached the imperial family waiting anxiously in the Hofburg – King John arrived at Vienna himself by train. A macabre ceremony was enacted in the middle of the night, at the Northern Station. Despite the hour and gloom of the occasion, the

platform was brilliantly lit. Franz Josef was there in full dress uniform
with green-plumed hat to greet his ally, now King of Saxony in name
only. The flowers laid out in welcome were really for a death. It was
Habsburg hopes of ever ruling the German-speaking world which were
being mourned.

The burial ceremony took place at Prague on 23 August 1866. The
definitive treaty concluded there that day (to replace the preliminary
peace signed between the two sides at Nikolsburg a fortnight before)
called on Franz Josef 'to recognize the dissolution of the German
League as it had existed hitherto, and to accept a new formation of
Germany from which the Austrian empire would be excluded'.

It was a turning-point in the history of Europe as well as the
German-speaking peoples themselves. From that moment the status of
the Habsburg monarchy as a great power was called into question.
From that moment, too, the Emperor's Austrian subjects had to wrestle
with the riddle of their own identity. Expelled by Bismarck from the
German family of nations, could they still think and feel as Germans at
all? What was their future now as Austro-Germans? Should they strive
for some national unity of their own; continue to serve simply as the
privileged servants of the dynasty, like a caste of political eunuchs; or
work for eventual absorption within a Greater Germany ruled from
Berlin? The problem survived both the German and Austrian empires.
More than seventy years later Hitler was to try, and fail, to impose the
last of those options which the Treaty of Prague had opened up.

In the immediate aftermath of the treaty, however, what mattered to
Franz Josef was stabilizing his defeated empire. This led, swiftly and
inevitably, to a new pact with the largest, most powerful and most
chauvinistic of the peoples of that empire, the Magyars. The year
before Königgrätz, the Emperor, anxious to guard his rear against
Prussia, had already put out feelers to Budapest for a political
settlement. His emissaries went, not to Kossuth who was still trying to
revive the 1848 rebellion from exile, but to the shrewd and pragmatic
leader of the conservatives, Ferenc Deák. There had been tentative
agreement on the need to give Hungary a much stronger national
profile, while preserving the unity of the empire and the prerogative of
the emperor in certain essential fields. Deák showed great farsightedness in asking no more, after Königgrätz, from a sovereign now
weakened and desperate in defeat. The result was the famous
Compromise of 1867.

Under this, defence, foreign affairs and the financing of both parties
were recognized by Budapest as 'common subjects' of the empire,
which left them essentially under the control of the Emperor. In all

other matters Hungary was to be ruled exclusively by her own laws. The split was formalized geographically as well as legally. For all internal purposes, Franz Josef's imperial orb was sliced like a great golden apple into two. The eastern Hungarian half was solidly based on the historic lands of the Magyars' great eleventh-century Christian king St Stephen, lands now greatly enlarged with greater dominion over non-Magyar races such as the Croats, Serbs, Slovaks and Rumanians. The western or Austrian half was simply what was left – a much less substantial affair shaped like a straggling crescent curving from Galicia through Bohemia and the Austrian heartland itself down to the Adriatic. Each half was given its own Prime Minister and government. Each raised its own domestic taxes. The raising of imperial taxes and levies for the common army was, however, to be debated afresh every ten years by the joint ministries and sixty-strong 'delegations' from the two national parliaments. If this sounded like a prescription for decennial mayhem, that was precisely what it turned out to be.

Nothing symbolized the structural imbalance of the division better than the baptism of the two halves. The Magyars had no problem. They called their new state within a state 'the lands of the sacred Hungarian crown of St Stephen'. The Austrians could think of nothing better for their half than 'the lands and kingdoms represented in the Imperial Council'. It was not much better when, after selecting as the boundary a dim little stream which runs south-east of Vienna called the Leitha, they referred to 'Cis-Leithania' (as opposed to 'Trans-Leithania'), as though the Habsburg monarchy had reverted to a couple of Roman provinces. Not until 1915, a year before Franz Josef's death, did they settle at last in Vienna for the simple word 'Austria', which, as an imperial concept, then had precisely three years to go.

The Compromise, though in large measure the result of Austrian blunders, cannot itself be damned as such. A blunder means a wrong choice between valid options. In 1867 Franz Josef had no choice. The ten million Magyars were the only compact unit of the multinational empire* who had both the power and the historical roots to shore the Monarchy up against Prussia. And the Dualist system, as it was known, certainly preserved unity of a sort until the empire disintegrated altogether in the great military and political earthquake of 1918.

---

* Its exact racial breakdown in the last imperial census of 1910 was:

Germans	12,011,081	Ruthenians	3,999,100	Slovenes	1,371,256
Magyars	10,067,917	Rumanians	3,224,728	Italians	771,054
Czechs	6,643,059	Croats	2,888,741	Others	979,990
Slovaks	1,967,520	Serbs	2,041,599		
Poles	4,977,643				

Yet, constitutionally, what was being preserved was paralysis. The clamour for similar self-government grew louder and louder from the other nationalities of the empire. But with so many Croats and Serbs locked away with St Stephen's crown, how could the Southern Slavs, for example, ever be satisfied as an entity? In any case, Franz Josef himself seemed permanently hobbled after taking this one giant step. The Compromise was a reform which put an end to other reforms. After 1867 it was a case of putting one's head down into the wind and slogging blindly on.

The Hungarians, on the other hand, could hold their heads defiantly high. Kossuth, the 1848 rebel with a price on his head, was now duly pardoned. How the Hungarian magnates thought of the Compromise was summed up by what one of their number exulted to the Italian envoy in Vienna: 'From now on, the future of the Monarchy belongs to us. We are the stronger ones.'[4]

Chapter Nine

AUSTRIA: THE STONE IDOL

The settlement with Hungary brought personal joy to Franz Josef and his wife, as well as relief for his empire. Their crowning in Budapest on 8 June 1867 was in many ways the ceremonial high point of their life on the throne together. Elisabeth, who had a passion for the fiery, irresponsible Magyars, and had helped to talk her husband into accepting the Compromise, never appeared more radiant or more regal than in her coronation gown of white brocade, fashioned by Worth in Paris, and fairly shimmering with diamonds and pearls. Her husband seemed to revel in the rites prescribed by a thousand years of tradition for each new king of Hungary – galloping like a young hussar up Buda's so-called Coronation Mound after the cathedral ceremony and brandishing his sword to the four corners of the earth in a pledge to defend the lands of St Stephen against all comers. It was heady, virile stuff and seems to have led to a fresh bout of love-making between the royal couple. Nine months later, on 22 April 1868, she bore their last child. She purposely returned to the palace in Buda for delivery, hoping that it would be a son whom she could christen Stephen. It was in fact a girl, named Marie Valerie, but none the less it remained her favourite.

This was fleeting sunlight. The clouds on their family life were gathering. Indeed one very black one rolled up in the very month of the Budapest coronation. On 30 June 1867 Franz Josef learned that his younger brother had been executed by his rebellious subjects in far-off Mexico. Four years before, Archduke Ferdinand Max had been persuaded by his ambitious Coburg wife, Charlotte of Belgium, and by that evil spirit of the Habsburg dynasty, Napoleon III, to be proclaimed Emperor of Mexico under what was supposed to be the firm military protection of French regular troops, plus some Austrian and Belgian volunteers. But as the inevitable rebellion against this unwanted foreign crown reached storm force, the protectors melted away before

it, leaving the hapless intruder to face the firing squad.* Relations
between the two brothers had usually been strained, and Franz Josef
had himself warned the restless, frustrated Ferdinand Max against this
hare-brained Mexican adventure. None of this lessened the blow when
it arrived in Vienna. It was to be the first of three such family tragedies
the Emperor was to endure before the century was out.

But it was a more intimate everyday sadness which by now numbed
Franz Josef's life. Those pictures, painted by court portraitists such as
Emil von Horowitz in the late 1860s and 1870s, showing the Emperor
and Empress riding out side by side in the woods of their various
palaces and gazing devotedly at each other across their horses' flanks,
were a mockery of the truth. It was becoming rarer and rarer for them
to be side by side anywhere, on horse or on foot let alone in the marriage
bed. Sisi, while never ceasing to love him in her fashion, had begun to
slip away in an agitated escapist world of her own. The longer the reign
and the marriage went on, the less did either empire or husband see of
their Empress. To begin with, though absent from the court, she stayed
fairly near at hand; at Gödöllö, for example, her favourite castle near
Budapest, among her favourite Hungarian subjects; or back in her
native Bavaria at the family home in Possenhofen or at Garatshausen,
rented from her elder brother Ludwig.

As the nerves grew tauter and the fits of depression darker, she
turned more and more to her horses to drain away the physical and
mental tension. At first the passion was for dressage and, in a small
private ring in the palace stables, she tried to learn the tricks of the
Vienna circus riders. Then a yearning for fox-hunting took over and so,
inevitably, she had to cross the Channel to fulfil it. In March of 1876
came the first long tour of the famous packs and hunting-boxes of
England, followed by similar trips to Ireland, where the ditches were
even deeper, and the banks and walls even higher. Back in the Hofburg,
Franz Josef paid the enormous bills for these expeditions without a
murmur, only concerned, in letter after letter, with worry for her safety.
Very occasionally there came the gentlest of rebukes for her personal
conduct after reports had reached the lonely husband that his wife had
been riding out alone with this or that dashing Englishman. Elisabeth's
beauty had indeed stirred as much excitement as her superb horseman-
ship.

When Elisabeth found she could no longer lose her depression in the
English mists, she turned to the Mediterranean sunshine instead. In

---

* Charlotte, who was away in Europe trying to raise help for her beleaguered husband, escaped
his fate, and lived on until 1927 when she died in Belgium, aged eighty-six.

the early 1880s the years of intensive cruising began, above all to Corfu, where she bought, again out of her husband's ever-open purse, her own villa. Greek ruins replaced Irish hunters as objects of distraction. There were times, of course, when the imperial couple were expected to appear together, at the great court balls and receptions of Vienna's winter season, for example.* Occasionally, they travelled abroad on official visits, though the Emperor went alone to Paris in 1867 and alone to Constantinople, the Holy Land and the newly-opened Suez Canal two years later. Holidays spent together anywhere outside the empire were even rarer. Thanks to her insatiable travel fever, separation became the rule. If this pricked her conscience now and then, it bruised his heart all the time. How he suffered can be judged from this typical letter, written in November 1887, when he was stag hunting at Gödöllö and she was cruising far away among the Greek islands on the royal yacht *Greif*: 'My thoughts are always longingly with you and I sadly work out the time, alas all too long, before we see each other again. I miss you in everything and everyone and, above all, I miss you myself.'[1]

By now, however, the Viennese comedy actress Katharina Schratt had come into his life – though probably never, despite the inevitable speculation, into his bed. The friendship endured to his death. The plumpish, blue-eyed 'Gnädige Frau', who was intelligent as well as womanly, lively yet discreet, provided him during the last thirty years of his life with that which he craved for above all else – someone to talk to.† It was a need which went beyond, and also stopped short of, the physical. This was an affair of morning coffee, not midnight champagne. Sympathy must go out to her as well. As the months and years rolled by, one is left wondering how on earth, at their regular morning chats, the lady from the State Theatre went on dredging up bits of Viennese gossip to freshen the ageing monarch for the series of audiences and the piles of documents which awaited him.

It was in this daily load of work that he sought ultimate relief. Indeed, the lasting image he left behind for posterity was not that of the saviour of the Monarchy, much less its victorious warlord or brilliant statesman (for he was neither of those). Even more than the demi-god

---

* There were two court balls during the carnival season. The less exclusive was the 'Hofball,' which could be attended by any member of society normally entitled to appear at court. Up to ten thousand guests turned up and no invitations were issued. The smaller, more select affair was the 'Ball bei Hof,' for the élite and the diplomatic corps only. This was by formal invitation only and ended with supper, presided over at small tables by various members of the imperial family. The Empress eventually allowed herself to be represented even here by the archduchess nearest in rank.

† His mother, Archduchess Sophie, died on 28 May 1872, aged sixty-seven and, with her, Franz Josef had lost his last intimate mentor.

of a sovereign (which he certainly was) he remains, in the mind's eye, as the empire's supreme bureaucrat, the once straight military back humped, like that of any desk clerk, by thousands of hours bent over his papers. The personification matches his character, for he was thorough rather than clever, with a mind attuned to routine and rules rather than experiment and improvisation; above all, a man for paperwork. Everything had to be on file, and practically every document which landed on his desk was marked with some comment or correction – even of spelling mistakes – in his neat, clear handwriting before it left to plough its way back through the machinery of imperial administration.

This meant getting up (from the plain military field-bed which he used from early middle age until his death) soon after 4 a.m. and then, after a breakfast which sometimes consisted only of a glass of milk, a three-hour stint on his state papers until 7 or 7.30, when most of his subjects were just awakening.[2] From 7.30 to 10 there would follow the daily palace conferences, primarily with the chiefs of his military and civil cabinets. Then, until 5 in the afternoon came the audiences – a procession of court officials, foreign ambassadors, generals, ministers, odd dignitaries from all corners of the eleven-nation empire. Even the short noon break for lunch was often taken alone at his desk, with one eye on the plain food (boiled beef with Bavarian beer was one of his favourite combinations) and the other on the file in front of him. Between 5 and 7 p.m. came the only real break, dinner with his family or guests. On an ordinary day it was the only meal served at table, and the only one followed by a little relaxation. But at 7 p.m. he would be back at his desk again for a final hour or two before going to bed, at a time when most of his subjects would be starting on their evening's enjoyment.

Two important consequences were to flow from this life-style which, over the decades, became as firmly set as the massive stones of the Hofburg itself. The first, which emerged in the final, and fatal, challenge of his reign, was his instinctive ingrained assumption that any crisis, however deadly it might appear, could be solved by a series of audiences and ministerial submissions. At the end, Franz Josef had spent so long merely presiding over the course of events that he had lost both the will and the ability to shape them. More of this later.

The other more evident consequence was an ever-widening remoteness from his subjects, especially after the turn of the century, when increasing frailty led him to abandon as many public appearances as he could decently escape. Yet the more his image receded, the more awesome it became in its unapproachability. Franz Josef ended as a stone idol for his peoples, to be worshipped, not touched. Not even the

Tsar of all the Russias stood so far above and apart from those over whom he ruled. A simple symbol of this lack of contact was the handshake. The Tsar, like the Emperor William and, even more so, the King of England, would dispense this at will. Franz Josef had his own fixed ideas as to who was worthy of the honour of pressing their monarch's flesh. Outside the family he shook hands only with his senior generals and ministers; with members of the highest nobility, whether young or old and whether they were officers or officials or not; with foreign envoys and distinguished visitors; and, finally, with his own ADCS.

Apart from the company of Frau Schratt, there was only one other setting in which the Emperor could relax, and that was at his beloved 'Kaiservilla' in Bad Ischl* where he had met and wooed Sisi, and where he returned every summer of his life. The little spa, perched some 1,500 feet up amid the lakes of the Salzkammergut, had been famed for centuries for its mud baths and sulphur waters (said to help in the cure of everything from heart complaints to bronchitis, from skin diseases to liver disorders, and from rheumatism to female sterility). What drew Franz Josef there, apart from its tranquillity and romantic associations, was displayed on the coat-of-arms which his ancestor Maximilian I had bestowed on the little town in 1514. This showed, and still shows today, simply a chamois astride two mountain tops, with a green tree jutting from a third peak in front of his nose. The surrounding forests of Ischl were a hunter's paradise, and stalking was the one continuous consuming passion of Franz Josef's private life.

Of course, half the court followed him to Ischl (also Frau Schratt, who had her own villa there). The work followed him as well, and so did some of the foreign sovereigns. But the stiffest of royal visitors relaxed under the general charm of the place. The delightful and relatively small 'Kaiservilla' was not the Hofburg; nor was the work-load quite as arduous, despite the stories of unremitting midsummer toil spread by some of his hagiographers. At Ischl, getting up at 4 a.m. often meant only the 'Frühpirsch' or early morning stalk, and one cannot kill, as he did, close on thirty thousand head of game in only the first fifteen years on the throne by firing from your desk. Franz Josef as a hunter, dressed in his comfortable green loden with coarse woollen leggings wound round above the heavy stalking boots, was the nearest thing to a human image which he ever presented to his subjects. Paradoxically, for him it was the closest he ever got to heaven on earth.

His family, which, by rights, ought to have brought distraction, was

* It had been designated 'Bad' Ischl in 1907.

a seemingly endless source of anguish instead. Nor was this confined to the quarrels with his ill-starred brother Ferdinand Max and the estrangement from his wife. In the closing years of the nineteenth century the name Habsburg became almost synonymous with scandal or tragedy. We have already mentioned, under another heading, the exploits of Archduchess Louise, who deserted her husband, the Crown Prince of Saxony, first for a Belgian tutor and then for an Italian musician. Her brother Leopold Ferdinand of Tuscany did the royal name no greater credit by renouncing all titles and privileges and ending up, as Leopold Wölfling, on the boards of a Berlin cabaret. Another of the Tuscan branch, Archduke Johann Salvator, after a rebellious spell in the army and a disastrous foray into Balkan politics, set the seal on his clownish career by marrying a dancer, Milli Stubel, changing his name to Johan Orth and embarking, like some royal 'Flying Dutchman', on restless ocean wanderings aboard his ship, the *Margarita*. He disappeared with it under the waves of the South Atlantic while negotiating Cape Horn in 1890, though he was not officially declared dead until 1911.

Neither was the Kaiser's immediate family in the so-called *Erzhaus* of Austria spared from taint. One of his nephews, Archduke Otto, was such a notorious and, above all, a blatantly public rake that even the permissive society of *fin de siècle* Vienna was shocked. (He died of syphilis in Vienna in 1906, comforted, not by his long-suffering Saxon wife, but by the loyalest of his string of mistresses.) Otto's brother, Ferdinand Karl, sinned in a milder but, to his imperial uncle, perhaps less forgivable way. This dreamy artistic youth, having tried to escape the army for the Vienna State Theatre, finally abandoned Habsburg responsibilities altogether by marrying one Bertha Czuber, daughter of a Prague university professor, and living in banishment as plain Herr Burg.

Closer to home still was the Emperor's only son, Crown Prince Rudolph, in whom scandal and tragedy were combined. Like many an archduke, he was dissolute. Like many an heir-apparent, he was impatient. Like many the son of a conservative father, he played with reformist ideas (in his case, the most dangerous of them all for the dynasty, namely the movement for total Magyar independence). Admittedly, in 1881, aged twenty-three, he had made a dynastically suitable marriage with Princess Stephanie, the gauche and unattractive sixteen-year-old daughter of King Leopold II of the Belgians. But the marriage did nothing for the succession by producing only one child, a daughter, Elisabeth. It did even less to settle Rudolph down. There was a streak of manic depression in him from birth (his mother's family, the Bavarian Wittelsbachs, were notorious for their mental instability and the Empress herself seemed, at times, to be drifting close towards it).

Even as a youth he had written fanciful last wills and testaments and, as the 1880s advanced, the hysterical outbursts and mumblings of suicide increased as drugs, drink and disease unhinged what remained of his reason. Unlike many who threaten the deed, he carried it out, killing the last of his many mistresses as well, like some Pharaoh resolved to take his most precious treasure with him to eternity in his coffin. On 30 January 1889 Rudolph shot the pretty, pathetically love-lorn Marie Vetsera and then himself in the snowbound shooting-lodge of Mayerling, in the Vienna woods. Fittingly, the corpses were found side by side in a locked bedroom. The Emperor, who at first was told that the Crown Prince had been poisoned, was devastated when he learnt the truth. Suicide and murder, even making allowance for a deranged mind, were not activities compatible with the son and declared successor of an Apostolic Majesty.*

The tragedy temporarily drew the Emperor, his wife and their two other children, the daughters Gisela and Marie Valerie, closer together. Katharina Schratt was also on hand to render solace. But the effect of Mayerling was to make Franz Josef feel more dispirited as well as more lonely than ever. His own direct issue would now no longer sit on the throne after him. The succession would pass first to his brother Karl Ludwig and, should he die before the Emperor (which, seven years later, he did), to his eldest son, the Archduke Franz Ferdinand. The Emperor was not at all happy with what he had heard to date about this reserved, unconventional nephew of his. He was to be made far unhappier later on.

Franz Josef's personal isolation was completed by a blow which fell even heavier than the loss of his son, because it was so utterly unpredictable. The temporary closeness to his wife over the Mayerling tragedy was only a brief check to their drift apart. An English ambassadress describes the situation in Vienna shortly before Rudolph's death:

The Empress is hardly ever seen. She hunts, fences, climbs to the top of mountains and goes to bed before dinner. She never shows herself at the theatre or any of the public functions but on a rainy day, when the Prater is

---

* From time to time attempts have been made to wash out this terrible blot on the Habsburg family escutcheon by claiming that the couple were the victims of a mysterious political murder. They are nullified by the half dozen or more last letters – plainly suicide notes – which the dead man wrote to close relatives and friends. To his father, however, he wrote nothing.

empty, she can be seen walking in the thickest of boots and wearing the shortest of green ulsters, with a billy-cock hat and a long buff fan spread out before her face. Her breathless lady-in-waiting tears after her and, in the distance, two detectives. She always has relays of ladies on the road, for nobody can stand the pace for long.

After Rudolph's death she became, to quote the same witness, 'like a ghost during her own life.' The palace guard had orders never to take notice of her carriage; the sentries presented no arms; anyone living or working in the Hofburg had orders, when meeting her in the corridors, to pass by without saluting or even looking at her.[3]

But, a ghost or not, she was still a loved presence in Franz Josef's life. Then, on 10 September 1898, the Empress Elisabeth was stabbed to death by one savage dagger thrust to her heart. She died, as she had for so long lived, a wanderer. The murder took place in Geneva during the few steps she was taking from her hotel, the Beau Rivage, to the waiting lake steamer. But if the setting was fitting, the deed itself was pure irrationality. The murderer, an Italian called Luigi Luccheni, gave his profession as 'personal anarchist' when interrogated by the Geneva police and declared that he had only killed the Empress of Austria, whom he had never seen before, as part of his 'fight against the great and the rich'. He added with demented pride: 'A Luccheni kills an empress but never a washerwoman.'[4]

Over the previous few years Elisabeth had become even more and more of a 'seagull', to use her own word. Her husband had grown glumly resigned to his seagull flying about all over the Mediterranean, always looking forward to the times, like now, in that September of 1898, when she was heading for the dry land of Vienna. The last letter he was ever to write to her – and which she never lived to read – expresses his touching gratitude that she was at least showing some signs of homesickness for the Villa Hermes which he had specially built for her in the great wildlife park of Lainz, on the outskirts of the capital. Now she returned, not to the Villa Hermes, but to Vienna's Kapuziner-kirche, to be buried in its crypt alongside long generations of other departed Habsburgs. Even in death, she managed to cause a commotion. The original inscription on her coffin read simply 'Elisabeth, Empress of Austria'. This made Magyar blood boil so furiously that, the same evening, the words 'and Queen of Hungary' were hastily added.

That outburst of the same Hungarian chauvinism which, more than thirty years before, had split the empire effectively into two, makes an appropriate transition back from the family to the political scene. Since the constitutional upheaval of 1867 Franz Josef had lost his next eldest brother, his only son and now his wife, each of them to violent deaths. To offset all this, the dynasty had gained nothing in the way of brilliant marriages producing new heirs. At most it could claim therefore to have stood firm and still. The Emperor himself was being held in increasing reverence as the fiftieth anniversary of his accession approached, while the succession was assured through Archduke Karl Ludwig and his sons. The same balance sheet showed up on the Monarchy's domestic and diplomatic fronts. Here too, the ground had been held, and no more.

Four years after the great Compromise with Hungary, there had been one last attempt to re-cast the entire framework of the Monarchy. It was inspired by the attempts of the Czechs, another 'historic race' of the empire,* to achieve for themselves in Bohemia the same sort of deal which the Magyars had won for themselves in Hungary. Franz Josef's Conservative ministry of the day headed by Count Hohenwart had worked out with the Czech political leaders a set of eighteen so-called 'Fundamental Articles'. These gave the Bohemian Provincial Assembly (or 'Landtag') a similar degree of independence to that now enjoyed by the Hungarian Parliament. A pure Bohemian ministry was to be created under the revived office of a Bohemian chancellor. The Czech language was to be made the official tongue in any district of Bohemia where the Czechs themselves were in a majority over the Germans and others', and Czech was to be placed on an equal footing with German as the languages of all central offices. Provision was made for the Emperor to be crowned King of Bohemia (one of his scores of ancient titles) in Prague and to proclaim these rights in his coronation oath. To camouflage what was a purely Czech dash to freedom, on 6 October 1871, the Bohemian reforms were dressed up in new federalist proposals for the Monarchy as a whole.

The result, as might have been foreseen (for the Czechs did not have the clout of the Magyars) was racial mayhem and a political débâcle. The German-speaking areas of Bohemia erupted in riots (a foretaste of Hitler's Sudetenland in the century to come). The Poles opposed the plan because it disadvantaged them, and the powerful Hungarians denounced it because it represented an increase of Slav influence within the empire. The same reservations were voiced by Chancellor

---

* Apart from the German-Austrians, only the Hungarians, Czechs and Poles counted as truly 'historic' nations in that they could look back over the centuries at times when they had ruled over miniature empires of their own. The other principal races were all, by comparison, 'non-historic'. This found visible expression in, for example, the empire's selection of foreign ministers. When not German-Austrian, these could be Polish (Goluchowski); Hungarian (Andrássy) or Czech (Czernin), but never Slovak, Slovene, Rumanian, and the like.

Bismarck in Berlin. The whole idea was dumped in the copious dustbin of the Monarchy's constitutional reforms. It was not surprising that Franz Josef never felt like lifting that particular lid again.

The fact that Bismarck's Germany had worked together with post-1867 Hungary to block any Slav expansion marked out a partnership that was to become increasingly crucial for Austrian, and indeed for European, history. Bismarck had found his ideal partner in Count Gyula Andrássy whom Franz Josef had made foreign minister in the Liberal governments he had appointed in the wake of the discredited and departed Hohenwart. Thus a Magyar was put in charge of the Monarchy's foreign affairs at a time when the Magyars had gained virtual independence in the Monarchy's domestic affairs. The result was a policy which – whether or not it ultimately served the interests of the empire as a whole – was fashioned to serve the interests of its Hungarian half. Containing Slav expansionism (which could only spell trouble from Hungary's millions of non-Magyar subjects) meant containing the supreme protector of the Slavs, tsarist Russia. There was only one power strong enough to help in that task, the new German empire which Bismarck had just conjured into life in the palace of Versailles after his victory against the French in the 1870–71 war. That same Prussia which, five years earlier, had inflicted an equally crushing defeat on the Habsburg monarchy, now had to be recruited as an ally to preserve its stability. For Franz Josef, this signalled resigned acceptance of the fact that Germany was unshakeable as the dominant force in central Europe and that the military verdict of Königgrätz could never be politically reversed.

The *rapprochement* between the two German-speaking empires was speeded up by Russia's intervention, already described, in the Balkan turmoil of 1875–78, ending with her defeat of the Turkish armies. At the congress of European powers which met in Berlin in June of 1878 to establish a new order in south-east Europe, Germany and Austria worked together to cut back the enormous territorial gains which Russia had exacted from Turkey – less for herself than for her Slav Balkan protégés such as Bulgaria and Serbia. It was with German backing that the Habsburg monarchy was now authorized to make its major thrust southwards against this south Slav world. Bismarck supported Austria's claim to occupy and administer, indefinitely, the two provinces of Bosnia and Herzegovina whose revolt against the Sultan had started the imbroglio. He also backed her request to station troops in a narrow tongue of land, the Sanjak of Novi Pazar, which separated Serbia from Montenegro and provided a ready-made land corridor for even deeper penetration of Slav territory.

Thus the German bolt was shot home to prevent Russia from breaking down Europe's eastern door. The same principle was formalized by the military treaty signed on 7 October of the following year between Austria-Hungary and Germany. This so-called Dual Alliance was purely defensive and directed primarily against St Petersburg. The two contracting parties bound themselves to come to each other's aid with all their military strength should either of them be attacked by Russia. Bismarck would have preferred a wider pact, automatically covering Germany in case of war against any other power (by which he meant France). But Austrian foreign policy under Andrássy's direction was only looking east. It was however agreed that if Russia *supported* any other country in war against either of the two allies, then the military clause would come into operation. Thus was spun the first and by far the firmest thread in that net of rival alliances which, in the end, destroyed the old European order.

For a while, both partners in the Dual Alliance kept a more tenuous thread open to St Petersburg. This was largely the doing of Bismarck who foresaw both the danger of France and Russia teaming up together and the perils for European peace of any Austro-Russian clash in the Balkans (both of which apprehensions were amply borne out by history). For a few years, (1881 to 1887) the so-called Alliance of the Three Emperors linked Vienna, Berlin and St Petersburg in a highly secret agreement which collapsed under the very Balkan rivalry Bismarck so feared. As described already, he also concluded a bilateral 'Re-insurance Treaty' of his own with Russia, only to stand by helplessly and watch it dropped from the Berlin end after his dismissal. There were moves towards a bilateral understanding between the two Balkan rivals themselves, as when, in October of 1903, Tsar Nicholas II came to stalk stag with Franz Josef at the Styrian shooting-lodge of Mürzsteg and joint police action to restore order in Macedonia was agreed. But these were like stones in a river bed which divert the water over short stretches yet without altering, let alone stemming, the main current. Long before Mürzsteg, the course of that current had been set.

By the end of the century Franz Josef, now approaching seventy, was resigned to constitutional challenges; he was also hardened to troubles inside the family. What he was not prepared for was a situation suddenly arising which combined both problems. This, however, was precisely what happened when the Archduke Franz Ferdinand, now Heir-Presumptive,* fell head over heels in love with a lady-in-waiting

---

* His father, Karl Ludwig, had died of typhoid in 1896, having ignored the pleas of his doctors on a trip to the Holy Land by drinking the waters of the sacred but very polluted River Jordan.

in the services of one of his cousins by marriage, the Archduchess Isabella. The affair erupted in the summer of 1899, when the Archduke was thirty-five years old and seemingly the very opposite of a tempestuous romantic. He had been a somewhat morose and introspective child and had grown up with a distrustful and sarcastic attitude to the human race (conditioned partly by a long and serious lung illness which had prompted most of his followers to switch their attentions rather too blatantly to the next in line for the succession, his debauched but handsome brother Otto). But if he was an unlikely royal Romeo, the lady of his choice made a very appealing Juliet. The trouble was that Countess Sophie Chotek (of Chotkova and Wognin), though of old Bohemian stock, was not nearly royal enough herself. The Habsburgs and, above all, a future emperor, could only marry inside the Monarchy into their own family; that of another Christian dynasty; or of the so-called 'mediatized' historic families first listed on 7 October 1825. Not even the Kinskys, the princely house to which Sophie's mother belonged, came within that implacably select circle.

But, for the Archduke, normally very conscious of his dignity, all this was swept aside by an infatuation which was psychological as well as physical. Though no classical beauty (and a little too tall and slim for the rounded tastes of the time), Sophie, with her huge dark brown eyes and perfect skin, was a handsome enough figure of a woman. But what set her apart from the rest was a serenity which promised balm for the nerves as well as comfort for the body. At all events (for human chemistry cannot be written out in words) he found the combination irresistible. Nor was he put off by the fact that she was turned thirty herself, quite an age by nineteenth-century marriage standards. As he wrote to one of his woman confidantes (after complaining that all the eligible princesses on the market seemed to be 'little more than chicks, one uglier than the other'): 'I can readily imagine the ideal woman as I would like her and with whom I could also be happy. She should not be too young, and her character and views should be fully developed . . .'[5]

For months the affair, which convulsed the closed circle of court society, made hardly any ripple outside. The general public were not to know, for example, that the scandal had broken after a tennis party given at the Archduchess Isabella's* Pressburg estate when the hostess, curious to see whose portrait it was in the lid of a watch left behind by Franz Ferdinand, prised it open only to see the features of her own lady-in-waiting gazing out at her. And only a select few knew, or

---

* Isabella was the wife of Archduke Frederick, and being by birth a Princess Croy, came of a 'mediatized' family which was acceptable to the imperial family.

guessed, that the bride the Archduchess longed the Heir-Presumptive to choose was the eldest of her own six daughters, Maria Christina. The battle between Franz Ferdinand and the Emperor – the nephew insisting on having both Sophie and the succession and the uncle demanding that he must choose between them – was, at first, also fought out in secret.

But as the year, and the century, turned, and more and more people were drawn into the conflict, the truth leaked out that the Monarchy was facing a crisis. Bishops, prime ministers (in both Vienna and Budapest), constitutional lawyers, Habsburg relatives and court pundits all wrestled throughout the winter and spring of 1899/1900 with the dilemma. Nearly all of the imperial family, echoing their master, were scandalized at Franz Ferdinand's demands. Frau Schratt joined in the indignant chorus against him. Only his stepmother, Maria Theresa,* a radiantly sweet-tempered woman for whom the Emperor had a very soft spot, pleaded his cause from first to last, arguing that the match could prove a good one and that somehow his domestic happiness (a rare thing in the dynasty) must be secured.

In May, after several stormy interviews with his uncle, the Archduke penned a final appeal to him which skilfully combined humility ('I turn again towards Your Majesty's fatherly heart . . . to fulfil for me that deepest and dearest of my wishes on which hangs the whole of my future existence . . .') with reassurances ('The Countess will never show herself either at court or in high social circles and will never make claims of any sort or seek to play a role . . .'), all rounded with a touch of moral blackmail by hints at the dire effects a refusal might have on his 'already tattered nerves'. That last sentence, raising up the spectre of another Mayerling, may well have tipped the balance in Franz Josef's agitated mind.

The outcome, at all events, was a victory on points for the nephew. Just before noon on 28 June 1900, in front of his Emperor, flanked by all adult archdukes of all branches of the Habsburg tree, Franz Ferdinand declared his forthcoming marriage to be morganatic and solemnly renounced, in an oath sworn to the cardinal archbishop of Vienna, all rights of succession for any children resulting from it. But he had kept the succession for himself, and he had also got his Sophie. They were married a week later at his stepmother's summer residence at Reichstadt in northern Bohemia. Neither the Emperor nor a single one of the fifteen archdukes who had attended the Hofburg ceremony,

* His father, the Archduke Karl Ludwig, was widowed twice in his life and married, for the third time, Maria Theresa of Portugal.

including his own two brothers, was present. It was the opening round in a long and exhausting family battle.

From now until the outbreak of war fourteen years later, court life in Vienna (and, as a consequence, social life throughout the empire) was dominated by the Archduke's struggle to secure a prominent role for his wife – in flat contradiction to the pledge he had made just before securing her hand. There were some concessions he never managed to wring out of that flinty grenadier who guarded Habsburg protocol, the court chamberlain, Prince Montenuovo. The ban stayed up, for example, against the couple appearing together in public in Vienna, even extending to private theatre performances. The Archduke was more successful on the armed services front. Though the emperor apologetically declined to allow Sophie to go with her husband to Innsbruck in August of 1909 for a great Tyrolean parade,* six months later the army were ordered to present arms in front of her and she was authorized to attend future military ceremonials (a fateful concession, as things turned out). Three months before, the Countess, who had been made a princess on the occasion of her wedding, had been further elevated by the emperor to the rank of duchess. That moved her one notch further forward in the baroque protocol ratchet of Hofburg court ceremonial. Henceforth, she would be called 'Highness' and take precedence after the youngest archduchess. A private card which has survived from the court ball of 1910 records the Duchess of Hohenberg making her first full-blown official appearance in the family circle – though still without her husband. At one of the four all-ladies tea-tables, she is shown as sitting between two of the daughters of her one-time employer, the Archduchess Isabella, who presided over the opposite table of the diamond formation. Malice – or a sense of humour – must have inspired whoever made the 'placement'.

If Franz Ferdinand was slowly getting as far as he could ever hope to get with the obsessive campaign of his private life, he faced an even harder battle on the political front. To say that the Belvedere (Prince Eugene's massive early eighteenth-century Vienna palace which was allotted to him as an official residence) was a rival centre of government to the Hofburg would be pitching it too high. It was, however, certainly a rival centre of ideas and pressures. Franz Ferdinand was a typical Habsburg inasmuch as his changes of mind and mood could be frequent and sudden. But there were two aims he held to throughout his life, and both were to be frustrated.

The first was to cut the Hungarians (whom he feared, distrusted and

---

* Marking the centenary of Andreas Hofer's peasant army victory against Napoleon's troops.

generally disliked) down to what he considered their appropriate size for the future stability of the Monarchy. The Hungarians, for their part, were taking the ten-yearly reviews of the 1867 Compromise as springboards for further leaps towards total independence. In 1897, for example, the Budapest government came within a whisker of abolishing the customs union between the two halves of the Monarchy altogether and securing tariff autonomy for Hungary. At the next review in 1907, an even fiercer battle broke out between the twin capitals of the empire. This time the Hungarians pressed for military independence as well – a national regular army with its own chain of command using its own Magyar language.* Though never conceding in full, especially on the vital military front, the Emperor was always prone to give away too much for Franz Ferdinand's taste. As for the uncle, he so feared tempestuous interference from his nephew that he went so far as to order that details of the 1907–8 negotiations be kept from him. Franz Josef had made a bargain with his Hungarian subjects forty years before and, however these subjects chose to inflate or distort the pledge, their king and emperor was resolved to stand by it. He was also doomed to do so.

The heir-presumptive made even less headway with his overriding ambition in the field of foreign affairs, which was to pick up the Monarchy's broken line to St Petersburg and to bring back into life the alliance of the three emperors. Here Franz Ferdinand reflected the farsightedness of Bismarck. Especially after Russia's defeat at the hands of the Japanese, he feared the political recoil of an intensified pro-Slav thrust in the Balkans and the collision with Austria's own ambitions there. The Monarchy's annexation of Bosnia-Herzegovina was the first of those major collisions. It is time to look at this seminal crisis of 1908 through Habsburg eyes.

There had never been any doubt, in the eyes of Franz Josef or any of his governments, that Austria's right to occupy and administer the two provinces, established by the Berlin treaty of 1878, amounted to a tacit international agreement that, one day, the Monarchy would take over the territories outright. The only questions to be answered were when and how. Both hinged on coming to an understanding in the matter with Russia. In 1897, when the Emperor had visited the new Tsar, Nicholas II, in St Petersburg, they and their advisers had paced warily around the problem when discussing co-operation between the two

---

* In 1868 this particular conflict had been resolved by having centralized control and a common German-language chain of command for all regular units of the Monarchy while creating, in each half, second-line infantry and cavalry forces allowed to use their indigenous tongue.

powers in the Balkans. The Austrian foreign minister of the day, Count Agenor Goluchowski, expressly reserved the right to annex. His Russian opposite number, Count Muraviev, did not dispute the right but stressed it would require 'special scrutiny at the proper time'.

Eleven years later the Ballhausplatz in Vienna decided that 'the proper time' had come. To begin with, the date looked right. It was both the thirtieth anniversary year of the occupation and the sixtieth anniversary year of Franz Josef's coronation, an event being marked with rapturous celebrations throughout the empire. Then there were political factors to consider. Pan-Slav agitation for a 'Greater Serbia' (which included the two provinces squarely in its sight) was on the increase and the 'hawks' of Vienna, headed by the army chief of staff, General Conrad, were growing correspondingly more clamorous for a showdown with Belgrade. Finally, there was a genuine, if somewhat arcane, constitutional problem. The liberal 'Young Turks', who had seized power in Constantinople that same summer, had announced the formation of a Western-style parliament for the whole of the Ottoman empire. Legal fiction still proclaimed Bosnia and Herzegovina to be part of that empire. What would happen if the provinces should be called upon to send deputies to that parliament? On which side should their subjects fight if a conflict developed over the issue? The danger to European peace had traditionally been Turkey as 'the sick man'. Ironically, the danger now came from a Turkey rejuvenated.

If the 'proper time' had come by 1908, so had the 'special scrutiny'. The personalities of the two men who now ran the foreign ministries in Vienna and St Petersburg have a great deal of bearing on the strange tale which unfolded in the summer of that year. Two years previously, political adventurers had replaced safe plodders at the diplomatic helm in both capitals. To make things more complicated, both newcomers had chips of differing sizes on their shoulders. The Austrian, Alois von Aehrenthal, was a mere Freiherr, moving in a Viennese high society which was fond of saying of itself: 'Life begins from count upwards.' More importantly, his grandfather, ennobled barely a century before, had been a grain merchant from Prague and, it was said, a Jew. Neither the racial nor the commercial connection were exactly social pluses. The grandson, a tall slouching-shouldered shortsighted man who had worked his way up as a career diplomat, was determined to do better.

His opposite number in St Petersburg was a much more dangerous character. Alexander Petrovich Izvolski was an obscure Kalmuk from the Mongol steppes of Russia, and looked it: squat, high cheeked, with eyes that readily narrowed into slits. His face, when he exploded with rage (which he frequently did), reminded Count Berchtold, the

Austrian ambassador at St Petersburg during the crisis and a sufferer of Izvolski's tantrums, of 'the picture of Ghenghis Khan as he had appeared in my childhood imagining, chief of the Tartar hordes, throwing his enemies into vats of boiling water'.[6]

This volcanic figure who, like Aehrenthal, had risen through the official ranks, had two ambitions. The first was to secure an attractive wife of noble birth. In this he succeeded, though only after several rebuffs.* The second, and even more raging desire, was to go down in history as the statesman who had fulfilled the age-old Russian dream of securing a permanent naval seaway into the Mediterranean through the Dardanelles. In this he was to fail abjectly, thanks to a combination of his own overconfidence and the slipperiness of his Austrian partner.

Izvolski had set the ball rolling on 2 July 1908 with a highly secret *aide-mémoire* outlining the basic bargain for a new entente between the two powers: Russia to accept Austria's annexation of Bosnia-Herzegovina in return for Austrian support over access through the Black Sea. As it was the season for spas in the Monarchy, the action moved there too. Berchtold, on leave from St Petersburg, joined the fashionable international throng at Karlsbad, where Izvolski was already established in the Hotel Cleopatra. It was in this unlikely setting that, on 30 August, Aehrenthal's reply was handed over. It was an acceptance in principle, though details needed to be worked out.

Then the life of the spa took over and, for three weeks, politics was pushed into the background by midsummer chatter and scandal. King Edward VII turned up from his regular August base at the neighbouring spa of Marienbad, invariably with a beautiful woman sharing his carriage. Berchtold visited his friends and relatives in their castles scattered throughout the surrounding Bohemian forests – the Lobkowitz in Eisenberg, the Clarys in Teplitz, the Czernins in Schönhof, the Hohenlohes in Rothenhaus, the Mensdorffs in Kulm – often taking the eager Izvolski with him. Finally, at a dinner party in Marienbad, Berchtold's wife Nandine invited the Russian to their own Bohemian hunting-lodge at Buchlau to meet up with Aehrenthal.

The full truth about the fateful Buchlau meeting of 15–17 September may never be known, since there were no witnesses to the talks and nothing was put down in writing. According to the Austrian version, as given at second hand in Berchtold's papers, the two foreign ministers, after long walks together in the castle park and hours of conversation

---

* One of the St Petersburg ladies who rejected him summed up her decision in later years with the delicious verdict: 'Not a day passes without my regretting not having married him; but there is never a night when I don't congratulate myself.'

alone in the smoking-room (under the antlers of three magnificent stags which crowned the fireplace) confirmed the pact outlined in their exchange of letters. Where Izvolski got it all wrong – or where Aehrenthal misled him – was over that critical how and when which their predecessors in office had left open eleven years before. The Russian, believing that there was no violent hurry in the matter and that further consultation would anyway follow before Austria acted, set out on a leisurely tour of European capitals. Aehrenthal immediately got down to business with his imperial master. Franz Josef had been told of the Russian approach at once while at Ischl for his usual midsummer stay and had approved the bargain. He was now to be the instrument of its execution. The annexation was announced, not by the Austro-Hungarian government to other interested governments, but in personal letters signed by the Emperor on 29 September for presentation by his ambassadors on 5 October to the heads of state of the major powers.

All of them were taken aback, and not a few of them irritated as well. We have seen how angry the German Emperor was at being caught napping over the announcement. King Edward VII, who had visited Franz Josef at Ischl as recently as 12–13 August (even persuading the old Emperor to take his first motor-car ride with him) was almost speechless at not having been let into the secret as a confidential matter between sovereigns. As for Nicholas II, he was so affronted on Russia's behalf that even this pacific and gentle Tsar kept Berchtold waiting for four weeks for his first audience over the crisis. (Franz Josef's letter had been handed over to, and presented by, Russian officials.)

But no one in Europe was as frantic and as furious as Izvolski himself. As the crisis dragged on that winter the European powers found face-saving formulas by which first Turkey was bought off (for 2½ million Turkish pounds) and then Russia herself was persuaded to swallow the *fait accompli* of annexation. Some of the bitterness was taken off the pill for the Tsar by the German compromise of 14 March whereby Austria would ask the European powers to sanction the annexation and also specifically request Russia not to make difficulties, which Russia would then agree to.

Serbia, who had mobilized for battle, was the hardest to pacify and the last to come to heel. But without the Russian army behind her she was little more than a fiercely-yapping terrier in Austria's path, and the Russian bear did not yet feel strong enough to move. Nicholas II had already said as much to King Peter of Serbia. Now, on 16 March, after a special council of war, the Tsar announced to his own ministers that he was not prepared to fight over the disputed provinces. For another fortnight Serbia held out, only giving up after military threats ʰrom Vienna were added to the warnings from St Petersburg. Finally, on 31 March, after General Conrad, to his delight, had been authorized by Franz Josef to fully mobilize five Austro-Hungarian army corps (one-third of the Monarchy's entire strength), Serbia stood her troops down, and formally agreed to 'renounce the attitude of protest and opposition which she has adopted since last autumn with regard to the annex-ation'.[7] After five exhausting months, the tension in Europe relaxed.

That same evening Count Berchtold gave an 'end of crisis' dinner party, complete with concert by the famous French pianist Risler, at the Austro-Hungarian embassy in St Petersburg. Izvolski was the only guest who could not share in the general relief. For him the outcome spelt personal disaster. He had been helpless to prevent Aehrenthal romping away with his part of the Buchlau bargain and unable to move an inch nearer towards his own share: neither France nor England had shown the slightest interest in even reopening the delicate question of warship passage through the straits. Izvolski swore revenge, at any cost.

But the impact of the 1908 affair went far wider than frustrating the ambition of one Russian minister. By her action, Austria had, at one and the same time, lost sympathy with England and France (who looked to the Monarchy to preserve peace in the Balkans, not disturb it); alarmed her German ally, while at the same time giving the totally erroneous impression that she had acted as Germany's tool; further alienated her uncertain ally, Italy; stoked up the Balkan fires and strengthened the bonds between Serbia and Bulgaria. At home, too, there was danger. The 'war party' had smelt blood but had been denied the kill. All of these factors cast their shadows towards 1914. The deepest was that thrown forward by Russia's humiliation. 'The Tsar', one of his officials noted during the crisis, 'has the feeling that a conflict with Germandom is inevitable in the future, and that one must prepare for this.'[8]

A sense of this implacable destiny broods even over the personal correspondence between the two sovereigns about the annexation. The monarchs always began their letters 'My dear Friend' and always ended them with the formula 'Please believe in the feelings of deepest friendship of your friend and brother'. But what comes in between is less harmonious. In his letter announcing the annexation, Franz Josef leans heavily on the greater weight of his years by appealing to the Tsar's support over a step into which he had been forced and had himself discussed 'with your blessed father and grandfather, who had agreed to it without protest'.[9]

The Tsar, in his reply (delayed for three weeks), makes it clear that despite his 'deep and heartfelt friendship' for the Austrian Emperor, he has to point out that, whatever his own father and grandfather may have said in their day, the situation in Bosnia-Herzegovina should not have been altered except 'by a decision of the signatories to the Berlin Treaty'.[10]

A few weeks later the Tsar's letter of congratulation on the sixtieth anniversary of Franz Josef's accession gave the latter the chance to spell out the problem more bluntly. The two rulers, he warned Nicholas in his reply, must always be careful to preserve their personal ties, since 'the national and geographical conditions of the two empires have been so different as to render it impossible always to go hand in hand to achieve one and the same end'. But he, Franz Josef, had always been sensitive to Russia's interests in the Balkans, as was shown by the fact that he had not sought to press home any Austrian advantage there 'at a time when you were fighting a hard war in the Far East'.[11] As can be seen, the monarchs were as disingenuous as their ministers.

The Austrian Emperor who wrote those letters and sat the long annexation crisis out was a tired man who was slowing down. He had already cut out state visits abroad because they were too much of a strain, as Edward VII had been obliged to accept four years before. On 24 April 1904 the British ambassador in Vienna, Sir Francis Plunkett, wrote to Buckingham Palace putting paid to any hopes that the Emperor might accept the King's invitation to visit England that summer:

There is, I regret to say, no doubt that the Emperor has aged considerably in the last six months and is obliged to take precautions which are new to him. For instance, the great Spring Reviews which His Majesty has the habit of holding are not be held this year . . .

The envoy added that the Emperor had been unduly tired even by a recent call just paid within the Monarchy on the King of Sweden at Abbazia. His doctors had therefore advised against the 'fatigue and excitement of a visit to London'.[12]

Fatigue and excitement were not avoidable in 1908 (quite apart from the upheaval over the annexation) because of the jubilee celebrations. In vain did Franz Josef drop the plainest hints to his fellow-sovereigns that their congratulations on the sixtieth year of his reign should be conveyed by letter or telegram. The German Kaiser (who else?) led the field in ignoring the hint and announcing his intention of coming with his Empress to present his compliments in person. At this, all the rulers, past and present, of the German world, followed suit and, on 7 May, there was a mass ceremony of congratulations in Schönbrunn Palace, followed by a gala banquet.

'I have reason to believe', wrote Plunkett's successor in Vienna, 'that the emperor is not very pleased at this visitation . . .'[13]

There were certain inescapable court functions, dictated by the calendar. These began with the ceremonies of New Year's greeting for the Emperor and the dinner he gave for the imperial family on New Year's Day; then came the two court balls and the so-called court dinners or 'Seriendiners' held between New Year and Easter; the Good Friday service itself, conducted in the Hofburg Chapel with the Emperor, for some reason, always dressed as colonel of his 8th Field Artillery Regiment; the Resurrection High Mass on Easter Sunday; and, in the late spring, the Corpus Christi celebration. This was the greatest public spectacle of them all, at which the Emperor (this time in the full-dress uniform of a field marshal) drove in his state coach to St Stephen's Cathedral and then, after the service, joined the procession, bareheaded and holding his candle, which wound its way on foot through the streets of the Inner City. Blessed Ischl gave an escape into informality for the summer months. The autumn in Vienna brought a few fixed ceremonies – the receiving of the parliamentary delegations, for example, and the military mass for the dead held in the Augustiner-kirche in November. Family obligations – attendance at weddings, christenings and funerals – were sprinkled throughout the calendar.

But everything not inescapable was avoided and so, in these last peacetime years, court life in Vienna presented a paradox as well as a dichotomy. On the one hand the reigning monarch withdrew as far as he could from the public gaze, retreating to that miniature arena of empire, his cluttered work desk. On the other hand his heir, more confident and more assertive as time went by, was always edging forward to get as much of the vacant limelight as he could decently take. Thanks largely to the efforts of Major Alexander Brosch von Aarenau, the head of his so-called 'military chancery', the Belvedere Palace had become, if not an alternative seat of power to the Hofburg, at least a second centre of influence.

It was, above all, through the selection of high office-holders in the Monarchy that this influence was felt. Franz Ferdinand in his time made and broke more than one key minister. It was partly due to him that Count Berchtold, the former ambassador to St Petersburg, replaced the mortally sick Aehrenthal as foreign minister in February of 1912. It was entirely due to him that, in December of that year, when the Balkan war was at its height, General Conrad was brought back as chief of staff. Conrad, true to form, immediately urged Austrian intervention to prevent the Serbs and their allies grabbing too much Turkish territory. (As we have seen, he had to content himself merely with rattling his sabre to persuade King Nikita of Montenegro to give up Scutari.) It is important to stress that the Archduke sponsored Conrad for his professional talents, not for his strategic ideas. Though he shared Conrad's fiery temperament and high ambitions for the house of Habsburg, Franz Ferdinand was always a moderating force whenever the talk was of military action in the Balkans. Treading warily in that minefield was the corollary to his political aim of reviving a dynastic treaty with the Tsar. Restraint, so far as the Archduke was concerned, was also plain common sense. To him the Balkans ('a few plum trees and a horde of rascals' as he once dismissed them) were not worth the risk of a major war which the Monarchy, in his view, was anyway not yet equipped to fight.

In the end, it was his own murder which was to embroil not only the Monarchy but all the major powers of the day in what began as just another Balkan crisis. Franz Ferdinand could not have sensed, in the early summer of 1914, that, thanks to a handful of that 'horde of rascals', Armageddon was about to engulf the European continent. He did, however, have a strange premonition that his own journey to Sarajevo would be a journey to death. At the beginning of May he invited the couple next in line to the throne, his twenty-seven-year-old nephew Charles, and Zita, the princess of Bourbon-Parma whom Karl had married three years before, to supper at the Belvedere. The future Empress Zita* described what happened:

It was just a small family meal, with ourselves as the only guests. Everything passed off quite normally – indeed quite merrily – until after supper, when the Duchess went to take the children up to bed. After his wife had left the room the Archduke suddenly turned to my husband and said 'I have something to say but I must say it quickly as I don't want your aunt to hear anything of this. I know I shall soon be murdered. In this desk are papers which concern you. When it happens, take them, they are for you.'[14]

To the young couple's protest that this must, surely, be a joke, their uncle replied that, on the contrary, he was in deadly earnest. He had only time to add that, fortunately, the special crypt being constructed at Artstetten was now finished† when Sophie reappeared. A strained attempt was made to resume normal conversation.

---

* Her husband became heir-apparent on his uncle's assassination, and succeeded to the throne, for a brief and tragic two-year spell, at the death of Franz Josef in November 1916.

† Apart from large estates in Bohemia, Franz Ferdinand owned a family property at Artstetten, just north of the Danube in Lower Austria. Knowing that his wife could never be buried alongside him in the Habsburg vaults in Vienna, he had built the Artstetten crypt, and it is here that their remains lie buried.

The Archduke had always been in two minds about the visit, which produced the last of the many brusque encounters to take place between him and the Emperor. The year before, Franz Ferdinand had been appointed inspector-general of the Monarchy's armed forces, a role which gave great influence, if not direct command, and which involved him almost automatically in major army exercises. It was in this capacity that, in September of 1913, he had agreed with General Conrad to attend the summer manoeuvres scheduled to take place in Bosnia the following June. As his wife had now been 'cleared' by the Emperor to appear with him on military occasions, he had arranged to take a delighted Sophie with him. That was the positive side of the visit.

On the negative side were those forebodings of doom which had surged up out of nowhere and also a bout of asthma, to which he had become increasingly prone. The Bosnian capital of Sarajevo lay in a mountain bowl which became oppressively hot and humid in mid-summer – the worst climatic conditions for the complaint. When he went for what was to prove his last audience with the Emperor (the date was probably 7 June, between 7.45 and 8.30 a.m.) he expressed misgivings about the trip. Franz Josef, who loathed scenes of any sort (and, most of all, confrontations with his explosive heir) gruffly left it to the nephew to decide. That, in effect, was a royal command to go.

The fact that the Emperor could have conceded straightaway or that the Archduke could simply have dug his toes in (as he had done on previous occasions by flatly refusing, for example, to pay a visit to Rome) is among the many might-have-beens of the assassination. At the other end of the story, the path to Sarajevo of the assassin, Gavrilo Princip, had been full of pitfalls and freakish escapes. The nineteen-year-old Bosnian-Serb fanatic (one of hundreds who haunted the seedier cafés of Belgrade vowing vengeance on the Habsburgs over the little marble-topped tables) had been armed and trained by the 'Black Hand' secret society formed after the Serbian humiliation of 1908. But its leaders, the most prominent of whom was the regicide Dragutin Dimitriević – now a staff colonel and head of Serbian military intelligence – left Princip and his band of amateur desperadoes very much to their own devices once they had been smuggled onto Bosnian, i.e. Austrian, soil.

On half a dozen occasions during the week's journey to Sarajevo the plot came within a whisker of detection or betrayal. And on 28 June itself, the first of the attacks on the Archduke, the bomb hurled at his car by Nedeljko Čabrinović as the motorcade was moving towards the town hall, failed when the missile bounced off the hood and exploded fifty yards behind its target. It was only due to the ultimate in flukes –

confusion about the safest route to be taken on the return journey with
the Archduke's car stopping to reverse at the very spot where Princip
and his revolver were waiting – that the assassin was able to fire off the
two shots with which he could hardly miss, even though he closed his
eyes as he squeezed the trigger. Minutes later both the Archduke and
his wife, seated next to him in the car, were dead. Their first full-blown
official appearance together inside the Monarchy had proved their last.
At least they had died as they had lived, side by side.

The story of what followed, told not so much in terms of the
governments of Europe but of the dynasties themselves, is recounted at
the end of this book. All that need be noted here is the greatest of the
Sarajevo ironies: the Habsburg monarchy had lost the one man who –
just conceivably, given a peacetime chance – might have saved it. In the
shorter term, Franz Josef had been robbed of the one voice for
moderation strong enough in any crisis to hush the clamour of General
Conrad and his war camp. The insulator of the perpetual Balkan
conflict had become instead its fuse.

Chapter Ten

ITALY:
THE MAKE-WEIGHT KINGDOM

Italy entered last, and very much least, into the Concert of Europe. The fabric of a modern nation-state, so suddenly woven in the famous *Risorgimento* of 1861 out of the peninsula's tattered ragbag of medieval principalities, may have had superficial constitutional unity. Yet it enjoyed neither political and cultural cohesion at home nor any real status abroad. The country was no longer that mere 'geographical expression' of Metternich's jibe. For decades to come, however, it was to remain an optical illusion as a European power.

The kingdom of Piedmont-Sardinia which we have already seen driving the Habsburgs, step by step, out of northern Italy, became the natural matrix of the new state. Turin, the chief city of Piedmont, was its first capital. Count Camillo Cavour, the Piedmontese statesman who had forged political union out of the rhetoric of Giuseppe Mazzini and the military exploits of Garibaldi, became its first Prime Minister. The house of Savoy, which ruled over Piedmont-Sardinia, provided its ready-made royal family when, on 14 March 1861, Victor Emmanuel II assumed the crown as the first King of the united Italy. Such a dynastic launch, though inevitable, had its drawbacks.

Throughout the centuries when Italy had been no more than a wellington boot of land, enclosed on three sides by the Mediterranean and on the fourth, northern, side by the Alps, the peninsula had always been divided into the relatively prosperous, cultured and sophisticated north and the primitive and desperately poor territories of the south. When the two halves became legally one, and the people of Naples and Palermo could claim the same nationality as the citizens of Florence or Milan; they could also demand the same standard of living. These economic and social contrasts have not been reconciled to this day. In Italy's founding years they erupted in riots and even open rebellions which threatened to tear the fledgling nation apart. Victor Emmanuel's ninety thousand troops of predominantly northern origin sent to garrison the south during the early phase were, in everything but name, an army of Piedmontese occupation, and were regarded as such. Only the Liberals in England, who had greeted the *Risorgimento* with ecstasy (and welcomed its standard-bearer, Mazzini, in London) imagined the Italy of 1861 to be a united country.

Turin's takeover of the peninsula also exposed and inflamed its cultural problems. As the name Piedmont conveys, the prime unit of the new state lay at the foot of mountains; in this case, it straddled the Alps between Italy and France. More especially, since it had been Napoleon III who stood as a very active godfather to the new nation, the French influence was, to begin with, overpowering. Cavour himself spoke better French than Italian and had separate secretaries to work in each language. Even when France became a rival rather than a sponsor, after the clash of colonial ambitions had arisen in Africa, these cultural ties remained strong.

The house of Savoy was itself the symbol of transmontane ambivalence. Its original coat of arms was the plainest imaginable, just a silver cross on a red shield. Yet there was never a better historical case in Europe for a dynasty to display (as several others did) an ornate eagle with two heads gazing firmly in opposite directions. The founder of the house, the romantically named Humbert with the White Hands, established his domains in the middle of the eleventh century between the River Rhône and the Lake of Geneva; only gradually did his successors extend their rule over the Alps and down into the Lombard plain, controlling the two key passes of St Gotthard and Mt Cenis. Though not the oldest royal family of Europe, they could claim to be the oldest in continuous succession. The last king of Italy, who abdicated in the middle of the twentieth century, was descended in direct male line from that count of Savoy who had set forth from Burgundy almost exactly nine hundred years before and carried the founder's name. The dynasty ended, as it had begun, with a Humbert.

Through the years the house of Savoy had married into most of the great families of Europe. In the thirteenth century, for example, all four granddaughters of Count Thomas of Savoy wedded kings, including Eleanor who, in 1236, married Henry III of England. Two hundred years later, Count Thomas's successor, Amadeus VIII, was not only promoted to duke by the Roman-German emperor but was elected Pope while still a layman, by the Council of Basle in 1439. (His spiritual reign as Felix V was, however, a disputed one and, after ten turbulent years, he withdrew from the Vatican and settled for a cardinal's hat.) Later, Habsburgs as well as Bourbons graced the family tree, whose most illustrious son, Prince Eugene of the cadet Carignan branch, won imperishable laurels as a soldier when he chased the Turks forever out of the Danube basin in the seventeenth century. Soon afterwards, the house of Savoy received its final promotion when, in a confusing redistribution of Mediterranean islands ordained by the European powers, the dukes of Savoy became first, kings of Sicily, and then, in 1720, exchanged that crown for the other island kingdom of Sardinia. Piedmont-Sardinia, the north Italian state which was to fight Vienna for the mastery of the Lombard plain and finally rule over the whole Italian peninsula, was born when the four black moors' heads of the Sardinian emblem were merged with the silver cross of Savoy.

More than the four black heraldic moors was transferred to a united Italy with the accession of Victor Emmanuel II. The Sardinian constitution of 4 March 1848 went over to the mainland as well, setting out the royal prerogatives by which the new kingdom was henceforth to be ruled. Notwithstanding the claim that they rested 'on the will of the people', these powers were authoritarian to the point of absolutism. Supreme executive as well as legislative and political functions were vested in the king alone. He was the head of state and the commander-in-chief of all forces on land and sea. He alone could sanction and promulgate all laws. He alone could convene, postpone or dissolve sessions of parliament, nominate and dismiss ministers. The grip for a very firm royal hand indeed had been established. Italy's growth as a nation would perhaps have been less turbulent, and her prestige in the world certainly less abysmal, had that grip ever been fully exerted. But the plain truth, even after making all allowances for the early problems faced by crown and government, was that the house of Savoy never produced a ruler worthy of meeting the challenge, let alone overcoming it. Their Italian kings remained what, with a few exceptions, they had always been in history, petty-minded princes with the politics of plain opportunism. In this, they followed to the bitter end the advice which their founder, Count Humbert, had passed on to them at his death in 1056: 'Never ally yourself completely to one side, one faction or one policy. Preserve intact all our bonds of friendship, family ties and political relationships, yet neither taut nor slack.'[1]

Victor Emmanuel II, the first of modern Italy's four kings, was the only one who looked worthy of those Sardinian prerogatives. He had the body of a bear and, on top of it, a domed forehead and bulging eyes which betokened an almost Bismarckian aggressiveness. The give-away were two enormous black moustaches whose finely-pointed upturned tips were trained to stretch more than half-way up his cheeks. This was the face of a vulgarian masquerading as a monarch. Behind the legend of the *re galantuomo*, the courtly soldier king, lay the reality:

an uncultured, indeed semi-educated, man, whose chief passions were hunting and the sexual act. His first wife, the Austrian Archduchess Adelhaid, died six years before she would have become Queen of Italy, exhausted by the demands of the marriage bed, aged only thirty-three. She had borne him eight children in thirteen years; bearing the last had cost her her life.

By now, 1855, it seemed likely that the house of Savoy had a promising future ahead of it and there was no shortage of possible bridal candidates for the widower, including a Russian grand duchess, a Hohenzollern princess, and one of the daughters of the Queen of England. But at this point in the story it is as though we are back in Belgrade with those Serbian monarchs who became besotted by their mistresses. Victor Emmanuel declined all royal offers in favour of a low-born woman who was to be his enduring and all-consuming love. This was Rosa, or 'La Rosina' as she was later known, the daughter of an army drummer called John Vercellana and as earthily coarse as the old-fashioned sergeants' mess. If this was unfortunate for the ancient line of Piedmont, it was a tragedy for the infant kingdom of Italy. What was needed above all in the years after 1861 was a sense of regal style and dignity, a court that the restlessly united Italians could gaze up to and the other monarchs of Europe could look straight in the face. With 'La Rosina', who, as Countess Mirafiore, eventually married Victor Emmanuel morganatically in 1869, this was simply unattainable. A precious source of national and dynastic prestige had been squandered.

The loss was felt all the more keenly when, only a year after the morganatic marriage, the court and the capital moved down at last to Rome, after a sojourn half-way down the country, at Florence. Rome, seat of the Caesars of old, and looking out on the Mediterranean, was the natural centre, both historically and geographically, for the new kingdom. Only a powerful combination of the Pope and Napoleon III had delayed the move for so long. The Vatican, far from leading the move towards unification, had bitterly opposed it. The Papacy knew that its own vast estates, which stretched from coast to coast across the centre of Italy, would inevitably be swallowed up in the new nation-state. On the ideological, as opposed to the nationalistic, level, it feared the triumph of liberal nationalism as a threat to the universal and ultra-conservative Catholic Church.

As for the self-styled Emperor of the French, his patronage of the *Risorgimento* had stopped dead at the gates of the Holy City, which he preferred to guard with his own troops as a symbol of the world power which he craved. We have seen one disastrous outcome of that craving in the Mexican adventure which had landed his dupe, Maximilian of

Austria, in front of a revolutionary firing squad. Now, three years after the Mexican disaster, had come the crushing defeat of the French armies by Prussia at Sedan, a blow which shattered the megalomaniac dreams of Napoleon III for good. For the Italian kingdom, on the other hand, it meant that, once again (as after Königgrätz, when Venice had been tossed into its lap), a Prussian victory on the battlefield had presented it with political spoils at home, for the French garrison had been withdrawn from the Holy City to fight on the Rhine. Cavour, who was avowedly anti-clerical and had always sworn to establish the capital at Rome, would have leapt at the chance. But this one great statesman of the *Risorgimento* had died in June of 1861, and his successors—Ricasoli, Rattazzi, Minghetti and Menabrea – were pygmies by comparison, the last-named being merely a royal aide-de- camp.

Lanza, the Prime Minister of 1870, dithered now in the crisis over the capital. As late as 1 August he was condemning any suggestion that Italy should profit by France's misfortunes to take Rome for herself. Victor Emmanuel, mesmerized by his old patron, could not believe that Napoleon III was heading for defeat, and even wanted to send troops to help him. It took a vote of the parliamentary Chamber, (passed by 214 votes to 152) to 'resolve the Roman question in accordance with national aspirations' to prod a hesitant government and a deluded king into action. On 20 September, a fortnight after the battle of Sedan, Italian troops marched into Rome on the pretext of 'preventing anarchy'. There was a brief clash with papal troops at the walls and then, with the loss of less than fifty dead, the Italians had won their proper capital. 'The word Rome, the greatest sound on the lips of man, is today rejoined with that of Italy, the word dearest to my heart,' the King declared in a dutiful proclamation.*

A protracted battle of another sort now began. Though laws were passed guaranteeing the sovereignty and independence of the dispossessed Holy See, the Vatican ignored them, and launched thunderous encyclicals against the 'sub-alpine invaders', a phrase which invoked all the foreignness of the house of Savoy. Victor Emmanuel added insult to injury in the Pope's eyes by setting himself up in the old papal residence of the Quirinal Palace. From that moment the society of Rome broke apart, seemingly implacably, into the two camps of 'blacks' and 'whites', the former still holding to the Papacy, the latter following the Crown. Some of the great families were split, out of passion or prudence, and sent representatives to both; others, like the

---

* The occupation was only to end formally in 1929, when a concordat was signed between the Italy of Mussolini and the Vatican.

Chigi, the Scotti, the Roccagiovane and, of course, the Borghese, who had produced popes of their own, clung solidly to the Vatican. So Rome began with two courts, two diplomatic communities, two social centres, two suns.

A graphic example of the situations this split constantly produced is provided by that same British governess whose memoirs of the Rumanian court have already been quoted. She also served in Rome at the height of the great political and social schism and describes what happened when the daughters of Don Carlos, pretender to the throne of Spain, arrived not at the invitation of the court but as guests of the Princess Massimo, another *grande dame* of the 'blacks'. The *'Consulta'*, as the Italian Foreign Office was known, had forbidden even remote contact between the Spanish princesses and Spanish diplomats accrédited to the court. On more than one festive occasion this led to the hapless envoy being obliged to break off in the middle of a dance and leave the floor and the house immediately either of the princesses entered the ballroom. Complained the governess: 'It spoilt many of the last balls of the season.'[2]

The feud, of course, ruined something far more important than dances. By splitting Rome into two, and draining away so much of its energies into what, to the outsider, appeared as a cantankerous parochial quarrel, it made it even harder for this anyway backward city to rival Paris or Vienna either as political capitals or as cosmopolitan centres of European culture. In the end the court and government were bound to win but, in the social sphere, there was no hope of this happening in Victor Emmanuel's lifetime. The inelegant king and his even coarser 'Rosina' were an embarrassment to the most ardent of royalists.

Some idea of how crude palace entertainment could be in a raw monarchy whose court was run on military lines without a royal lady and whose king was without any of the social graces, is given by a British minister's wife who attended one of Victor Emmanuel's Florentine balls shortly before the move to Rome:

Italy being so democratic, the guests consisted of every class of people, mostly men. I saw some in coloured ties and trousers, some in jackets and hob-nailed boots, women in the most impossible attire, with striped blankets over their shoulders in the guise of a shawl. Some wore neither, and a camelia in their hair seemed to be the only effort at any kind of ornament which they had made. It was impossible even to approach the room in which refreshments were, for a free fight went on there all the time. I was told that the knives and forks were chained to the buffet, and that many who left had the necks of bottles sticking out of their coat pockets. . . .

Punctually at twelve o'clock the king, followed by his suite, retired from his dais, which he had never once left, the ropes were withdrawn and, to my utter astonishment, every diplomat seized hold of his wife or daughter and rushed helter-skelter down a small back-stairs to the court where their carriages were standing, before the crowd streaming down the grand staircase could block the way.[3]

Dignity could only come to the Italian court when Victor Emmanuel had left the scene. In January of 1878 the first King of Italy died, aged fifty-eight, of malaria caught from the notorious Roman marshes. His bitter adversary, Pope Pius IX, who was to die himself only a month later, relented sufficiently for the monarch to receive the last sacraments. The 'whites' glimpsed fresh hope in the person of Crown Prince Humbert, now his successor.

One symbol of the change was the new ruler's title: he styled himself Humbert I, thus marking the dynastic transition from Piedmont to Italy. A different atmosphere soon swept through the corridors of the Quirinal, which now had a proper queen as mistress. Humbert's wife, Margherita, was in fact his first cousin. Neither had wanted the other. Humbert had hoped to follow in his father's footsteps by marrying, for political reasons, into the 'enemy house' of Habsburg. But the plan quite literally went up in flames when the lady of his choice, the Archduchess Mathilde, set fire to her crinoline with a forbidden cigarette when dressing for a Vienna ball one evening in 1867. It was General Menabrea, Victor Emmanuel's military aide (and Prime Minister of the day) who suggested the sixteen-year-old Margherita of Savoy, daughter of the Duke of Genoa, as a substitute. Though she had enjoyed anything but an agreeable start in life (her mother, Princess Elisabeth of Saxony, had added to Europe's royal *chroniques scandaleuses* by eloping with a palace major), Margherita had grown into a serene and cultured young woman who loved art and literature and spoke French and German better than Italian. Though not beautiful – she had too prominent a nose and too fat a neck to fulfil the classic requirements – she looked handsome and stately enough as a consort at their Turin wedding in 1868.* Moreover, within eighteen months, she gave birth. It was the only child to spring from a marriage which lasted for thirty-two years, and the infant looked ominously frail and puny. But, as signified by the hundred-and-one-cannon salute which thundered out from the fortress of Sant'Elmo on 11 November 1869, it

---

* Turin had rioted when it was announced that Humbert's father, in keeping with the nationalistic ethic, would be buried in Rome's Pantheon. The wedding in the Piedmont capital went some way to soothing local feeling.

was a boy, baptized as Victor Emmanuel III, the title the infant was destined to rule with for forty-six years.

Humbert and Margherita had already endured, as Crown Prince and Princess, eight years of the royalist versus papalist feud in Rome. Their apartment at the Quirinal soon became the real focus of 'white' activity, and royalist leaders such as the Duke of Sermoneta immediately began to stage their private balls around the young couple. Gradually the royalists gained the upper hand, not merely because their social life was so much more relaxed and amusing, but because it became increasingly underpinned by international recognition. By 1876, two years before Victor Emmanuel's death, England, Germany and France had all raised their missions to ambassadorial level and European royalty, including Queen Victoria's heir, the future King Edward VII, had visited the new Italian capital and paid their respects to its strange court.

Humbert's accession set the stage for the triumph of the 'whites' and with it the acceptance, albeit still somewhat condescending, of Italy into the old European hierarchy. This was primarily the work of two people: the new Queen as regards the prestige of the palace, and the Sicilian-born Francesco Crispi as regards the kingdom's political profile. The royal couple got off to the best of emotional launches during their grand goodwill tour of the kingdom in the first months of their reign. On 19 November, when driving side by side through Naples, in an open carriage, a madman named Giovanni Passanante, founder and sole member of the 'Universal Revolution', lunged at Humbert from the crowd with his dagger. Margherita shouted out to Benedetto Cairoli, the Prime Minister of the day, who was seated opposite them in the coach, to leap across and take the blow (he was wounded while obeying the imperious command, but not seriously). The Queen then joined in the general drubbing of the lunatic assailant by pounding him with the only thing she had to hand, a bundle of posies held in her lap. The dramatic escape did wonders for the popular image of the newly acceded pair. It also put paid to a brief experiment in political permissiveness which Cairoli himself had indulged in, and for which he was now judged to be paying some divinely ordained penalty. He fell from power the following month and, for the rest of Humbert's reign, Conservatism held sway against Republicans and Socialists.

Rome now had an established social season revolving around a brilliant and imperious centre. The season began when Humbert lit the palace Christmas tree on 24 December and ended at the close of carnival time in the spring. Its high points were the court balls, when over a thousand guests crowded the Quirinal. The coarse muddle of

Victor Emmanuel's day was over and done with. The King and Queen would enter on the stroke of eleven to the sound of a royal fanfare. The opening quadrille was danced by couples selected in advance for their birth or distinction. Humbert, in contrast to his wife, was unimposing in physique and shy in manner, an unambitious plodder who seemed to derive little joy from his position. Indeed he once exclaimed, only half-jokingly, 'I would have made an excellent police inspector. That ought to have been my vocation!'[4]

Though that may have been a fair judgement on his native talents, it gave a false impression of bourgeois stolidity as regards his habits. Humbert's private life was far more reprehensible than his father's. Victor Emmanuel had at least stayed loyal to his 'Rosina', even defying both the court and the Vatican by taking her as his morganatic wife. The son was more fickle with his mistresses. He began with the Duchess Litta, a handsome woman seven years his senior who had ensnared him before his marriage and whom he then imported into the palace so that the affair might conveniently continue. (There was one awkward moment when the Queen and the Duchess, who were on predictably icy terms, appeared at a court ball, both wearing magnificent pearls given to them by the King.) But in the 1880s, when the Duchess was into her fifties, Humbert dropped her without compunction (though not without tantrums on her part) for other loves. The most ravishing of these was the widowed Countess Vincenza of Santa Fiore, 'La contessa fatale', as she was dubbed. Like the Duchess Litta, she too was a lady-in-waiting. There were times when Humbert treated the palace more like a handy trysting place than a seat of royal power and dignity.

Margherita's priorities were different. She revelled in putting the throne where it belonged and surrounding it with Italy's 'spiritual aristocracy' as well as with selected noblemen and officials un-swervingly loyal to the house of Savoy. The latter were political diehards almost to a man. One and all were subject to the novelty of a rigorously enforced etiquette. Three bows, made walking backwards, were prescribed for retiring from the royal presence. The Queen gave her own acknowledgement by making a long semicircular curtsy on entering or leaving the room; the gesture had been invented, it was said, by Marie Antoinette. As Humbert had a larger privy purse for his kingdom than Queen Victoria possessed for reigning over the British empire, there were funds enough for lavishness. No less an exacting critic than the future chancellor of Germany, Bernhard von Bülow, who served for four years (1893–97) as ambassador in Rome, was full of praise for Margherita's work:

The Italian court was well kept up. The King disposed of palaces in Rome and
Turin, Florence, Naples, Venice, Milan and Palermo which are among the
finest in the world. The household was brilliant and distinguished. The
courtiers were polite, and not in the least stiff or pompous.[5]

But he went on to stress that an Eulenburg or a Fürstenberg – those
courtiers whom we have seen in Berlin exercising great influence over
the monarch while remaining unaccountable either to the parliament
or government of the day – would have been unthinkable in Rome. The
household was essentially non-political, as symbolized by the King's
chief aide-de-camp, General Ponzio Vaglia, a plain soldier who did his
palace duties and no more. The Queen herself had the highest public
profile of anyone at court. Since she detested parliamentarians in
general and socialists in particular and nurtured in her salons the
spiritual leaders of the loyalist-nationalist camp, she might be said to
have exerted an indirect influence on the political scene, like some
brilliant light shining obliquely through a curtain. Her husband was
ruled out both by his passive temperament and his meagre talents from
any powerful role. Cavour had once said, comparing elected government with dynastic rule: 'The worst Chamber is better than the ante-
chamber.' Despite the vast power which the constitution had vested in
the monarchy, that maxim continued generally to apply. Whenever
strong leaders were at the helm, it was enforced without reservation.
The strongest of these in the Humbertian era, and one of the half-dozen
master builders in the long-term construction of the kingdom was
Crispi, an unusual man who had followed an unusually twisting path to
power. Though born in Sicily in 1819, he was of Albanian descent and
there was something of Balkan granite as well as Sicilian molten lava in
his make-up. He had started off as a semi-educated revolutionary, a
Garibaldian red equipped with the gift of demagogy and a boundless,
blustering self-confidence. He was, above all, an opportunist, prepared
to serve any cause that would further his personal ambition. When
Italy began to settle down under the monarchy, he decided that the
most promising and proper cause was the house of Savoy. His famous
phrase: 'The monarchy unites us; the republic would divide us',
marked the epitaph of his radicalism and the motto of his future
political career. His idol and would-be model was Bismarck, and it was
to the Iron Chancellor, among other European leaders, that, in August
of 1877, Victor Emmanuel dispatched his Sicilian devotee, then
minister of the interior, on one of the most hare-brained secret missions
of the century.

Foreign policy was, in theory, and occasionally in practice, a special
preserve of the Crown and now, in the last year of his reign and life and

with only the weak Cairoli as his Prime Minister, Victor Emmanuel suddenly lunged out in a bid to overturn the continental balance of power single-handed. One aim of Crispi's mission to London, Vienna and Berlin was to try and fish something for Italy out of the turmoil that had erupted in the Balkans with the Russo-Turkish war: if Austria were to make gains at the expense of the Ottoman empire, might not Italy be compensated with the 'unredeemed lands' of the Trentino and Trieste which were still part of the Habsburg monarchy? When put forward to the Concert of Europe by a raw and relatively weak newcomer, who had nothing to offer or command, the proposed bargain was utterly unrealistic. 'Take Albania', Disraeli snapped when Crispi told the English Prime Minister that his sovereign needed more territory.

If Crispi's first proposition was extravagant, his second, expounded only to Bismarck, was pure fantasy. Italy and Germany, according to Victor Emmanuel's plan, were to slice up the continent between them. Italy would get, in addition of course to Trentino and Trieste, parts of the old duchy of Savoy, including Nice, at the expense of France. Germany was to expand southwards into the Austrian lands and eastwards into Champagne and Burgundy. By this re-drawing of the map of Europe, Crispi wrote, Victor Emmanuel II hoped 'to crown his days with a victory which will give our army the power and prestige it lacks in the eyes of the world'.[6] The only effect of this political gibberish, duly presented to Bismarck at, of all places, the Austrian spa of Gastein, was to convince the Iron Chancellor that Victor Emmanuel must be mentally retarded and that Italy herself was something of a sick joke in the power game.

Nor did Italy fare any better when she paraded herself in more conventional style at the Congress of Berlin shortly afterwards. She desperately wanted to grab something out of that grand diplomatic mêlée and only pronounced her hands 'clean' after she had been forced to accept that they were empty. Her amateurish foreign minister, Count Corti, raised the question of the Trentino but got the same reply from Bismarck that Disraeli had given to Crispi: look to Albania instead. For Italy, the most worrying result of the congress was not that England expanded further into the Mediterranean by taking Cyprus, nor even that Austria had moved further south in the Balkans by occupying Bosnia-Herzegovina. It was that France was being encouraged to expand further into Africa, and notably into Tunisia. When the French duly went ahead and moved into Tunis two years later, the house of Savoy realized it must urgently find support against these colonial ambitions of its former ally, even if this meant joining the camp of its historic foe, Austria. Bismarck was always keen on burying hatchets all round once he had wielded and wiped clean his own Prussian one. Though he regarded Italy as a negligible addition to his Austro-German bloc, he was, therefore, prepared to have her in the Teutonic fold in order to smother the dangerous enmity between Rome and Vienna.

The outcome was the treaty, signed on 20 May 1882, by which Italy joined the central powers, thus turning the Dual Alliance into a triple one. There were special provisions concerning any further Austrian moves in the Balkans which were to play their role in the final and fatal crisis of old Europe in the summer of 1914. All that need be noted for the moment is the protection the treaty gave Italy against both her old enemy Austria and her new rival France. If Italy were attacked by France, the all-powerful Germany would come to her aid. Bismarck did not think much of the reciprocal pledge of Italian support: 'Our aim is to spare the forces of Austria rather than win those of Italy,' he noted at the time.[7] Moreover, as he had commented scornfully when Italy made her first approach to him: 'Her promise will prove valueless unless it is in her interest to keep it.'[8] In this, as in so many other matters, events were to prove the Iron Chancellor right.

For the time being, however, it was very much in Italy's interests to join sides with the most powerful military bloc on the continent, even if this did bring the house of Savoy into incongruous partnership with the house of Habsburg.* It meant that, henceforth, Italy was a fully-fledged entrant into the European power game. What she needed above all in the 1880s and 1890s to make her a fully-equipped player in that game was a colonial empire. This she set out to achieve, now that her mainland base on the continent was secured against both France and Austria. Still afraid to grab Libya, the one obvious major prize available in North Africa, the Italians started, remotely and modestly, by establishing bases at Assab and Massawa down the Red Sea. In 1887, when Crispi, aged sixty-seven, finally became Prime Minister for the first time, their East African adventure, together with much else, moved to a tumultuous climax.

Crispi was the political symbol of the Italy of his day: arrogant, naïve, oversensitive, overambitious, corrupt, immoral, the whole concoction kept aloft like a hot-air balloon with seemingly inexhaustible gusts of grandiloquent rhetoric. But he was, for all that, a great

---

* The alliance treaty had been preceded by a state visit paid by the Italian royal couple to Vienna in October 1881. It was something of a muddle from the very beginning where, on the platform of the South Railway Station, Franz Josef and Empress Elisabeth offered the customary Austrian embrace of a kiss on one cheek while their guests responded in Italian style by kissing on both. But this famous 'bacio di Vienna' had none the less been exchanged.

patriot and had now put aside his revolutionary ideas to become a devoted monarchist as well. Indeed, he dreamed of doing for the house of Savoy the glorious things that his idol, Bismarck (whom he continued to visit after the great man's fall) had done for the house of Hohenzollern. The Iron Chancellor, even more acerbic in retirement than he had been in office, was still unimpressed. The Italians, he remarked, had a large appetite but very poor teeth.

All the dangers inherent in the Italian predicament exploded, one after the other, under Crispi's feet. First, the feud with France culminated in an all-out trade war between the two Latin neighbours. Italy, with her basically agricultural economy, was by far the harder hit when the French barred imports of Italian oil, fruit and vegetables. Thousands of farmers were ruined and in Sicily the French boycott also delivered the last blow at an already declining sulphur industry. Economic ruin led to political turmoil. In the winter of 1893–94 the Sicilian volcano, which had been rumbling with unrest for two decades, finally erupted. Strikes turned into riots, riots led to arson and bloodshed. The peasants flocked to enrol in a movement known as the 'Fasci Siciliani'. It began to look as though Sicily, where Garibaldi had launched the unification of Italy three decades before, would become the place where his work would fall apart. The middle classes were alarmed and the court panic-striken by the power of this proletarian ferment.

Crispi, who had been temporarily out of office when the troubles first started, was recalled by a desperate King Humbert, proclaimed the 'man of the hour' and given all the emergency powers he needed to meet the challenge. The result was a swift and savage campaign of repression worthy of any embattled Caesar of old. Crispi despatched fifty thousand troops to his homeland, set up military tribunals with powers of summary justice, suspended all civil rights, suppressed all left-wing parties and closed down all inconvenient newspapers. In the seven months of the emergency a thousand Sicilians were jailed and a hundred times that number deprived of the right to vote. But by the summer of 1894 the authority of King and government had been restored. The victory had come very handily for Crispi in his private affairs, where it had helped to blot out well-documented accusations of his criminal involvement in recent banking scandals. In the political sphere he found himself re-launched – more prestigious, more ambitious, more thirsty for glory than ever. With the home front subdued, there was only one course that restlessness could take – across the seas to Africa.

To this course he was also being propelled by the generals. They had convinced the King and Queen that the army needed a battle. It was getting larger and larger all the time, yet had nothing more heroic to do than guard the Alps (against the allied Austrians as well as the hostile French) and wage civil war against Sicilian peasants. Moreover, the humiliation of an East African defeat at Dogali in 1887, when a column of five hundred Italian soldiers from Massawa had been wiped out after venturing into the Ethiopian interior, still remained to be avenged.

They made the same mistake nine years later when, after attempting to set up the Ethiopian ruler, Menelik, as their political pawn, the Italians again forsook their Red Sea bases and drove inland to crush him by force. It was one of the most disastrous military bungles of the century. Crispi held all the strings in his hands in Rome, telling neither his ministers nor his cipher of a commander-in-chief, King Humbert, what he was about. As the Prime Minister was himself now seventy-five years old, and was as muddled as he was devious, those strings got steadily more entangled. Instead of receiving sufficient funds and clear directions, all that the East African commander General Baratieri got from Crispi was a stream of telegrams taunting him with timidity. The breaking-point came when the hapless general heard that the Prime Minister had determined to replace him. Throwing patience and prudence to the winds, he led almost his entire command across country to the heights above Adowa, where Menelik's army was encamped. The Italian brigades, cut off from their Red Sea bases and operating in unknown terrain with faulty maps and treacherous guides, were easy meat for the Ethiopian forces. At a series of engagements fought on 1 March 1896 they were separated and cut to pieces a column at a time. Though Baratieri escaped to tell the doleful tale, six thousand of his men were killed. As a modern authority has put it: 'In one single day, as many Italians lost their lives as in all the wars of *Risorgimento* put together.'[9]

Though Adowa was far from being the end of Italy's colonial adventures, it was the end of Francesco Crispi. From being the toast of Italy he became, overnight, its shame as the nation unloaded all its own complexes and frustrations over his head. In vain did his staunchest champion, Queen Margherita, urge the King to keep him on and mount a bigger and better expedition of revenge against Menelik. For once, Humbert ignored the advice. A major disaster demanded a major scapegoat if the prestige of the army and the Crown were not to be totally undermined. Crispi was dropped and went, broken and bitter, into retirement. Ironically, the Sicilians he had tyrannized were the only people who continued to sing his praises, right down to his death in 1901.

By then the Humbertian era had itself come to a violent end. Italians were already established as the great assassins of the day. It was an Italian, Ieronimo Caserio, who had stabbed the president of the French Republic, M. Carnot, to death at Lyon on 24 June 1894; four years later the Empress Elisabeth of Austria had fallen to the dagger of Luigi Luccheni on the shores of Lake Geneva. Now, another Italian fanatic turned his weapon on his own sovereign. On Sunday 29 July 1900, Gaetano Bresci, a thirty-year-old peasant's son who had embraced the cause of revolution while working in America, pumped three bullets into King Humbert as the monarch was driving away, unguarded, from an evening gymnastic display at Monza. By the time the royal coach reached the nearby palace, where his unsuspecting Queen was waiting, Humbert the Good was dead. Margherita had been the royal symbol and inspiration of that blinkered authoritarianism for which he had been killed. During a brief interregnum she now presided alone over a régime which had only a few hours to live. Nothing was left undone to try and create a legend out of this worthy but totally unremarkable monarch who had died, in her own grandiloquent words, in 'the crime of the century'. The only concession she made in private to the frailty of her husband was to allow his long-term mistress, Duchess Litta, to spend a few moments alone with his corpse.

The interregnum had come about because the new King, at sea on his yacht, could not be traced for a day and a half. Victor Emmanuel was sailing around the Aegean with the bride he had married four years before. She, as we know from the saga of King Nikita and his family, was Elena Petrovich of Montenegro. Though it had not seemed a brilliant match for the heir to the Italian throne, there was much which had made it plausible. To begin with, it was time to put a stop to the inbreeding in the house of Savoy and seek some new virile blood which this statuesque daughter of the Black Mountains could certainly provide. There was also, to put in the reckoning, the physical appearance of Victor Emmanuel, the product of that inbreeding. The puny infant of 1869 had grown up to be an insignificant midget of a man, barely five foot tall. Even built-up heels and high-peaked military caps could not produce an acceptable royal figure, and his Montenegrin bride always towered over him like a giraffe. Such was the strangely assorted couple who, escorted by torpedo boats, came ashore at Reggio Calabria on 31 July as the new King and Queen of Italy.

Victor Emmanuel III, as he was styled, was the most spiteful, as well as the meanest-favoured, of his line. He was also, though erudite and not unintelligent, the dullest of them, if his private hobbies were any guide. His chief passion, apart from hunting, was collecting coins. The brilliance of Margherita's court was extinguished accordingly. Gone were the three bows and the glittering balls. The palace took on an atmosphere more like the villa of a worthy '*grand bourgeois*'. Indeed, he did move his Roman home to a villa, the Villa Ada, a modest country house set in ten acres of forest on the hills overlooking the capital. The Quirinal he treated as his office. To begin with he travelled to and from it with the regularity of any business commuter. Later, when he realized that Italy, when not in acute crisis, more or less ran herself, the absences grew longer.

The little King's dislike of what he called 'high society' was fixed partly by the realization that he could never cut a dash in it himself. But there was also his prim moral disapproval of its idleness and infidelities. Royal mistresses, an established feature of court life since the birth of the kingdom forty years before, disappeared from the scene promptly and for good with his accession. Victor Emmanuel remained devoted to his Montenegrin princess throughout a long, happy and fruitful marriage that was rare in the Europe of his (or any) day. His love for her managed to show itself even in the most formal of settings. At the state banquets which they were obliged to give for foreign royalties, he issued strict orders that the flower arrangements should be placed low enough so that he could always see his wife across the table.[10]

Elena's own tastes and character matched and intensified this domesticity of the new court. She was never happier than in the rustic Villa Ada (which they renamed Villa Savoia) cooking meals herself for the King and even helping their few servants with the housework. She was, on the other hand, never truly at ease in the formal world of the Quirinal palace, over which her mother-in-law had so resplendently presided. The Queen Mother and the King's cousin, the handsome Duke of Aosta, henceforth provided all the brilliance that was to be found in the royal scene. Indeed, for some years the Duke (who was married to the high-born Princess Hélène of Orleans) could hope to provide the succession to the throne as well. It was not until June 1901, five years after their wedding and a year after their accession, that Elena produced her first child and that was only a girl, Yolanda, to be followed a year later by another girl, Mafalda. Only in September 1904 did a son appear at last; the infant, christened Humbert, assumed the Savoyard succession in the direct male line.* Their growing absorption with family life made the little King and his Montenegrin wife (dismissed as 'a shepherdess' by the Duchess of Aosta) even less

---

* He ruled for a bare thirty-four days in 1946 before being deposed after a referendum. In all Elena bore her husband one son and four daughters, one of whom, Joanna, married King Boris of Bulgaria.

enthusiastic about their duties at court. Madame Waddington, the American wife of a prominent French diplomat who left several volumes of memoirs behind her, declared on a visit to Rome in the year of Humbert's birth that the Quirinal was now so unlike a royal palace that one might well have gone to the wrong house. As for the great carnival ball in February of 1904, it was 'extraordinarily simple, if not democratic'.

Democratic was precisely what Rome had become, much to the distaste of this transplanted daughter of the greatest democracy. Victor Emmanuel had watched his father's most effective prime ministers, Depretis and Crispi, either juggling with or blatantly suppressing the country's growing socialist movement. His father's assassination by a revolutionary fanatic seemed to him to sound the death-knell of all such policies as well. Henceforth, the monarchy would survive and flourish only by liberal, even populist policies in the economic and social fields. This meant that he as king must put aside his absolutist prerogatives and appear as the very opposite of a haughty *Roi Soleil*. When a byzantine courtier of the old school, discussing the ravages of Italian earthquakes and floods, once assured Victor Emmanuel that his presence alone would bring relief to his suffering subjects, the little King brusquely replied: '*Non diciamo sciocchezze*' ('Let's not talk rubbish!').[11] That was the mood of his '*Roma democratica*'.

The King was fortunate to find, in Giovanni Giolitti, the perfect statesman for his political tastes. Giolitti had headed the government for a few months in 1892–93 under King Humbert before returning as a long-serving Prime Minister in 1903. Indeed, as he held that office, with two short breaks, right down to 1914, this can properly be called the Giolittian decade of Italian politics, years when the King withdrew, quite contentedly, from the centre of the national stage. Giolitti, who was sixty-one when his great era began, was a northerner, descended from a long line of Piedmontese bureaucrats on his father's side and a family of assorted liberals on his mother's. He himself had entered politics through the civil service and, in many ways, he ran the country like the permanent secretary of a great department of state. What mattered to him above all else was that the machinery of government should function efficiently for the maximum good of the country. To this end friction had to be minimized, extremist views reconciled, enemies blandished, supporters rewarded, force used only when legally authorized and strictly necessary, and everyone sucked up and held fast by self-interest in the system over which he presided.

Though a man of the left, he was in fact a man without party, almost without partisan feeling, let alone passion. Social justice was needed not so much as a moral imperative regardless of the consequences but because it made economic and political sense. The old policies of reaction had only weakened the nation by dividing it. The landless peasants and the factory workers of a burgeoning industry were dangerous to crown and country only if excluded from public life; let them in and give them responsibility, Giolitti argued, and they will in turn become conservative because they will have a material stake of their own to defend. It was all a far cry from the heady rhetoric of Crispi and the bigoted conservatism of the court in Queen Margherita's heyday. But, for a while, Italy seemed content to relax under this regime of calm and pragmatic liberalism. Giolitti himself was a relaxing, fatherly figure. 'Tall and broad-shouldered, wearing a T-shaped white moustache and goatee [beard] he lacked – when as almost always he appeared in his broad-brimmed fedora and his Uncle Sam coat – only a cigar and a tumbler to complete his resemblance to a Kentucky colonel.'[12]

The military picture is not inappropriate. By a careful tactic, adapted to any new emergency, Giolitti rarely failed to marshal a sufficient army of supporters in the assembly. Where persuasion failed, bribery was used, both at the polls and in the distribution of office. If a ministerial post was the price of keeping a faction happy, a place would be found in his government for the relevant nominee. He wooed the Socialists by accepting the minimum reform programme set out in their 1900 congress in Rome. When they proved sulky, he made overtures to the clerical right, even backing down on a bill to legalize divorce just to keep the ardent Catholics in his ranks. When unrest appeared on the streets (and he faced a serious general strike in 1904) he surmounted even this challenge like a cautious commonsense bureaucrat. Where the impetuous Crispi sent the troops in, Giolitti merely put them on display until tempers cooled.

It all added up to a decade of parliamentary dictatorship in which impressive results were achieved all round. His social reforms in the field of taxation, public health, industrial welfare and education culminated in the great universal suffrage act of 1911–12, under which all males who were either ex-servicemen or over thirty were given the vote, thus raising the electorate at a stroke from three to eight million. The Giolittian age was also – despite its crop of financial scandal and spectacular bankruptcies – a decade of economic boom. Italy had never been too far below Concert of Europe standards as regards population, and by Giolitti's time she had reached thirty-five million. Her crippling lack was of natural energy supplies – in those days primarily coal – to fuel her industry. Even Crispi and Giolitti between them could not raise

Italian coal production to more than a beggarly million tons a year, compared with Germany's 277 million and the 292 million of Britain (from whom she imported 90 per cent of her needs). But hydroelectric power began to make its serious contribution in the first years of the new century.* Output rose, wages rose and – miracle of miracles by Italian standards – for ten consecutive years the national budget actually showed a surplus. Only one thing was lacking in Giolitti's efficient beehive; the taste of dramatic glory. For a people like the Italians, with their worship of the *bella figura*, it was a deficiency which could not be denied for long.

It was inevitable, given the prevailing background of the 'scramble for Africa', that Italy would one day join that scramble full tilt by grabbing Libya. It was, to begin and to end with, the only prize which could bring consolation and self-respect after the disaster at Adowa which was itself supposed to have brought victorious revenge for the earlier Eritrean defeat at Dogali. This compounded humiliation throbbed like a boil and had to be lanced if the body politic were ever to feel at ease. Gradually the very fact that Giolitti operated so quickly and unobtrusively came, in this context, to be held against him. The critics who derided him for creating an '*Italietta*', a 'Little Italy' of bourgeois materialism and narrow horizons, grew steadily louder and drew more and more applause. Though prosperous, the country became convinced that it was bored.

During Giolitti's time Italy had greatly increased her economic stake in Libya, mainly through the investment of the Banco di Roma. But this peaceful penetration was dismissed as effeminate unworthy stuff by the patriotic agitators. Their cause received a powerful boost when in 1910 the nationalist movement turned itself into a People's party at an emotional launching congress in Florence. Men like Prezzolini, Corradini and Papini formed the political leadership of the new party, which had nailed the cause of imperialism to its banner. But its real inspiration came from that genius among windbags, and lord among libertines, the Italian poet Gabriele d'Annunzio. From his exile in France, d'Annunzio, in books like his 'Songs of Death and Glory', called on his countrymen to act as something they yearned to be but could never become: Nietzschian supermen. He both symbolized and nurtured all that was deadliest in the Italian spirit, the pathetic yearning for recognition, for a glory that would smother the realization of their own inadequacies. How that glory was to be achieved was never

---

* Output rose from 100 million kilowatt hours in 1898 to a massive 2.5 billion by 1914, helping to feed the rapidly growing automobile industries, like Fiat, in the north.

spelt out by this demon calling from afar. His exhortation to his fellow-countrymen to 'man the prow and sail towards the world', summed up the bombastic vagueness of his message.

By 1911, however, other factors had set both the sailing time and the course for d'Annunzio's golden barque. Patriotic hysteria had mounted with the fiftieth anniversary of Italy's unification under the Savoyard monarchy. To mark the half century, the little King had inaugurated in March the huge and hideous monument to his grandfather, Victor Emmanuel II, which was to disfigure the skyline of Rome from that day to this. But the decisive impulse for action came four months later, from North Africa itself, and arose out of the squabbles of the other colonial powers. On 1 July, Franco-German rivalry in Morocco, which had flared up six years before with the Kaiser's famous horseback ride in Tangier, became inflamed again when a German gunboat, the *Panther*, dropped anchor in Agadir harbour, ostensibly to protect the lives of German subjects there threatened by unrest. A major international crisis erupted and diplomatic calm was only restored in November, when Germany backed down over France's claims in Morocco in return for one hundred thousand square miles of the French Congo. Giolitti could not afford to wait that long. He knew, as soon as France and Germany fell openly at each other's throats in Morocco, that a unique moment had arrived for Italy to make her long-meditated move into Libya. Such were the imperialist *mores* of the day that no European power would have felt anything but puzzled contempt for Italy had she acted otherwise. It was Giolitti's calculating mind which drove him into the adventure, not a heroic heart. He fought his wars overseas as he had fought his reform campaign at home, because it made compelling commonsense at the time.

Few episodes show Italy's King in such a faint and feeble glow as the Libyan war of 1911–12. He was opposed to the whole idea (mainly, it seems, because the Italian Socialist party, on whom he thought his crown depended, had come out, almost in isolation, against it). It was Giolitti who personally prepared the campaign in great secrecy with San Giuliano, his capable foreign secretary, and the general staff, during the midsummer months, when the King was mostly out of the capital. It was Giolitti who, at the end of September, finally talked the monarch into sending an ultimatum to Turkey, the nominal suzerain of Libya.[13] The King concurred in the most Giolittian manner by agreeing that this would perhaps be 'in the best interests of the country'.[14]

If Victor Emmanuel had cut a reluctant figure in the run-up to the war, the little ruler in the toy-blue uniform remained almost insignificant while it was being waged. He never once set foot on the battlefield, and it was left to his cousin, the Duke degli Abruzzi, to show the colours of Savoy in action, by leading an Italian fleet to an early naval victory against a Turkish flotilla. That quick success, accompanied by initial military advances along the coast, proved, however, a false harbinger. To the surprise of the Italian commander (the unenterprising General Caneva, who was more used to manoeuvres in the Po Valley) twenty-five thousand indigenous Arab guerrillas joined the Turkish garrison forces in putting up determined resistance. Despite the annexation of Libya by royal decree in November – another bold initiative which Giolitti had to drag out of the King – a year of bloody stalemate unfolded in the desert.

'*Tripoli-Trappola*' (a trap); the cry was heard at home while Italy's allies scoffed. As the German ambassador in Rome wrote to his chancellor, Bethmann-Hollweg: 'Since people have seen that the African adventure is not just a carnival caper and that the Arabs don't shoot with confetti but with bullets, popular enthusiasm is dying down.'[15]

The enthusiasm waned still further – both of Italians for their own war and of the outside world for Italy – when Caneva's army, goaded by costly ambushes, began to take terrible reprisals against the Arab irregulars. The liberal Italian image, so carefully preserved in the consciences of the Western democracies, was shattered.

In the autumn of 1912, diplomacy came to Caneva's rescue and the Concert of Europe pulled Italy out of the '*Trappola*'. After three months of niggling peace talks in Switzerland, Turkey was persuaded to recognize Italy's rule over Libya and the Dodecanese islands (Rhodes had been taken by Italian forces in May of that year) in return for a large cash indemnity. The Treaty of Lausanne, signed on 18 October, brought the crisis to a formal end.* The reason why four powers from both camps – Germany, Austria, France and England – brought pressure on Turkey to yield was the war which had just erupted in the Balkans, triggered off by Montenegro's attack against the Ottoman garrison there. The course of this Balkan war has been fully recounted elsewhere. What remains to be noted here is how each phase in the death and dismemberment of the Turkish empire was interlocked. This new conflict which had engulfed Turkey-in-Europe speeded the settlement of the war over Turkey-in-Africa. But it was the Italian attack against Libya in 1911 which had encouraged the Balkan states in

---

* Italy was recognized as the *de facto* political sovereign, while the Sultan retained his not unimportant religious authority.

the first place to band together and draw their swords against the engulfed Sultan a year later. Italy's victory in Libya, won at such a heavy cost in blood, treasure and prestige, thus also became one of the chain of fuses which led to the Great War.

Italy's posture as Europe drifted towards that holocaust symbolized both the character and the predicament of the nation. She approached the final crisis upside down, yet signalling wildly to both rival camps that she was, in fact, right side up. The fundamental nonsense was the partnership with Austria – however qualified by special reservations – through membership of the Triple Alliance. When the little King's collateral ancestor Charles Felix of Savoy, had died in 1831, his death-bed instructions to his successor, Charles Albert, supposedly consisted of two words: 'Hate Austria!'[16] That message could never be smothered under a diplomatic parchment which Italy had only signed because of her sudden friendlessness in the colonial contest with France; there was simply too much to keep that hate alive. The '*Tedeschi*', as the Italians called them, had been the prime enemy throughout the struggle for unification. They still sat in the South Tyrol (Alto Adige for Italy) and Trieste, which had to be wrested from them if that unification were to be completed. The irredentist drive to secure those territories had received fresh impetus from the rise of the Italian Nationalist party and the inspired claptrap of demagogues like d'Annunzio. As regards Trieste, feeling began to run even higher when, in August of 1913, the Austrian governor of Trieste, Prince Conrad Hohenlohe, issued his inflammatory decrees which sacked from civil office all Italians who did not hold Austrian nationality.

By this time, as we have seen in the context of the Balkan wars, the rivalry between Rome and Vienna stretched right down the Adriatic. Because of his beloved Elena (and that was about her only influence on Italy's foreign affairs) Victor Emmanuel III always espoused the interests of his Montenegrin father-in-law, King Nikita, and that meant working against the interests of the Habsburg empire. There was a similar clash of interests over Albania, a natural target for Italian expansion.* Indeed, in the wake of Austria's fateful annexation of Bosnia-Herzegovina, Italy had even come to a secret agreement with the great rival of her Habsburg ally, Nicholas II of Russia, on co-ordinated policies towards 'the European East'. This was the so-called Racconigi Bargain of October 1909, named after the castle south of

---

* Benito Mussolini converted the long-cherished prospect into reality by invading the country over Easter of 1939, still under the standard of the same little King.

Turin where the Tsar had visited Victor Emmanuel. (It was the two foreign ministers, the vengeful Izvolski and Tommaso Tittoni, and not the two sovereigns, who had inspired the idea.)

Italy kept the Racconigi pact a secret from her Triple Alliance partners and Austria was temporarily put off the scent by Tittoni signing a more or less identical agreement with Vienna only a few days later! But even before suspicions were aroused as to anything Italy had put on paper with the rival camp, the Italians had been written off, by both Germany and Austria, as an effective or reliable ally. Among the hawks of Vienna, the contempt verged on the vitriolic. 'A useless force' was how the Austrian chief of staff, General Conrad von Hötzendorff, described the country which had signed the paper alliance. It must be added that both he and the Austrian heir, Archduke Franz Ferdinand (who detested Hungarians, Italians and French in that order), did all they could to expose it as a farce. The Archduke refused outright even his Emperor's pleadings to visit Rome and so put some semblance of dynastic blessing on the diplomatic link. As for General Conrad, so far from backing Italy over the Libyan war, he actually urged a preventive attack against her while she was preoccupied in the African deserts. (He had even advised similar action when Italy was distracted by the great earthquakes of Reggio and Messina.) The Italians were well aware of these views and of the danger they represented. As a result, throughout the Libyan campaign they did not withdraw one man from those divisions which faced Austria in the north. These defences, it is worth noting, were strengthened in 1912 by a 'Maginot Line' of about one thousand steel pillboxes, manufactured mainly in France![17] Such was the grotesque background to the last formal renewal of Italy's membership of the Triple Alliance on 5 December of that same year.

Germany, though always sceptical of what Chancellor Bülow had described as Italy's perpetual '*Giri di Walzer*', did what she could to keep her in the fold, following Bismarck's original precept of ensuring damage limitation for the main ally, Austria. The Kaiser was particularly active as a goodwill broker. Always true to form, the German emperor had mortally offended the little King by turning up on a state visit with an escort of herculean grenadiers who seemed to have been hand-picked to emphasize his host's diminutive stature. But, the predictable jests apart, the Kaiser tried right to the end both to bring the houses of Savoy and Habsburg closer together and to draw Italy more deeply into the military network of the alliance. In September 1913, for example, he received all three chiefs of staff after their attendance at the German autumn manoeuvres to discuss what concrete pledge of help Italy could give. The result was Italy's promise, in March of 1914, to send two cavalry divisions to help Germany fight on the Rhine.

The Kaiser's last idea was to combine military with dynastic fusion by inviting Victor Emmanuel III and Franz Ferdinand to meet at joint naval exercises of the Triple Alliance.[18] The date envisaged was the autumn of 1914.

Part Three

MONARCHIES ON THE WINGS

Chapter Eleven

RUSSIA: THE ALIEN GIANT

Two things about imperial Russia troubled the other European powers. The first was dynastic and was summed up by Queen Victoria in a letter to her eldest daughter in Berlin soon after 'Vicky' had married the Prussian Crown Prince Frederick. 'The Romanoffs', the Queen declared contemptuously, 'are not to be compared with the houses of Brunswick, Saxony and Hohenzollern.'[1] If the 'Grandmother of Europe' could place three German kingdoms, two of them light-weights in political terms, ahead of the court at St Petersburg, how could the Romanovs be compared with her own ancient crown, or that of the Habsburgs? The lineage of the Russian ruling family did indeed leave something to be desired. It only dated from 1613 when Michael, the sickly sixteen-year-old son of Fyodor Romanov, became the new Tsar. Moreover, far from inheriting the throne through marriage or from the extinction of an affiliated line, he had been elected at a time of chaos and crisis by a coalition of Cossacks, army commanders and 'boyars'. In that same year James I sat on the Stuart throne of England which, through the Tudors and the Plantagenets, stretched back to the Middle Ages in one complex yet connected royal line. As for the Habsburgs, whose house had borne the same name ever since its foundation, they could look back, in 1613, on nearly three and a half centuries of continuous rule and were eventually, in 1758, to become Apostolic Majesties to boot, reigning thus by God's grace as well as by descent.

The second troubling aspect of Romanov Russia was far more important: its essential foreignness. This was stamped firmly enough on the dynasty itself. The other great courts of Europe had been linked for centuries (*mésalliances* apart) by marriages between a hundred or so royal and princely houses, all of which, Protestant or Catholic, reigning

or mediatized, had a cosily familiar ring. But what was one to make of
these Romanovs and, even more, of the much older house of Rurik
which had preceded them, with names like the princes of Uglich,
Mozhaisk and Rylsk, the grand dukes of Suzdal, the khans of Polovtsky
in its lineage – to say nothing of the one imperial entrant, none other
than John VIII Paleologus, Emperor of Constantinople? A family tree
full of such weird and exotic branches remained remote in its roots even
after it began to put out welcoming offshoots to West European courts.

This process had started in the early eighteenth century when the
dynasty was almost exactly a century old. The genealogical table of the
Romanovs was transformed with almost brutal suddenness. Its
monotonous sequence of outlandish Slav titles was broken for good
when, within the space of twenty years, German names (most of them
equally outlandish, especially to a Slav) came to predominate instead.
Princess Charlotte of Brunswick-Wolfenbüttel was the first to enter the
picture in 1711, closely followed by Duke Frederick of Holstein-
Gottorp in 1725. Württembergs, Saxe-Weimars, Oldenburgs and
Hesse-Darmstadts followed (among others) in phalanxes over the
following generations as the Russian house became genetically more of
a German one.

This startlingly rapid dynastic blood change was the counterpart,
indeed the product, of equally startling transformations in the political
and cultural scenes. In the thirty-six years (1689–1725) of his reign,
Peter the Great (the first tsar to be styled 'emperor') tried – and partly
succeeded – in turning Russia from an Asiatic into a European state.
He himself travelled to Western Europe in search of the tools and
technical skills needed to modernize his country. Equally unprecedented for a Romanov, he built a navy, which, in itself, signalled an opening
to the wider world. To symbolize and perpetuate the shift in Russia's
centre of gravity, he moved the capital to St Petersburg on the Gulf of
Finland, where thirty thousand labourers perished building, upon a
chain of nineteen islands, a stupendous array of ministries for his
bureaucrats, mansions for his courtiers, and palaces for himself. In
appearance, it was a city of the western Catholic world, not the eastern
Orthodox one. St Petersburg was not dubbed 'the Venice of the north'
for nothing. Italian architects like Rossi and Quarenghi and the
massive, elaborate balance of their baroque style had stamped their
hallmark on it. The Cathedral of Our Lady of Kazan was modelled
after the great basilica of St Peter in the Vatican, a tribute to the
Church of Rome which would have been regarded as little short of
blasphemy by the rulers of old Muscovy.

Peter even tried to change the life-style of his subjects by decree, ordering his nobility, for example, to copy everything Western from shaving off their beards to drinking coffee rather than tea, all in an attempt to make Europeanized gentlemen out of them. From here it was a steady progress to a nineteenth-century court, which was not only fluent in English, French and German, but often spoke them better than its native Russian and, worse still, thought in a mixture of the cultures.

The end result was a schizophrenic nation, uncertain of its own identity at home and fitting in nowhere abroad. The novelist Joseph Conrad, himself a blend of spirits, captured the essence of this Russian floundering in a famous essay written in 1905:

This despotism has neither a European nor an Oriental parentage: more, it seems to have no root in either the institutions or the follies of this earth. . . . It is like a visitation, like a curse from heaven falling in the darkness of ages on the immense plains of forest and steppe lying dumbly on the confines of two continents: a true desert harbouring no Spirit either of the East or the West.[2]

However 'western' the St Petersburg of the Romanovs became, Russia itself remained, in the European conscience, part of that heathen Slavic menace against which the Teutonic knights had fought for centuries. The reverse of this perception was equally deeply etched in the Russian psyche: images of the time before Peter I when Muscovy, as the seat of the world's only independent Orthodox ruler, was held by its leaders to be the world's only truly Christian kingdom, fighting the double schisms of the Catholics and the Protestants to the West.

A great Polish-born novelist, writing in impeccable English, has just been quoted describing the rootless nature – alien to all other European systems – of Russian despotism. But it was a Russian intellectual, Peter Chaadayev, writing seventy years before Conrad, who first put on paper for his fellow-countrymen some of the harsh truths about their irrelevance and isolation as a nation:

Situated between the two great divisions of the world, between East and West, one elbow resting on China, the other on Germany, we should be able . . . to embrace in our own culture the histories of the whole world. But this is not the role that Providence has assigned to us. . . . The experience of the ages has meant nothing to us. . . . Alone among the peoples of the world, we have given nothing to the world, we have learned nothing from the world. We have contributed nothing to the progress of the human mind, we have only disfigured it. There is something in our blood which rejects all true progress. . . . Today, we are nothing but a lacuna in the intellectual order.[3]

As though to hammer home the point he was making, Chaadayev had

written *his* famous essay in impeccable French. The tsar of the day,
Nicholas I, convinced that he must be mad, placed him under house
arrest and ordered special medical supervision.

This silenced Chaadayev; but the tormented debate between the
'Westernizers' and the 'Slavophiles' which his words touched off
continued, sometimes on the surface, sometimes just beneath it, until
the end of the Romanov empire. It entered the political arena with the
question: should Russia go back to the old-style paternalist rule of the
tsars before Peter the Great, or go forward with the foreign experiments
he had introduced and the giant bureaucracy he had interposed
between monarch and people? It invaded, just as powerfully, the
diplomatic field, for the worship of all things Slav, and the desire to
protect and promote them, also fed the nationalist springs of pan-
Slavism in the Balkans.

In both domestic and foreign affairs, the Russian giant had limped
awkwardly through the nineteenth century. Serfdom (which, per-
versely, had not begun to emerge until the middle of the fifteenth
century, at a time when it was on the wane elsewhere) was not
abolished until 1861 as part of the reforms of the liberal-minded
Alexander II. Even when it belatedly came about, emancipation proved
a messy compromise, which left all of the conservative landlords and
many of the newly-created smallholders dissatisfied. The same surge of
reforms saw the establishment of a European-style judiciary in Russia,
with proper procedures for appeal. Local and provincial administration was also transformed with the setting up of new types of
assemblies, the so-called 'zemstvos', where the peasants had representation of their own, even if the landlords still dominated the scene.

These seeds, sown by the humane and well-intentioned Tsar,
produced some poisonous fruit. Revolutionary terrorism sprang into
being in Russia alongside the great reforms. As so often, long overdue
concessions from the rulers were judged by the ruled not so much by
what they gave as by what was still left to give. Above all else, the
clamour grew for reform in the central apparatus of national government which even the progressive Alexander II had been careful to keep
as his own autocratic preserve. The university students, influenced by
Western socialist ideas, took their revolutionary creed, first to the
grumbling peasantry and then to the factory workers of Russia's
burgeoning industry. One wing of their new 'Land and Freedom' party
favoured gradual and basically peaceful transformation of the old
order. Its radical rivals, who split off as the so-called 'People's Will',
chose the shorter and bloodier route of assassination. On 13 March
1881 this faction claimed its prime victim when Alexander II was fatally

wounded by an anarchist's bomb, hurled as part of a carefully-planned multiple street ambush in St Petersburg. By an irony typical of the Russian scene, the murdered Tsar had signed, only a few hours before, another set of potentially deeper reforms which touched the constitution itself. The measures were buried with his mutilated body.

Russia's relations with the Concert of Europe which had emerged after the defeat of Napoleon were just as tortuous as her development at home. True to Chaadayev's verdict, she always seemed the odd one out. She waged repeated wars against the Ottoman empire but, as we have seen, the most ambitious of these, the Crimean War of 1853–56, ended in defeat at the hands of England and France; while after the most successful, the Balkan campaign of 1878, the spoils of battle had been taken away from her by international pressure. It was this painful experience at the Congress of Berlin which drove home to the Tsar and his ministers how vulnerable Russia was in her isolation, and the conclusion of the Dual Alliance between Germany and Austria a year later only deepened this feeling of lonely unease. Apart from the shaky monarchical bond of the League of Three Emperors, her only link with the rest of Europe was in Bismarck's secret 'Re-insurance Treaty'; and when the Iron Chancellor fell from power in 1890 and the line to St Petersburg was left dangling by his successors,* Russia's sense of isolation became intolerable. New alignments were forming in Europe and she would either have to involve herself in them, or be crushed by them.

It was at this point that the dynasty came to play a crucial role in shaping Russia's destiny. The tsar of the day was Alexander III. He was an ox of a man who could tie pokers into knots and rip packs of cards in half with his hands. His broad six-foot-three frame was topped by a high-domed head out of which two large blue eyes gazed confidently, almost contemptuously, at the world around him. It was the face of a born despot, and the terrible fate which had overtaken his father lessened any inclination to temper these natural leanings. The reactionary influence of his former tutor, Constantin Pobedonostsev, the procurator of the Holy Synod, did the rest.

The iron-hard pattern of the new reign was set in the accession manifesto: 'The voice of God commands us to stand resolutely by the task of governing, relying on Divine Providence, with faith in the strength and truth of autocratic power which we have been summoned to enforce and protect against all encroachments for the good of the

* See supra, p. 96.

people.'[4] Whether in the fields of education, justice or local government, the reformist wheel was spun sharply back. Those who had striven with his father to move it forward, like the Grand Duke Constantine, abandoned the struggle and, in his case, departed in voluntary exile to Paris.

But if the hand of Alexander III suppressed all movement at home, it set Russia on an historic new course abroad, and it was his own likes and dislikes, as much as political considerations, which provided the impulse. We are dealing here with a pure example of personal dynastic diplomacy. His was a complex personality, taciturn, brooding, distrustful and given to bouts of prolonged idleness. But one of the biggest riddles of his make-up was his loathing of the Germans, which we have already seen displayed in his fierce opposition to the election of Prince 'Sandro' Battenberg as Prince of Bulgaria.* Reaction to his father's regime, which had included many Baltic-German officials, may have played a part. So, almost certainly, did his resentment against Bismarck, which dated from the Prusso-Danish war of 1864. (There is an interesting parallel here with the Prince of Wales in England. Alexander III, like the future King Edward, was married to a daughter of King Christian of Denmark, and the Empress Dagmar of Russia, like her sister, the future Queen Alexandra of England, did everything in her power to egg her husband on against Prussia.)

But what probably sealed the matter for the Tsar was that he simply could not stand his bombastic cousin, William II, who had succeeded to the Hohenzollern throne in 1888, seven years after his own accession. Alexander had to be dragged even to the briefest of encounters with the German Kaiser, and avoided them whenever possible. The League of the Three Emperors had lapsed in 1887, largely due to conflicts of interests in the Balkans, but, as far as Alexander's personal feelings were concerned, it became a non-starter from the moment one of those emperors was William II. Again, there is a parallel with the Heir-Apparent's sentiments in England. But whereas, in the 1890s, the Prince of Wales could do no more than express distrust of a Prussian-dominated Germany and distaste for his brilliantly awful nephew who ruled it, Alexander could translate his feelings into action.

The Tsar, through ministers whom he could appoint and sack at will, controlled foreign policy as he controlled everything else in his country and there was, as yet, no Parliament or National Assembly to question his decisions. Though not often seen on the bridge, it was he who now set Russia's course.

* See *supra*, p. 48.

The minister whose task was to orchestrate the move towards France was Nikolai Giers. He was an experienced seventy-year-old diplomatist whom the Tsar had kept in charge of the Foreign Office in St Petersburg since 1882. The political climate in Paris was propitious. For the entire French nation, the humiliation of the crushing defeat of 1870 at Bismarck's hands remained an open wound that no scar would ever cover until the lost provinces of Alsace and Lorraine were won back. Much had been done over recent years to give France some semblance of the military muscle needed to gain her vengeance. Charles de Freycinet was the man who, as minister of war, had expanded the French army, reorganizing and re-equipping it from top to bottom. Now, in the spring of 1890, only a few weeks after Bismarck's fall, he had once again become French Premier, with Alexandre Ribot as his foreign minister. Neither came to office as a compulsive Russophile. Indeed, Freycinet had angered the Tsar on more than one occasion in the past while, had it not been for Anglo-French tensions in Egypt, Ribot would just as soon have sought closer ties with London as with St Petersburg. But the popular mood, foaming under a new wave of chauvinism, was all for an alliance with Russia and the government soon rode on top of it. A significant step forward came in May of 1890 when the French police swooped on a gang of exiled Russian revolutionaries and arrested them in the act of manufacturing bombs which were doubtless intended for the Tsar and his advisers. Alexander III immediately conveyed his formal thanks. The air was clearing.

The way in which, from now on, the Tsar constantly prodded his ministers down the road to Paris is one of the most remarkable features in the making of this Franco-Russian alliance. It was the Tsar who brushed aside Giers's fears over the abandonment of the German alliance, forbidding his foreign minister even to broach the question of a renewal with Bismarck's successor, Leo von Caprivi. It was the Tsar who, in July of 1890, ordered that Raoul de Boisdeffre, the chief of the French general staff, should be invited, as his personal guest, to attend the Russian midsummer manoeuvres at Tsarkoe Selo and Narva. The French government could hardly miss the significance of this gesture. Ever since his spell as assistant military attaché at St Petersburg eleven years before, Boisdeffre had been a passionate advocate of closer Franco-Russian staff links. Before he left Paris for the manoeuvres, the General was instructed by Freycinet to sound the Russians out as to how far they were prepared to go to help France if she should find herself once again at war. Germany was not mentioned by name. There was no need.

The process by which, over the next four years, France and Russia finally joined hands through the secret military convention of 1892, followed by the even more closely shrouded alliance of 1894, need not be told here in all its byzantine complexity. It resembled a lobster quadrille in that, from the start, four negotiating partners were moving around each other. It was Boisdeffre and his Russian opposite number, General Obruchev (married to a French heiress with a handsome château near Bergerac in the Dordogne), who hammered out the basis for the military agreement, beginning with a fortnight of almost daily talks at the midsummer manoeuvres of 1890. It was Ribot and Giers who, a year later, when a French naval squadron arrived for a spectacularly successful visit to Kronstadt, worked out the draft of the political pact. But always at the centre of the quadrille, directing the step of the Russian partners, stood the commanding figure of the Tsar. As a modern authority has put it:

The desire for the alliance [in St Petersburg] was there from the summer of 1890. It was Alexander's desire, not that of his foreign minister. And such was the stubborn persistence of this crowned head, once the mind was made up, that, while the various impediments and hesitations would be the occasion for long delays and setbacks ... Alexander's disposition to proceed along this path, albeit in his own way and in his own time, would never waver until the goal had been achieved.[5]

One can, of course, argue that, even if Alexander III had been only lukewarm over a pact with France, the two countries would have slowly been pushed together by all the centripetal forces swirling around them. There was, for example, the renewal of the Triple Alliance between Germany, Austria and Italy, which, as related elsewhere, had been carried out at Italy's insistence on 29 June 1891. There were even suspicions in St Petersburg at the time that England might become linked in some way with the three central powers – a prospect which would have imperilled both France's ambitions in the Mediterranean and Russia's hopes for the Dardanelles. France and Russia, each threatened by any or all of these combinations, would naturally seek mutual protection. Moreover, the path towards their alliance had been liberally strewn, from the French end, with arms deliveries and above all with loans. These totalled some three billion francs by the beginning of 1891, an enormous sum in the currency of those days.

Yet despite all these external factors, an alliance would have been impossible to achieve in Alexander's lifetime had this imperious and strong-willed autocrat been opposed to it. As it was, he now went to extreme lengths to help it along, even standing bareheaded in his Peterhof Palace in July of 1891 while his orchestra played the 'Marseillaise' in honour of the visiting French officers. It had taken a lot of agonizing before this personification of absolutism had agreed to pay formal respects to the marching song of revolution. 'After all,' he had pointed out to Giers beforehand, 'I can't invent another national anthem for them.' He tried to placate the spirits of his horrified ancestors by putting his cap back on after the opening bars, motioning the orchestra to stop with the French command, 'Assez, assez.'

The main clauses of the pact in its final form were as clear as they were secret.* They are also brief enough to be quoted in full:

1. If France is attacked by Germany, or by Italy supported by Germany, Russia shall employ all her available forces to fight Germany.
   If Russia is attacked by Germany or by Austria supporting Germany, France shall employ all her available forces to fight Germany.
2. In the case of the forces of the Triple Alliance or any one of its members being mobilized, France and Russia, at the first indication of the event, and without a previous agreement being necessary, shall mobilize all their forces immediately and simultaneously, and shall transport them as near to the frontiers as possible.[7]

The alliance, though it offered defence protection for both parties, clearly favoured France. Germany, her supreme enemy (with whom Russia, it must be stressed, did not have a single serious quarrel anywhere in the world), was placed by clause 1 at the centre of the stage. If Russia became embroiled in a straight conflict with Austria who was her principal adversary among the major powers, France was not bound to come to her aid. (The French pointedly reminded the Austrians of this restriction during the Balkan Wars crisis of 1912–13.)

The second clause embodied a requirement which the French had put in their very first draft. This had been drawn up by Freycinet and Ribot on 23 July 1891, the very day the French squadron dropped anchor in Kronstadt. It is well worth re-reading. It helps to explain why, in the climate of 1914, the even graver Balkan crisis of Sarajevo could and did lead to a world war instead of being confined to a regional one. The French wanted to make certain all along that, when war with Germany came (and in the nation's mind, as opposed to its will, it was a case of when, not if) the Russian colossus who was now their ally would lumber into action as speedily as his massive slow-moving limbs would allow. They thus in effect substituted mobilization by Germany or Austria for actual aggression as the flashpoint of war. Well might General Boisdeffre say to the Tsar soon after the military part of the agreement had been signed:

---

* The Tsar had insisted that only himself and the French president, M. Carnot, should know the full terms, apart from the principal negotiators. The French Cabinet, he maintained, should be told only in general terms that an 'entente' had been agreed.

To mobilize is to declare war. To mobilize is to force your neighbour to do the same. . . . To allow your neighbour to mobilize a million men on your border without mobilizing in return is to deny yourself every possibility of movement.[8]

This was indeed the military-political code of the day where general, as opposed to partial, mobilization by a major power was concerned. None the less, a strong-willed ruler could break the convention to avert disaster. Even that emergency escape had now been blocked to Russia, as Alexander's son and successor was to discover to his cost twenty years later. It is time to look at the future Nicholas II.

The Tsarevich was the first to survive infancy of the six children which the Empress Marie Feodorovna (as the Danish-born Dagmar was styled) bore Alexander between 1868 and 1882. He was a shy and gentle youth, totally overshadowed by the commanding figure of the Tsar. The physical presence of Alexander III must have exerted an even more powerful effect on the son than his father's iron will. Nicholas was a slight youth with a handsome but somewhat effeminate face which his full beard did little to harden. He probably never forgot the herculean display of strength which his father had put on, one day in October 1888, when the imperial train, with all the family on board, ran off the rails near Kharkov. With his bare hands, the Tsar held up the caved-in roof of the dining-car where they had been sitting, and then braced it on his giant shoulders long enough for his wife and children to crawl free onto the track. Even if one is quick-witted and of independent mind (and the twenty-year-old Nicholas was neither) one does not argue with a father like that. His four uncles* were equally huge and equally bellowing, so that no tender consolation was to be found among the grand dukes.

The upbringing of the Tsarevich had been the routine one of spartan discipline with hard beds, cold water for washing and never quite enough to eat – and this amidst all the luxury and extravagance of the eight royal palaces which would one day be his. Languages had to be learned (he grew up speaking fluent French and German while his English was flawless), as did fencing, riding, dancing and shooting. But the key figure among all his tutors was a baleful one: Constantin Pobedonostsev, the high priest of absolutism who poured his creed of the unchallengeable divine right of monarchy into the head of young Nicholas just as, twenty-five years before, he had cemented it in the

---

* In order of age, the Tsar's brothers were Vladimir, who among his other posts was commander of the imperial guard; Alexis, grand admiral of the navy; Serge, governor of Moscow and, if that were possible, even more reactionary than the Tsar; and Paul, who was relatively insignificant.

mind of his father. Thus, though the Tsarevich was a gentle and well-meaning youth, there was not one shred of liberalism in his upbringing or his own convictions. The concessions he later made, as ruler, to his people were wrung out of him on the twin mangles of violence and panic.

The procurator-general of the Holy Synod (for Pobedonostsev clung on to that office until 1905) was presumably as concerned about the morality as well as the sanctity of his royal charges. But here the Tsarevich slipped through his bony fingers. After the customary induction into the night life of the young Russian nobility (which, in St Petersburg, meant attendance at balls, theatres or operas, followed by sessions of gambling, drinking and womanizing lasting until dawn), Nicholas settled down with Mathilde Kchessinska, a delectable seventeen-year-old dancer from the imperial ballet. Their liaison acquired almost bourgeois domesticity when he installed her in a modest two-storey house (rented in fact from the composer Rimski-Korsakov) and the prince and his ballet-girl began to give regular private supper parties like any young married couple. He continued meanwhile with his duties as an officer of the guards, which were nominal, and his functions as Heir-Apparent. These, thanks to his own retiring nature and the contempt in which his father held him, were even slighter. (When it was proposed to Alexander III that his son might be appointed president of the great Trans-Siberian railway project, the Tsar had at first protested that Nicholas, then turned twenty, was still a child, with 'only infantile judgements'.)

Child or not, Nicholas continued to live the lazy, indulgent life expected of a Tsarevich until, in 1892, the year he set up house with Mathilde, he decided that he would marry a childhood friend four years his junior, Princess Alix of Hesse-Darmstadt. His parents, St Petersburg society and – when they heard about it – the Russian people were all distinctly cool to the idea. The princess in question may well have been a granddaughter of Queen Victoria's (she was named, in phonetic German, after her mother, Princess Alice of Great Britain and Ireland); for all that, the small grand duchy of her father was not at all what the Emperor and Empress of Russia had in mind as a match for the Tsarevich. What antagonized Alexander III and his Danish wife even more than the undeniable modesty of Hesse-Darmstadt was the equally undeniable fact that it was German.

Yet Nicholas, who soon abandoned his ballet dancer and all other temptresses in his curious passion for this German princess (curious because she was neither particularly beautiful nor particularly charming) was not to be put off, even though he also had to contend with her

reluctance to embrace the Russian Orthodox faith. In the spring of
1894, in the congenial romantic setting of a family wedding at Coburg
to which nearly all Europe's Protestant royalty (including the old
Queen of England herself) had flocked, Nicholas got permission to
propose, and persuaded Alix to accept. It was one of the few occasions
in his life when he displayed a sustained effort of will, carrying forward,
until victory and against strong parental opposition, his personal battle
for happiness. So far as the husband picking a wife was concerned, he
turned out to be right: the marriage between them remained both
passionate and devoted right down to its savage ending. But for a future
tsar picking his future tsarina, the choice was a dismal one, for the
German Alix, when transformed into Alexandra Feodorovna, proved
as universally unpopular as her Danish mother-in-law was loved.

Their path to the throne was strewn with gloomy omens. To begin
with, Nicholas was obliged to celebrate the marriage itself in the
shadow of his father's coffin. On 1 November 1894, less than six months
after the engagement, Alexander III died unexpectedly of kidney failure
at the early age of forty-nine. One of his final acts had been to receive
the young couple in his Crimean palace of Livadia to give his blessing to
their union so they could become formally betrothed. He remained a
tsar to the last moment of his life and the last inch of his huge frame,
now crumpled up with disease. Though unable to rise from his
armchair, he had insisted on donning full dress uniform as the only
fitting garb in which to greet a future Russian empress.

It was just as well this formidable man never heard the panic-
stricken words his twenty-six-year old successor poured out within
minutes of becoming 'Emperor and Autocrat of all the Russias' as the
first of his many titles ran. Seizing his brother-in-law Grand Duke
Alexander by the arm, once they were away from the death chamber,
Nicholas wailed:

Sandro, what am I going to do? What is going to happen to me, to you . . . to
Alix, to mother, to all of Russia? I'm not prepared to be Tsar. I know nothing
of the business of ruling. I have no idea even how to talk to ministers.[9]

The first thing he had to do, of course, was to get married. The
wedding, originally planned for the spring of 1895, twelve months after
the engagement in Coburg, was now hastily arranged to take place only
a week after his father's funeral. Most of the sixty-odd royal mourners
who had come from all courts and corners of Europe for the lying-in-
state and the burial stayed on for the marriage, celebrated in the chapel
of the Winter Palace on 26 November, the birthday of the widowed
Tsarina. She dominated the first months of their married life, which

was spent under her eye in cramped quarters in St Petersburg's Anitchkov Palace. It was not an auspicious start. To the tensions between mother and daughter-in-law, Dowager and Empress, were added the fundamental antipathy between the temperaments of these two royal ladies; the older woman confident, cheerful and outgoing by nature; the younger one neurotic, withdrawn and suspicious. Though there could only be one throne, two courts instantly began to form underneath it.

The coronation, held in May of 1896 in Moscow (St Petersburg may have been the empire's modern capital but only its ancient one was a fit place to crown a tsar) also brought disturbing auguries. As he was preparing to receive the sacrament before the ceremony, the chain of the Order of St Andrew slipped loose from his uniform and fell on the altar floor. It was speedily retrieved and, as the mishap took place in the sanctuary, it was easy to hush it up. This was in glaring contrast to the disaster which took place in broad daylight on 18 May, when the festivities were into the fourth day. A huge crowd had gathered in the Khodynka meadow, an exercise ground of the Moscow garrison, for the traditional open-air feast. Hundreds of barrels of free beer and tens of thousands of free coronation mugs had been provided for the populace, many of whom had been drinking at their own expense all night so that they could scarcely stagger by the time dawn broke. Then, before the wagons had time to unload, a rumour flew round that both the beer and the souvenirs were in short supply and it would be a case of 'first come, first served'. Pandemonium broke out as half a million revellers surged towards the booths across a field crisscrossed with infantry trenches. Hundreds of men, women and children – the exact number was never revealed, and probably never established – were trampled to death before police and Cossacks could check the stampede and restore order. Thousands more were jammed into Moscow's hospitals so that the size of the catastrophe stared everyone in the face. None the less, Nicholas allowed himself to be talked out by his uncles of his first impulse, which was to go into retreat and pray for the dead, and instead was persuaded to appear with the Tsarina at a sumptuous ball given in their honour by the French ambassador, the Marquis de Montebello. The envoy had gone to extravagant lengths to prepare a function worthy of the occasion (a hundred thousand roses, for example, had been brought in by train all the way from the south of France) and, so the uncles had argued, Russia's solitary ally, secured only the year before, could not be gainsaid so early in the partnership. The upshot of it all was that while the dead and injured were still being sought out on the Khodynka field, the Tsar and Tsarina, brilliant in sashes, decorations and jewels, were opening the festivities at the French embassy with a stately quadrille.

Those outside the building were not to know that he was ashen with grief and that her eyes were red from weeping. Nor did the gestures they made the following day – doing a round of the hospitals, donating a thousand roubles from the private purse to the family of each victim – repair the damage. The fact remained that the Tsar and his German wife had danced while his ancient capital had grieved. Within days of his coronation the new Little Father of the Russians had been moved a step away from his people. The gap was to widen steadily.

Chapter Twelve

RUSSIA: END OF THE LINE

The last Romanov, whose fate it was to see his realm disintegrate as the first of Europe's three doomed empires, and finally to be slaughtered alongside his entire family, cuts a doleful as well as a tragic figure in history. Like all the tsars before him, he occupied a position unique among the dynasties. In one way he stood further apart from the ordinary people even than the venerable Franz Josef. In another sense he stood closer than any other sovereign to his subjects, for he was responsible to each and every one of them, and this not by constitution but, more powerfully, by legend. The accepted wisdom of ages held that he could do no wrong. Yet neither could he allow any wrong. If the times were harsh, it was because even he had to bow before divine providence. If an injustice prevailed, it was because the 'Batiushka-Tsar' had not been told about it. That was why the catastrophe on the Khodynka meadow had done such harm. He *had* known. His will for his people's good, deemed one of the elements of the universe, had been seen to flicker and fail.

Nicholas II, who was only twenty-six years old when he came to the throne, certainly had the best of personal intentions. Goodwill positively shone out of those childishly frank blue eyes of his. It oozed much more reluctantly through the cracks in the conservative framework which encased him. It is true that, despite the historic reforms of his grandfather, and despite his father's failure to extinguish either the liberal spirit in Russia or its revolutionary movement, the idea of firm rule from the top remained embedded in the Russian mind. The nation still more or less expected that their Tsar's strong hand would spend more time applying a knout across their backs than benevolently stroking their hands. As one observer put it, remarking on the phenomenon of Alexander III: 'The Russian people love a masterful head of household; in short, what is expressed by the untranslateable word "khuzain". The American expression "boss" comes perhaps nearest to rendering its meaning.'[1]

Nicholas was certainly no 'khuzain', either to his family or his subjects. There was a clear sign of this at his own coronation. He had wanted to use the twelfth-century Kievan cap of Monamakh partly because it was so historic but partly because, at two pounds in weight, it was so light. Instead, ceremonial tradition obliged him to use the vast crown of Catherine the Great with its two thousand diamonds, which was more than four times as heavy. He rightly feared it would prove too much for his small head to support comfortably during the coronation and, as it turned out, afterwards. Yet this glittering artefact also symbolized the enormous power which had descended upon him. Unlike other monarchs, who were crowned by their archbishops or metropolitans, the Tsar of Russia placed the crown on his own head and then briefly on the brow of his tsarina. The last Tsar's problem was that, though born to autocracy and though dedicated to it, he was no autocrat by nature and could never steel himself to become one.

A distinguished and well-disposed British ambassador to his court – one of a series of such envoys who served at St Petersburg – summed up the case in his 'annual Report for Russia for the Year 1906'. The verdict stings through all the diplomatic grease in which it is wrapped:

If in the eyes of many he does not rise fully to the exigencies of the present situation, and does not always act with the required firmness and decision, nor take a bold initiative indifferent to the opposing currents of so many different waves of opinion, it is doubtful if many of his critics would, if placed in similar circumstances, be able to meet and overcome successfully the difficulties which beset the Throne . . .[2]

The German Kaiser, not restrained by such professional inhibitions, put it more bluntly and more profoundly in this annotation, written in French, on a report for his own envoy in St Petersburg at the same period: 'L'empereur n'est pas faux, mais faible. La faiblesse n'est pas la fausseté, mais elle en tient lieu, et elle en remplit les fonctions.'*[3]

His weakness was, if anything, made worse by his wife's affectionate yet remorselessly nagging campaign to cure it. This was to culminate in the following advice, offered during the final crisis of imperial Russia: 'Be Peter the Great, be Ivan the Terrible, be Tsar Paul. Crush them all

---

* 'The emperor is not false, but weak. Weakness is not falseness, but it takes its place and fulfils its functions.' One is left wondering whether William II really devised such thoughts, or simply borrowed them.

under your feet. . . . Now don't laugh at me, you naughty one!'[4]

There are few more desperate and depressing sights than an ambitious wife trying to load more and more weight on her husband's shoulders than these were designed to bear. When such a mismatch between marital pressure and natural capacity takes place between an empress and an emperor throughout the crucial years of their empire's life, the result could only be national as well as personal tragedy. Instead of leaving her 'Nicky' to argue the toss with the crowd of ministers, officials, grand dukes and foreign envoys who surrounded the throne, she eventually began to interpose herself between him and his advisers, thus creating yet another layer of hesitation and vacillation for the wretched young ruler to flounder about in.

Another political drawback to their relationship was the drooling sentimentality she always imparted to it. Like her attempts to turn Nicholas into a Russian superman, this also runs through her six hundred and thirty letters to him which have survived. They are all in English, for she never mastered Russian, and their tone is babylike. She rarely signs herself 'Alix'. It is usually 'Wify', 'Girly', 'Sunny' or 'Own', and the rest of the text is in the same key. The language of the nursery comes out almost as strongly as the language of the bedroom, for they were indeed both lovers and children to the end. 'I do so endlessly love my very own Boysy dear' is a typical effusion. Yet, ironically, by wrapping him in this sweet and soft affection, she countered her own efforts to put more spine into him. In short, she did more harm by cocooning than by hectoring.

It was at her insistence that he left St Petersburg and spent months on end at Tsarkoe Selo, fifteen miles south of the capital. Here they had two palaces, the blue and white one of Catherine the Great and the Alexander Palace in which she set up home. This was their private world. It was also a dream world of grottoes and lakes, flowered terraces and lawns, pony-traps and donkey-carts, rowing-boats and tennis courts, all far removed from the real Russia it was supposed to represent. Only here did Alexandra feel secure from St Petersburg society, whose immorality shocked her as much as its hostility frightened her. So the gulf widened. Apart from a resident handful of favourites and hangers-on and the changing flux of ministers driving out to Tsarkoe Selo, the capital kept its distance. Hatred for the intense, suspicious, seemingly cold and very foreign Tsarina deepened.

The only escape for the Tsar into more bracing masculine company was when he went to lunch or dine with one of his regiments. Yet even here, for all his devotion to the army (and all his dependence on it) one senses that he was never completely at ease, and that a good half of him was itching to get back to the cosy boudoir of the Tsarina. A letter he wrote on 7 August 1896 as a young-married to his mother is very revealing:

My dearest Mama,

The review on August 6 left a very sad impression on me, though everything went off very well. In the morning, before getting into the carriage, I had one of my fits of nerves which reminded me of the old days when I got them before every review. I felt green and trembled all over. When four battalions and the Artillery had drunk my health I felt better and tried to look cheerful, especially when talking to the officers after lunch . . .

He ends by telling the Dowager Empress that his constipation has ended, thanks to 'three pills which Alix gave me. I feel so relieved and well, just as you probably do after a confinement.'[5]

It is hard to find a trace of Ivan the Terrible anywhere in all this. The pity of it was that Nicholas, for all his perfect English, had the habits of the tsars of old. Whenever he could get out of uniform, he did so, and usually worked at his desk in a peasant-style blouse, with sagging breeches and soft leather boots. At least in that respect he embodied the soul of Russia.

His reign, even before the catastrophe which began in 1914, was marked by traumas and defeats on all three fronts of government – the military, the domestic and the diplomatic. The great military disaster was, of course, Russia's swift and savage defeat at the hands of the Japanese in the Far East. The initial challenge had come from Russia, who took on the role of China's protector after the rickety Manchu empire had been vanquished and partly occupied by Japan in 1895. The Japanese, at that stage unwilling to risk confrontation with St Petersburg, withdrew their armies southwards along the Pacific coast; by 1898 Russia had installed herself in their place in the great Chinese warm-water anchorage of Port Arthur.* When the Russians moved first into Manchuria and then began, in 1903, to advance down the Korean peninsula, a clash became inevitable. Nicholas, as usual, vacillated, talking now of peace and now of war.

The Kaiser's was one of the most insistent voices urging him into battle. Indeed, as the voluminous 'Willy-Nicky' correspondence shows, the German Emperor, realizing that Nicholas was a far softer target than Alexander III, began to bombard his cousin almost from his coronation with advice and exhortation on every subject under the sun. To push the Tsar now into war against Japan served a dual purpose.

* This harbour had long tempted Russian admirals. Vladivostok, their own Pacific port, was ice-bound during the winter months.

First, it satisfied the Kaiser's own obsession with the 'Yellow Peril' which had surfaced again only three years before in his notorious speech over the Boxer rebellion.* But it also suited Germany's purpose in leaving her in even greater command of the European continent while Russia's energies were drained away on Asian battle-grounds. Both elements, the heroic and the strategic, enter into this exhortation of William II:

It is the great task of the future for Russia to cultivate the Asian continent and to defend Europe from the inroads of the Great Yellow Race. In this, you will always find me at your side, ready to help you as best I can. . . . I would let nobody try to interfere with you to attack from behind in Europe during the time you were fulfilling the great mission which Heaven has shaped for you . . .

The Kaiser then went right over the top by sending Nicholas an allegorical portrait, which he had had specially composed, to represent both the Tsar's sacred task and his relationship with his German cousin. In the picture a transfixed and radiant Emperor William stands in shining armour holding a great crucifix aloft. Nicholas – the one who was supposed to be doing all the fighting – crouches humbly and admiringly at his feet, clad in Byzantine garb. It was the sort of unhinged, megalomaniac gesture which so appalled their uncle, King Edward VII of England. The sensitive Nicholas found these histrionics equally distasteful. Indeed, at heart he disliked the Kaiser almost as much as his father before him. 'C'est à vomir!' he had written to the Dowager Empress when breaking the news gently to his Danish mother that he had been obliged to make William II an admiral in the Russian navy.

In the end, it was neither the Tsar's cousin in Berlin nor his divided generals and ministers in St Petersburg but the Japanese themselves who made up his mind for him. Under cover of darkness on the night of 5–6 February 1904, Japanese destroyers slid into the outer harbour of Port Arthur and struck with their torpedoes two battleships and one heavy cruiser of the Russian squadron lying at anchor there. It was only a modest dress rehearsal for the attack on Pearl Harbor nearly forty years later, but the outcome was the same. The news of the attack – in this case a telegram sent to St Petersburg by Admiral Alexeyev, whom Nicholas had appointed viceroy of the Far East – was itself a declaration of war between the two rivals.

'May God come to our aid,' the Tsar entered that night in his diary.

---

* See *supra*, p. 99.

But even had it so desired, divine providence would have found it very hard to help the Russians in the brief conflict which now opened. Geography was all against them to begin with. The Japanese had short and direct supply lines to the battle area. The Russians had to haul every man and every shell along the five-thousand-mile Trans-Siberian railway which, apart from being only single-track, still had a gap at Lake Baikal. Thus, though the Russian army was nearly six times the size of the Japanese, their opponents could throw 150,000 men into action immediately on the Asian mainland, outnumbering the Russian forces based in Manchuria. A divided Russian command, which meant that the vice-regal Alexeyev in Port Arthur was constantly at cross purposes with General Kuropatkin, who led the land forces, further lengthened the odds. The calibre of Russian generalship on the ground, which mostly varied between the barely competent and the positively calamitous, did the rest. In January 1905 Port Arthur fell to the Japanese.

This still left a large Russian army intact in the interior; but the lethal blow now came from the sea. On 27 May 1905, Rozhdestvenski's Baltic Fleet, which had sailed half way across the world in a bid to smash the much-ridiculed Japanese navy once and for all, was instead ripped to pieces itself by Admiral Togo's awkward-looking top-heavy ships. Within an hour the accurate and rapid gunnery of the Japanese, backed up by their torpedoes, had sent four Russian battleships, seven cruisers and five destroyers to the bottom of the Tsushima Strait. Five other Russian warships were captured. Only two vessels, a cruiser and a destroyer, escaped to Vladivostok to tell the mournful tale.

The battle of Tsushima was the greatest and most decisive naval action since Trafalgar a century before. Its effects, as far as the loser was concerned, were even more drastic. Not only did it end the war almost at once (with President Theodore Roosevelt in Washington acting as the mediator, and thus foreshadowing America's entry into the world arena); it also marked the beginning of the slow end inside imperial Russia itself. 'I fear we all shall have to drain the bitter cup to the dregs,' Nicholas had written to his mother.[6] He never dreamt that those conventionally emotional words would prove stark prophecy.

Defeat in the Far East did not spark off the great revolution of 1905. It did, however, fan the flames once the conflagration started and, what was worse, helped them to spread from the streets to the warships of the Russian navy, the service which had been totally demoralized by the Tsushima disaster. The new wave of violence began when the Japanese war was only six months old. In July of 1904 the minister of the interior, Vyacheslav Plehve, fell, like his predecessor two years before, to a terrorist's attack. It was Plehve who, as a professional policeman, had supervised the round-up of hundreds of suspects after the killing of Alexander II. It was Plehve, a rabid anti-Semite, who had condoned bloody pogroms against Russia's five million Jews. Yet though it was one thing for a minister of the interior almost to invite assassination, it was another thing for the assassins to succeed in accepting the invitation by literally blowing this symbol of reaction to pieces with their bomb. In another of those ironies with which the decline of the Romanovs is sprinkled, the victim's only imaginative act while in office turned out to be lethal for the dynasty after his death.

Plehve had conceived the bold idea of founding, with government money, the so-called 'Assembly of Russian Factory and Mill Workers' which, though dedicated to improving housing and working conditions, was primarily designed to draw the sting from the revolutionary movement and attract its followers into an officially sponsored organization. The man placed in charge of it was Father George Gapon. He was a police informer, which made him acceptable to Plehve; a worker-priest, which made him acceptable to the St Petersburg masses; and a mystical idealist which, he hoped, would make his deeds acceptable to both God and the Tsar. Such was the strange individual who, in January of 1905, when the news of Port Arthur's surrender had swollen the existing industrial unrest, decided to lead a mass march on the Winter Palace. It was the old legend, the old illusion. If only the Little Father of all the Russias could be persuaded to receive his people and hear their grievances, all would be set right in the world. In the event, as we know, all went catastrophically wrong.

On the morning of Sunday, 22 January, five columns of marchers, two hundred thousand strong in all, converged on the Winter Palace to present a petition to their tsar. Gapon, who led the main column, was convinced that the march, which he had announced to the authorities a fortnight before, had been authorized. In fact, orders had been issued to arrest him and his principal helpers though, for reasons best known to himself, General Fullon, the chief of police, decided to ignore these instructions. The catastrophe unfolded in a similar vacuum of confusion. The police actually cleared the streets for a procession they were supposed to ban. The Tsar, whom the procession was all about, slipped out of St Petersburg to Tsarkoe Selo (doubtless on his wife's persuasion) in order to escape being publicly petitioned by a man he had just described in his diary as 'a kind of socialist priest'. It was embarrassment he hoped that he was sliding out of, not danger. Nobody had warned him of what might be in store with such a vast

emotionally-charged throng converging on his palace and he had not
the wits to sense the peril himself if the crowd, finding their 'Little
Father' not at home, were turned away empty-handed.

Something far worse than disappointment awaited the marchers. As
the hymn-singing, icon-waving, noisy but entirely respectful mass of
humanity closed in on the square and showed no sign of withdrawing,
the commander of the guard finally panicked and ordered his men to
fire their first volley not over the heads of the crowd, as was the
customary dispersal procedure, but slap into their bodies. Volley after
volley followed and the killing continued late into the afternoon as
Cossacks and other mounted troops of the Petersburg garrison hunted
down groups who had fled the corpse-strewn palace square. 'Bloody
Sunday' had entered its mark on the Russian calendar, and the stain
was never to be removed.

Sir Charles Hardinge, whom we shall soon be seeing a lot more of as
King Edward VII's principal diplomatic adviser, was serving as British
ambassador in St Petersburg at the time. In a long letter which he sent
home to the King's private secretary, Sir Francis Knollys, a few days
after the catastrophe, he not only gives some unfamiliar details about
the drama but also draws the right conclusions from it. As his embassy
was situated on the corner of one of the bridges leading to the palace, he
was virtually an eye-witness of events. Of the placid, almost reverential
mood of the workmen as they formed up there was no doubt. They
were, he wrote:

a most peaceful crowd in their Sunday clothes, all of whom were hoping to see
the Emperor and they went straight to the square of the Winter Palace, the
approaches to which were blocked by troops. There they stood for hours and I
am told that those nearest to the entrances stood with their caps off, for fear
that they might come into His Majesty's presence with their heads covered. A
really touching simplicity.

As for the start of the slaughter, it seems that the Far East war even
played a baleful role here. He continues:

About two hours later, the crowd refusing or being unable to disperse in the
streets adjoining the Palace and the soldiers being irritated by some of the
crowd jeering at them and asking why they were not in Manchuria, a company
of one of the Guards regiments was brought up and fired into the crowd at a
distance of about 20 yards, naturally causing terrible destruction. . . . The
sight of the killed and shrieks of the wounded were beyond description. What
seems however indisputable is the fact that . . . no provocation was given. I am
quite convinced that a few London policemen could have easily managed that
crowd.

As for the consequences, the perceptive Hardinge, writing only a week after the tragedy, set them out thus:

I cannot help thinking that the Emperor missed the chance of his life-time. His Majesty knew that these thousands of workmen were coming to present to him a petition setting forth their grievances, and if he had received at the Winter Palace a small deputation and promised to give them then what has since been promised in his name, he would have obtained the undying loyalty and admiration of the lower classes of his subjects. Now it has gone abroad that, when his subjects came to present their grievances to the 'Little Father', they were mown down by his troops and a gulf has been created between the Emperor and his people which will not be easily forgotten.*[7]

Not only was the gulf never forgotten; it was never bridged, apart from brief flashes of patriotic fusion. The legend that Tsar and people were one, already damaged by the affair of the Khodynka meadow and by the royal family's stubborn isolation at Tsarkoe Selo in the ten years since had now been shattered. Father Gapon personified the new violent hostility as he had personified the vanished mood of humble pleading. The worker-priest, who had escaped the Winter Garden carnage, was now a rabid revolutionary, denouncing 'Nicholas Romanov, formerly Tsar and now soul-murderer of the Russian empire'. Gapon's origins as a police agent made him too suspect as a flag-bearer of rebellion. (He was indeed sentenced to death by the real underground, the Socialist Revolutionary Party, and murdered by their agents in Finland the following April.) Yet his fury echoed, accurately enough, the angry disillusionment of the people. A year of violent chaos had begun.

The first counter-blow against the old order was struck in Moscow where, on 4 February 1905, the Grand Duke Serge, until recently governor-general of the city and one of the most hated men in the empire, was blown to pieces by a bomb hurled on top of his carriage as he was driving out of the Kremlin gate. The student, Kaliayev, who had thrown the bomb, refused to plead for pardon, on the grounds that his execution (which duly followed) would further serve the cause of the revolution. Only the day before, Nicholas had been deliberating with his ministers how to meet the main political clamour of the hour, which was for the creation of some form of elected assembly to function

---

* The 'real culprit', according to Hardinge, was Prince Vassiltchikov, commander of the Guards Division, who was 'on the spot himself and gave the order to fire'. He is said to have refused an immediate order from the Grand Duke Vladimir to cease firing on the grounds that 'he could not be responsible for the safety of his troops, or of the town unless they used their arms'.

alongside the Tsar, even if only in an advisory capacity. This was the start of a grim game of tag which continued throughout 1905, whereby political concessions, hard-wrung out of the ruler, chased, and usually failed to catch up with, the violence erupting throughout the country.

While, in St Petersburg, the grand dukes and the ministers agonized over whether the Tsar should give up any of his autocratic power, and if so, how much, the factory workers gave their verdict by simply downing tools. Within a month of the Winter Palace slaughter (the rumours of which went far beyond even the reality) half a million of them were on strike. When troops attempted to get them back to work, riots and shootings, which claimed hundreds more victims, took place. The ugliest scenes of all took place in the Black Sea port of Odessa, where in June an all-out civil war had broken out between soldiers and police on the one hand and armed strikers, arsonists and anarchists of all labels on the other. On the fifteenth of that month the conflict spread from the streets to the fighting ships when mutiny broke out on the new battle-cruiser *Potemkin*, and this pride of the Black Sea fleet was seen steaming into Odessa harbour with the Red Flag flying from her mast. That was the signal for a fresh round of fighting, with the *Potemkin*'s guns crashing wildly into the city at points where the mutinous sailors hoped their shells might help their comrades battling ashore. (As the crew had either killed or locked up every single officer on board, in a row which had been sparked off by a ration of bad meat, their aim was uncertain.)

The Odessa mutiny sharpened the debate at a divided court where, for example, the Grand Duke Nicholas Nicolaievich was arguing in favour of political concessions, whereas both the Montenegrin-born grand duchesses were firmly, and stridently, in the larger camp of the reactionaries. Sergei Yulievich Witte, a government veteran who had been minister of communications and then of finance as far back as 1892, had been recalled by Nicholas to conduct the peace negotiations with Japan and now emerged as the key figure in the tussle. He had successfully battled in Washington for a treaty, signed on 5 September 1905, which did not inflict excessive humiliation on Russia, and was immediately rewarded for his services by being made a count. It was thus a politician greatly elevated in prestige as well as in status who returned to St Petersburg ten days later, amidst the growing expectation that he was the magician who could also bring about peace at home.

This bear of a man, who had inherited from his Dutch father a physique which even put that of the late Alexander III in the shade, was a conservative down to the marrow of his huge bones. He once said: 'I

have a constitution in my head but as to my heart . . .', and at that point
he broke off and spat on the floor. But in the month which followed his
triumphant return from America he had to get the idea of a constitution
fixed not only in his own head but in that of the Tsar. By the beginning
of October the capital was paralysed by strikes. It was not just the
factories which had stopped working. The trains had stopped running;
electricity, gas and water supplies were cut off; the printing presses
were shut down and hardly a shop was open. Workers' Soviets, inspired
by such figures as Vladimir Ilyich Ulyanov, soon to call himself Lenin,
were wresting ground-roots political control out of the chaos. If their
mock parliaments were not to take over, Witte realized that the Tsar
would have to establish a mock parliament of his own. The only
alternative was an all-out military dictatorship. This not only meant
the certainty of further bloodshed. It also raised the anxious question
whether the soldiers would, always and everywhere, obey an order to
fire on the rioters who were now claiming them as class comrades in a
struggle for freedom.

The upshot was the imperial manifesto of 30 October 1905 which, on
paper (and, to a limited degree, in practice), changed Russia from an
absolute into a semi-constitutional monarchy. The limits were considerable. In particular, the Tsar kept complete control over defence
and foreign affairs and over the appointment and dismissal of
ministers, who remained responsible to him and not to the Duma, as
the new national parliament was called. None the less, this body was
guaranteed a veto power on legislation in that, in future, no law could
take effect without its consent. The manifesto also promised freedom of
conscience, speech, assembly and association to the people. Even the
paper promise was a giant step forwards (or backwards, depending on
the point of view) for an autocrat by birth and by nature to take. The
Tsar's behaviour at the moment of decision is described in an account
given later by Witte himself to the British embassy and duly reported to
Buckingham Palace:

Witte went down to Peterhof and there explained his point of view to the
Emperor. He says that the Emperor behaved with great dignity as well as
simplicity. With his pen in his hand he said nothing about his ancestors . . . but
simply this, 'I opposed the reforms because I thought in my conscience that
this was best for the country's good; and now I grant the reforms for the same
reason.' Then, with a firm hand, he signed the Manifesto. People present were
in tears, and so was Witte himself when he told the story.[8]

As for what had brought about the complete somersault in the Tsar's
thinking, a recapitulation of events is graphically set out in one of the

longest and most revealing of all the letters that he wrote to his mother, who was staying at the time in her native Denmark until the revolution had subsided. Here are some extracts:

My dearest Mama,

I do not know how to begin this letter. . . . A month ago yesterday we returned from Transund and everything was comparatively quiet. . . . All sorts of conferences took place in Moscow which Durnovo [the minister of interior] permitted, I do not know why. Everything was being prepared for the railway strike. The first one began in and around Moscow and then spread all over Russia, practically at once. Petersburg and Moscow were entirely cut off from the interior. For exactly a week today the Baltic Railway has not been running. The only way to get to town is by sea. How convenient at this time of year! From the railways the strike spread to the factories and workshops and then even to the municipal organizations and services and lastly to the Railway Department of the Ministry itself. What shame, just think of it! . . . .

God knows what happened in the universities. *Every* kind of riff-raff walked in from the streets, riot was loudly proclaimed – nobody seemed to mind. . . .

It makes me sick to read the news. Nothing but new strikes in schools and factories; murdered policemen, Cossacks and soldiers; riots, disorder, mutinies. But the ministers, instead of acting with quick decision, only assemble in council like a lot of frightened hens and cackle. . . .

Through all these horrible days, I constantly met Witte. We very often met in the morning to part only in the evening, when night fell. There are only two ways open: to find an energetic soldier and crush the rebellion by sheer force. . . . That would mean rivers of blood and in the end we should be where we had started. The other way out would be to give the people their civil rights . . . also to have all laws confirmed by a State Duma – that, of course, would be a constitution. Witte defends this very energetically. . . . He put it quite clearly to me that he would accept the Presidency of the Council of Ministers only on the condition that his programme was agreed to, and his actions not interfered with. . . . He and Alexei Obolensky* drew up the Manifesto. . . . There was no other way out than to cross oneself and give what everyone was asking for . . . [9]

The Tsar was right in his prediction that Witte, as Russia's first Prime Minister, would soon 'find out what he was in for'. The conservatives and ultra-reactionaries cold-shouldered him as a traitor; the revolutionaries fought his pragmatism tooth and nail as a threat to their political extremism. And so the violence grew even worse. In the next two months more naval mutinies had to be put down, in the Baltic as well as, again, in the Black Sea. There were riots and further mass

---

* Prince Obolensky, a member of the council of empire.

pogroms in the Ukraine. The unrest spread to all the outer bastions of the Russian empire – the Baltic provinces, Poland and Finland. In December, in a move inspired by Lenin and his Bolsheviks, students and workers fought the army for ten days for control of the old capital, Moscow, until crack troops arrived from St Petersburg to restore order.

Having failed to deliver the peace he had promised, Witte was forced to ride roughshod over his own constitution as well as over his people. In April of 1906 the old 'fundamental laws' of the monarchy were reissued alongside the already discredited manifesto. There was only one concession to the spirit of the new age. From clause 1, 'To the Emperor of All the Russias belongs the supreme autocratic and unlimited power', the words 'and unlimited' were now left out. It represented Witte's last attempt to face both ways at once. His energies were exhausted; even more so his credit with the Tsar. He was bundled out of office on 23 April, four days before the opening of the first State Duma which he had helped to create. 'All Russia is one vast madhouse,' he declared before taking himself off abroad.

Whether or not that verdict was exaggerated, it was certainly true that, with his departure from the scene, Russia had lost one of her sanest as well as ablest statesmen. Goremykin, his successor, was an idle and somewhat clownish reactionary, who made no secret of his contempt for the Duma – which, significantly enough, had been inaugurated in a frigid ceremony in the Winter Palace itself. 'Let them babble,' he told the new British ambassador, Sir Arthur Nicolson, who was appalled to find that the Tsar's First Minister at this crucial juncture was nothing more than 'an elderly man with a sleepy face and Piccadilly whiskers'.[10]

It was scarcely surprising that the parliamentary experiment of the Romanovs never recovered from this grudging, bloodstained and muddled start. The first State Duma lasted only three months before the Tsar dissolved it; the second (February to June 1907) only a month longer before suffering the same fate. In each case the reason was the same: deadlock when far-reaching reforms demanded by the Assembly were rejected by a government answerable only to the Tsar. The third and fourth Dumas, which ran from 1907 down to 1914, survived only because, thanks to a new franchise weighted against the peasants, they were more conservative in composition and were prepared to accept the overriding principle of autocracy. But the deadly gap between Nicholas and his people widened all the time. As one of his more intelligent female cousins wrote later, from her exile in America, of those final years:

Russia still writhed and stumbled. The wave of revolts and uprisings . . . had cowed the Emperor and the ruling class into bewildered and sullen inertia. They had long since lost contact with the true thoughts and interests of the country. . . .

On the other hand, the mouth-pieces of the so-called public opinion, those men who, by high-sounding formulas, had so impressed the densely ignorant masses – they too lacked competence and initiative. They had neither sufficient moral force nor experience necessary to build up a new system. Their mental store was limited to theories, often excellent but inapplicable to realities. . . . From the very beginning, the effort peacefully to liberalize Russian absolutism was doomed to failure.[11]

In following the fate of the Dumas we have jumped over the one event which, in the agonizing period of the Far East war and the revolution, brought both great joy to the royal couple and a temporary boost to their standing with their subjects. On the afternoon of 12 August 1904, the cannon at the Peterhof and at the ramparts of the Peter and Paul fortress of St Petersburg boomed three hundred times, instead of, as on four occasions, stopping at a hundred and one. After producing four girls in a row – Olga, Tatyana, Maria and Anastasia – Alix had finally given birth to a son. All over Russia guns and church bells took up the greeting. It was no ordinary event for the dynasty. Indeed, the infant, christened Alexis Nicolaievich, was the first male heir born to a reigning tsar for more than two hundred years.

For the parents the event was momentous enough in its own right – not simply as the crowning of a devotedly passionate marriage but also as the assurance (or so it seemed then) that the crown would pass to their own child instead of to the Tsar's younger brother Michael.* This made the discovery, only a few weeks later, that the tiny Tsarevich was suffering from haemophilia even more agonizing to bear, especially for the mother. It was she who had unsuspectingly brought the disease with her to St Petersburg, inherited from another unsuspecting carrier, her grandmother, Queen Victoria of England. This turn of events was ironic as well as tragic. As the mother of an heir to the throne, Alix was in a position to act with much greater assurance towards a St Petersburg society which had hitherto been mocking in its hostility. Yet the need to cosset the precious infant, who grew up bleeding profusely and suffering great agonies at the slightest knock or bruise, only turned her still further inwards to the family retreat at Tsarkoe Selo and made her anxiously compliant husband even more remote as tsar.

* Paul, the son of Catherine the Great, had abolished the system whereby female Romanovs could succeed to the throne.

The final element in this lethal domestic tragedy was, of course, the appearance of Gregory Efimovich, better known as Rasputin, on the St Petersburg scene. This drunken and lecherous Siberian monster (his nickname meant 'dissolute') was bogus as a *starets* or holy man, but extremely effective both as a talker and an amateur hypnotist. The combination of a master confidence-trickster wearing the robes of a monk, claiming both the gift of healing and the second sight of prophecy, proved overwhelming from the moment when, in the summer of 1906, with the sickly Tsarevich barely two years old, Rasputin came into the mother's presence. According to Maurice Paléologue, the exceedingly able and well-informed French ambassador in St Petersburg, it was the Montenegrin-born Grand Duchess Militza who recommended this baleful fraud to the imperial family. She and her sister Anastasia, soon to marry a Russian grand duke herself,* were as naturally inclined to the occult as they were to intrigue. They had already tried in 1900 to introduce a French mystic, one Philip of Lyons, to the Russian court.[12] He left little lasting impact. With Rasputin, it was to be a different story.

There is no need to go over his familiar tale again except in outline: how, by seeming to cure the Tsarevich from some of his bleeding bouts, Rasputin gradually appeared not only as an emissary of God to the distraught mother but as her evil confidant and even, in wild rumour, her lover, to the outside world. What is needed, as with the case of the German Kaiser's withered arm, is to view the matter in perspective. William II would have been a vainglorious imperial demagogue (and his country an unstable fireball of energy) with or without that disability. Nicholas II would have remained a weak ruler estranged from his people, and his wife an almost universally detested German intruder with or without the complication of the mad pseudo monk. Indeed, the influence of Rasputin on the Tsarina, and through her on Russian political life, did not become a public issue until 1912. By then, as we have seen, even the pseudo-liberalism of the 1905 reforms had been throttled back, leaving the Tsar a vulnerable and isolated autocrat who was every bit as frightened of his power as he was jealous of it.

By then also the greatest of his Prime Ministers, Peter Arkadyevich Stolypin, a pragmatic, clear-eyed monarchist who might have stopped the domestic rot, given time and a free hand, had been removed from the scene by yet another assassin's hand. The Russia of 1912, with autocracy sitting unsteadily on top of anarchy like the shaking lid of a

* See *supra*, p. 8

boiling kettle, was already a doomed construction. All Rasputin did
was help topple it altogether. Even so, it was only when the sufferings of
a world war rebounded on the domestic scene that the final collapse
came about. Rasputin himself was then already dead, destroyed by his
princely enemies in a murder which was exceptionally gruesome, even
by Russian standards.

It is time to turn to the long and steady run-up to that war and to the
role Nicholas played in it. Defeat at the hands of the Japanese had
bruised the pride of Russia at home and lowered her prestige abroad.
Nor had the Romanov dynasty as a whole come very well out of it. As
the British ambassador in St Petersburg reported to King Edward VII,
of the numerous grand dukes alive in 1904–5, no more than two had
seen fit to go to the Far Eastern front.[13] The conflict gave the German
Kaiser one of the best chances he would ever get to drive a wedge
between Russia and England, since the latter had signed a defensive
treaty with Japan only two years before the war broke out and was now
obliged to take up a stand of awkward neutrality. The massive military
and naval battles being fought out in Asia also gave the Kaiser the
opportunity to do what he most savoured, namely, parade himself as
the wise strategist. William II made the most of both openings in his
bombardment by personal letters of the Tsar.

One typical missive, written on the eve of hostilities, eggs Russia on
with the assurance that 'Everybody here [Berlin] understands perfectly
that Russia, following the laws of expansion, must try to get at the Sea
for an iceless outlet for its commerce.[14] In the sentence immediately
before, the Kaiser accuses the British of 'blowing at flames where they
can', impervious to the fact that that is precisely what he is doing
himself. The unfortunate Dogger Bank incident of October 1904 lent
fresh winds to the Kaiser's campaign; it was in the wake of it that he
first floated the proposals for an alliance between Germany and Russia
which surfaced briefly again in some imperial yacht diplomacy at
Björkö Fjord the following July.* The Kaiser then spoke as Supreme
War Lord to his cousin, working out for him exactly what strengths and
dispositions he would need to fight the Japanese on land. Finally, after
the fall of Port Arthur and Russia's crushing defeat at sea, he offered
himself as the supreme mediator ('Should you think that I could be of
any even smallest use to you for the preparatory steps to bring about
peace, pray dispose of me at your leisure')[15], having scorned King
Edward's offer of the same services a year before, when they might have
salvaged Russia's position.

---

* See supra, p 101.

But this fleeting dynastic *rapprochement* between Berlin and St Petersburg counted for little compared with the basic political impact of the Japanese war, which was to turn Russia's face back from the Pacific to the Adriatic and the Mediterranean. Apart from the folly of starting the Far Eastern war, Nicholas II bore little personal blame for the disaster. He was operating, with bad generals and severe logistical problems, in a remote terrain against unknown oriental opponents. What he can be judged by, however, is his performance on the Balkan arena on to which Russia had now recoiled. This was her familiar European back yard; most of the small nations who inhabited it were her own little Slav brethren, whose monarchs and ministers were all well known. Above all, the greater nations involved, Austria-Hungary and her German partner, were Russia's ancient rivals in the long tussle over the carcase of the Ottoman empire. Here, at a game his ancestors had prepared for him, the Tsar held a powerful hand. He played it indifferently during the two great flare-ups which preceded Sarajevo: the annexation crisis of 1908 and the Balkan Wars of 1912–13.

Like all the other European heads of state involved, Nicholas II was both astounded and offended by the abrupt notice given in the Emperor Franz Josef's personal letter of 5 October 1908 that he had decided to proceed at once with the outright annexation of Bosnia-Herzegovina.* He was almost equally offended by King Ferdinand's simultaneous announcement that this princeling intended henceforth to be called tsar of an independent Bulgaria. Yet Nicholas had also been confounded by being told, for the first time, that his own grandfather, Alexander II, had more or less signed away the two annexed provinces to the same Franz Josef forty years before. The whole dynastic imbroglio is set out in a letter which Nicholas, fresh under the impact of events, sent to his mother (then visiting her sister, Queen Alexandra, in England) on 8 October:

Brazen impudence gets away with anything. Ferdinand has done a stupid and very untimely thing. Obviously Austria pushed him to do it – and the main culprit is Achrenthal.† He is simply a scoundrel. He made Izvolski his dupe when they met and now puts things quite differently from the way he did then. . . .

But there is something else which is really most distressing and which I had no idea of until now. The other day, Charikov, our ambassador at Constantinople, sent me some secret papers dating back to the Berlin

---

* See *supra*, p. 150
† Austrian minister of foreign affairs and one of the partners in the rogues' conspiracy with his Russian opposite number at Buchlau on 15 September 1908.

Congress of 1878. It appears from them that, after endless controversy, Russia consented to a possible future annexation of Bosnia and Herzegovina by Austria.

I have now received a letter from the old emperor [Franz Josef] calling my attention to a promise given by Anpapa [sic]. What an awkward situation! . . . . You will understand what an unpleasant surprise this is and what an embarrassing position we are in . . .[16]

The situation was made even more embarrassing by the arrival in St Petersburg on 28 October of the delegation from Belgrade which had come to plead for armed help for Serbia in her confrontation with Austria. To underline the dynastic link as well as Russia's pan-Slav ties, Crown Prince George, bearing a letter to the Tsar from King Peter, had accompanied the Serbian Prime Minister Pašić and his attendant swarm of officials and academics. Both the Crown Prince and the Prime Minister, who remained several weeks on their lobbying mission, were received more than once in the Winter Palace, but were given little comfort. Russia, with the Far East catastrophe and her own revolution barely two years behind her, was in no mood and in no condition to risk a major conflagration. There were various dark hints about other possibilities in the future but, for the moment, Serbia was told that she must sit on her bayonets and bide her time. The German ambassador in St Petersburg, Count Pourtalès, reported on 13 November, when the Serbian delegation was still in the capital:

I am convinced that His Majesty the Emperor of Russia and his government have done the cause of European peace a great service by warning the Serbian Crown Prince and the other Serbian emissaries to stay calm and refrain from any precipitate action. . . .

Even though the waves of pan-Slavism are currently swelling up higher . . . they quite clearly realize here that war would bring financial ruin for Russia as well as a re-kindling of the revolution with unpredictable consequences . . .[17]

As for that other dynastic aspect of the problem – the relentless efforts of the German Kaiser to curry favour with the Tsar and turn him away from the Anglo-French camp –, this campaign had suffered a severe setback with the annexation crisis. Nicholas, like every other onlooker, imagined that it was Germany who had pushed Austria into the adventure in the first place. As we have seen when viewing this seminal crisis from Berlin and Vienna, the assumption was totally false. Both the Kaiser and Chancellor Bülow were taken aback by the abruptness of the Austrian move and, though very concerned that the issue should be settled in Austria's favour, wanted this to happen peacefully.

By the end of the year the Tsar had come to accept his mistake. The annexation, he wrote to his German cousin on 28 December, had produced 'an uproar of indignation' in Russia and this had been directed not just at Austria but also at Germany as the 'power behind her back'. But, the letter continued: 'Now this belief is gradually losing ground here because people have seen that your country was taken by surprise in the same way as was Russia.' The Tsar ended by appealing to the Kaiser in the name of 'their old friendship' to help damp down the crisis by 'making them understand at Vienna that a war down there is a danger to the peace of Europe'. If William II could do that, 'then war will be avoided'.[18]

The Kaiser and his ministers were just as anxious to avoid a military conflict over two Balkan provinces, which had been tacitly accepted by the powers as being an extension of the Habsburg empire for the past forty years. But, as we have seen, they were ready in Berlin to give total political support to their allies over the annexation affair. It was this support which emboldened Austria to issue her ultimatum to Serbia in March of 1909, at which point in the poker game both King Peter and the Tsar threw in their cards. Nicholas described the moment in another of his revealing letters to his mother (which, unlike those to his wife and to the Kaiser, were always written in Russian):

This affair, which had been going on for six months, has suddenly been complicated by Germany's telling us that we could help to solve the difficulty by agreeing to the famous annexation while, if we refused, the consequences might be very serious and hard to foretell. Once the matter had been put as definitely and as unequivocally as that, there was nothing for it but to swallow one's pride, give in, and agree.[19]

The Tsar was, as usual, sitting out at Tsarkoe Selo when he wrote that. The Dowager Empress was still in Buckingham Palace when she read it. This epitomized the detachment of the Romanovs from what had been yet another crucial challenge to their prestige. The criticism against Nicholas II over the crisis of 1908–9 is not that he did not solve it single-handed or brazen it out at the poker table, as his powerful father might have done. The charge is rather that he gave no leadership at all to his ministers and merely wailed for help abroad.* It all helped to strengthen Austria – and her mightier ally Germany – in the fateful

---

* An interesting statistic: volume 2 of the second series of the French diplomatic documents on pre-war events, which covers the first five months of the annexation crisis (October 1908–February 1909) does not carry one single reference to the Tsar. He is only mentioned casually in the next volume, which deals with the end of the affair. This despite the fact that France was Russia's only ally.

belief that Nicholas and his Russia would always back down.

If Nicholas can be reproached for lethargy over the annexation affair, it was his ill-judged initiatives which were mostly at fault when the next test arrived four years later, as the Balkan states went on the warpath. The course of this two-phased conflict has already been described from the standpoints of the different countries in the region who were involved. During the first phase, which saw the lightning victory of the Balkan partners over the Turks, the Tsar, like the other monarchs watching from the outside, could do little but stare in amazement. But he does deserve credit for realizing the dangers inherent in the situation from the start. Thus on 21 October 1912, when the Turks had just been swept out of northern Albania by the Serbs and Montenegrins, and pushed right back to the approaches of Constantinople itself by the Bulgarians, Nicholas wrote to his mother:

In spite of Alexei's illness,* I am watching the war between the Christians and the Turks very carefully and I rejoice at their brilliant success against the common enemy. The chief difficulty will come at the end of the war, when it will be necessary to face the reconciling of the legitimate rights of the small countries with what remains of Turkey-in-Europe . . .[20]

The 'brilliant success' of the little Balkan states had, in fact, spared Nicholas a very awkward dilemma. When the conflict was still brewing, he had taken what sounded like a strong line with the British ambassador at St Petersburg, who reported at the time: 'He had spoken of . . . the danger of Russian sympathy for the Balkan Slavs forcing his hand should Servia [sic] or Bulgaria become engaged in war with Turkey . . .'[21]

In fact, the Tsar was all the time running scared from involvement in the Balkan imbroglio. This was not least because his only partners, the French, had made it plain that they were not to be counted on for military support in any such intervention. On 12 September 1912, shortly before the fighting had broken out, the French Prime Minister had warned the Tsar's envoy (none other than the egregious Izvolski, who had been relieved of the Foreign Office and transferred to Paris in 1910), that France would give Russia her 'most vigorous diplomatic support' should a Balkan war lead to tension between the great powers. But, the French statesman had continued: 'At this stage of events, the French government would not be able to secure, either from Parliament

---

* The Tsarevich had just recovered from his first serious attack of haemophilia. His condition, which was so bad on 10 October that Holy Communion was administered, improved almost miraculously. The Tsar makes no mention of Rasputin to his mother.

or from public opinion, the necessary approval for any form of active military measures.'[22]

However, the French statesman added, the moment Germany gave armed support to Austria in any escalating military involvement of the powers, France would instantly mobilize at Russia's side. Of course; it was Germany, and Germany alone, who had been in France's sights ever since her pact with Russia had been concluded nearly twenty years before. Nicholas was therefore hobbled from the very beginning over military intervention in the drawn-out Balkan crisis. Where he went sadly wrong was to overestimate his personal and political influence over the combatants. His prediction to his mother that, once victorious, the Balkan partners would start squabbling among themselves, proved all too accurate when these duly started to mobilize against each other in the summer of 1913. On 8 June of that year, Nicholas decided to assert himself once and for all as grand patron of all the Slavs by sending personal telegrams to King Peter of Serbia and Ferdinand (now self-styled tsar) of Bulgaria, threatening them with dire vengeance should either of them refuse his mediation and declare war on the other. The clenched fist showed through the kid glove of diplomatic parlance: 'I want to make it clear that the country which starts such a war will stand responsible for it to the Slav cause, and that I reserve for myself complete freedom of action as regards the attitude which Russia would adopt towards the outcome of such a criminal fight.'[23]

As already recounted, Ferdinand ignored both glove and fist and rashly embarked on the war against his partners which led to military and political disaster for his country. This folly, which came close to destroying Ferdinand, had also humiliated Nicholas. The Tsar was determined to do better whenever another challenge arose in the Balkans and, without dreaming how close that ultimate challenge was, he seems to have been preparing for it during these last months of European peace. To begin with, the pace of Russian rearmament was stepped up rapidly, with eager French assistance. Nicholas also drew Serbia closer and closer into his calculations. The Serbian Prime Minister Pašić, whom he received in audience on 2 February 1914, was asked outright how many soldiers his country could now put into the field. When Pašić replied that Serbia could provide half a million well-equipped soldiers the Tsar commented: 'That is enough. That is no bagatelle; with that one can do a lot.'[24]

The other way in which the Tsar tried to brace Russia up was to go beyond the Anglo-Russian accord of 1907 and persuade England to enter into the same obligations towards Russia as she had undertaken with France. The idea, originally floated by Poincaré on a visit to

Russia in August 1912, was pressed hard again by Nicholas in the spring of 1914. On 3 April of that year he even offered England an all-out defensive military alliance. Failing that (and there was little hope that England would, in fact, go beyond the existing 'entente') he fell back on a long-standing suggestion for closer naval co-operation. The British ambassador in St Petersburg, now Sir George Buchanan, reported the Tsar's arguments after a long audience with him:

'It might . . . be advantageous to arrange beforehand for the co-operation of the British and Russian fleets. By the year 1917 he hoped to have eight Dreadnoughts in the Baltic, and, in the event of war, the Germans would have to detach more than that number of ships to watch them. . . . The existence of a Russian fleet in the Baltic would ease the situation for the British fleet in the North Sea.' Surely, the Tsar had urged, the existing Anglo-Russian understanding over Persia could be extended, either by a general staff arrangement or 'by some written formula which would record the fact of Anglo-Russian co-operation in Europe'.[25]

The Tsar's efforts on the naval front were rewarded that same midsummer when Admiral Sir David Beatty led the First Battle Cruiser Squadron of the Royal Navy, headed by the *Queen Mary*, *Lion*, *Princess Royal* and *New Zealand* up the Baltic to anchor at Kronstadt, and took his officers to pay their respects to a delighted imperial family at Tsarkoe Selo. The date was now 21 June 1914. London had remained doubtful and evasive about the Tsar's other request for 'some written formula'. However, events set in train only seven days after Beatty's visit soon swept all doubts and evasions aside, for Europe as well as for England.

In these final years of peace, two patriotic events had put a momentary sheen on the Romanov presence. The first was the hundredth anniversary of Napoleon's great battle at Borodino. The Tsar went to the famous battlefield to attend the celebrations, whose centrepiece was a military review where every single regiment which had fought there against the French was represented by a unit from its present establishment. Russia's great enemy of a century ago, who had become her great ally of the present, had also been tactfully invited to send a delegation, thus emphasizing the contrast between yesterday and today. Nicholas was still full of emotion when he described the scene to his mother a fortnight later:

No description of the battle can ever produce an impression comparable at all to the one which moves one on setting foot on the soil where the blood was shed of fifty-eight thousand of our brave men. . . . Some of the old redoubts and batteries had been faithfully reconstructed by our sappers. . . . Moreover, a number of old men who still remember the coming of the French had been assembled. Most important amongst them was the veteran Sergeant-Major Voitiniuk, one hundred and twenty two years of age, who had himself fought in the battle! Just imagine, to be able to speak to a man who remembers everything, describes details of the action, indicates the place where he was wounded, etc., etc.[26]

No wonder, as the Tsar wrote from his hunting-lodge at Bialystok, that he had been 'sad to leave the place'.

The other event which rallied the people in a spasm of shared identity with their rulers was the three-hundredth anniversary of the dynasty itself, which fell in March 1913. The celebrations got off to an uncomfortable start when, at the opening Te Deum in St Petersburg's Kazan Cathedral, Rasputin was found to be occupying one of the privileged seats reserved for the Duma. Fortunately the Duma's president, Michael Rodzianko, was even more muscular than the Siberian peasant and, after a brief altercation, during which the *starets* unsuccessfully tried out his powers of hypnotism, he found himself being lifted bodily out of the chair by the back of his crimson silk tunic and kicked out of the church.

But it was the Empress herself who caused the most comment and the most anxiety. As a stately presence, she had improved considerably on her earlier image, once savagely described in these words by one of the haughty noblewomen at her court:

She was at a disadvantage in a ball gown. Her complexion left much to be desired and she had red arms, red shoulders and a red face which always gave one the impression that she was about the burst into tears. . . . She danced badly, not caring for dancing, and she was certainly no conversationalist. Nothing seemed to interest her, nothing aroused her attention, and her whole appearance suggested one of those Byzantine empresses . . . who slowly and with measured tread walked from their palaces at Constantinople to the Cathedral of St Sophia. Everything about her was hieratic, to the very way she dressed in the heavy brocades of which she was so fond, and with diamonds scattered all over her, in defiance of good taste and common sense . . .[27]

The Alexandra Feodorovna of 1913, mother of five children, including a Tsarevich, had become a far more composed and mature figure; yet still, anywhere outside her family circle, she remained an empress of ice. By now heart problems which left her easily exhausted had cut her off even more from social and ceremonial life. The British ambassador, present, of course, at all the tercentenary celebrations, wrote to Buckingham Palace on 9 March:

They have, I fear, been a great strain for the Empress Alexandra, who has been far from well of late. Her Majesty attended the 'Te Deum' at the Kazan Cathedral, the Gala Representation at the opera, the Ball given by the 'Noblesse' of St Petersburg and will also, I believe, assist at the Dinner in the Winter Palace this evening, to which between two and three thousand people have been invited. Both the Gala Opera and the Ball were magnificent sights; but it was pitiful to see what an effort it was for the young Empress to sit through even part of them. One could see how she was suffering and occasionally almost fainting, as if she had a difficulty in breathing . . .[28]

From St Petersburg, Nicholas and Alexandra, together with their children, set out on a pilgrimage to follow the route taken by Michael Romanov three hundred years before on his way to the Volga town of Kostroma, where he was elected to the throne. It was a time of strange contrasts. Especially in the countryside, the imperial family were greeted with frenzies of loyalty; peasants waded up to their waists into the Volga to catch a glimpse of their Tsar gliding by in his steamer. Yet in the factories seven hundred thousand workers were on strike in this tercentenary year. By the New Year the number had topped a million, with police and Cossacks in action against demonstrations in what was beginning to look like a re-run of 1905.

Surely, the ambassadors of the major powers in St Petersburg reported home, a Russia crippled by these domestic problems was in no condition to fight a war. Maurice Paléologue, representing the country most interested to get Russia onto the battlefield, felt he ought to analyse the question for his foreign minister. Was it true that, if the Tsar went to war, 'he would do well to fit a clamp on his imperial crown so that it would not be swept away by the winds of revolution?'

After a long exposition, the envoy came to the conclusion that autocracy was still firmly in place in Russia and, if it were ever threatened, war would have little or nothing to do with it. That prophecy[29] was written on 21 May 1914. It may have been just what Paris wanted to hear; but it was not much of a forecast for the hurricane which lay just ahead for the Romanovs and their Russia.

Chapter Thirteen

ENGLAND:
THE WIDOW'S HERITAGE

The role played by the crown of England during the long prelude to the Great War was a curiously uneven one. From her widowhood in 1861 down to her death forty years later, Queen Victoria had to make her own decisions. She held stubborn and consistent prejudices in foreign affairs and struggled, with mixed fortunes, to turn these into government policies. Her son, Edward VII, brought with him to the throne in 1901 precisely the opposite prejudices towards the European power game, which he, on the other hand, succeeded in influencing throughout his nine-year reign, blatantly, and, at times, unconstitutionally. The last of the pre-war sovereigns, George V, simply opted out of the game altogether. It was only when catastrophe stared the entire continent, including his own kingdom, in the face that he was brought by his ministers unavailingly into play.

For the Queen, foreign policy was basically family policy. That family was spread far, wide and high. Its links ran in straight or zigzag lines to almost every court in Europe, except to the Habsburgs in Vienna. This complexity brought problems for the 'Grandmother of Europe' when the different members of her august blood got involved in political quarrels. But her approach was always simplified by the overwhelming weight of German wood in the family tree. She was herself entirely German by blood, with nothing but Hanover, Mecklenburg-Strelitz, Brunswick, Saxe-Coburg and the like in her ancestry. She had double-looped this Germanic knot by marrying, in 1840, Albert of Saxe-Coburg-Gotha, the insignificant little principality which marched into European history up the altar steps. She placidly converted the dynastic connection into a political one. Accordingly, any clash of interests between England and the German states had to be avoided or played down. If German interests clashed with those of third countries, then the German cause must be upheld. Even when the 'dear little Germany' of her husband's day, which embraced so many cosy

and harmless states like the Coburg of Prince Albert, was forged, on
Bismarck's anvil, into the fearsome, Prussian-dominated, German
empire, the Queen still did her utmost to give it preference where she
could no longer show it affection. It was as well that she was spared the
final confrontation between the great land empire of the Hohenzollerns
and her own empire of the oceans.

The most pressing, and most obvious, way to link the dynastic with
the political was to marry her eldest son and heir to a German princess.
These existed in profusion across the Channel; but the search for the
right candidate, launched around 1858, when the bridegroom-to-be
was only seventeen, proved heart-rendingly frustrating for his mother.
To start with, 'Bertie' (as he was known in the family) had already
developed that voracious taste for female beauty, elegance and wit that
was to stay with him to the last day of his life, drawing European gossip
and scandal in its wake like the tail of a comet. Then there was the
problem of religion. England's future Defender of the Faith could not
pick out a Bourbon or a Habsburg to bring home to Windsor even had
he so desired. So the search began for a Protestant beauty with charm
as well as looks. The Crown Princess of Prussia (none other, of course,
than Queen Victoria's eldest daughter, Vicky)* was immediately
roped in to help. 'Why won't Pcss. Marie become a Protestant?' Queen
Victoria bemoaned early in 1861. The reference was to Princess Marie
of Hohenzollern-Sigmaringen, the pick of the European bunch on all
grounds except the unbridgeable one that she belonged to the southern,
Catholic branch of the Prussian royal family and had no intention of
abandoning her faith, even to become Queen of England. (It was her
kinsman, Prince Charles, who in 1866 became Prince of Rumania.)

Another early favourite was Princess Elizabeth of Wied, whom we
have already met in later life as 'Carmen Sylva', the enchantingly
talented and scatty wife of that same Rumanian king. Before the match
to King Carol, she had been ruled out for the Prince of Wales as being
altogether too dowdy and, as Vicky reported, 'certainly the opposite to
Bertie's usual taste'. One by one, as Queen Victoria's daughter in
Potsdam and her Coburg uncle, King Leopold of the Belgians in
Brussels, went the rounds of the European courts, candidate after
candidate was struck from the list. Princess Hilde of Dessau, Princess
Marie of the Netherlands, and another Princess Marie (of Altenburg)
were among those eliminated either because they were too dim, or too
frail, or too plain, or all three at once. The poor Altenburg girl was
blackballed for being so badly dressed as well.

* See *supra*, p. 83.

It was Vicky who steered her mother into moving reluctantly away from Germany and northwards to the court at Copenhagen. Princess Alexandra was the eldest daughter of Prince Christian of Schleswig-Holstein-Sonderburg-Glücksburg, who was heir to the throne of Denmark. She was said to be as pretty as she was Protestant and Vicky was accordingly asked by Queen Victoria to make an inspection. From Strelitz, on 4 June 1861, the Prussian Crown Princess wrote enthusiastically to her mother:

I never set eyes on a sweeter creature. . . . She is lovely. . . . Her voice, her walk, carriage and manner are perfect, she is one of the most lady-like and aristocratic-looking people I ever saw. . . . I know you and Papa would be charmed with her . . .[1]

Bertie himself confirmed the verdict in a specially contrived 'sightseeing' meeting with the chosen one in Speier Cathedral in September of that year. Despite a drawn-out battle by the Coburg clan to keep the marriage in the German camp, if not in their own family, their engagement was announced a year later, and the couple were married on 10 March 1863 in St George's Chapel, Windsor. During the brilliant ceremony the Queen kept almost out of sight in Catherine of Aragon's closet above the aisle, dressed in her black widow's weeds. The last time she had been in that Windsor Chapel was fifteen months before, to attend the funeral of her own beloved Albert.

Within a year of the wedding power politics drove straight across the new dynastic link. Otto Bismarck, now Prime Minister of Prussia, launched the first of his lightning expansionist wars by invading the border provinces of Schleswig-Holstein whose sovereignty was a matter of byzantine dispute between Berlin, Copenhagen and the local princelings. Queen Victoria's new daughter-in-law was Danish but her own daughter was Crown Princess of Prussia and it was that side which the Queen took, without hesitation, from the first moment. 'With regard to this sad S. Holstein question . . . my heart and sympathies are all German . . .', she wrote to the Crown Princess on 27 January 1864, when the quarrel was brewing.[2]

And when battle commenced and the Prussian cannon went into action, Vicky wrote back with the righteous complaisance of any good *Junker* wife: 'I can see nothing inhuman or improper in any way in the bombardment of Sonderburg; it was necessary, and we hope it has been useful.'[3] In this, she had merely carried out an earlier pledge to her mother: 'I see myself in duty bound as a good wife – and as a really devoted and enthusiastic Prussian.'[4]

Her mother's position was, however, much more complicated. 'Alix', as Princess Alexandra was known, was distraught with grief and fury against Prussia in general and Bismarck (whom she never forgave) in particular. Her newly-married husband was bound to share her emotions and to resist, therefore, the efforts which the British government was making to urge compliance on the Danes. So, on 17 May, we find the Queen writing to her foreign secretary of the day: 'It strikes the Queen that it would be *very* useful if Lord Clarendon would take an opportunity of seeing the Prince of Wales and *preparing* him for what the Danish Government, in *all* probability, will have to consent to . . .'

The Prince of Wales was, in fact, pleading to be allowed to act as an intermediary in the conflict – a request which, along with his many later pleas to be given a personal role in his country's diplomacy, came to nothing.

The Queen directed that the Prince's offer should be accepted only 'with extreme caution' and that, in the meantime, he should be warned against 'any violent abuse of Prussia'. He should be reminded, she told Lord Clarendon, that 'he is bound by many ties of blood to Germany and only, quite lately, to Denmark'.[5]

But the Queen also had problems with her Whig Prime Minister, Lord Palmerston; with the Tory opposition; and with Parliament and public opinion in general. 'Any surrender of the integrity of Denmark would be very unpopular in this country,' her government warned.[6]

Palmerston used much stronger language to his notoriously pro-German sovereign:

The Germans are acting like a strong man who thinks he has got a weak man in a corner, and that he can bully and beat him to his heart's content. . . . But it sometimes happens . . . that the wicked giant finds that his intended victim meets with unlooked-for support.[7]

Denmark did not get 'unlooked-for support'. The crisis threatened to escalate into a major conflict when Prussia brought in Austria on her side and there was even talk of sending the English fleet into the Baltic to do battle for the Danes. In the event, due as much to the more cautious elements in the Cabinet as to the efforts of the Queen, England remained neutral and Denmark was abandoned to her fate. None the less, referring to newspaper criticisms about the Queen's one-sided intervention in the dispute, Palmerston had felt bound, when it was all over, to send her this blunt warning:

It would be a great evil if public opinion were to divest Your Majesty of that proper and essential protection which the Constitution secures for the

Sovereign by making the responsible Ministers answerable for all that is done or not done . . .[8]

The Queen gave only a guarded response. But two days later, using her mocking sobriquet for her Prime Minister, she snorted, in a letter to her Coburg uncle in Brussels: 'Pilgerstein is gouty, and extremely impertinent.'[9]

It now became steadily more difficult for the Queen to proceed with the task which her husband had bequeathed to her – namely, to have England marching always together with a Germany which was strong, united, friendly and liberal. The problem, of course, was Bismarck, who was building up both the strength and the unity under Prussia's dominance but not necessarily the friendliness nor the liberalism. He shocked the Queen as well as the rest of Europe by swiftly turning on Austria, his ally in the Danish conflict, in order to drive the Habsburg monarchy out of the German confederation for good. When that contrived quarrel blew up, the Queen was at first all for taking the Austrian side, even to the extent of bringing in England and France against Prussia. But the speedy and crushing triumph of Prussian arms at Sadowa in July of 1866, already described elsewhere, put paid to such thoughts. The fact of Prussian hegemony had to be accepted, however unpalatable in many respects.

War, any war which might align England against Germany, remained her nightmare. Indeed, when Bismarck, having disposed of Denmark and Austria, started setting his sights unmistakably on France, the Queen even advocated a preventive alliance with Prussia, simply to keep the two powers from each other's throats. Again, she underestimated Bismarck's ruthlessness. Her daughter Vicky complained, after it was all over, with England having again stayed neutral:

I think in the *main* grievance Germany is right and her feeling *legitimate*; for in my mind I cannot help thinking England *could* have and should have prevented the war – by a rebuke and a threat to the party who was the aggressor.[10]

The nagging fear of an Anglo-German clash of interests surfaced afresh five years later, when the Balkans started to heave with rebellion against the Ottoman empire. The war which Russia, as protector of the little Slav nations, fought and won against Turkey in 1877 and the international distribution of the spoils at the Congress of Berlin a year later have already been looked at from the standpoint of the various nations closely involved. England was mainly concerned in the final solution to keep the paws of the Russian bear away from Constantinople and to protect the recently-opened Suez Canal; this, plus the

acquisition of Cyprus, was duly achieved for her at the Congress by
Lord Beaconsfield, the ennobled Benjamin Disraeli. But the Queen's
mind throughout was exercised more by family than by strategic
matters. Both she and her daughter had felt the familiar twinges of
dynastic unease from the beginning: 'The Oriental affair is very
disagreeable,' the Queen wrote to Vicky on 29 May 1876.[11]

The Prussian Crown Princess agreed: 'The Oriental Question does
fidget one in the extreme,' she wrote back on 10 June, adding, 'I am so
afraid of England and Germany being estranged by it.'[12]

Germany, the daughter assured her mother later that year, was not
supporting Russia's aggressive stand in the Balkans or, if she was, it
was only because England was 'hanging back' on an alliance with
Berlin.[13] The old dream and the old reproach again.

As Russia and the Austro-German camp were now moving towards
confrontation in the Balkans, it followed that the Queen's passionate
partisanship for Germany should bring with it growing coolness
towards Russia. This had always existed and stemmed from a certain
dynastic *hauteur* as well as broader considerations such as the strategic
conflict along the Himalayas. A few weeks after her marriage to the
Prussian Crown Prince, a high imperial order for ladies was conferred
on Vicky from St Petersburg.

'So you have got the order of St Catherine,' the Queen sniffed on
hearing the news, adding graciously, 'You can wear it with the others if
you like.'[14] (It was, of course, no longer any business of Queen
Victoria's what decorations her daughter wore at the court of
Potsdam.)

Later that year the Queen's air of condescension became even
heavier as she told her daughter: 'Our princes never admitted the
Grand Dukes of Russia having precedence over them . . .'[15]

As for the other great continental dynasties, the Queen would have
certainly admitted that the Habsburgs and the Bourbons were, to put it
mildly, on a level footing with the obscure little Coburg house whose
name she had carried since the marriage to Prince Albert. But, thanks
mainly to the great religious divide, there was as good as no contact
with the court in Vienna. There was much intermarriage between the
aristocracies of England and Austria-Hungary, while the upper-class
Hungarians, in particular, were almost embarrassingly Anglomaniac.
But the Austrian Emperor himself might almost have lived on the moon
so far as contact with Queen Victoria was concerned. They occupied
their thrones for fifty-three years in parallel and during all that time
they met but fleetingly – once, for example, for a few minutes of general
conversation at Innsbruck railway station.

As for the Bourbons, their last ruling remnants had, of course, disappeared from the scene quite early in Victoria's reign. She found that she could get on surprisingly well with Louis (nephew of Bonaparte), the president of the French republic who had revived the monarchy and proclaimed himself Napoleon III in 1852. This was due not least to the intelligence, charm and beauty of Napoleon's new bride Eugénie. The French couple had captivated Prince Albert and Victoria on a visit to London in April of 1855, and there followed, in August of that year, a very successful family return visit to Paris.* But, in 1870, Napoleon was deposed and had fled to England with Eugénie after his disastrous defeat at Prussia's hands, and the French empire became again a republic. Ardently republican it remained, which did not endear it to the Queen, especially after it began to forge its close links – at first financial and then political and military – with the already suspect Russia.

In the last years of her reign it looked as though her worst fears about this unholy and unnatural partnership would be realized. She had already envisaged war with Russia when the Balkan crisis was at its height in 1878 and even threatened resignation rather than let the Tsar into Egypt. A letter to Lord Beaconsfield in May of that year contained the sober words: 'The Queen ... must own to disbelieving any *permanent* settlement of Peace until we have fought and beaten the Russians.'[16] Twenty years later it looked for a while to her – and indeed to her ministers – as though England might have to confront the recently allied strengths of Russia and France over a squabble, not in the Balkan mountains, but in the swamps and deserts of Africa. In 1898 a French military outpost at Fashoda on the Upper Nile had refused to yield, on orders from Paris, to British troops pushing down from the reconquered Sudan. Throughout October of that year war fever mounted, stirred by the jingoists on both sides of the Channel and it seemed that France might push the crisis to the limit; Russia, so the reports went, was egging her on.

On 28 October the Queen enquired anxiously of Lord Salisbury:

Ought we not to ask the Russians if the reports are true, and further get assurances of support and understanding with the other powers, Italy, Germany and Austria? But surely the French will not let it come to that?[17]

In the event, they did not. The French government backed down the

---

* The watchful Parisians noted straightaway the difference between their own *parvenue* Empress and a monarch born to the purple. At receptions, Eugénie would give a fleeting glance behind her before sitting down, just to make sure that the chair was there. Victoria, knowing it would be, just sat.

following month. The offending outpost was evacuated and the Fashoda war scare died away as quickly as it had arisen, like a flash flood in the wadis of those African deserts surrounding it. None the less, if any political punter of the day had been asked to wager on a continental partner for an England now emerging out of her long, calculated isolation, the money would have been all on Germany, with France nowhere in the market. Fashoda seemed to have brought Prince Albert's political vision a good deal sharper and closer. Indeed, there had already been much talk of, and one important diplomatic move towards, an Anglo-German alliance. This was launched in London in March of 1898 by the British colonial secretary, Joseph Chamberlain, leader of the pro-German faction in a government divided on the issue.

That it all came to nothing was due partly to England's clinging reluctance to commit herself; partly to reservations about a Germany with whom she was already locked in world-wide commercial battle, with a deadlier naval rivalry fast looming up; and partly to hesitations in Berlin. But William ii, the Queen's most difficult (and most dangerous) grandson was also to blame in that, over the years, he had personified and magnified all the most unpalatable aspects of his nation.

The Queen's own doubts about him went right back to the days when, as a five-year-old brought to pay his respects to her at Osborne, he had refused to get in the back of the pony-cart, insisting on sitting in front instead. Two years later, she wrote, on 'dear little William's birthday', the hopeful prayer: 'May God preserve him and may he grow up good, clever and liberal-minded in his views.'[18] That prayer of 1866 remained unanswered, especially after 'dear little William' came with such unexpected speed to the German imperial crown little more than twenty years later. From then on, it was the European continent he wanted to drive, not the Osborne pony-cart. The Queen fumed at his display of arrogant tactlessness, such as the famous snub delivered to her own 'Bertie' in Vienna in October of 1888.* Like her ministers and subjects, she winced and shuddered as the Kaiser let fly, one after the other, with his vainglorious speeches. But, by the end, what probably troubled her most about her imperial grandson was his passion for intrigue and his talent for deceit.

That he revered her in his twisted fashion is beyond doubt, though the affection was always cloying and overdone. One of his last Christmas messages to her was typical:

May Heaven shield your precious life and health from all evil . . . for the

* See *supra* p. 104 above.

maintenance of the peace of the world. . . . Come what may, I shall always be glad to assist anybody for the preservation of Peace and Goodwill among men![19]

Yet all the time it seemed to her that he was constantly at work behind the scenes making not peace but trouble, with England as the principal target. She almost certainly died in ignorance of how William had exploited the Chamberlain approach by claiming, in a letter to the Tsar, that England had made him 'enormous offers' of an alliance. If he turned these offers down, he had asked, what would Nicholas II give him in return?[20] But, without knowing the details, she was well aware of her grandson's overall game. The draft of her letter for the Tsar dated 1 March 1899 reads:

I am afraid William may go and tell things against us to you, just as he does about you to us. If so, pray tell me openly and confidentially. It is so important that we should understand each other and that such mischievous and unstraightforward talk should be put a stop to . . .[21]

None the less, that same November, William, accompanied by his Empress Dona, came over to England for a harmonious visit to Windsor and Sandringham. It was the last such peaceful family reunion. The next time William came to see his grandmother it was in January 1901, to her death-bed at Osborne House. Even here, he wanted to get into the driving seat. Much to the annoyance of his uncle Bertie, who was about to become King of England, he insisted on holding on to the Queen until her dying breath and even on measuring her afterwards for her coffin. It was a typical blend of histrionics and genuine feeling.

The death-chamber at Osborne is the place from which to look back on the Queen's enormous reign, to summarize the personal influence she had had on the course of European affairs. On the strictly family front, which, apart from the key link of Vicky in Berlin, consisted mainly of intrigues over minor crowns, she enjoyed mixed fortunes. She won a battle against her Belgian Coburg relatives over filling the throne of Greece, which became vacant in 1862; the unsuitable, childless Duke Ernest finally withdrew as a candidate in favour of her nominee, Prince William of Denmark, brother of Bertie's bride. But, as we have seen, she was less successful elsewhere in this game of Balkan princelings. She had failed to get her protégé, Sandro Battenberg, reinstated to the Bulgarian throne and failed again to prevent his being replaced there by Foxy Ferdinand. The supreme dynastic setback was, of course, none of her doing: the tragedy of her Prussian son-in-law's death after ruling for a mere hundred days as the second ruler of Bismarck's new German empire. Her Vicky had been transformed almost immediately from Crown Princess to widowed Empress; her husband's funeral had also buried the Queen's rosiest hopes of Anglo-German unity.

With the exception of her bellicosity towards Russia, Queen Victoria stood always on the side of peace. However, as that stand was struck largely in the Europe of Bismarck's ruthless expansionism it did not count for much. Most of the Queen's attempts to block the Iron Chancellor's ambitions with her barriers of dynastic loyalty proved sadly, almost pathetically, futile. Thus, old King William I of Prussia simply ignored the appeal she sent to him in the spring of 1866 not to wage war on Austria, 'the responsibility of which will rest on you alone'.[22] She had no better luck when she tried to head off the next of Bismarck's wars, the 1870 campaign against France, by proposing a mass démarche of monarchs. Why, she suggested to Lord Granville on 15 July of that year, should not the emperors of Russia and Austria, and the kings of Holland, Belgium and Italy, join with her in making a combined appeal for peace?[23] The answer, as she was slow to learn, was that the new Europe was being forged by Bismarck's 'blood and iron' and not by any magic circle of crowns. Occasionally her ideas bordered on pure fantasy, such as her suggestion to solve the entire Balkan problem by uniting all the provinces of Turkey-in-Europe into one Christian, neutral state – a scheme which Lord Beaconsfield gently talked her out of.[24]

Her direct personal influence on the affairs of her own empire was equally mixed and, on the whole, marginal. It was the then Mr Disraeli who, in a letter written as far back as May of 1859, had suggested to her the fundamental imperial assertion, namely that she should associate her own name with that of her Indian subjects.[25] But it was not until 1873 that she seriously considered the idea herself, and not until 1 January 1877 that she was finally proclaimed Empress of India at Delhi. Even then, though she became captivated by the Orient (learning Hindustani and importing into her palace various very pampered Indian servants), it was only towards the end of the century that she began to think in imperial as opposed to European terms.

This process was accompanied by agonizing setbacks. The Sudan of the 1880s provided the most painful example. The mystic soldier-adventurer, General Charles Gordon, had been dispatched to Khartoum with inadequate resources and even more inadequate instructions to save the English inhabitants of that remote desert city from the dervish army of the Mahdi, who was rolling up the vast country in a holy war against the white Christian invader. As early as February of 1884 the Queen started trembling for Gordon's safety and, throughout the next eleven months, she pounded away at her Prime Minister, Gladstone, and his government to send reinforcements to the Sudan. 'Surely Indian troops might go from Aden,' one such demand went. 'They could bear the climate. You have incurred fearful responsibility.'[26] When, in January of the following year, Khartoum fell and the news of Gordon's death came through, the Queen did more than privately share the anguish of her people; she made it public, and placed the blame where it lay. In an unprecedented move, she sent her telegram of rebuke to Gladstone and his responsible ministers *en clair* so that everyone should know her feelings: 'These news from Khartoum are frightful, and to think that all this might have been prevented and many precious lives saved by earlier action is too frightful.'[27]

However, the point to note is that the Queen-Empress had not been able to prevent the tragedy herself, despite the strongest personal pressure exerted over the best part of a year. At the very end of her reign came an even deeper imperial humiliation when, in 1899, the Boer War broke out. Unlike the Sudan crisis, this also had a powerful European reaction. Germany, with William II very much to the fore, stirred the Boers on. French and Russian newspapers joined the German press in a chorus of condemnation. Only the Austrian Emperor Franz Josef, for some reason, showed sympathy for the English case, but the Habsburg monarchy was of little use in this connection. By the time the old Queen died it was clear, not only that imperialism had its drawbacks, but that England's isolationism had to end. She needed allies in Europe if her huge commitments outside Europe were to be protected.

It is time to look at Victoria's heir, who was soon to play a lifelong personal part in securing those allies. During his mother's lifetime he had to struggle to get even into the wings of the diplomatic stage. We have seen how, during the Prusso-Danish war of 1864, he had pleaded in vain to be given some role as mediator. He was not only shut out from the action (wisely in view of his emotional pro-Danish prejudices); he was also excluded from official information about the crisis. When he pressed to see the relevant Foreign Office dispatches, his mother refused point-blank, giving as her reason: 'The Queen cannot help objecting to the *principle*, which would thus be admitted, of separate and independent communication between the Prince of Wales and her government.'[28]

She was just as adamant about any verbal briefings about the situation: 'The Queen would not wish Lord Clarendon to enter into too many details or say *anything* of a very *confidential* nature . . .'[29]

It would be very wrong to suppose that, because of these official barriers, the Prince was ill-informed about foreign affairs. He always had his own friends, in office and opposition. He had a wide circle of relatives and other informants on the continent. In London, as the leader of society, he had privileged access to the houses and confidences of the diplomatic corps. For all this, however, the so-called 'Battle of the Boxes' was not simply a matter of personal pride. If he wanted to know exactly what the government of the day was up to, there was no substitute for full, regular and unimpeded access to its secret papers. This was only formally secured in 1886, and it was none of the Queen's doing. The future Prime Minister, Lord Rosebery, a personal friend of the Prince, and a fellow member of the Turf Club, happened to be doing a five-month spell as foreign secretary that year, and took the opportunity to hand Bertie something which had lain unused in the Foreign Office for twenty-five years, the special golden key which had been made for his father to open all government dispatch boxes. So, at the mature age of forty-five, the Crown Prince was given official access to crown secrets. The Queen was angry at the action taken behind her back, for she was repeatedly assuring herself and anyone who cared to listen that her son was really not fit to rule. She saw that it would be imprudent to revoke the privilege once granted; but she also took care, to the end of her days, to share precious little else with her son and heir.

Deprived for so long of playing a part in what fascinated him most – foreign affairs – the Prince of Wales had grown instead into a parallel role, that of the leader of English and continental society. The parallelism is important to stress. The Europe of those days was dominated by its leading families: say a thousand of them, counting the more recently ennobled plutocracy ·and 'meritocracy'. It was their members who provided the vast bulk of the chancellors, prime ministers, foreign secretaries, ambassadors, courtiers, generals and financiers who kept the power game revolving. It was in a sense immaterial whether one met them at international conferences, from which the Prince was clearly excluded, or at the race-courses, spas, regattas, pheasant shoots, grand weddings or funerals at which the Prince equally clearly stood out. He was able to gain their confidence not merely because he was the Heir-Apparent to the greatest empire on earth but because he had a talent, almost a genius, for cultivating friendships with those of all nationalities and temperaments. His many tutors, despairing of his mulish reluctance to get down to his studies, all noted how good he was with people with whom, from childhood, he had always felt more at ease than with books. The friends chosen for him as a boy by his pedantic, well-meaning Coburg father, were all conventional enough: boys from Eton, like Charles Carrington, asked over to nearby Windsor Castle as companions. But after the death of his father, the Prince Consort,* and, even more, after his own marriage two years later, Bertie set about choosing his own friends, and most of these were far from conventional.

In Norfolk, where the Prince had purchased the 7,000-acre Sandringham estate, the guests included from the beginning some of the straightforward East Anglian shooting set, such as Lord Suffield of Gunton Hall, or the Earl of Leicester from Holkham. But as time went on the circle was widened to embrace a social jumble of visitors who looked almost hilariously out of place in an English sporting country seat.

In December of 1873, Bishop Magee of Peterborough arrived for the weekend. He had been invited not to shoot but to talk, at which, being an Irishman, he excelled. Any fears he may have felt at being out of place in his episcopal gaiters vanished when he was introduced to his fellow-guests. As he recorded:

I find the company pleasant and civil, but we are a curious mixture. Two Jews, Sir Anthony de Rothschild and his daughter; an ex-Jew, Disraeli; a Roman Catholic, Colonel Higgins; and Italian duchess who is an Englishwoman, brought up a Roman Catholic and now turning Protestant; a set of young lords and a bishop. . . . We are all to lunch together in a few minutes . . .[30]

That Sandringham guest list gives a good flavour of the Prince's social tastes. Variety was the keynote. A talent to amuse – combined wherever possible with the means to entertain – was the password. The Prince could just tolerate around him women with little else to commend them but outstanding beauty. But the men had to have wit as well as money or distinction. That combination accounts for the Prince's many Jewish friends. They amused him with their stories as well as indulging him with their lavish parties. He gave them in return something far more precious in the England of the day – acceptance, through his patronage, into the highest social circle of the land. In 1881 he even attended, in a synagogue, the wedding of another Rothschild – Leopold – a departure which caused much delight among Jewish circles, and much head-shaking among Anglican ones.

He extended similar patronage to the wave of Jewish South African diamond millionaires like the Wernhers, who followed the Jewish bankers up the Prince's magic bean-stalk. To these eager climbers were

---

* Prince Albert died on 13 December 1861 of typhoid fever. Three weeks before the ailing father had struggled to Cambridge, where Bertie was an undergraduate, to read the son a final sermon on a life-style which was already laced with scandal.

added home-grown non-Jewish tycoons like the grocer-yachtsman Thomas Lipton (whom he knighted into the bargain) and a swarm of other successful figures from Victorian industry, bureaucracy and the City. Though his own prime aim in this was to seek distraction, the breadth of his choice also reflected that spontaneous passion for people which had been with him since childhood. Whatever the motive, the result brought even more benefit to his crown and country than to himself. The Queen his mother had become, in the eyes of her subjects, a dowdy recluse in widow's weeds; a remote figure on the postage stamps, most of them, appropriately, being penny blacks. The Prince and his graceful young bride not only enlivened the social scene; they opened it up as well.

This was best epitomized in the 'Marlborough House set', named after the handsome mansion in Pall Mall that was their London home.* It immediately became the fulcrum of social life in and around the capital. Society (those born into it and those pressing to enter it) now had what they yearned for – a fixed season revolving around a fixed sun and moon. The royal pattern has not much changed to this day: autumn, Christmas and the New Year at Balmoral and Sandringham for stalking and shooting; the late winter months tempered by at least one visit to warmer climes; then the main London summer season of presentation balls, country house parties, Ascot, Henley and Cowes; and so (in the Prince's case after another August trip abroad) into the autumn again.

The role that sport played in all this (and pheasant-shooting in particular) was central. Then as today, the old families struggled to keep inherited standards up; then as today, the *nouveaux riches* struggled to move alongside them by outdoing them with sporting bags and lavish entertaining. Edward, whether as prince or king, was an exemplary sportsman in the purest sense of the word. Though only a moderate performer himself, he delighted in shooting alongside the best in his kingdom and, when doing so, sought neither flattery nor concessions from them.

Belonging to the Marlborough House set (frowned on as 'fast' by the Queen) had two drawbacks: it cost a lot of money and it sparked a lot of scandal. Both problems afflicted its august leader. Bertie never had enough money. His regular official income did not exceed £115,000 a year for the first twenty-seven years of his married life and was only, after a long fight, raised by Parliament in 1890 to £150,000. There were

---

* It had been designed in 1710 by the great English architect Christopher Wren for the equally great English soldier duke whose name it bore.

useful windfalls from time to time, like the prize money brought in by his greatest horse Persimmon, which won both the Derby and the St Leger in 1896, causing the whole empire, let alone the whole country, to erupt with patriotic joy. (Could one have imagined his mother, at any stage of her reign, beaming with pride in the winners' enclosure of a racecourse?) Even greater triumphs followed in 1900 when he actually headed the list of winning owners. But the huge bills had to be met all the time that the wind was not blowing the right way and the Prince was perpetually pressed by his creditors and moneylenders.

Here, his Jewish banker friends again entered the scene, above all the immensely shrewd and loyal Ernest Cassel, an obscure immigrant from Cologne who, after a meteoric career in the City, became the Prince's chief financial adviser. This he remained also throughout the nine-year reign of his royal patron which was to come, always 'managing investments' in such a way that Edward, as prince and king, mysteriously came out on top, whatever the vagaries of the market. What Cassel wanted in return was the familiar demand for social acceptance. At one point it was a demand which he quite literally presented: when asked by Sir Edward Grey in 1908 to help the Bank of Morocco out of trouble with a £500,000 loan, Cassel agreed on condition that the Grand Cross of the Order of the Bath be added to the other grand crosses (of the Royal Victorian Order and the Order of St Michael and St George) which he could already pin on his breast. He scandalized the foreign secretary, but eventually got his half-million-pound sash.*

What the Prince's friends, Jewish or otherwise, could not always shield him from was scandal. Nearly all of this concerned the women in his married life, for he was the very model of genial but remorseless infidelity. Such was the reputation he had earned for himself that he was judged guilty even when, in all probability, he was innocent – as when, in the divorce trial in February 1870 of Lady Harriet Mordaunt, he was accused by the evidently deranged woman of being one of her many lovers, 'often, and in open day'. On other occasions there could be little doubt of his involvement, as when, in the autumn of the following year, he had to negotiate, through discreet intermediaries, for the return of some letters he had written to the notorious Parisian courtesan, Giulia Barucci, described by the lady herself as 'the greatest whore in the world'. Once it was his gambling set of men friends who

* Cassel's place in society was consolidated when his only child, Maud, married a man of good if not brilliant family, Mr Wilfrid Ashley, with King Edward in attendance. When, eventually, the daughter of that marriage, Edwina, married Lord Louis Mountbatten, the Cassel blood, and the Cassel millions, mixed in with royalty.

landed him with distressing publicity. This was the so-called Baccarat
Case of 1891 when he was obliged to appear in the witness box in a libel
action to decide whether a lieutenant-colonel in the Scots Guards, Sir
William Gordon-Cumming, had or had not cheated at cards at a
country house party attended by the Prince the year before. To the
Queen (and nephew William, who penned a typically infuriating letter
of reproach from Berlin) suspected cardsharpers were no company for
the heir to the throne. It was part of the penalty for leading a very mixed
society, and setting it a very fast pace.

More important for the Prince's future (both his own and his
country's) than the leadership of English society was that, long before
he came to the throne, that pre-eminence was extended throughout the
European continent as well. In his time that continent was the world
which counted, and he only made two trips in his life outside it. The
first, in 1860, was a tour of the United States, which had been added on
to a visit to Canada at the express request of the then American
president, James Buchanan. As no heir to the English throne had
crossed the Atlantic before, let alone visited the one-time American
colonies, it was a stiff challenge for the nineteen-year-old Prince. By the
time he set sail for home again after nearly a month on American soil,
even his parents – so niggardly with their praise – were obliged to admit
that Bertie had been an enormous success. That was due primarily to
his own informality, curiosity for the new in people and places, respect
for riches and zest for life, qualities all shared to the full by his hosts. As
for the impact of America on the Prince, he never shed the memory of
the sheer size, strength and vitality of the country and its people.
Detroit, Chicago, Cincinnati and Pittsburgh, each appeared in turn as
another giant furnace of energy, giving a welcome correspondingly
warm. At St Louis, where his arrival coincided with the annual autumn
fair, a hundred thousand people turned out to see 'Baron Renfrew', his
very transparent incognito, ordained for the journey by the Queen. In
New York (according to his own unscientific estimate) three times that
number jammed the Broadway area to see him drive past. The ball in
that great city which ended the tour was vast in proportion. Three
thousand guests had been invited. Another two thousand gatecrashers
came along as well and part of the floor collapsed under the weight of
flesh, fur and jewellery. The Prince's only regret was that he was
obliged to dance with the wives of the leading industrialists present,
instead of with their daughters.

The tour did more than establish Bertie (hitherto regarded as
something of a pleasure-seeking lightweight) as an international

personality in his own right, a vote-winner in democratic terms.* It left him with an enduring affection and admiration for the transatlantic half of the Anglo-Saxon race. This was of relatively little consequence diplomatically for, during his lifetime, the United States, of its own volition, played only a modest role in world affairs. It all helped, none the less, to build bridges for the future. In the shorter term, both as Prince and King, Edward paid back his hosts of 1860 in his own golden coin of patronage. Any American man or woman who fulfilled the personal requirements listed above was always sure of a place in his circle. Given the determined campaign of American heiresses, daughters of the New World's leaders, to graft themselves onto the social stalks of the Old, that was no mean return.

The only other occasion in his life when he strayed far from the European continent was when he visited India, at Disraeli's urging, in 1875. This journey lasted seven months, not four weeks, and instead of the fast-moving informal excitements of the American tour, he was subjected to ponderous ritualistic repetitions of the same durbars, elephant processions, banquets, firework displays and investitures up and down the subcontinent. He returned unawed by the magic of the Orient and equally uncaptivated by the mystique of the Raj. 'As regards myself, I must tell you frankly that I could never consent to the world "Imperial" being added to my name,' he wrote the following year to Disraeli when his mother finally assumed the style Empress (without taking him into her confidence first).[31] As for his friends, all that the Marlborough set noted and bemoaned was that the whole of the autumn and winter season of 1875–76 was unbearably dull because its leader had gone absent, half-way across the globe.

His indifference towards imperial glory was the other side of the coin to his passion for Europe. The continent was both his personal playground and his field of diplomatic campaign and the contrast with his mother's approach to the European power conundrum was plain from the first. He never shared either her instinctive warmth towards all things German nor her corresponding coolness towards Russia. As far back as 1866, when his sister-in-law Princess Dagmar of Denmark was married to the future Tsar Alexander III, he had successfully appealed to be allowed to go to St Petersburg for the wedding. That he had dynastic politics in mind as well as pleasure is shown by a remarkable phrase in a remarkable plea he sent to the Prime Minister of the day, Lord Palmerston: 'I should be only too happy to be the

---

* 'Come back in four years and run for President', was one enthusiastic shout he had heard from the New York crowds.

means in any way of promoting the "entente cordiale" between Russia and our own country . . .[32]

The next two decades provided more dynastic summonses to St Petersburg and the Prince strove to exact some political goodwill out of each occasion. Thus, in March 1881, when Alexander III became Tsar after the murder of his father, the Prince positively steamrollered Lord Granville, the foreign secretary, into agreeing that the Order of the Garter – probably the most coveted decoration in the world – should be given the new Russian ruler as a special mark of goodwill. On 28 March the Prince bestowed it on his brother-in-law himself, at a somewhat fraught ceremony in a Winter Palace heavily barricaded against any further terrorist attacks.

Alexander III proved as big a trial for England, through his increased penetration of Afghanistan, as he did for his own subjects, through his increased repression at home. But his early death on 1 November 1894 provided a double opportunity to start afresh. Not only was there another funeral for the Prince to attend; there was a family wedding as well. The new tsar, Nicholas II, was betrothed to one of the Prince's German nieces, Princess Alix of Hesse, and it was arranged that the joyful occasion should follow immediately on the mournful one. This time the Prime Minister (now Lord Rosebery, the Prince's old friend) positively urged him to make all he could out of the dual ceremony. The Prince obliged by charming the kindly but ineffective new Tsar ('as weak as water') who had now become his nephew twice over. He also stamped his own personality afresh on the great international gathering in St Petersburg. It was a concourse which already recognized him as its arbiter in matters of protocol, fashion and taste and was soon to experience him as the royal diplomatist *par excellence*.

Apart from his purely dynastic feeling that these two courts, now doubly linked by marriages, could and should not preside over hostile governments, there were two other considerations which drove the Prince more and more into a pro-Russian stand. The first was the steadily increasing strength and arrogance of Wilhelminian Germany which, as described already, was personified by the antics of the Prince's other imperial nephew, William II. Quite apart from the commercial, political and military challenge which this Germany represented and quite apart from William's own behaviour – which gyrated between cloying sentimentality and downright insults – there were family barriers between the two men. The Prince could never forgive or forget the dismissive treatment which his own sister Vicky suffered at her son's hands once William had reached the throne.

The other factor which constantly impelled the Prince towards

Russia was, of course, his own feelings towards France, Russia's ally and partner in the European power game. Bertie's adoration for France and all things French was a lifelong love-affair. It had begun with that visit with his parents in August of 1855 to the recently proclaimed Second French empire of Napoleon III and Eugénie. It was not simply the stag hunt in St Germain and the ball in Versailles which had dazzled the fourteen-year-old. The erotic charisma of the brilliant court and capital, full of beautifully gowned and scented women also left its lasting mark on a boy just reaching puberty. Nothing could be more different from, or more preferable to, the sedate and stuffy world of Windsor. He had found in France the culture of civilized hedonism which fitted his tastes and temperament like a glove.

It was an infatuation which simply overrode the republicanism which followed the Second Empire's collapse. If henceforth Edward, as prince or king, no longer had a fellow monarch to support in Paris, he was none the less sure of always finding fellow spirits there, as well as the fiercest anti-Prussians on the continent. Quite apart from his increasingly frequent trips *en garçon* to sample every sensual and cultural delight the city had to offer, the Prince also neglected no opportunity to press home his political ideas. The most notable example was his speech at the opening of the Great Paris Exhibition of 1878, over whose British section he had presided. Speaking partly in French (which he had completely mastered), he nailed the Union Jack firmly alongside the *tricolore* by telling his audience 'and the whole of France' that the prosperity of their two countries was something of essential and reciprocal interest.[33] The path towards that other 'entente cordiale', the truly historic one with France, had been traced in his heart and mind long before, early in the new century, he reached the throne at last.

Queen Victoria's long life and enormous reign ended soon after half-past six on 22 January 1901 when, after a mild stroke, she died peacefully in her bedroom at Osborne. The Prince of Wales, from that instant King, shared the nation's grief at the passing of his mother. He did not, however, share its awed bemusement at the realization that, after sixty-three years, seven months and two days, the monarch of England was no longer 'Ma'am'; that laws, promulgations, military and civil commissions, ambassadorships and all other public appointments were no more at Her Majesty's command; and that loyal toasts throughout the empire were no longer raised to 'The Queen, God bless her'. Though his mother's death had never, for an instant, been desired by him, he had long yearned for its consequence, the throne. There had been a long, frustrating wait on its steps. He was two months over fifty-nine when he mounted those steps and he was determined to waste not a single minute.

A brisk indication of this came after the lying-in-state at Osborne, when the convoy of vessels, headed by the *Alberta*, with the Queen's coffin on its quarterdeck, steamed across the Solent on its way to Portsmouth and the state funeral at Windsor. The new King, sailing just astern in the *Victoria and Albert*, suddenly noticed that his royal standard was flying at half-mast. When summoned to explain, the yacht's captain could only observe, somewhat lamely, that the Queen was dead. 'The King of England lives,' his sovereign retorted, and the standard was promptly hoisted up high in the sunshine. That was precisely where Edward intended to keep it flying. The gesture did not pass unobserved by his nephew, the German Kaiser, who was standing at his side, dressed, like his uncle, in the uniform of a British admiral of the fleet.

One of the things the new monarch had been mulling over throughout the long evening of his mother's life was what he should call himself when the crown was his to wear. She had died hoping and believing that he would reign as King Albert, thus immortalizing on the throne the name of the beloved consort who had stood alongside it. But their son had decided otherwise. 'I have resolved to be known by the name of Edward, which has been borne by six of my ancestors,' he announced to the Privy Council which had assembled at St James's Palace to hear the Archbishop of Canterbury read out the oath of accession. It was a significant change. The ruler who had nothing but German blood in his veins had distanced himself from the Coburg connection which had strangled his childhood and from the Germanic atmosphere which had smothered his mother's court.* Moreover, in so doing, he had passed over the Hanoverian era of his ancestors and had deliberately conjured up the image of Tudor England. In his quick temper, his humour, his love of display, his sensuality and zest for pleasure there was, indeed, much of the Tudor about him – above all, perhaps, in the fierce pride in his island kingdom and his own prerogatives.

Writing of the heritage Queen Victoria had left behind, the Kaiser, after returning to Berlin, enthused in a letter to his uncle: 'What a magnificent realm she has left you, and what a fine position in the world!'[34]

---

* Ironically, to the end of his days, his English was touched with the strong burr of a German accent.

That the uncle never bothered to use the imperial title which went with that world position ('King of England', he once declared, 'is good enough for me') always puzzled and irritated the Kaiser – so proud of Germany's imperial glory which was but a few decades old. Edward's approach was the ultimate in English understatement; not surprisingly therefore, it was quite incomprehensible to the master of Teutonic overstatement.

But if Edward VII was happy to concentrate on his England, he was determined that it should never be a Little England. One would have to go back centuries to find a predecessor who knew as much about the continent of Europe as he did. One would search in vain for a ruler who was just as cosmopolitan as he was patriotic. Moreover, his was all first-hand experience and knowledge. The mother had striven to keep abreast of the fast-moving European situation through her worn and sometimes leaky family channels and by the literally millions of words she poured out in her letters and journals. The son had followed those developments with his eyes on the continent, branching out far away from family connections (numerous and important though these were) into a network of friends and confidants spread over half a dozen countries. It was above all through people that he operated rather than through correspondence and, once he came to the throne, a powerful cabal of king's men soon emerged in England and abroad.

His informal palace cabinet at home was headed by his private secretary Francis Knollys, a Victorian rather than an Edwardian figure who had entered service as far back as 1870 with the then Prince of Wales. His tact and cool judgement were always in demand to damp down the royal fireworks, while ensuring that, wherever possible, his master had his way. In the field of foreign affairs which King Edward was to make his own, there was a trio of special advisers. The first was Lord Esher, who counselled the King on army matters. The second was Admiral 'Jackie' Fisher, himself a reincárnation of England's buccaneering sea captains of Tudor times. He endeared himself to the King because he loved the ladies as much as he detested the Germans. However, the admiral's favourite recipe for dealing with the menacing new German fleet – namely to sail into the Baltic and sink it – was always too strong, even for Edward VII's palate.

As for diplomacy itself, the King's great favourite and protégé here was Charles Hardinge who, partly through the royal patronage and partly through his own acumen and driving ambition, shot up like a meteor in the Edwardian heavens. A medium-grade Foreign Office official of forty-three when the King came to the throne, he was promoted under-secretary in 1903, ambassador to St Petersburg in

1904, permanent under-secretary back home again in 1906, and then made viceroy of India (with the accompanying peerage) four years later. His envious contemporaries accused him of careerism. If so, one can only say that his heart always seems to have been in the right place for his king and country, as well as for himself.*

Hardinge was by no means the only Foreign Office man to go where he went because he had caught the King's eye. So long as Edward VII reigned, key ambassadorial posts were appointments that he powerfully influenced, instead of merely rubber-stamping. It was, for example, on the King's outright insistence that Sir Cecil Spring-Rice was sent as envoy to Persia which, because of its proximity to India, was then of cardinal importance. The Paris embassy was the continental plum, made even juicier by the King's special love for France. Sir Francis Bertie (later Lord Bertie of Thame) was to hold that enviable post under two kings for a remarkable thirteen years and was sent there in the first place in 1905 by Edward VII.

Selected envoys who served at his own court of St James were also gathered under the royal wing. The King had a particularly soft spot, for example, for Whitelaw Reid, who came to London as American ambassador in 1905, made solid good sense on professional matters and entertained lavishly on the social scene at his residence, Dorchester House. Then, as now, such appointments were political rewards for prominent campaign backers of the incumbent American president, and quite a queue of hopeful tycoons was soon forming in Washington to take over the coveted London post. The King, however, would not hear of a change and caused such pressure to be applied on President Taft that Ambassador Reid was duly informed by the White House that he could now consider his assignment as indefinite. On hearing the news the King wrote to the reprieved envoy expressing his personal joy 'that one whom I have learned to know as a friend will not now be leaving my country'.[35]

As for the major European powers, the King was well served at his court by Count Benckendorff, the Tsar's ambassador from 1903 right down to the Russian revolution. France had already sent one of her greatest diplomatists, Paul Cambon, to London in 1898; he remained *en poste* throughout the King's reign and beyond, always a powerful factor in bonding and then cementing the Anglo-French connection. The Austrian, Count Mensdorff-Pouilly, who served in London from 1904 onwards, became so anglophile that his Emperor Franz Josef took to referring to him as 'the British ambassador in Vienna' and

---

* He ended a glittering career as ambassador in Paris from 1920 to 1922.

there were even family links with the King.* The King, though not the Count, was to be spared the personal pain of England and Austria suddenly and unexpectedly finding themselves at war in the summer of 1914.

There was only one exception to this cosy and familiar 'coterie' of envoys to the Court of St James; but it was a grievous one. Count Paul Metternich, the German ambassador in London for much of the King's reign, was a rather gloomy and taciturn fellow who came to understand all English misgivings about his country, yet lacked the charm and personality to dispel them. For that matter, the King's ambassadors to Berlin proved a mixed lot. It was strange that his talent for picking effective people should have faltered in the one area it mattered most.

---

* Mensdorff and King Edward were second cousins. The ambassador's grandmother, Princess Sophie of Saxe-Coburg-Saalfeld, was the sister of the King's paternal grandfather, Duke Ernest of Saxe-Coburg-Gotha.

Chapter Fourteen

ENGLAND:
THE UNCLE OF EUROPE

The King's foreign secretaries faced a formidable task if they wished to pursue policies which ran counter to the wishes of the monarch and his circle. Lord Lansdowne, the foreign minister Edward VII had inherited with Salisbury's last government, and who remained in office for a critical five years, gradually developed very much the same ideas as his sovereign; the only friction which arose between the two men was over who was to play the leading role in carrying those orders out. Lansdowne was the prototype of the feudal grandee. Besides Bowood, his English seat, and his town house in Grosvenor Square, he owned large estates in Scotland and even larger ones (over a hundred thousand acres) in Ireland. He had switched parties on his tranquil journey through politics but Prime Ministers of both complexions seemed pleased to employ him as a resplendent pillar of empire. In his Whig days, Gladstone had made him governor-general of Canada. Soon afterwards, as a Conservative, he was appointed by Salisbury to the supreme lay post any man could hold under his sovereign, viceroy of India. By the time he became foreign secretary at the turn of the century he was, therefore, a man not used to sharing the limelight.

What pointed Lansdowne along the same diplomatic path as the King (though he trod it much later and with far more hesitation) was his ancestry: his maternal grandfather, Count de Flahault, had been one of Napoleon's generals and he himself spoke perfect French. But he was also nudged along the path, as that language puts it, *par la force des choses*. As already mentioned, it was the Boer War (ended at last in May of 1902 with the conclusion of peace terms in Pretoria) which had helped to convince England that she could no longer stand isolated from both the rival power blocs of the continent. The year before, the last in the long series of desultory and mutually suspicious treaty soundings between England and Germany had petered out. This left, at some time or another and in one form or another, only the Franco-

Russian alternative. France and Russia had been in the minds of the British statesmen throughout the last round of discussions with Baron Eckhardstein, then German chargé d'affaires in London, who had started the last Anglo-German ball rolling in March of 1901 with an 'unofficial' approach to Lord Lansdowne about an alliance. The foreign secretary had been prophetically pessimistic at the time: 'When each side comes, if it ever does, to formulate its terms, we shall break down; and I know Lord Salisbury regards the scheme with, to say the least, suspicion.'[1]

In November, when Lansdowne came to spell out the 'virtually' insuperable difficulties of a full-blown treaty with Germany, he put, high on the list, 'the certainty of alienating France and Russia'.[2] Among the other objections given in his memorandum were the risks of alienating both the British colonies (and her great ex-colony, the United States of America) and the problem of carrying either Parliament or public opinion with the idea of a German alliance. On the government side, therefore, the indecisive feelers from Berlin had been written off six months after they were first put out.

Yet while writing off the German option, Lansdowne remained curiously hesitant in plumping for its only alternative. He was well aware that the global issues which England surely needed to settle lay primarily on the Franco-Russian side. With France, an accommodation had to be reached over rival interests in the Mediterranean; with Russia, the problems lay further east, in Persia and Afghanistan, both of them causeways which led up to the ramparts of the Indian Raj. After the huge expense, as well as the huge embarrassment, of fighting the Boer War, there was no longer the money in the exchequer, let alone the will among the government, to sustain displays of naval and military might against the empire's rivals on all world fronts. Like a box being squeezed in from the outside, it was these pressures beyond Europe which were forcing England into her European commitment.

For all the credit Lansdowne claimed afterwards as the supreme architect of the Anglo-French entente, it was Paul Cambon, the French ambassador in London, who made the running from 1901 onwards. It was not until New Year's Day of 1903 that, his hand forced by upheavals in Morocco, Lansdowne decided to follow up Cambon's approaches in earnest.[3]

What a contrast to his sovereign who, on the eve of the Franco-Prussian war in 1866, when a twenty-five-year-old Prince of Wales, had told the French foreign minister of the day, M. Drouyn, that 'The general interests of Europe could best be served by an "entente" between England and France.'[4] When Edward minted that phrase which, nearly forty years later, he helped to turn into reality, the future Marquess of Lansdowne was an obscure youth.

Enough had happened on the personal and family plane during that same fateful year of 1901 to reinforce the King's long-standing conviction that Wilhelminian Germany could never be a comfortable partner. In February he had left for Germany, his first journey abroad as monarch, to visit his sister Vicky, the Dowager Empress, at her castle at Friedrichshof, in the Taunus mountains near Cronberg. She was already mortally ill and in intense agony with cancer of the spine which, with true Victorian fortitude, she referred to as 'lumbago', spurning any pain-killing drugs. In these circumstances the Kaiser, her son, was expected to ensure that this reunion between his estranged mother and his suspect uncle would be as tranquil as possible. Instead, he put on a characteristic circus performance, dashing backwards and forwards across the snow-laden woods from nearby Homburg in a sledge drawn by a pair of prancing Hungarian greys, thus forcing the King to don the tight-collared Prussian uniform he detested for luncheon, and obliging him, as a fellow monarch, to pay a return visit.

Worse was to follow when, six months later, King Edward arrived in Germany again to attend the funeral of his sister, who had died on 5 August. There had been a row even over her funeral arrangements. According to Chancellor Bülow, the Kaiser had simply overridden his mother's last request that her naked corpse should be wrapped in a Union Jack and sent back to be buried in English soil. There was to be an even greater row later on over the smuggling out from Friedrichshof of her letters, which she had wished to be added secretly to the Windsor archives. In death, as in life, the English Princess Royal, briefly a German Empress, personified the growing strife between the two countries of her birth and marriage. Yet the funeral itself, held under leaden skies at Potsdam on 13 August, displayed the old links, rather than the new rivalries, between the two dynasties. Just as the Kaiser and King Edward had stood side by side, both dressed as admirals of the Royal Navy for Queen Victoria's water-borne cortège from Osborne, so now again, in the procession to the Friedenskirche, they both marched in the blue inform of the Prussian Dragoon Guards, of which the old Queen had been colonel-in-chief.

As soon as the funeral was over the King left for his cure at Homburg, which had been planned well before his sister's death. Queen Alexandra accompanied her husband to the German spa but stayed there barely a day before travelling on northwards to join her own family in Copenhagen. This was typical of that sad if civilized routine, developed between them many years before his accession, whereby, once all joint appearances required by protocol or social nicety had been absolved, husband and wife went their separate ways.

Left alone to his friends and his pleasures, the husband soon realized that there were two things wrong with Homburg. The first was that, now he was King of England, the German crowds would no longer leave him in peace but would jostle him from the moment, at 7.30 each morning, he appeared outside the Park Hotel to walk to the mineral springs. The old life, which combined grandness with informality, was over, at least here. The second and even bigger drawback was that, if he was in Homburg, he was in Germany, and that meant he was in the clutches of his imperial nephew. The inevitability of a political meeting between the two sovereigns had been foreseen, and Lord Lansdowne had accordingly furnished his master with a guidance memorandum ranging from a joint policy in Morocco to relations with the ruler of Kuwait, the sheikdom at the head of the Persian Gulf which the Germans had chosen as the terminus of their projected Berlin-Baghdad railway.

The encounter, which duly took place at the Kaiser's castle at Wilhelmshöhe on 23 August, was a disaster all round. Despite an understanding that there would be no ceremony, in view of the court mourning, the Supreme War Lord had been unable to resist the temptation to jam the streets with fifteen thousand troops assembled simply to honour (and impress) his uncle, who was once again corseted in his uniform as a Prussian colonel-in-chief. The King was not only tired after the four-hour train journey from Homburg. He was also famished, with nothing but the breakfast eggs of the Park Hotel inside his rapacious stomach. Not until after two o'clock, when the last unit had marched past at the salute, could he get into the castle, and lunch. At their talks in the park afterwards, the Kaiser, his tail right up, was constantly on the attack. He irritated his uncle by resurrecting the phrase 'perfidious Albion'. He annoyed him even more by showing that he was better informed about the British government's plans for Malta than the King himself. It was rare for King Edward to be caught napping in this way and it followed an earlier lapse when, just after the funeral, he had simply fished Lord Lansdowne's guidance memorandum out of his pocket and handed it over to his nephew to study – a gaffe that would have cost any junior diplomat his career. It was no wonder that, in the castle park, the Kaiser was on top throughout the discussion; no wonder that Lord Lansdowne in London was horrified; and no wonder that it was a very tired and out-of-sorts King of England who, after another four-hour train journey, regained his sanctuary at the Park Hotel Homburg late that night.

The return visit which the Kaiser paid his uncle in the autumn of the following year proved an equal strain. The invitation was a private and family one, to attend the King's sixty-first birthday at Sandringham on 9 November, and to combine the anniversary with a week of Norfolk pheasant-shooting, which conveniently approached its apogee at that point in the season. But, as the King knew perfectly well that his nephew preferred politics even to pheasants, he had amply catered for that side of the occasion as well. The Prime Minister, Mr Balfour, accompanied by Mr Chamberlain and Mr Brodrick (the ministers for the colonies and for war respectively) had all been asked to Sandringham for the opening weekend, to be followed on the Monday by a shooting-party which included the foreign secretary, Lord Lansdowne, and his wife. 'Tout se bornera à un grand massacre de faisans,' Lansdowne had assured Cambon before leaving London.[5] In view of the ministerial team on parade for the Kaiser, the envoy, then still pressing Lansdowne hard to open Anglo-French talks, must have been glad of the assurance.

In fact, Lansdowne was right. On the political front, the Kaiser only succeeded in putting greater distance between himself and the King's ministers by, for example, trying to persuade Mr Balfour that it was really a good thing all round for Germany to be building herself such a large fleet. It was a similar tale on the family front, where the imperial nephew, without willing it or even realizing it, only managed to widen the personal gulf between himself and his uncle. To the King and his English guests, all in their well-worn, loose-fitting shooting tweeds, he was a constant eyesore in that crisp, military-style uniform of his, whose special design (high leather boots, stiff hat and khaki cape) seemed, ominously, to reflect the harsh parade grounds of Potsdam rather than the peaceful green coverts of East Anglia.

Moreover, just as at Wilhelmshöhe the year before, the nephew had taken to informing his uncle about England's imperial affairs, so now at Sandringham he suddenly started playing the instructor again – this time on a subject about which his host was stumped from the start. When the King proudly showed him his new automobile, the Kaiser suddenly asked whether it was driven by petrol or by any other fuel. King Edward, to whom the underside of a car was as remote as a crater on the moon, confessed he had no idea. At this, his guest launched out on a dissertation as to how German scientists were already busily developing potato spirit for the internal combustion engine and, later that week, he flummoxed his uncle completely by producing an array of bottles with chemical samples (doubtless rushed over from the Fatherland for the purpose). To any other sovereign of Edwardian

Europe, let alone to King Edward himself, there was something disturbingly odd about a fellow-ruler who dabbled in advanced science and knew all about propulsion systems. Like the shooting uniform, it was all too redolent of Prussian Germany.

The Kaiser was, as ever, oblivious to it all and left England (after an extended visit to the pro-German 'Yellow Earl', Lord Lonsdale, at Lowther Castle) 'personally quite satisfied'[6] with his whole trip. 'Thank God he's gone!' sighed the uncle as, on 20 November 1902, his nephew boarded the *Hohenzollern* again and steamed back across the North Sea for home.

And so 1903 came round, the *annus mirabilis* of King Edward's endeavours and, partly as a result of those endeavours, one of historic change for his country. As we have seen, Lord Lansdowne had begun the new year with a grudging acceptance that the time may well have come at last when the Foreign Office ought to pay some heed to the persistent French overtures for a colonial settlement. His sovereign, well aware of the pace at which the Foreign Office operated, and knowing that the Prime Minister was even more hesitant than Lansdowne over leading England into her great leap out of 'splendid isolation', decided to take that leap himself. Already on 6 March of the previous year, the King had personally instructed his ambassador in Paris, Sir Edmund Monson, to sound out Loubet, the president of the French republic, about the possibility of a royal visit to Paris. But, with the postponed coronation looming up,* his calendar was too heavily charged and a week later the King was obliged to inform Paul Cambon, Monson's opposite number in London, that the idea would have to be dropped.[7] Lansdowne, who had been kept informed throughout, was accordingly instructed to cancel the project officially. But now, when Edward VII returned to the charge a year later, neither Lansdowne nor Monson nor anyone else in the accepted chain of command was even consulted.

It is at this point that the most colourful of all the 'king's men', the sixty-year-old bachelor, Marquis Luis Augusto Pinto de Soveral, enters the scene. Soveral, who had been Portuguese minister in London (with one short break) since 1891, was a small star in the diplomatic sky. Yet he shone larger and brighter than them all in the Edwardian social firmament. The 'Blue Monkey', as he was affectionately dubbed, was the greatest party-goer and ladies' man of an era famed for its lavish entertainment and sophisticated philandering. This

---

* This should have taken place on 26 June of the previous year but had to be cancelled at the last moment when the King went down with acute appendicitis.

extraordinary figure, with his heavy black moustache, beard and eyebrows, always set off against white gloves and white buttonhole flower, bowled over the wives while beguiling the husbands he was cuckolding. His charm never sank into what the English would instinctively condemn as Latin greasiness. His wit was never barbed with spite or sarcasm. Above all, though privy to all manner of secrets, he proved the soul of discretion. This quality was urgently called for when on 1 March 1903, after a private summons to Buckingham Palace, he drove back to his legation at 12 Gloucester Place as fast as his carriage could go to send an urgent message to his sovereign in Lisbon, King Carlos I. He copied the telegram in his diary, one of the hundreds of fascinating personal documents about the era which he and his descendants refused to reveal to anyone until special access was given some seventy years later. For the first time the full degree of King Edward's audacious secrecy in planning his 1903 tour was revealed.

The telegram begins, in translation from the Portuguese:

Highly Confidential. H.M. the King summoned me today and told me the following. 'My doctors have advised me to take a rest after the arduous work I have been doing recently and so I have decided to make a cruise in British waters. However, political considerations of the highest order oblige me to pay a visit to the King of Italy in Rome and the President of the French Republic in Paris. As the relations between your country and mine are so cordial . . . I have decided – if this is agreeable to the King of Portugal – to begin at Lisbon, where I would sail discreetly.'

[Soveral's message continued in reported speech:] H.M. intends to leave on 30 March and to remain in Lisbon three or four days. . . . The royal yacht will be escorted by two cruisers. H.M. the King asked me to maintain the utmost secrecy about this. Here nobody suspects a thing, *not even the Queen herself and not even the King's Private Secretary.** This extreme discretion is necessary in view of the effect which these visits will produce on the powers of the North.[8]

The last phrase was taken to mean, in the first instance, Germany, though keeping the secret for as long as possible from his nephew in Berlin could never have justified the King's behaviour. The explanation was, quite simply, that he had determined to set out on a personal exercise in royal diplomacy and to bypass all normal channels in the process. That, in doing so, he had declined to tell either his wife or the utterly trustworthy Francis Knollys what he was about to do could be passed off as decisions which, though extraordinary, affected only his own palace domain. But to launch himself on such a crucial journey at a time when his government stood, still hesitating, at the diplomatic

---

* Author's italics.

crossroads of Europe, challenged all constitutional practice. To do so without informing any member of that government, from the Prime Minister and foreign secretary downwards, was to drive a coach and horses clean through that constitution.*

No English sovereign of modern times had ever embarked on such an important journey abroad. None before – and certainly none ever since – would have dared to launch such an adventure entirely single-handed. Nor would the King himself have attempted any such solo move on the home front. But on the continent, and in the field of foreign affairs, the 'uncle of Europe' surmised – quite rightly – that he could move unchallenged in what everyone accepted to be his own royal parish. As a final affront to established practice, he horrified Lord Lansdowne by taking neither him nor any other minister on the journey. Instead, Charles Hardinge was plucked from his Foreign Office desk to accompany the sovereign as a sort of diplomatic aide-de-camp. Lansdowne, understandably gritting his teeth, released Hardinge so late that the excited under-secretary barely had time to pack.

The triumph of the King's spring tour of 1903 was achieved by methods just as personal and unorthodox as those used in its preparation. Lisbon, where the royal party arrived on 2 April on board the *Victoria and Albert* for a five-day stay, was but a ceremonial launching-pad. By now, belatedly let into the secret on 11 March, Sir Edmund Monson in Paris had fixed the King's dates with President Loubet; similarly hurried arrangements had been made with the Quirinal Palace for the visit *en route* to Italy. The British diplomats had not, however, got very far with the King's most pressing desire for his Italian trip, which was for a meeting with the ninety-three-year-old Pope Leo XIII in the Vatican – and this for the very good reason that the Prime Minister and the Cabinet back home were opposed to it. In their view, England's sixteenth-century break with the Papacy was as absolute as ever; the Defender of the Protestant faith could not possibly be seen together with the Holy Father.

Yet such was the awesome authority of the King that his government dared not oppose him outright. A flurry of telegrams passed between London and the royal yacht as the *Victoria and Albert* (now accompanied by a miniature fleet of eight battleships, four cruisers and four

---

* Another telegram in the Soveral papers, sent on 4 March when rumours of the visit were beginning to leak in Lisbon, confirms the King's extraordinary behaviour. 'His Majesty has not yet consulted with the Queen nor with his Ministers,' the envoy wrote. 'Moreover, the King of Italy and the French President know nothing yet.'

destroyers) steamed via Gibraltar and Malta, eastwards across the
Mediterranean. The outcome of the Vatican problem was an agreement by Mr Balfour and his government to tender no advice; to step out
of the picture completely; and allow the King to act on his own
responsibility. So, on 29 April, King Edward VII, the first English
sovereign to set foot in Rome since the Saxon Ethelwulf more than one
thousand years before, had his meeting with the Supreme Pontiff. They
chatted amiably about everything from the situation in Somaliland and
Venezuela to the Pope's one visit to London as a priest in 1846. In an
early tribute to what later generations came to call the 'ecumenical
spirit', Leo XIII expressed his gratitude for the religious tolerance which
prevailed throughout the British empire. As a courtesy to the Italian
government, the King decided to return directly to the Quirinal Palace
instead of his own embassy, thus trying to suggest that his controversial
call on the Vatican had been a purely personal episode in a state visit
between sovereigns.

The little King of Italy, on his throne for less than three years, was
possibly too raw to appreciate such subtle courtesy. But, as a newcomer
to the game, he could not fail to have been impressed by the massive
English serenity which his guest exuded; nor, as a Mediterranean ruler,
by that armada of a Royal Navy escort casually drummed up to bring
him to Naples. For his part, William II had been fidgeting for weeks as
to whether King Edward's visit might in some way weaken Italy's
loyalty to the Triple Alliance, and had organized his own counter-blow.
Two days after the uncle left Rome, Victor Emmanuel was obliged to
appear on the same railway platform again, to greet the imperial
nephew. The workmen had barely had time to change the street
decorations from the Union Jack to the German black, white and red.
To make matters worse, the sun had disappeared and it was pouring
with rain. By now King Edward was nearing Paris, the prime and
ultimate target of the whole grand tour.

On the last of Queen Victoria's private visits to Nice in January
1899, the good people of Nice, who, for decades, had revered their most
august and valuable patron, had been heard to hiss 'Vive Fashoda' as
her carriage rolled along the promenade. This, in a nutshell, was the
problem facing her son as, precisely on the scheduled minute of 2.55
p.m. on 1 May 1903, his special train pulled in to the Porte Dauphine
station of the Bois de Boulogne. That very ugly confrontation on the
banks of the Upper Nile was, to many Englishmen and Frenchmen,
merely the extension on the world stage of a conflict that had raged
between their two countries for centuries in Europe. Captain
Marchand of the Fashoda outpost may have looked incongruous

alongside Jeanne d'Arc and Napoleon Bonaparte; but, to the French, his was a new name on the same roll-call. The two nations had been conditioned to regarding each other as historic enemies. The change which was most needed now could not be wrought by bureaucrats working at their desks on convention clauses. It had to come from the emotions and the heart of the people if any paperwork produced later on by their governments was to have any meaning. That was what Edward VII set out to do, and triumphantly succeeded in doing, during those four springtime days in Paris. There was no point in having a plan for such a delicate exercise in public relations. He relied on what his Coburg father would have called 'Fingerspitzengefühl' or, less expressively, intuitive improvisation.

Things got off to a mixed but not too discouraging start on the drive in. Captain Ponsonby, at the rear of the processions, provoked plenty of anti-English shouts with his scarlet military uniform, which acted, quite literally, as a red rag to the Gallic bull. But, up at the front, the King was drawing polite cheers from a Parisian crowd who remembered and liked him well from his many visits to their city as Prince of Wales *en garçon*. (He was still without his wife now, as King.) The trick was to convert 'Vive Edoard' into 'Vive l'Angleterre'.

It was accomplished not so much by the prepared speeches delivered at state banquets as by off-the-cuff remarks in less august settings. A dedicated theatre-goer, he had pleased his hosts by declining to hear the Comédie-Française perform one of the standard classics such as Molière's *Le Misanthrope* ('They really must *not* treat me like the Shah of Persia!' he had snorted at the mere suggestion.) He had plumped instead for a daringly novel play, *L'autre danger*, in which the hero falls in love with a ravishing sixteen-year-old girl who turns out to be his daughter by a former mistress. It was just the stuff he would have savoured as Prince of Wales. He not only clapped it heartily now but made a point of congratulating Jeanne Granier (who played the girl) with outstretched hand in the foyer: 'Ah Mademoiselle! I remember how I applauded you in London. You personify all the grace, all the esprit of France.' The words, spoken, of course, in French, were meant to echo far outside the foyer, and they did. The next day, the capital's leading newspaper described the episode as 'a charming act of gallantry by this most Parisian of kings'.[9] He was making the flattering, sentimental point of his personal attachment to the city, and the next day he drove it home.

It was a Saturday, and had been declared a holiday in his honour, which was enough in itself to produce good humour among the workmen released from their benches and the schoolboys escaping from their desks. Despite Ponsonby's unfortunate experience, the King had no qualms himself at appearing in his scarlet English field marshal's uniform for the great military parade. The crowd proved him right. There was far more cheering as he drove through the predominantly working-class suburb of Vincennes than he had ever heard in the elegant Faubourg St Honoré.

The happiest stroke came on the way back to the embassy for lunch. A brief stop had been arranged at the town hall, where the mayor and municipal council were waiting to pay their respects. The mayor, M. Deville, struck the right note by welcoming 'the return of an old friend who has not forgotten us because we have not forgotten him'. The King responded, again in his perfect French, with interest: 'I shall never forget my visit to your charming city and I do assure you that it is with the greatest pleasure that I find myself among you again here, where I always feel just as though I am at home.' In later years, one or two variants were produced for the magic phrase 'tout à fait comme chez-moi' and claimants even came forward to say that they had suggested its use. Success always has many fathers. It seems safe, however, to treat the town hall speech – which went round the capital like lightning – as vintage, improvized Edward VII.

These, at all events, were the episodes which put human warmth into the high-flown language of the King's official toasts ('A divine Providence has designed that France should be our near neighbour. . . . There are no two countries in the world whose mutual prosperity is more dependent on each other. Our great desire is that we should advance together in the path of civilization and peace.') When he left Paris on the Monday morning, along the Avenue Marigny and across the lovely Alexander III bridge to the Western railway station, there was no more shouting of 'Fashoda' and 'Marchand'. It was cheering all the way, and the hawkers of souvenir pins and brooches showing the two heads of state had a field day.

His conjuror's trick had come off. For the Parisians, at least, that 'sale pays', England, had become identified with 'notre bon Edouard', its King.[10]

We will come in a moment to King Edward's much-disputed significance as a diplomatic factor in the overall European balance. Suffice it to say here that those who have dismissed the 1903 Paris visit as of no importance beyond creating 'an atmosphere of goodwill'[11] miss the central point by quarrying in and judging entirely from later official documents. The Foreign Office only began serious work on an Anglo-French agreement three months after the King's visit, and it took a further nine months before the famous 'Convention and Declarations' of 8 April 1904 were concluded. Apart from the central bargain whereby France gained a free hand in Morocco in return for accepting English predominance in Egypt, the final text covered territorial disputes ranging from the banks of the River Menam in Siam to the Iles de Los, opposite Konakry 'ceded by His Britannic Majesty to France'.[12] It was, of course, bureaucrats, not the King, who hammered out such details. None the less, the Convention they shaped never became a formal treaty. The obligation to France lay only in the secret but non-binding military discussions which developed later between the two general staffs, powerfully sponsored by the King and partly conducted by his personal adviser for army affairs, Lord Esher. But the obligation remained a moral one which public opinion had to endorse if put to the test. Thus, at the root of everything lay the changed mood between the two peoples which reflected and sustained the strengthening relationship between the two governments. That change had been primarily the King's doing.

The 'entente' of 1904 was historic in that it marked Britain's entry, as the last of the great powers, into the European system of rival alliances. As yet, however, she only had one foot across the Channel. For the rest of the reign, both King and Cabinet concentrated on defending and extending the foothold.

The need to defend the new Anglo-French alignment came more speedily than anyone expected, though the quarter from which the challenge came – Berlin and the Potsdam Palace – caused no surprise. On 31 March 1905, just under a year after the conclusion of the Entente Cordiale, the Kaiser made that famous horseback expedition up into Tangier which has been described already from his side of the affair. The French and British governments were at first inclined to dismiss the Kaiser's antics as clownish theatre. However, they soon realized that this was the opening shot in a campaign by Chancellor Bülow to sabotage, not only the untested colonial pact between France and England, but to prevent that pact spreading out to embrace Russia. The fact that the Tsar's forces had been plunged, only six weeks before, into what was to prove a disastrous war with the Japanese, probably accounted for Bülow's timing, though his own explanation in later years was predictably disarming and slippery.* Whatever the exact calculations were in Berlin at the time, the King was concerned that his nephew, in four hours on Moroccan soil, might undo much of the work he and his ministers had laboured for two years to bring about. He wrote to Lord Lansdowne:

---

* See *supra*, pp. 100–1.

The Tangier incident was the most mischievous and uncalled-for event which the German Emperor has ever been engaged in since he came to the throne. . . . He is no more nor less than a political *enfant terrible* and one can have no faith in his assurances . . .[13]

Three weeks after the Kaiser's escapade, as German pressure mounted in Paris and many of the Socialist deputies in the French Chamber began to lose their nerve, the dimensions of the crisis were plain to see. Théophile Delcassé, the foreign minister who had piloted the 1904 entente from the French side, came under fire and threatened to resign. The rumour reached King Edward on 23 April just as the *Victoria and Albert*, which was taking him on his annual Mediterranean cruise, was pulling in to Algiers. He immediately reacted by despatching from the yacht a personal telegram to Delcassé 'strongly urging' the minister to stay on, not least because of the 'loyal and trusted relations which existed between them'.[14] The long-suffering Lord Lansdowne later described the King's action, with acid restraint as 'a very unusual step'. It was, of course, much more than that. For a sovereign to meddle in the domestic politics of another country without either going through that country's head of state or even consulting his own government in the process was unconstitutional behaviour carried to the ultimate of audacity.

In fact, despite the King's attempt to calm things down and stiffen French resistance during a two-day stay in Paris on his way home, on 6 June Delcassé did resign, in the face of German threats of war unless France agreed to an international conference on Morocco. It was an undeniable triumph, if short-lived, for German diplomacy. Bülow had temporarily succeeded in one of his main objectives, casting doubts in London over the value of their new alignment. As Lansdowne wrote to the Paris embassy a month later: 'Recent events have, I am afraid, undoubtedly shaken people's confidence in the steadfastness of the French nation.'[15]

The King was himself down in the dumps for a while, contemplating the damage: but he soon got to work, alongside his ministers, with the cement trowel. It was at his initiative that the visit of a French naval detachment to Spithead, already scheduled for that coming August, was turned into a major display of Anglo-French solidarity, with lunches in the City and even at Westminster Hall for the visiting officers as well as a frenetic programme of festivities at anchor in Portsmouth. This was clearly the way ahead. The French ambassador, Paul Cambon, reported, after a weekend of political discussions at Windsor Castle in January 1906 (with the new Liberal Prime Minister, Sir Henry Campbell-Bannerman and his new foreign secretary, Sir

Edward Grey in attendance) that though official silence ought to be maintained for the time being over Anglo-French 'identity of interests' in the face of any German aggression, both the King and his ministers had agreed to press ahead with the vital joint staff talks.[16] The entente was changing quietly from its frock-coat into uniform.

If defending the new Paris-London alignment was fraught with problems, extending it to St Petersburg was no easy matter either. It was, in strategic terms, a natural extension. France, England's first continental partner, had already been locked for the previous ten years into a cast-iron military alliance with Russia, while Germany, the main target of their pact, was growing more powerful and more strident with every month that passed. For the King, of course, an understanding with Russia meant the realization of the task he had repeatedly volunteered for as Prince of Wales – keeping a line open to the vast, unpredictable realm of the tsars, whose sheer size and weight of manpower would count heavily in any conflict.

The ink on the 1904 Convention with France was barely dry when Edward VII told his diplomatic *adlatus*, Hardinge, of his determination to 'bring off a similar arrangement with Russia'.[17] Before April was out, the King was developing the same theme in Copenhagen with his new-found ally and future protégé, Alexander Izvolski, then Russian ambassador at the court of Denmark. The ambitious envoy, realizing that his own career might well hinge (as indeed it did) on such unexpected royal connections, made the King's policy doubly his own. When, just over two years later, he became Russia's foreign minister, thanks largely to King Edward's sponsorship,* he was in a position to turn aims into action. Yet the difficulties, more global than European, were more formidable even than those which the Anglo-French Convention had had to bridge.

To begin with, the bitter taste of the Russo-Japanese war still lay in the mouths of Russia's ultra-conservatives. Not only had that conflict produced, in the Dogger Bank incident of 1904,† a very nasty flare-up in Anglo-Russian relations. England's whole Far Eastern stance seemed to St Petersburg to be ambivalent for, in 1902, she had signed a treaty with Japan, mainly to safeguard her interests in China. Cautious and regional though that pact had been, it made London's professions

---

* See *supra*, p. 149.

† On the night of 21 October 1904, the Baltic Fleet of Admiral Rozhdestvenski, ploughing its way across the North Sea to annihilation in the Far East, mistook some English trawlers for Japanese vessels and opened fire, causing death and injuries. The unhappy affair was wound up four months later with a £65,000 damages award.

of strict neutrality as between England and Japan sound rather dubious, and the Kaiser had had a field day, in his letters to the Tsar, lambasting and parading 'Uncle Bertie's duplicity'. German influence at the St Petersburg court was, in any case, powerful, not least due to the family connections of the Empress. Moreover, quite apart from the Japanese entanglement, the direct strategic rivalries between Russia and England – notably the struggle for control over Persia and Afghanistan – were both long-standing and massive.

Finally, there was an ideological complication. Though the Entente Cordiale had been an agreement between monarchy and republic, both nations stood on the same broad platform of democracy. A similar move towards Russia, however, raised the hackles of every liberal in England for whom the Tsar was the personification of repressive autocracy. When the new Campbell-Bannerman government came to power, liberal was also spelt with a capital 'L'.

Even Edward VII, itching as he was to help along his second *rapprochement*, saw the dangers of acting too soon. Nicholas II, accompanied by the Tsarina and their baby daughter Olga (the first of their five children) had come to Balmoral in 1896 and there had been a plan for King Edward and Queen Alexandra to return the private visit ten years later. The Liberal government were all for it, despite the political upheavals which were shaking the Russian monarchy to its foundations in 1906. But a memorandum written by the King on 22 March of that year shows that it was his decision alone to postpone it:

I honestly confess I can see no particular object in visiting the Emperor in Russia this year. The country is in a very unsettled state and will, I fear, not improve for some time to come. I hardly think that the country at home [England] would much approve of my going there for a while . . . What advice could I possibly give the Emperor as to the management of his country? What right have I to do so, even if he were to listen to me, which I very much doubt . . .?[18]

Six days later, Sir Edward Grey wrote to the King's private secretary pleading that, in England's urgent political interests, the visit should only be postponed. This one letter of 28 March 1906, coming as it does from a Liberal foreign secretary, is enough to dispose of suggestions, made in later years, that his sovereign was nothing more than a royal commercial traveller in diplomacy. Surely, Sir Edward argued, if there was no more bloodshed in Russia, the King might manage some sort of meeting, perhaps at sea in the Baltic. He went on:

An entente with Russia . . . is the thing most to be desired in our foreign policy. . . . It will complete and strengthen the entente with France and add very much to the strength and comfort of our position. *But it all depends on the Tsar, and he depends on the King.*[*][19]

The King, who had throughout done all in his power to nudge along good relations with St Petersburg (by helping to smooth down the Dogger Bank incident, for example) duly obliged two years later. Unlike his Paris visit of 1903, which was a solo ice-breaking operation, his voyage to the port of Reval (now Tallinn) in the summer of 1908 only put the sovereign's seal on a pact already concluded by their ministers.[†] None the less, the meeting on 9–10 June between the two monarchs and their families on board their respective yachts, *Victoria and Albert* and *Standart*, was more than a private occasion. Admiral Fisher, who was in the King's party, may have played court jester by dancing the hornpipe on deck until he nearly dropped before his august audience, but he also had some straight talking with the very able Russian Prime Minister Peter Stolypin, who had come with the Tsar: 'Your Western frontier is denuded of troops and your magazines are depleted. Fill them up, and then talk of fleets.'[20]

For the most part, however, the discussions held on the two yachts were more general and genial. Broad policy was debated and honours were exchanged in between the family talks. Each sovereign made the other an admiral of his fleet, though as nearly all of poor Nicholas's navy lay on the Pacific sea-bed, he got by far the better bargain. The main object of the exercise was to make this strange new partnership between the lion and bear look natural and relaxed. This was no small thing in view of the stifling security protections imposed to protect the Tsar; even the women singers performing on a special steamer anchored nearby would have been stripped and searched for bombs had not Captain Ponsonby, visualizing enraged headlines in the liberal newspapers at home, intervened to spare them. When the visit was drawing to a close, Prince Orloff, aide-de-camp to the Tsar, assured Fisher that the King's descent on Reval had transformed Russian feelings towards England 'from suspicion to trust'.[21] That was a courtier pitching things rather too high. But there can surely have been no doubt that, when Nicholas II looked back on his earlier venture in

---

[*] Author's italics.

[†] The Anglo-Russian Convention was finally signed, after long months of negotiation, on 31 August 1907. Russia declared Afghanistan to be outside her sphere of influence and agreed to deal with the Amir only through British authorities. To balance this substantial gain, which brought peace of mind over India, England lost her free hand in Persia, the largest and richest northern region of which was declared a Russian sphere of influence. Needless to say, the Shah was not consulted over this imperial carve-up.

'yacht diplomacy', the exhausting and disastrous meeting at Björkö with the German Kaiser three summers before, he must have sighed with relief at the contrast.

If Edward VII's course with France and Russia was smooth almost all the way, it was a very different tale with the rival camp of the central powers. His personal relations with the doyen of European monarchs, the Emperor Franz Josef (who was already over seventy when Edward came to the throne) were always cordial. The fastidious and puritanical old Emperor had, it is true, little in common with King Edward's life-style – neither his gargantuan appetite for *haute cuisine*, nor his passion for the turf and for travel, nor his patronage of social climbers, nor his cult of personal diplomacy, nor, least of all, his flaunting of a succession of beautiful mistresses. Yet there was a bridge which over-arched all these contrasts of taste and temperament: the mutual respect of two *grands seigneurs* who were both, in their different ways, professionals to their fingertips at the royal game and between whose empires there stood not a single serious direct clash of interests. The relaxed relationship was symbolized by the place where most of these informal meetings* took place – Bad Ischl, Franz Josef's summer paradise, where the King would call in for a day or two during his annual August trip to the continent.

Apart from keeping the lid on the Balkan powder keg, the Habsburg monarchy had only one other main service to perform for England: to urge restraint on Berlin, above all in the deadly business of fleet-building. In 1907, and again in 1908, Hardinge and Aehrenthal (who had come to Ischl at the King's suggestion) had polite but inconclusive discussions on this with the Austrians, predictably, trying to keep out of the Anglo-German tussle. But stories spread by Austrian courtiers years later that King Edward used his time with the Emperor to try and prise Austria-Hungary loose from her German alliance seem very wide of the mark. At all events there is no hint of any such grave and stressful clash in the only accounts which have survived (in the Mountbatten family papers) of what the King himself put on paper about those Ischl meetings.

These are contained in the letters he sent back to his old and trusted friend Sir Ernest Cassel about his midsummer tours, letters written

---

* King Edward had paid one state visit to Vienna – and a very successful one – in 1903, the first time the city had seen an English monarch since Richard Coeur de Lion had been captured there on his way home from the Crusades. As the old Emperor could never be persuaded to undergo the rigours of a return visit to London, all further meetings had to be elsewhere.

when the events were still fresh in his mind and in which political secrets are freely discussed – including the German naval problem. All he says of this allegedly sinister 1908 confrontation at Ischl is that he had 'found the kind old Emperor in the best of health' and that, as regards the international scene, his host was 'much interested as well as agitated in regarding the news from Constantinople', (i.e. the Young Turk rebellion). The King went on: 'I took the Emperor for his first motor car drive which he greatly enjoyed and will I hope in the future not object to that mode of locomotion.'[22] This is hardly the tone or the language of a man who had been trying to overturn the entire political balance of Europe between showers in the Salzkammergut and who was now smarting under his failure. The Emperor Franz Josef was an Olympian among monarchs whom even Edward VII would have thought twice about lobbying, let alone trying to suborn from the strongest and oldest of all major European alliances.

As for the King's relations with his imperial nephew who presided over the business end of that alliance in Berlin, it was the same old story which Edward had endured as Prince of Wales. There could never be a close 'rapport' between the two men. Yet, for all his histrionics and manic suspicion of his uncle, the Kaiser, to his dying day, was still emotionally tied by Grandmama Victoria's bonnet-strings to England. The King's reign is thus marked by a series of episodes at which sentimental goodwill generated by family gatherings (or even family anecdotes exchanged by letter) struggled in vain to smother those military, political and commercial tensions which were steadily mounting beneath the surface between the two countries.

This love–hate relationship has already been examined from the German side. So far as the King was concerned, his golden rule, throughout the nine years of his reign, was to see as little of his nephew as he could and, when he was obliged to meet, to leave it to his advisers to tackle this disagreeable business of battleships. One of the reasons why the King wanted others to argue the naval toss for him may well have been an awareness of his own inadequacies when it came down to debating all the details of fleet construction which his technically-minded nephew had mastered. Thus, at Cronberg in August of 1906 and again at the same German castle two years later, it was Hardinge who did all the detailed political talking. His discussion partner on the first occasion was state secretary Heinrich von Tschirschky (deputizing for a sick Chancellor Bülow) and, on the second occasion, the Kaiser himself. This proved too hopelessly a lopsided match even for the capable Hardinge, who at one point was squashed by the following imperious rebuke: 'Your own documents are wrong. I am an Admiral of the British Navy which I know all about and understand better than you, who are a civilian with no idea of these matters.'[23] Whatever the documents showed, one cannot help feeling that by exposing a mere permanent under-secretary to that sort of treatment from an emperor and supreme war lord, King Edward was asking too much of his advisers and doing too little himself. His own conversations at these Cronberg meetings seem mainly to have been confined to the chitchat of fellow-sovereigns: how should the Duchess of Hohenberg be treated once Archduke Franz Ferdinand came to the Austrian throne; who should succeed Sir Frank Lascelles as the King's ambassador in Berlin? (The choice, as we saw at the beginning of this book, had fallen on Sir Edward Goschen, who was not immediately palatable to the Emperor because of his Jewish origins and who was anyway utterly miserable at being uprooted from the Vienna embassy.)*

State, as opposed to private, visits had to be exchanged by two courts so closely linked in blood, however brittle the personal contact between the sovereigns and however hard and loud the hammers were banging away in their rival dockyards. In November of 1907, William II and his Dona had been fêted at Windsor Castle (where one banquet included no fewer than twenty-four royal heads, many of them crowned). The Kaiser, as so often, did his best to counter his own damaging record and tried on this occasion to transfer the family spirit of Windsor to the political arena of London's Guildhall. Urging the need for closer Anglo-German ties on his distinguished audience, he produced, on 13 November, one of his effective phrases: 'Blood is thicker than water.' This went down well. Cynics might, however, have reflected that, once spilt, blood leaves the deeper and more obstinate stain.

For all the King's reluctance to drag himself and his relentlessly anti-German Queen Alexandra to Berlin, the return visit simply had to be made, and this eventually took place in February of 1909, the last full year of his reign. It was a testing phase in Anglo-German relations which had been stretched to breaking-point at times during the previous year. The Kaiser's newspaper gaffes in the autumn of 1908 (and notably his notorious *Daily Telegraph* interview of 28 October)† were only the foam on the waves of far deadlier currents underneath. That same autumn, a divided Liberal Cabinet in London was agonizing over what sort of armed help, and how much of it, England

---

* 'I shall have to go,' Goschen lamented prophetically on hearing of his transfer. 'I cannot refuse the King. But I am certain my mission in Berlin will end in failure for there will be no means of avoiding catastrophe.'[24]
† See *supra*, p. 110.

should give France should that country find herself at war with
Germany. Through his close friend and military adviser, Lord Esher
(who was also a member of the imperial defence committee), the King
was pushing, as hard as he could from the sidelines, the case for fighting
alongside France with everything England could throw in. Asquith,
Haldane and Grey were each broadly of this view. But there were those
(headed, ironically, by the young Winston Churchill, then president of
the Board of Trade) who were all for keeping out of it. On 8 November,
Esher gave a secret private briefing to the French military attaché,
Colonel Huguet, on the tussle and made it clear where the King stood.
As Huguet's ambassador, Paul Cambon, reported ten days later to
Paris:

Even if all the members of the Cabinet . . . do not favour giving us the help of
both the British Army and the British fleet, we have on our side, together with
the King, all the most influential Ministers.[25]

The arguments over wartime help for France were just about the
most closely-guarded secret in the country. Nothing, on the other hand,
could have been more public than that other great controversy sparked
off by the German threat. This concerned the programme to equip the
Royal Navy with ten per cent more battleships than the two next
strongest fleets in the world combined.* In that same November of
1908 (on the 23rd, to be precise) Mr Asquith had reiterated in
Parliament this doctrine of the so-called 'two-power naval standard'.
The debate soon spread from Parliament to the nation, and was to
culminate in the cry 'We want eight [extra Dreadnoughts] and we
won't wait'. This was the fraught state of Anglo-German relations
when, on 8 February 1909, the King and Queen crossed the Channel on
Alexandra, the smaller of the two royal yachts, bound for Calais and
Berlin. He was pining for the winter sun of southern France; she was
dreading this descent on the Prussian capital which had once crushed
her fatherland. Bismarck's lightning war against Denmark may have
taken place forty-five years before, but Queen Alexandra had neither
forgotten nor forgiven.

It is impossible on this occasion not to feel some sympathy also for
the Kaiser. He had tried so hard to make the visit a success yet, through
no fault of his own, so many things went wrong. The preparations,
which he had supervised down to the last detail, seemed to include
every compliment and to leave nothing to chance. To make his Danish
aunt feel at home, he had installed a concert piano (she was a capable

* In 1908, Germany – and America!

player) in her suite of rooms in the Potsdam Palace and hung the walls with pictures of Sandringham and Copenhagen. In the study of the King's suite, he had placed not only a portrait of Queen Victoria but also figures of England's great naval heroes, Nelson, St Vincent and Howe. Both uncle and nephew were after all, like Nelson, admirals of the British fleet, an honour which the Kaiser had once declared made him 'quite giddy'. As for the ceremonial planning, that had been executed with Prussian thoroughness, now trained for nearly forty years to do things in the imperial style. Yet the best staff work cannot cope with gremlins, and these popped up from the start.

At Berlin's Lehrter station, for example, the King was expected to descend from his own carriage near the front of the train, where the imperial welcoming party was waiting at a precise spot marked on the platform. For some reason, however, the King decided to alight with his Queen from her carriage, which was much further back. Emperor, Empress, royal princes and princesses, aides and officers all had to dash a hundred yards in full regalia along the train to offer their greetings. There was an even more embarrassing slip-up when the carriages in the procession to the palace got too close to one another. In the ensuing mayhem, the horses of the ceremonial coach bearing Queen Alexandra and the Empress decided they had had enough and refused to move an inch. There was nothing for it but to transfer the two royal ladies, before the eyes of an astonished populace, to an ordinary carriage behind. To cap everything, two cavalrymen of the crack 'Garde du Corps' escort were thrown off their horses, which then galloped around loose.

Both uncle and aunt did their best with the programme of state dinners, court balls, formal luncheons and gala opera performances which followed over the next three days. But though the King did well with some impromptu remarks to Berlin's stolid aldermen in their huge pseudo-Gothic Rathaus, it was noticed that he read out his banquet speeches from a prepared text, quite against his normal custom. This was taken as a sign that he was under strain and that the bitterly cold weather (which had caused part of the open-air programme to be abandoned) was doing him no good. There was dramatic evidence of this after a large luncheon party at the British embassy on the second day of the visit. The King, wearing a tight-fitting Prussian uniform, was chatting on a sofa with the English-born society beauty Daisy Cornwallis-West, who had married the German Prince Pless but who none the less still regarded Edward VII as her real monarch (needless to say, to the Kaiser's fury). The account she gives in her memoirs is supported by other eye-witnesses:

Suddenly he coughed and fell back against the back of the sofa and the cigar dropped out of his fingers, his eyes stared and he could not breathe. I thought, 'My God, he is dying; oh, why not in his own country?' I tried to undo the collar of his uniform. . . . Then the Queen rushed up and we both tried; at last he came to and undid it himself.[26]

All the guests withdrew as the King's physician, Sir James Reed, was fetched from a nearby room. After a quarter of an hour the hushed company was called in again and everything was pronounced to be in order. Both the doctor and his patient knew otherwise. What the King had just survived was a violent bout of that chronic bronchitis which, before long, was to kill him.

Despite this scare, the amended programme was completed and according to the Kaiser's report to Chancellor Bülow[27] (there is no other evidence, even second-hand, available) the King at last raised the dreaded question of Anglo-German naval rivalry himself. In this brief exchange, held only a few minutes before the King's train pulled out, the Kaiser depicts himself as assuring his uncle that, despite what 'some Jingos in England' were claiming, the German fleet threatened nobody; moreover, the Emperor reported, King Edward had quite accepted this. The truth was probably that, having at long last brought himself to raise in person the danger of German fleet building, the King felt in no mood and in no condition to start an argument about it. By the winter of 1909, he may well have felt towards his nephew's fleet as he did towards his own bronchitis: both dangers were now chronic, incurable and lethal.

So far we have followed King Edward in palaces and castles; in ceremonial processions and at court balls; at gala banquets and operas; and in the state-rooms of imperial yachts. Yet we cannot leave the monarch or his era without mentioning the special touch he brought to international affairs, his spa diplomacy. It was at the spas that the social and political trails of the Edwardian landscape, which were always crossing one another, converged and became one – above all, at Marienbad, tucked away in the pretty Eger valley of Bohemia at the heart of the Habsburg empire. The King chose it partly because it had all the easygoing cosmopolitan atmosphere of that empire and partly because, though the castles of the German Kaiser lay conveniently *en route*, it lay outside his nephew's domains and therefore sheltered from all those sudden theatrical descents of his. Every midsummer from 1903 until King Edward's death, Marienbad was transformed, for three weeks, into a cross between the stage of a Restoration comedy and the anteroom of a Byzantine court. Of those who flocked to it, some came for serious political business; some to exchange diplomatic chitchat; some for gain; some for notoriety; some to lose weight; and some – perhaps the majority – just to be seen and say they had been seen.

The Prime Minister of Republican France trying to talk the King into building a bigger British Army against Germany would brush shoulders on the hotel stairway with a Hungarian horse-breeder trying to sell that same monarch some racehorses for his stables. The Foreign Minister of Imperial Russia, in Marienbad to get the King of England's help over some dangerous Balkan muddle, would have to elbow aside tailors from Berlin busy sketching the cut of his latest coat to copy in their autumn catalogues. Inventors with a patent to proclaim; financiers with a scheme to float; famous journalists who had the King's ear for their news and views; humbler colleagues who never spoke a word with him but still made a summer's living by writing a few lines each day about his movements; a special muster of chefs, doctors, police chiefs, musicians, actors and other entertainers – all these formed the busy cosmopolitan background against which the King's party moved.[28]

Seated at his desk at the Hotel Weimar in the middle of this maelstrom, and trying to protect his master from undue exposure to it, was the King's personal secretary, Frederick ('Fritz') Ponsonby. His memoirs form one of two essential source-books on Edwardian Marienbad.[29] Some idea of the force and variety of the human torrents which bore down upon him comes through in his record of one morning's interviews on his sovereign's behalf. The first visitor was an Austrian countess requiring a special dispensation from the monarch to exempt her dogs from the strict quarantine laws of his realm. Then came an American tourist, complaining about unfriendly treatment from one of His Majesty's consuls. He was followed by a sculptor seeking a commission to do a bust of the King, and an eccentric Austrian army officer who was hoping to get royal sponsorship for a telescopic sword scabbard he had invented. Finally, when all these callers had been assuaged or fended off, a beautiful Viennese lady was announced who informed him quite simply that she wished to have the honour of sleeping with the King. When Ponsonby protested that this was out of the question, she reflected for a moment and then suggested that, in order not to waste her train fare, perhaps the King's secretary might deputize for his master. It was a very angry and disillusioned lady who was sent politely packing over this proposal as well.

The incident is typical of the way in which legend was always racing ahead of reality as regards the King's amorous exploits. The only acknowledged mistress of his to visit him at Marienbad was Lillie

The marriage that shook an empire and divided a dynasty, Archduke Franz Ferdinand with his newly-wed morganatic wife Countess Sophie Chotek. The Emperor sent jewels and good wishes to the bride, but was conspicuously absent from the ceremony.

The long and the short of European royalty, the diminutive (despite his raised cap) King Victor Emmanuel III of Italy and Queen Elena, one of the statuesque daughters of the King of Montenegro. The picture shows the contrasting but blissfully happy couple opening the Turin exhibition in 1911.

The veteran King Carol of Rumania entertaining 'en famille' his mighty northern neighbour Tsar Nicholas II of Russia at Constanza in June 1914. During the last few weeks of peace, King Carol cherished the hope of a marriage link between the two houses.

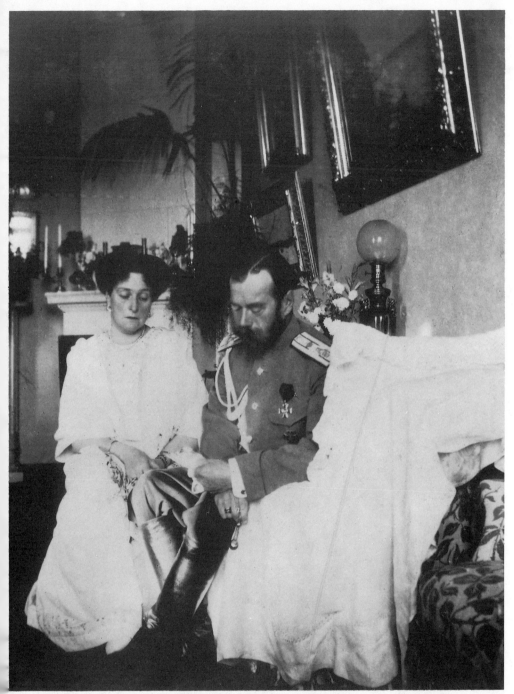

The private agony: Tsar Nicholas and his German-born wife Alexandra at their palace of Spala in October 1912. The letter they are reading is said to be a message from the bogus monk Rasputin telling them that the Tsarevich would survive the latest of his haemophiliac attacks. Alexandra's blind faith in the hated Rasputin proved a large nail in the Romanov coffin.

The public pomp: Nicholas II and Alexandra in national dress at the Romanov tercentenary celebrations of 1913.

(*Left*): The Colonel of the Hussards, Olga, and the Colonel of the Uhlans, Tatiana, the two young Grand Duchesses, eldest daughters of the Tsar, on the right and left of their father at Peterhof.

(*Below*): Strong family ties which failed to check a steadily growing Anglo-German rivalry: *from left to right*, Duke of Connaught, Duke of Saxe-Coburg and Gotha, Queen Victoria, William II, Empress Augusta, Frederick and Prince of Wales.

Edward VII at his 'continental court' of Marienbad, being visited on 16 August 1904 by Franz Josef of Austria.

King Edward VII mixing politics with pleasure at the daily morning gathering in front of Marienbad's mineral baths. In this picture, specially painted by a local artist, the most interesting promenaders are, to the King's right, King George of Greece and the insufferable 'Foxy Ferdinand' of Bulgaria; and, on his left, the Marquis of Soveral, the Portuguese Ambassador in London and the King's closest male friend, and Sir William Harcourt. A little further to the King's right stand the Abbot of the local monastery, Tepl, (who has donned a top hat over his robes) and, wearing their fezes, a Turkish 'delegation' headed by Hakki Pasha.

Imperial cousins and 'look-alikes', Prince George of Wales (later King George V) and Tsar Nicholas II. Their fates, however, were to be very different.

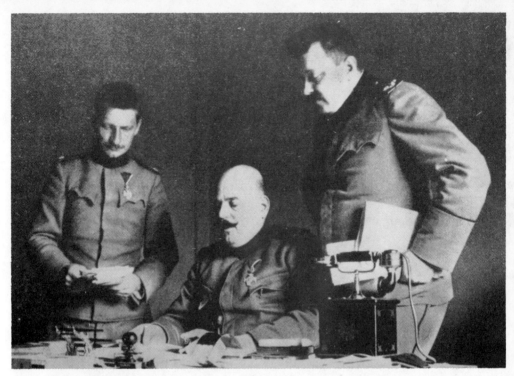

Colonel Dragutin Dimitriević, the former officer regicide of 1904 who rose to be head of Serbian army intelligence, pictured here with his aides. Dimitriević or 'Apis' ('the Bull') as he was nicknamed, was a key figure in the secret anti-Austrian terrorist movement and the main wire-puller behind the Serbian students' conspiracy which led to the assassination by Gavrilo Princip of the Austrian heir-presumptive, Archduke Franz Ferdinand, and his wife at Sarajevo on 27 June 1914. 'Apis' thus helped to trigger off the greatest war the world had seen.

All looking different ways: a symbolic military manoeuvres picture of the Austrian Emperor Franz Josef (*centre left, facing the camera*); his nephew and heir, Franz Ferdinand (*next to him, back to camera*); and various aides and generals, each of whom has his eyes on something different.

Langtry, the actress of stunning good looks and cheerfully lax morals who had first captivated him back in 1877 but who, by now, was very much a fading flame. Yet any attractive woman seen beside him in his carriage or next to him at table – at Marienbad as everywhere else – was automatically placed by gossip next to him in bed as well. Queen Alexandra was certainly a sorely-tried spouse, though never, in the furtive sense of the word, deceived. One excuse that can be made for the King is that Europe swarmed with mothers and daughters of society, all of them yearning, like that Viennese beauty, to 'have the honour', and also of hostesses only too willing to arrange matters at country house parties. As Prince and King, Edward was overwhelmed with opportunities as well as temptations, both of which, one suspects, were denied to some of his more puritanical critics. A second point in the errant husband's favour is that, unlike many of his own subjects (and nearly all of his mother's) he never indulged in hypocrisy. Indeed, his conviction was that, by following the style of the vanished Bourbons and declaring his society mistresses openly, he was going as far as he could towards preserving royal dignity all round.

The *haute volée* of England did not follow their leader to Bohemia. For most of them mid August (which was when the King, absurdly disguised as 'The Duke of Lancaster', descended on Marienbad) was anyway the time for the Scottish grouse moors. It was the second layer of English society who got their look-in at Marienbad, topped off by politicians, Balkan kings and continental aristocrats in no predictable sequence or order. The most prominent of the statesmen was the French Prime Minister Georges Clemenceau who, on 15 August 1909, came for a highly political lunch at which he urged the King to pledge an expeditionary force of 110,000 men to help France fight the battle they both sensed was coming against German militarism. Considering that the balcony of the Hotel Weimar, where the two men were talking, was in the middle of a Habsburg empire which was bound hands and feet in alliance to Germany, both the meeting and the conversation took distinct liberties with Franz Josef's unfailing kindness and hospitality.

None of the Tsar's Prime Ministers appears to have made the pilgrimage to Marienbad, but his foreign minister (and the King's own political protégé) Izvolski was always there, often shadowed by Alois Aehrenthal, the man who had duped him over the famous Buchlau conspiracy of 1908.* The King's own ministers, especially those not attached to the grouse-butts, became increasingly frequent holiday visitors: Campbell-Bannerman, for example, the leader of the 1905

* See *supra*, p. 149.

Liberal government who was an old Marienbad devotee; Lord
Haldane, his war minister; and the upwards-striving chancellor of the
exchequer, David Lloyd George.

The only monarch of note to put in an appearance was the old
Austrian emperor himself, who, on 16 August 1904, paid a courtesy
visit to this foreign monarch who had set up a midsummer court in the
midst of his domains. The spa, for the first and last time in its history,
was decked out with triumphal arches of double-headed Habsburg
eagles alternating with lions and unicorns. For once, Scotland entered
the Marienbad picture: the King had had grouse of the 'glorious
twelfth' rushed by car, rail and steamer all the way from its moors to the
kitchens of the Hotel Weimar, just in time for the dinner offered to the
Emperor, a guest in his own empire. That was King Edward's one
moment of truly regal hospitality at Marienbad, though lesser
princelings were always turning up. Among the more familiar of these
(and certainly, for the King and his party, the most trying) was
Ferdinand of Bulgaria, always eager to score first with the European
gossip when they met for the morning promenade and glass of spa
water at the famous Kreuzbrunnen. However, not even this ceaselessly
intriguing busybody, self-styled tsar by the time of the King's last visit
in 1909, could spoil the cosiness of the place.

The season, of course, continued after that last visit had been paid
but, as a political centre, Edwardian Marienbad died with King
Edward, though the era to which he gave his name is commonly
extended to 1914. For seven years, it had had its brief moment in
European history. Inasmuch as England had been nudged just a little
closer each midsummer to France and Russia, the spa had also played
its modest role in shaping that history.

The other continental resort regularly favoured by the King was
Biarritz, the little seaside town facing the Atlantic at the foot of the
French Pyrenees. If, as his reign approached its end, his stays here
(usually straddling March and April) became even more precious to
him than the August descents upon Marienbad, it was because, at
Biarritz, he could relax, undisturbed, with the most precious person in
his private life. Alice Frederica Keppel might have been created by
providence, working to a formula, as the perfect mistress for a monarch
such as Edward VII. Unlike Lillie Langtry, she came out of the top
drawer of society, being the youngest daughter of an admiral and
Scottish baronet, Sir William Edmonstone, and the wife of the Hon.
George Keppel, third son of the seventh Duke of Albemarle. Unlike
Lillie's principal successor, Daisy Countess of Warwick, who was an
exhausting and indiscreet 'salon' socialist, Alice was supremely good at

calming the King's nerves as well as keeping his secrets. She had a superb sense of humour; she shared his own great gifts of friendship; she sincerely loved him; and, with a face and figure of almost Latin sensuality, she could more than satisfy all the passion of her ageing royal philanderer. To cap it all, her husband, who was almost penniless by the standards of Edwardian big spenders, proved the most complaisant of partners. George seemed quite content to bask in the reflected glory of his wife's position and was certainly always relieved to know that the family's debts were, in the last analysis, backed by the King, through his financial amanuensis, Ernest Cassel.

'La Favorita', as she was dubbed, came into the King's private life in February of 1898 and she dominated that life from then on until his death. But though she appeared almost everywhere with him at the London season, and though Queen Alexandra came stoically to accept the situation as being the least of evils for both herself and the King, the liaison had its awkward edges in England. Count Mensdorff, for example, who seems to have invented her nickname, would groan into his diary whenever she was a guest at his Belgrave Square dinners, thus causing the fastidious Austrian ambassador problems of 'placement'. (Alice's triumph on this front came when she was once seated next to the Kaiser on one of his private visits to England.) Then there were certain old families, self-appointed guardians of the nation's morality, who refused throughout to accept her in their homes – the Salisburys at Hatfield House, the Portlands at Welbeck Abbey, the Norfolks at Arundel Castle.

This was where, for both of them, that annual escape to Biarritz came so strongly into the picture. The Hon. Mrs George Keppel may have travelled to Dover only as 'La Favorita'; but when she stepped into her sleeping car at Calais (having been whisked, unquestioned, through customs by the *chef de gare*) Alice was treated like a Madame Pompadour of the vanished Bourbons. Once in Biarritz, she *was* queen. All was done discreetly, with Sir Ernest Cassel again earning his multiple knighthoods. Alice would stay at the Villa Eugénie, which the financier rented from year to year at mounting cost, and where his sister did the formal honours as hostess. Conveniently near by was the great Hotel du Palais where the King had a specially appointed suite of rooms (including the novel luxury of a telephone) on the first floor. High society was not reluctant to follow its monarch to southern France to get away from the long tail of an English winter, and the holiday-makers were all Alice's friends. A typical sample was the lunch party which the King took by car into Spain on 21 March 1906: the Duke of Devonshire, the Duchess of Roxburgh, the Earl and Countess of

Dudley and the American-born Consuelo, Duchess of Marlborough.

Such trips into and across the Pyrenees, for picnics whenever the weather allowed, were the speciality of these stays. It was the same mountain border with Spain which provided Edwardian Biarritz with its own little moment in European history.

We have seen how furious the Kaiser was when, on 9 March 1906, King Alfronso XIII of Spain announced his engagement to Princess Victoria Eugenie of Battenberg. For once, concentrating his wrath on 'these pathetic and corrupt Latin peoples',* the Kaiser missed the chance to fire at his favourite target, Edward VII. Victoria Eugenie was the King's niece (a daughter of his youngest sister, Princess Beatrice of Battenberg) and from the moment, at a Buckingham Palace ball in the summer of 1905, that Don Alfonso became enamoured of the young lady, her uncle had stepped in behind the scenes as a determined matchmaker. Catholic Spain was something of a floater on Europe's political waves. Her monarch was not without influence, and his choice of bride therefore not without significance. The Kaiser himself had grasped the point and had been parading princesses from Germany's Catholic royal houses like thoroughbred fillies in a horse-ring in the hope that one of them would catch Alfonso's eye.

Why this genial young royal sportsman (he was reckoned one of the six finest shots in Europe and was one of its most intrepid pioneer motorists) should have broken with centuries of religious and political tradition by choosing an English Protestant remains – despite his obvious infatuation – something of a riddle. King Edward wasted no time in trying to probe the romance; all he was concerned with was fulfilling it, and Biarritz proved the ideal stage. A German kinswoman of the King's, Princess Frederica of Hanover, had her permanent home there, the Villa Mouriscot, and it was arranged that Princess Ena (as Victoria Eugenie was always called) should go and stay there in January of 1906, to be wooed by her conveniently adjacent suitor and decide whether she wanted to be Queen of Spain. The twenty-year-old Alfonso needed no further encouragement, driving across the border almost daily from San Sebastián at breakneck speed in his Panhard Phaeton car.

When the proposal was duly made and duly accepted (the betrothed pair planting two fir trees in the Villa Mouriscot's gardens to mark the occasion) it was a delighted King Edward back in England who went on to stage-manage the formal proceedings. It was he who decreed that the ceremony by which his niece would embrace the Catholic faith (an

* See *supra*, p. 107.

essential precondition of the match) should be held discreetly in a 'neutral' chapel at Versailles; he who approved the Catholic Bishop of Nottingham, Monsignor Brindle, as her religious instructor for the conversion; and he who dealt firmly with the domestic clamour raised by bodies such as the Protestant Alliance. (He evaded their objections in characteristically deft style by declaring that the Battenbergs, being a 'foreign family', were not subject to the Royal Marriages Act of 1772.) Finally, three days before the public announcement in Madrid, King Edward arrived in Biarritz himself, to congratulate his niece and see her off to San Sebastián, where Monsignor Brindle from Nottingham was waiting at the chapel of the Miramar palace to give her her first communion as a Catholic. This arrangement, it was felt, would placate public opinion in England.

King Edward was not, however, present for the ceremonial climax of the romance, the wedding, which was held on 31 May 1906, in Madrid's ancient church of Los Gerónimos. It was just as well, for this marriage, which he had worked so hard to bring about, got off to the most dreadful start. As the couple were driving back to the palace an anarchist's bomb was hurled at their carriage. The bride narrowly ecaped death within minutes of becoming Queen of Spain; as it was, her bridal gown became bespattered with the blood of some of the visitors who died around her. She impressed her new subjects by maintaining an English sang-froid throughout.

A year later there came a political pact with Spain which complemented this dynastic link between the two countries. It was drawn up in the Spanish port of Cartagena (the King, mindful of anarchist bombs, having declined to travel to Madrid) and, in essence, it pledged Spain to join with both France and England in maintaining the status quo in the western Mediterranean. This modest-sounding arrangement sufficed to put paid to the Kaiser's attempts to draw Spain into the German camp in the event of a European war. King Edward, who had proceeded to Cartagena from Biarritz, for once intervened in the detailed mechanics of diplomacy by persuading both his own Cabinet and the French government to add a third exchange of notes between themselves to their separate notes with Spain. In this way, he argued, Spain would have a link with the Entente as such and not simply with its two partners. Even the professionals gave him full credit for the idea.

The combination of Biarritz and Alice Keppel had come to mean so much to the King that it was surely fitting that he should have enjoyed their combined magic once again in the last spring of his life. He arrived at the Hotel du Palais for what was to prove his final visit on 10 March

1910. For more than a week the bronchial trouble which had assailed him in Berlin the year before kept him indoors and Alice Keppel (at the Cassel villa as usual) had to arrange little dinner-parties with Soveral and the other intimates in the spare bedroom of the hotel suite which had been turned into a private drawing-room. She was worried and so, though he never admitted it, was he. Though up and about again by 21 March, he seemed more disinclined than ever to leave Biarritz and more determined than ever to pack in as many and as varied excursions as possible before departing. He stretched out his stay for more than six weeks, despite pleas from Queen Alexandra to come away from 'that horrid Biarritz' and the mounting constitutional crisis at home.* He left at last on 25 April, after a spectacular farewell from the municipality which included a miniature military tattoo. As he took a final look at the Atlantic from his hotel balcony, he was heard to mutter that he might never see Biarritz again.

He looked fit enough, especially to his sun-starved subjects and, for a day or two, all seemed well. Then, at Sandringham, on Sunday 1 May, he took a last fatal liberty with that treacherous chest of his by roaming around the estate in a chill, damp Norfolk wind. Back in Buckingham Palace he started to cough horribly as the bronchitis took decisive hold. The oxygen cylinder was brought to his bedroom; the family started to gather. When, on 5 May, he was not at Victoria station to greet the Queen, who had hurried back from Corfu, the whole nation was alerted and further dissimulation became impossible. That evening a bulletin was issued warning that the King's condition 'causes some anxiety'. Defiant to the end, he went on puffing at those cigars, the size of small capstan bars, which had wrought such havoc on his chest and lungs.

The next morning, the wording of the bulletins moved from 'grave' to 'critical'. It was clear that the ample hour-glass of his life was running dry. It was an enviable end. Apart from having around him his wife and children, who had continued to love him despite his tantrums and infidelities, any special friend who wanted to see him was admitted to his rooms; and these included, by a generous gesture of the Queen's, Mrs George Keppel. Thus, during that afternoon, Luis Soveral, his greatest man-friend, and Alice, his greatest love, were among those who came to say goodbye. His last recorded words, though not of fond reminiscence, were also happy ones. After long hesitation, his horse trainer had allowed Witch of the Air, one of the King's promising two-

---

* On 14 April 1910, Mr Asquith (who had been obliged, two years before, to travel all the way to Biarritz to kiss hands on his appointment as Prime Minister) had introduced his famous bill to curtail the residual powers of the House of Lords.

year-olds, to run in the 4.15 at Kempton Park. It won by half a length, beating the favourite. 'I'm very glad,' the royal owner managed to whisper when given the news. Death came just as Big Ben was chiming the quarter hour before midnight on 6 May 1910. It was a Friday, apparently the day he had always sensed that he would die.

Long after the Windsor Castle funeral (attended, as befitted the 'Uncle of Europe', by nine reigning sovereigns and, following them, fifteen files of imperial, royal, serene and grand-ducal highnesses) the debate continued as to how influential he had been as a monarch. In his case, that meant only one question: what personal influence had he brought to bear on the diplomacy of his day? Not surprisingly, those long-suffering ministers he had so often ignored or side-stepped were prominent among his derogators. In 1915, for example, a scholarly work appeared which gave the late monarch his full share of credit for the concept and creation of the Anglo-French 'entente'. After reading it, Lord Balfour, Edward VII's second Conservative Prime Minister, wrote to Lord Lansdowne, his foreign secretary, dismissing this idea as 'a foolish piece of gossip'. 'So far as I remember,' Balfour continued, 'during the years which [sic] you and I were his Ministers, he never made an important suggestion of any sort on large matters of policy.'[30]

Even allowing for the fact that Balfour never had the privilege of reading Soveral's secret diary on the famous royal foray of 1903, the verdict – typical of this remote and complacent figure – is simply fatuous, for it confused the role of officials with the role of monarchs. Paul Cambon, the astute French ambassador in London (and universally accepted as one of the principal working architects of the alliance) got it dead right when he declared, of King Edward's role: 'Any clerk at the Foreign Office could draw up a treaty, but there was no one else who could have succeeded in producing the right atmosphere for a *rapprochement* with France.'[31]

However vital that atmosphere was in 1903, the King's influence stretched back long before, and extended long past, that *annus mirabilis*. The Danish war of 1864 first implanted in him the fear that Bismarck's Prussia, by dominating the continent, would also imperil England. After his brilliant but unstable nephew became Kaiser of imperial Germany, that fear became a sober conviction and he sought to insulate the danger by enveloping it, bringing England steadily closer to the governments and the armed services of both France and Russia. The picture, one of broad brush combined with minute dabs, has been detailed above. His reputation can surely rest upon it.

If further evidence were needed of the influence he had exerted, it was provided by the vacuum he left. George V was a far better family man (as well as a far better shot) than his father. But he had neither the temperament nor the desire to intervene in foreign affairs. Europe bored him as much as it had absorbed Edward VII. He paid one obligatory state visit to Paris but, despite the conventional encomiums, its greatest impact was to mark the contrast between the personalities of father and son. George V, an admirably honest and conscientious ruler, was an empire man first and foremost. He gazed at a setting sun, whereas his father, perhaps without fully realizing it, had looked to another horizon which awaited England beyond her empire.

The Kaiser alarmed George V just as he had alarmed Edward VII, but there were never the same electric sparks flying between the two men, if only because King George was determined not to compete. When political matters arose – for example at that Berlin wedding of 1913 with which we opened this narrative – he was quite happy to agree with whatever the Kaiser said, so that family peace and harmony should prevail.

Quite by accident, and through the congenial instrument of his beloved shotguns, he did manage to forge a useful, and potentially powerful, connection with the one European court which had really eluded the personal grasp of his father – that of the Habsburgs in Vienna. An invitation to the Court of St James had, for years, been the ambition of that darkly-smouldering royal volcano, the Austrian Heir-Presumptive Archduke Franz Ferdinand, in order to set the seal of European social acceptance on his morganatic bride Sophie. From 17 to 21 November, thanks to the assiduous lobbying of the Austrian envoy in London, Count Mensdorff, the Archduke got the next best thing, a five-day private visit to Windsor Castle to shoot pheasants in the Great Park and discuss the international scene in the smoking-room with (among others) the lords Lansdowne, Rosebery and Salisbury and Sir Edward Grey.[32] The visit was a tremendous success. The dignified Sophie charmed everybody and her grateful husband departed a different man. As Queen Mary wrote to one of her German aunts a week after her guests had left:

The Archduke was formerly very anti-English but that is quite changed now and *her* influence has been, and is, good, they say, in every way. All the people staying with us who had known *him* said how much he had changed for the better and that he was most enthusiastic over his visit to us and to England . . .[33]

There were even plans for a return visit to be paid by King George and Queen Mary to Blühnbach, the Archduke's favourite autumn shooting retreat in the mountains above Salzburg. The date they had in mind was September 1914. But Gavrilo Princip was soon to put paid to those royal plans for the coming year, along with the plans of millions of their commoner subjects. The time has come to see how, after Sarajevo, the dynasties of old Europe slid into a catastrophe which all had helped to prepare, which none had wanted, and none could stop.

Part Four

END GAME

Chapter Fifteen

FATAL GAMBITS

It remains to bring together, for the first and last time, all of these emperors and kings at once, and to see how they performed in the closing act of this European tragedy, which was to sweep some of their weightiest crowns off the world stage for ever. Before we come to that, however, it is worth looking at the event which triggered off the final crisis, the assassination at Sarajevo of the Austrian Heir-Presumptive, Archduke Franz Ferdinand and his wife. It was a remarkable happening, for it was both predictable and haphazard.

Ever since 1908, when the Austrian annexation of Bosnia-Herzegovina had inflamed pan-Slav feeling in Serbia and also pushed it further down the path of terrorism, it seemed only a matter of time before some crime of vengeance would strike down a Habsburg governor or even a Habsburg prince in the lost provinces.* And of all the secret societies which were sharpening their daggers against the dynasty, the 'Black Hand' of Colonel Dragutin Dimitriević seemed the most likely to be involved, not only because it stood on the lunatic fringe of extremism but also because its leader, the regicide of 1903, now held the key post of chief of Serbian military intelligence. He thus disposed over the information, the control channels, and the weapons. There was no need to expose his own officers on the task, for the Belgrade of 1914 swarmed with student refugees from Bosnia who spent at most one-third of their time over their books, and the remaining two-thirds plotting bloody retribution against the Austrians over the little marble-topped tables of Belgrade's 'kafanas'. It just happened that the 'Golden Sturgeon' was the particular café where the plot to murder the Archduke was hatched and that the two principal students involved were called Gavrilo Princip and Nedelkjo Cabrinović.

* Already on 15 June 1910, Bogdan Zerajić, one of the founders of the 'Mlada Bosna', or revolutionary Bosnia Youth movement, had tried to kill the governor of Sarajevo, General Varešanin. The General survived five bullets; the attacker committed suicide.

Having found its volunteers, the Black Hand proceeded to arm them with pistols and bombs; instruct them in the use of the weapons; and then smuggle them down a regular underground route by river and remote field paths into Bosnia. According to an account based on contemporary Serbian documents but only published forty years later,[1] the burly Colonel 'Apis', finding himself under suspicion, tried at the last minute to call the operation off. By then, however, the conspirators were already ensconced in hiding in Sarajevo and refused to back down. Even if this version of the Black Hand's second thoughts were true, it does not diminish the guilt of Serbian officers and Serbian organizations in the affair, a guilt for which the Belgrade government (still headed by the venerable Pašić) was obliged to take some responsibility. The chief wire-puller himself, Colonel Apis, was not the only one who, over the coming weeks, discovered that it was easier to provoke catastrophe than to contain it.

As for the haphazard aspect of the Sarajevo killings, vain attempts to cancel Princip's mission – assuming these were really undertaken – represent only one of many bizarre muddles in the affair. To begin with, it was uncertain until the morning of 7 June 1914 that the Archduke would go to Sarajevo at all. Though the journey (to attend the summer manoeuvres in Bosnia of the 14th and 16th Austrian Army Corps) offered Franz Ferdinand a rare opportunity to travel officially within the empire with his beloved Sophie, he had developed an unaccountable reluctance to go, even amounting to an alarming prophecy, made to his young nephew Charles, of his own death.[2] Three weeks before he was due to set off, the Archduke expressed these reservations in an audience with the Emperor. Nearly always he had his own way in such matters, if only because his aged uncle hated scenes. On this occasion, without actually ordering the visit, the Emperor made it clear by his tone that he desired it. So off the Archduke set, his premonitions not eased by the fact that the electric lights fused in the saloon car of his Trieste-bound train, thus forcing him to travel by the funereal gleam of a few candles.

If it had been touch and go whether the victim himself would be in Sarajevo, the way in which the assassins reached their destination was even chancier. For part of the route, the underground 'tunnel' of Colonel Apis, ran smoothly. But there were also hold-ups, any one of which could have betrayed the conspirators to the swarms of Austrian police agents covering the area. At one point Cabrinović, travelling alone by rail on the last leg of the journey, found himself sitting right next to one such agent who happened to know his father and engaged the nervous youth in conversation. At another point the bombs and revolvers, stuffed in a black sugar box which was simply covered with newspaper and tied round with string, were removed from the station waiting-room at Doboj junction and had to be retrieved from a tailor's shop in the town. At yet a third point, the village of Priboj, the local 'tunnel' operator, who was the local schoolmaster, asked Princip point-blank whether he was heading for Sarajevo to kill Franz Ferdinand. After a moment's hesitation, Princip admitted that he was. In this way two uninvolved peasants living in the schoolmaster's house learned the secret. They kept it though they paid for their silence eventually on an Austrian gallows.

Events in Sarajevo on the fatal day were just as haphazard. Counting a local 'back-up team', the killers on the ground numbered six young fanatics. Had they all done their job, six revolvers would have been emptied of six bullets, six bombs would have been thrown, and six doses of cyanide would then have been swallowed to put the plotters beyond the reach of interrogation. As this was all to happen on the 525th anniversary of the great Serbian battle of Kosovo (none the less emotive for being a defeat), it was an appropriate moment for such heroics. As it turned out, only two of the six converted their fiery words into deeds. Cabrinović hurled his bomb at the Archduke's car as the motorcade entered the city along the main Appel Quai which ran alongside the mud-green Miljačka river. It bounced off the rolled-back hood, wounding only passers-by and officers in the car behind.

Then came the ultimate unpredictability. Princip, the most dedicated of the band, was convinced that, once that bomb had gone off, the police clamp-down would be so tight as to preclude any second attempt. None the less, he felt there was just a chance that the authorities might allow the Archduke's procession, which had driven on to attend a fraught ceremony of welcome at the town hall, to drive back along the same vulnerable route. So he simply crossed the road and waited at the road junction opposite. His faith in Austrian inefficiency was justified beyond his dreams. Mistakenly, as it turned out, the procession did set off back down the Appel Quai, and the error was communicated to the chauffeur just as the Archduke's car was approaching the assassin's second stand. Indeed, in a frantic change of course, it reversed straight into the barrel of Princip's revolver. Even turning his head away as he pulled the trigger twice, he could not miss his target. It was shortly before eleven o'clock on the morning of 28 June 1914. A quarter of an hour later, both the Archduke and his wife were dead. What was to be the greatest war in history had been touched off by the greatest of flukes. Franz Ferdinand had been killed by an overpowering combination of new Slav fanaticism and good old-fashioned Austrian muddle.

Whether sped on its way by flukes or not, one of Princip's bullets had struck down, in public and in cold blood, the heir to one of Europe's most venerable thrones. Moreover, the killer had not been a motiveless madman like Luigi Luccheni who, sixteen years before, had stabbed the Archduke's aunt to death merely because his path had crossed with hers on the shores of Lake Geneva that September morning. Princip was a political assassin who had sworn with Cabrinović to kill his victim three months before when on 27 March 1914, the two youths, sitting on a Belgrade park bench, had solemnly shaken hands on the murder pact. Moreover, though he was later to express regret from his prison cell* for killing a woman, he felt not a twinge of remorse in assassinating Franz Ferdinand, any of whose various personal plans for a reconstruction of the Habsburg monarchy ruled out that independent Greater Serbia of which Princip and his powerful helpers ardently and genuinely dreamed. His deed had thus struck a blow at the dynasties, rather than the governments, of Europe. The crowned heads reacted accordingly – all of them with shock, though only some of them with grief.

All sent messages of condolence to the Emperor Franz Josef and all ordered either requiem masses or periods of court mourning, or both. In Belgrade, the capital which knew it would meet the full force of any hurricane which now blew up, the court was still reeling from the sudden and unexpected departure, on health grounds, of King Peter, an exit which, as we have seen, amounted to an abdication. It accordingly fell to Crown Prince Alexander to announce an eight-day period of mourning, beginning on 29 June. Apprehension over what was to come was probably tempered by momentary relief that the most dynamic of the hated Habsburgs would never mount the throne.

If, in Belgrade, they were careful to conceal any such sentiments, King Nikita in neighbouring Montenegro made absolutely no secret of his. Returning to Cetinje after the assassination, he held a small requiem service in his palace chapel there, to which, of the entire diplomatic corps, only the Austrian chargé d'affaires had been invited. His French colleague reported of the King's attitude: 'Though he cannot approve of the deed itself, he is delighted with the result.'[3] The mood in the Montenegrin capital seems to have been catching. The Serbian minister, M. Gavrilović, discussing the outlook on the night of 28 June, was heard to exclaim: 'That bullet will bring liberty to the whole Serb race.'[4]

---

* Princip, because he was under age at the time, got away with a twenty-year prison sentence. He served less than two of them before dying of tuberculosis on 24 April 1918, in the last year of the war he had precipitated.

In fact, the only Balkan monarch who was deeply saddened, for personal as well as political reasons, by the Archduke's death, was the seventy-five-year-old King Carol of Rumania, who was at a race meeting and nearly fainted when he heard the news. It had been to his palace at Sinaia that the Archduke had come in 1909 on the first official visit he had been allowed to make outside the Austrian empire with his morganatic wife. As described above, Carol was hoping to reap a massive reward out of this relationship once his guest had mounted the throne in Vienna: only if an Emperor Franz Ferdinand could succeed in curbing Magyar power might the disputed Rumanian lands in Transylvania be won back. This hope, too, had been ended with Princip's revolver, and Carol showed how hard the bullet had struck him. He ordered a four-week long court mourning and donned Austrian army uniform to attend the memorial mass.

In Italy, a country the Archduke had detested as one of the grave-diggers of his empire, King Victor Emmanuel and his Montenegrin Queen went through all the formalities of condolence and remembrance, and the little King would certainly have felt some surge of empathy when he thought of the assassination of his own father fourteen years before. But the popular mood was summed up by a cinema audience in Rome who stood as one man to sing the Italian national anthem when the film was interrupted to announce the Archduke's murder.[5] The Italians, like the Hungarians, had been delivered from a powerful and dedicated foe.

Of the monarchs in the entente camp, it was King George v, the Archduke's host at Windsor Castle only seven months before, who gave the response which was both appropriate and genuinely felt. He had immediately ordered a week of court mourning on hearing the news, and Prince Arthur of Connaught was sent to represent him at a requiem mass in Westminster Cathedral. Equally impressive to the racing fraternity, was the announcement that he had cancelled his annual attendance at Newmarket's big midsummer race meeting the following week. In his private diary King George, after recording the news about 'poor Archduke Franz Ferdinand and his wife', added: 'It will be a terrible shock to the dear old Emperor and is most regrettable and sad.'

The government echoed those royal sentiments. At the conclusion of question time in the House of Commons, the Prime Minister, Mr Asquith, moved a 'humble address' to ask the King to convey to the Austrian emperor Parliament's 'abhorrence of the crime and their profound sympathy with the Imperial and Royal family and with the governments and peoples of the Dual Monarchy'. Mr Asquith went on to pay a personal tribute to the Austrian monarch: 'The unperturbed,

sagacious and heroic head of a mighty state, associated with us in this
country in some of the most moving and precious chapters of our
history.'[6] There was no thought here that, a bare five weeks later, the
Marlboroughs and the Prince Eugenes of the twentieth century were to
find themselves marching into battle against each other.

If the reaction in London was the most measured, that in Berlin was,
from the start, the most explosive. Like so much else in that neurotic
capital, it centred on the Kaiser himself. William II had made a
consistent play for the sympathies of Franz Ferdinand, using the same
instrument as the Rumanian king – namely, the Archduke's morganatic wife – but playing for even higher stakes. With a personal friend
installed one day in the Hofburg, the Kaiser could look to the Dual
Alliance between Berlin and Vienna being laid down between the
dynasties, as well as the governments, across the heart of Europe.

There was, as always, a histrionic element in the Kaiser's response.
He still made a habit of sending messages of remembrance to the
Austro-Hungarian embassy or even appearing himself, in Austrian
uniform, on each 30th of January, the anniversary of Crown Prince
Rudolph's death; and that was a Habsburg he had barely known.
Franz Ferdinand, on the other hand, he had met only ten days
previously, when he had visited the Archduke and his wife at their great
Bohemian estate at Konopischt. The private diary, only recently made
known, of the Archduke's secretary on duty for that occasion totally
contradicts, if further contradiction were needed, the *canard* which was
later spread around that the two men had plotted a European war at
this last meeting of theirs. The rumour fed largely on the fact that
Grand Admiral Alfred von Tirpitz, the creator of the Kaiser's navy,
had accompanied his royal master. However, as the secretary, Baron
von Morsey, who prepared all the arrangements, records, there were
two far less ominous reasons for the admiral's presence. Franz
Ferdinand was, it was true, eager to meet the famous admiral, being a
keen naval enthusiast himself. But the reason why Tirpitz wanted to see
Konopischt was disarmingly simple. Like the Archduke, he had a
passion for roses and, in twenty acres of the vast grounds of
Konopischt, Franz Ferdinand had created the largest and finest rose
garden to be found anywhere on the continent, a garden which, in
mid-June, was at the peak of its beauty and fragrance.[7]

But now, in the wake of the assassination, the German Emperor
became the key figure in deciding what could have proved an important
factor in the unfolding drama: should the funeral of his murdered friend
be turned into a European event by the simultaneous presence in
Vienna of almost all the monarchs or crown princes of Europe, together

with some of their advisers? Both as the closest and most powerful of the victim's royal friends and as the sovereign of the Monarchy's principal ally, the Kaiser had been the first foreign ruler to whom Baron Rumerskirch, the Archduke's aide, had telegraphed from Sarajevo. The message reached William on board the *Hohenzollern* in Kiel harbour, where he was presiding over Germany's annual international regatta. (It was the season for royal yachting; Tsar Nicholas was cruising in northern waters in the *Standart* when the news reached him.) The regatta was immediately broken off and all vessels of any nationality present lowered their flags to half-mast. As Franz Ferdinand had been an admiral of the Kaiser's fleet, the battle-flag of Austria-Hungary was then hoisted up on every German warship to fly, also, of course, at half-mast, alongside the German colours. It was the first of a great panoply of mourning ceremonies which unfolded in Berlin, where the Kaiser now returned.

He clearly wanted to attend the funeral in person, accompanied by one or more of his sons. This, to begin with, was the general expectation in Vienna. The presence of the German Kaiser would automatically involve the kings of Saxony, Bavaria and Württemberg, all of whose houses had close family ties with the Habsburgs and, in their wake, dukes or princes from all the other German courts. As it could not be an all-German affair, the other royal houses of Europe would then have to be represented as well. If he did not come himself, so informed speculation ran in the Vienna press, then the Tsar of Russia would send his brothers, and George v of England would nominate the Duke of Connaught. Whatever the dead man's personal relationship with Italy had been, the house of Savoy would have to send a high representative to the funeral of its ally's Heir-Presumptive. King Carol of Rumania would certainly come in person to mourn his friend. The King of Montenegro would presumably send the preposterous Crown Prince Danilo. In the end, all the speculation was in vain. None of them came. It was announced that the funeral, to be staged as a one-day affair on 3 July, preceded by only a brief lying-in-state, would take place without a single royal mourner from abroad.

Among the reasons falsely cited for this decision was the desire on the part of the Emperor and his court chamberlain to render as little honour as was possible to the dead man and his morganatic wife. On the day, Prince Montenuovo certainly did not step one inch outside the strictest bounds of protocol to bury his old antagonist;* but sheer spite

---

* This should not be exaggerated, however. To set Sophie's casket on a stand eighteen inches lower than that of her husband was not a deliberate slight on Montenuovo's part. At a court so ossified with the old Spanish-style ceremonial, a wife like Sophie had to be shown to be morganatic, in death as in life.

had not dictated the arrangements. A more plausible explanation can be found in the field of security. The Austrian authorities had made a total hash of protecting one archduke in Sarajevo. A full-scale funeral would have brought dozens of crowned heads to Vienna at a smoke-laden time when any lunatic, let alone another Bosnian fanatic, might well be tempted to match Princip's deed, or even emulate it by killing a ruling emperor or king. What carried most weight was Franz Josef's own frail state of health, which had brought with it his steadily-mounting distaste for fatiguing ceremonies of any sort. The eighty-four-year-old monarch had gone down two months previously with one of his severe bronchial attacks and had only been finally cleared on 23 May, when his private physician, Dr Kerzl, had issued the final bulletin on the illness. The Emperor had just reached his summer retreat in Bad Ischl when the telegram from Sarajevo had forced him back to Vienna again.

It could be argued that, had the crowned heads of both the rival camps in Europe, with some of their leading courtiers or officials, met over the Archduke's funeral bier, their coming together in a common act of remembrance might conceivably have checked the juggernaut of mobilization which they ordered, and which crushed all hope of peace a month later. If the Emperor's yearning for peace and quiet can be blamed for this missed opportunity, that same longing found even more fateful expression in what he did next. On 7 July, only four days after the funeral, he went back to Bad Ischl and did not return to the capital again until his empire was already at war. Whether Franz Josef was himself reluctant or quite ready to wage that war, and whether, in either case, he envisaged it as a localized or a general conflict are questions to which there will probably never be any final answers. This particular riddle of the obelisk will be scrutinized briefly below.

But whether he played an active role or not, his absence from his capital throughout those three weeks of July, when the Balkan crisis grew into a European conflict, must leave him with a portion of passive guilt over the catastrophe. Wherever he was, he retained, of course, the prerogative of ultimate decision. Only on his authority could a declaration of war be made. What he lost by retreating to Ischl was the power of initiative. This passed to his ministers back in Vienna who, in turn, passed it on to a handful of their own officials. Not once did the Emperor call them all together, or even assemble representative groups, to hear the debate as to what should be done and, having heard the discussion, make up his own mind. Instead, individual ministers – notably Count Berchtold, the minister for foreign affairs – journeyed to Ischl to present a case about which he himself was partisan. The only colleague of his who was fairly regularly at the 'Kaiservilla' during those weeks was the finance minister, the Polish-born Leon von Bilinski, whose department was responsible for the administration of Bosnia-Herzegovina. Bilinski later claimed he had suggested to the Emperor that a return to Vienna might be desirable in view of the gravity of the situation. According to him, the Emperor replied that this was not necessary as from Ischl they were anyway in telegraphic and telephone communication with the capital.[8]

Not only were telegraph machines and telephones (especially the relatively primitive versions of 1914) inadequate instruments with which to follow and guide an immensely complex and fast-developing crisis: the mere fact that the Emperor's end of the line was in the study of his peaceful villa in a peaceful spa must, by itself, have created a certain remoteness from reality. It would have been hard to envisage a holocaust in this genial yellow-washed building where he had lived with his beautiful Sisi and where, after her death, he had returned alone every midsummer to stalk his deer. (He was still out stalking in July 1914, at least until the third week of the month.) The submissions came from Vienna and the submissions were approved. Thus an autocratic monarchy moved into war, and into destruction, not by Crown councils, with the ruler at the head of the table, but by ministerial conferences, with the autocrat far away amid the lakes of the Salzkammergut.

As for the leading men of the Monarchy, these, to begin with, held contrasting views as to what Austria should do. The loudest voice calling for military action against Serbia without delay was, predictably, that of the Austrian chief of staff, Conrad von Hötzendorf who, as we have seen, had been itching for years to draw the sword against Belgrade. Now the ideal, indeed, for him, the imperative, summons to that lightning 'preventive war' against the South Slav menace had come. He tells in his memoirs how, the day after the assassination, he tried to persuade the Foreign Minister, Count Berchtold, to agree to immediate mobilization against Serbia, which seemed to him 'inevitable, however little it suited the Monarchy at present'. Berchtold, while agreeing with the general that 'the moment had come to solve the Serbian question', was against precipitate action. Public opinion, he argued, must first be prepared and, in any case, they ought to wait for the results of the official investigation into the murders.[9]

At the opposite end of the scale to Conrad stood, to begin with, a very formidable opponent, Count Stephen Tisza de Boros-Jenö, the Prime Minister of Hungary. After Deák and Andrássy, Tisza was the greatest statesman ever to come from the Magyar half of the Dual Monarchy and in 1914 he towered over all his colleagues in Budapest and Vienna. For months past, he had been trying to persuade Berchtold to calm the chaotic Balkans down by luring King Ferdinand of Bulgaria firmly into the Austro-German camp, thus containing Serbia politically. Rumania too would have to be wooed away from Belgrade, to make the isolation of the Serbs complete.

On Monday 29 June, the day after the assassination, Tisza had hurried to Vienna, not only to convey his condolences to the Emperor but also to ensure that his long-term peace plans had not been overthrown by the Sarajevo murders. When he saw Conrad clamouring for immediate war and Berchtold himself talking, in only slightly less ominous terms, of achieving 'a solution' with the Serbs, Tisza threw all his considerable weight on the side of moderation. He warned the foreign minister that any such war with Serbia would be 'a fatal mistake' and then wrote to the Emperor himself in the Hofburg, warning the sovereign against any 'intention to make the horrible crime of Sarajevo the occasion for the final reckoning with Serbia'.[10] Back in Budapest, Tisza wrote another letter in similar vein to Franz Josef, urging the monarch to stay with the long-term peace plan and induce the German Emperor (then still expected to be in Vienna for the funeral) to support it as well.[11] At the same time, Tisza embarked on a peaceful propaganda campaign of his own, aimed at St Petersburg, whom he rightly saw as the key to the crisis. In a special interview with a Russian paper, published on 1 July, he stressed that both Hungary and Russia were 'completely dedicated to peace and concerned to preserve calm in Europe'. The Balkans, he added in a pointed appeal for non-intervention, should be left to the Balkan states.[12] It can be seen what a tragedy it was that Tisza never met the Emperor again in the critical weeks ahead.

It is at this point, when the scales of peace and war were finely balanced in the Monarchy, with Tisza on one side, Conrad on the other, and the Emperor and the foreign minister still not finally committed, that William II enters upon the scene. How far he tipped the balance is still a matter of debate. How far he really meant to tip it remains, like almost everything concerning the Kaiser's true intentions, also an unsolved riddle, despite all the confident conclusions some historians have seen fit to draw.

The German emperor's first recorded entry on the scene comes, appropriately for him, in a scribbled entry in the margin of a diplomatic dispatch. On the afternoon of 30 June his ambassador in Vienna, Count Heinrich von Tschirschky, reported on the widespread feeling in Vienna that 'a final and fundamental reckoning should be had with the Serbs'. The envoy, clearly thinking that restraint was appropriate,

went on 'I take the opportunity on every occasion to advise calmly, but very forcefully and seriously against over-hasty steps.'

This proved too much for the Kaiser, not merely because he was still under the full emotional impact of his friend's murder only forty-eight hours before, but also because his ambassador in Vienna had taken it upon himself, without instructions from Berlin, to intervene decisively in Austrian policy by pulling hard on the brakes. The Emperor took up his pen and wrote the equivalent of a second and contradictory telegram in the margin. Next to the reference to the 'final and fundamental reckoning' he minuted 'Now or never'. Alongside the rest of the dispatch he dashed off the following reproof to the author:

Who authorized him to act in that way. . . . It is none of his business as it is entirely up to Austria what she intends to do in this affair. Tschirschky will kindly drop this nonsense. Matters must be cleared up with the Serbs *and that soon!*[13]

An imperial rebuke of that vehemence would certainly have caused the German ambassador to change his tune. The Emperor's fiery remarks would have been noted, on their way to Vienna, by both the German Foreign Office, which had been following the same pacific line, and by the very modestly-gifted chancellor, Bethmann-Hollweg. It is thus fair to assume that the Kaiser's marginalia stiffened the general attitude in Berlin. But that is no reason to conclude that, on 30 June 1914, the German Emperor already wanted Austria to invade Serbia, as opposed to simply repeating the formula used so successfully six years previously – namely to force complete political submission on Belgrade by the threat of invasion. The Emperor's insistence on speedy action reflected, apart from his own volcanic temperament, the very practical consideration that any showdown with the Serbs ought to come in the immediate wake of the assassinations, when general sympathy for Austria would be at its height.

Far, far less can the Kaiser's marginal comments on one telegram be taken as signalling the start of any conscious and deliberate march by Germany towards an all-out European war. Yet that is the construction which some of the modern revisionist historians, seeking to pin the blame for that war almost exclusively on Berlin, have put on the Kaiser's scribbled words. One such writer, who has produced three tomes of research on the subject, concludes:

The entire constitution of the Prusso-German Reich determined that the onus of deciding the issue lay with the Kaiser himself. . . . When William II received Tschirschky's preliminary report . . . he covered the document with un-controlled marginal notes which – this time – made world history. His drastically formulated wish to dispose of the Serbs 'soon' and his 'now or never' supplied the decisive catch-words for subsequent German policy in the July crisis.[14]

This is to swing a massive thesis on a very small and squeaky hinge. As we shall see, three weeks later, when that July crisis was reaching its climax, the Kaiser scribbled precisely the opposite comments on his telegrams, when welcoming what he thought was a peaceful solution through what he supposed to be an acceptable Serbian climb-down. If his marginalia had the force of imperial authority on the first occasion, why not on the second? Even if they were not followed then, why can they not be accepted as evidence that he was simply behaving now as he had behaved throughout his life – all bombast on the surface, but all doubt and uncertainty underneath?

Far more weight can certainly be attached to the response in Berlin given, both by the Kaiser in person and his ministers, to feelers put out from Vienna over the nature and degree of German support should the situation worsen. Here, we are dealing not with off-the-cuff comments seen only by German eyes, but with formal communications to a fellow monarch and an allied government. These responses have gone down in history as Germany's 'blank cheque' to her Austrian ally to count on unlimited support, no matter what the consequences. The verdict is a fair one, provided one leaves open the possibility that Berlin never expected the cheque to be cashed in full.

The feelers put out from Vienna were two-pronged, one dynastic and one diplomatic. Berchtold, knowing he could not throw any gauntlet down in Belgrade's face without the assurance of German backing, had drafted an aggrieved yet somewhat tentative letter for Franz Josef to send to his fellow monarch. This missive was far from bellicose; indeed, for the most part it recapitulated the Tisza programme for pacifying the Balkans by the diplomatic isolation of Serbia, an operation which now seemed more necessary than ever in view of 'the frightful catastrophe at Sarajevo'.

The only hint of toughness came at the end:

After the last dreadful events in Bosnia, you too will be convinced that a friendly settlement of the hostility which divides Austria and Serbia can no longer be contemplated and that the peaceful policies of all European monarchs are threatened so long as the source of criminal agitation in Belgrade lives on unpunished.[15]

This draft of Berchtold's was signed by the Emperor on 2 July and delivered in Berlin three days later, together with a government-to-government memorandum covering the same points but ending with a slightly more menacing reference to Austro-Serbian relations in the wake of Sarajevo: 'It is all the more necessary for the Monarchy to rip apart with a determined hand the strings of the net which its enemies are weaving over its head.'[16]

Both the imperial letter and the supporting memorandum were taken to Berlin by Count Alexander Hoyos, Berchtold's *chef de cabinet*, and given to the Austro-Hungarian ambassador, Count Ladislaus Szögenyi-Marich, to present to the Kaiser at the Neues Palais in Potsdam. William II now found himself right at the centre of the political arena and, predictably, had a moment of stage fright. He would have to consult his chancellor, he told the envoy, before giving a reply to the appeal for support implied in the Austrian Emperor's letter. After all, he added, such an appeal 'raised the prospect of a serious European complication'.[17]

That was on the morning of Sunday 5 July. By the afternoon the Emperor had found (or been given) his lines, and he read them confidently enough. Austria, he told Szögenyi, must not delay, whatever action she had in mind concerning Serbia. Then, according to the envoy's report to Vienna that evening, the Kaiser had continued:

Russia's attitude will no doubt be hostile but he had been ready for this for years and, should war between Austria-Hungary and Russia be unavoidable, we could rest assured that Germany, our old and faithful ally, would stand at our side. Russia at the present time was in no way prepared for war, and would think twice before resorting to arms.

The pledge of unconditional support was repeated in the Kaiser's reply to the Austrian Emperor, which was signed on board the *Hohenzollern* three days later. This letter, which had been drafted by the German Foreign Office, ended by assuring Franz Josef: 'You will find me and my Empire standing faithfully at your side in this dark hour, in full accord with our old and proven friendship and with the obligations of our alliance.'[18]

This pledge is always – and quite rightly – placed at the core of that share of the blame which the Kaiser and his advisers must bear for the catastrophe already looming up on the European horizon. However, the dismissive reference to Russia being anyway unprepared for war and therefore reluctant to wage it, a comment which follows in the very next sentence to the pledge, is rarely given the weight it deserves. As always, the Kaiser was striking a heroic pose while pronouncing policy. In only three weeks' time he would be bitterly regretting the Potsdam promises of 5 July and trying frantically to escape their consequences, like a bear struggling to break out of a pit he has walked straight into.

But the point to note is that, even when he made the original commitment, the Kaiser had half-convinced himself that he would never be called upon to deliver. The valid charge against William II is not that he deliberately plotted a world war and engineered its outbreak. The true indictment is worse: he helped to bring it about by sheer fecklessness. It was stupidity, not evil, but, as Talleyrand had once said to another emperor: '*Sire, c'est pire qu'un crime, c'est une erreur.*'

Before setting out for Kiel on the morning of 6 July to begin his annual cruise in northern waters, the Kaiser summoned army and navy officers – all senior men, though none of topmost rank – to the Neues Palais so that he could inform them about the latest turn of events. That these were political briefing sessions and not war councils was confirmed by the officers concerned, one of them General von Falkenhayn, putting pen to paper immediately after the audience. Falkenhayn, who was Prussian minister of war, wrote to the German chief of staff, General von Moltke, on the evening of 5 July that, so far as he could make out, the support which had been promised to Austria was for some sort of 'energetic political steps' on the part of the Dual Monarchy. Neither the Austrian Emperor's letter nor the Vienna memorandum 'spoke of any warlike issue'. Moreover, both he, Falkenhayn and the German chancellor doubted whether Austria was 'really in earnest' even about non-military measures.[19]

Lieut.-General Bertrab of the army general staff and Admiral Capelle, the acting secretary of the navy, who were briefed separately by the Kaiser early the following morning, both gave a similar picture – though in their case they spoke shortly after the war had been fought and lost by Germany. Bertrab stated of his audience:

No orders were given either then or as a result of the interview. In fact, His Majesty emphasized the point that he did not consider it necessary to give any special orders as he did not believe there would be any serious complications as a result of the Sarajevo crime.

Capelle's account ran parallel:

The Kaiser said he did not believe there would be any great warlike complications. In his opinion, the Tsar would not . . . place himself on the side of the regicides. Moreover, Russia and France were not prepared for war . . .

The reason why deputies and second-line service officers were called into the Kaiser's presence (and why Falkenhayn had to write a letter) was that, at this crucial juncture, when the Supreme War Lord was pledging unqualified support to his Austrian ally, the men at the very top of Germany's military machine were all far away from the capital on holiday.

One of the two key figures, the chief of staff, General von Moltke, was in indifferent health at the time and had been in the Bohemian spa of Karlsbad for the cure ever since the middle of April. His Austrian opposite number, General Conrad, had visited him there in civilian clothes on 12 May. The firebrand of the Monarchy describes in his memoirs[20] how the two men had held the sort of broad professional discussion which would have been normal between two closely allied chiefs of staff in either European camp. There was no talk of imminent war, and no expectation of it. Two days later, Moltke left Karlsbad to take up his duties but returned to resume his cure on 28 June, a few hours *before* hearing the news from Sarajevo. He remained at Karlsbad a full month, until 25 July. Only then, when Austria was about to declare war on Serbia, did he hurry back to Berlin. During the critical four weeks between these dates, he led the normal tranquil life of an ailing and elderly spa guest. The local police registers show no special movements and no special visitors, beyond two military messengers from Berlin to bring the General up to date.

Moltke's deputy, General von Waldersee, also left Berlin on holiday two days after the Kaiser's departure. He was, in his own words, 'ready to jump',[21] but evidently saw nothing to jump about until Austria delivered her ultimatum to Serbia a fortnight later. As for Admiral von Tirpitz, the head of the German navy, he was on holiday at Tarasp in Switzerland from 2 July right down to 27 July, and thus only returned to Berlin when a European, as opposed to a localized Austro-Serbian, conflict was looming up. His absence in the remote Swiss Alps, had he really been expecting, let alone planning, a major war, would have been even more difficult to explain, since naval preparations for battle are even more complicated than military ones. It should be noted that all these midsummer holidays, cures and official leaves were, just like the Kaiser's own cruise, prearranged well before Sarajevo, and proceeded on their untroubled course for a month after Sarajevo. It would be preposterous, therefore, to maintain that they constituted a massive and calculated programme of deception, to be called by a later generation 'disinformation'. The reasonable inference to be drawn from these absences is also the most likely one. As July progressed, those left behind in Berlin* became gradually convinced that Austria would, after all, steel herself to take a very tough line with Serbia; but they were neither convinced nor anxious that, within a week or two, that tough line would draw Germany herself into war.

---

* The chancellor, Bethmann-Hollweg, spent most of the month on his estate at Hohenfinow, from where he could easily make trips to the capital. His vice-chancellor and minister of the interior, Clemens von Delbrück, was on holiday until recalled on 23 July.

The Kaiser moved temporarily away from the centre of the stage
when he boarded the *Hohenzollern* in Kiel harbour for his annual cruise
in Norwegian waters. It is on that same day, 7 July, that the action
shifts back to Vienna, with the holding of a special ministerial council
on the Sarajevo crisis. The Austrian foreign minister was now
undergoing a psychological repeat of his behaviour during the
annexation crisis of 1908. Now, as then, the assurance of German
backing had put some steel down the spine of this normally amiable
and vacillating aristocrat. Now, as then, when he was serving as
ambassador to St Petersburg this heroic mood was to culminate in his
country flinging an ultimatum at Belgrade. However, quite apart from
the difference in the outcome of the second crisis, there was a contrast in
the preliminaries. In the summer of 1914, Berchtold had to struggle,
both with his colleagues and his Emperor, to get his challenge out in the
first place.

That Berchtold was still thinking of this challenge as meaning, at
worst, a localized war with Serbia is plain from his conduct as chairman
of the meeting.* In his opening remarks he even seemed at pains to
avoid using the word 'war' in any context. Ought we not to decide, he
asked, whether the moment has not come when 'a show of force might
put an end to Serbia's intrigues once and for all'. It was 'most
satisfactory' that both the German Emperor and the German
chancellor had solemnly promised full support in the event of 'a warlike
complication with Serbia'. He was not persuaded that any 'passage of
arms' with that country must involve the Monarchy in a conflict with
Russia. The Russians were concentrating on the long-term political
penetration of the Balkans, so Austria had to get in first by ensuring 'a
timely final reckoning' with Serbia.[22]

Tisza, who spoke next, insisted that the Monarchy should only resort
to military action, even though this now seemed more probable than a
week ago, after all attempts by diplomatic means to achieve satisfaction
from Belgrade had failed. He would not concur in a surprise attack
against Serbia. He would never, as Hungarian Premier, agree to the
'annihilation of Serbia'; nor, for that matter, would Russia, who would
'fight to the death' before allowing it. What the Monarchy should aim
at – and this was entirely her business, not Germany's – was 'a
diplomatic success, with the severe humiliation of Serbia'.

As, in the discussion which followed, all the others doubted whether
a purely diplomatic victory was possible, or even desirable, Tisza then

---

* The others present were the prime ministers of the two halves of the Monarchy, Count Tisza
and his Austrian counterpart, Count Stürgkh; the joint ministers for war and finance, Krobatin
and Bilinski; the chief of the general staff, General Conrad, and the deputy chief of naval staff,
Rear-Admiral von Kailer.

tried to meet his colleagues half-way. The demands to be made on Serbia should, he agreed, be hard, but not so hard as to make them palpably unacceptable; nor should they be in the form of an ultimatum. Looking around the table and weighing the drift of the discussion, Tisza had clearly come to the conclusion that his colleagues were ready to do precisely what he had warned them against. He therefore insisted that he should be consulted over the note to Serbia, which should be drafted 'with the utmost care'. Moreover, when Berchtold told him that he proposed to leave for Bad Ischl the next day, to discuss the note, Tisza replied that, before returning to Budapest, he would draft a personal memorandum of his own, to be laid before the Emperor alongside the foreign minister's presentation. Accordingly, Berchtold delayed his departure for twenty-four hours.

Tisza's long memoir amounted to a vehement appeal to the monarch to exhaust every peaceful possibility before drawing the sword:

It must be made possible for Serbia to avoid war by accepting a severe diplomatic defeat. . . . A note in moderate, but not threatening language should be addressed to Serbia which should set forth . . . our precise demands. . . . Should Serbia give an unsatisfactory answer, or try delaying tactics, an ultimatum should follow, and once it has expired, the commencement of hostilities. . . . Should Serbia yield, we must accept this solution in good faith, and not make her retreat impossible.[23]

It was not surprising that, with this powerful handbrake being applied to his war chariot, Berchtold failed to carry the Emperor all the way with him at their postponed audience. The foreign minister spent one and half hours with his royal master on the morning of 9 July. In the brief and fragmentary parts of his personal diary which have survived (even the copies of the extracts only take us, mysteriously, down to 21 July when the world crisis was still over the horizon) Berchtold recorded: 'I read Tisza's memorandum to the Emperor. I pleaded for requirements designed not so much to castigate Serbia as to create practical control for us. The Emperor gave his consent, concerned that a weak stand on our part could discredit our position with Germany.'

Writing after the war which he had helped to unleash was over, Berchtold claimed that the Emperor had declared that Austria 'could not go back'. According to his post-war account, there was still, however, no clarity as to how far, or how fast, Austria should go forward. The Emperor wanted to be neither too precipitate nor too dilatory. He accepted there were drawbacks in delaying military preparations but these could be partly made good by delivering a very short-termed ultimatum to Serbia should the need arise. If Franz Josef even referred to the fervent appeal just delivered into his hands from his Hungarian Prime Minister, we are not told. Nor does Berchtold mention any firm guidance. The old monarch had received a submission from his foreign minister and had half-nodded at it in the delphic fashion in which he had ruled his empire for decades past.

For Berchtold, however, the imperial half-nod was enough. Immediately on his return to Vienna on 10 July he put in train what he had had in mind ever since Hoyos had returned, triumphant, from Berlin: the drafting of a note to Serbia couched in the most drastic terms and coupled (as opposed to followed) with a forty-eight hour ultimatum.

The Foreign Office official put on the job of preparing the text was Baron von Musulin who, in his post-war memoirs, was somewhat coy and vague about his part in the operation – not surprisingly, since he was then in a position to survey the catastrophe he had helped produce, a catastrophe which included the elimination of his own Austrian empire from the map. Musulin occupied the desk for religious affairs at the Ballhausplatz at the time but was pulled away from this and set to work on the Belgrade draft partly because the man who ran the Serbian department, Baron von Flotow, was away on holiday and it was not thought necessary to disturb him. Moreover, Musulin was known to have a deft pen when it came to wrapping threats in diplomatic verbiage: six years earlier he had composed the decisive notes to Belgrade over the annexation crisis – yet another echo of 1908 resounding in the summer of 1914!

Musulin's account, written from memory, makes only one interesting contribution to the affair. He claims that, when his draft for each of the succesive demands to be put to Belgrade was discussed by 'all the ministers present' (unnamed), on each and every occasion they considered whether Serbia would and could accept, and that 'in each case the formulation of the relevant paragraph was only finally agreed upon once this question had been answered in the affirmative'. As a result, 'We in the Foreign Ministry did not believe that the ultimatum would bring about war.'[24] As we shall see when looking at the text Musulin finally produced for his masters, this was either deliberate deception; unconscious self-deception; or plain stupidity.

Before throwing his diplomatic grenade at Serbia, Berchtold had to wait for several things to happen. First, he had to study the report on the assassination which was being compiled on the spot by one of his legal counsellors, Dr Wiesner. After only forty-eight hours in Sarajevo, Wiesner telegraphed a hurried and somewhat ambivalent verdict: namely, that though the crime had been prepared in Belgrade with the help of Serbian officials, there were no grounds to prove, or even to suspect, that the Serbian government as such was in any way involved. Berchtold used what was helpful to him in the report and simply ignored what was unhelpful.

Second, the foreign minister had to get Tisza's agreement to pulling the pin out of the grenade itself. This he secured in principle on 14 July, the day after Wiesner sent in his report. The Hungarian Prime Minister now reluctantly abandoned his opposition to an ultimatum accompanying the note but insisted that, in the event of war, Austria should formally renounce in advance any major territorial claims on Serbia. (Here, Tisza, like any Hungarian statesman, was worrying primarily about any border changes which might threaten the sacred Hungarian lands of St Stephen.) That same evening, Berchtold reported the essence of this discussion in a letter to his Emperor. The text, he told the monarch, 'was now being settled'. As to the date for its presentation, that would have to take account of the visit which the president of the French Republic, M. Poincaré, was due to pay to Russia beginning on 20 July. To present the challenge when the leaders of the two rival European allies were meeting at a state occasion might be considered gratuitously provocative; moreover, as Berchtold went on to point out, it would provide them with the chance to confer on the spot and thus increase the chances of Franco-Russian interference.

So much for the ultimatum and its timing. As for the outcome of all this, the foreign minister bluntly warned his Emperor that the text of the note now being finalized 'is such that we must reckon with the probability of war'. There is no record of any response, let alone restraint, from the old autocrat at Bad Ischl. What he had read was yet another ministerial submission from Vienna about the crisis. A lot could happen yet to ward off trouble, or contain it. Containment had, after all, been Franz Josef's guiding motto ever since his two fateful plunges of the Italian war and the settlement with Hungary nearly half a century before.

Having got what he wanted out of Tisza, and having secured acquiescence, by silence, out of the Emperor over the probability of war with Serbia, Berchtold now kept all the cards close to his own chest, bluffing the opposing players about his true game and even, in this final stage, concealing the details from his own German partner. Thus, the French ambassador in Vienna, M. Dumaine, felt at first able to report that Austria's demands 'seem to be acceptable to the dignity of the Serbians'.[25] His Russian colleague, M. Shebeko, was so calmed by similar reassurances that, despite his doubts deep down, he left his post and was on home leave when the crisis broke. The British ambassador, Sir Maurice de Bunsen, reported on 17 July that, at a talk with

Berchtold, the Austrian foreign minister had been charming; had invited the envoy and his wife to come out and stay at Buchlau; had chatted about some of his racehorses in training; 'but never mentioned general politics or the Serbians'.[26]

The shrewder men in the entente camp were not fooled by such disarming airs. In that same telegram, Bunsen, for example, had warned London of the 'uncompromising mood' in Vienna and had concluded: 'I cannot yet believe that Austria will resort to extreme measures, but I think we have an anxious time before us.' Two days later M. Dumaine had changed his tune and was telling Paris: 'The tenor of the note and its imperious tone will almost certainly ensure rejection by Belgrade. Then military operations will begin.'[27]

On 20 July, the British foreign secretary, Sir Edward Grey, spoke at length about the rumbling crisis to Prince Lichnowsky, the very popular diplomat who had succeeded the glowering Count Metternich as German ambassador in London. Lichnowsky said he was not quite clear what was going on in Vienna but that he personally regarded the situation as 'very uncomfortable'. Both men agreed that, whatever she intended, Austria should first make public her case against Serbia. Grey pointed out that this would make it easier for outside powers, such as Russia, to counsel moderation. He ended by saying how he 'hated the idea of a war between any of the great powers, and for any of them to be dragged into war by Serbia would be detestable'.[28] Little did the foreign secretary dream that, in only a fortnight's time, His Britannic Majesty's government would be dragged into such a war itself. The mind of that government was anyway concentrated meanwhile on other things, above all the grave constitutional crisis caused by the challenge of Sir Edward Carson and his Ulstermen over Irish Home Rule. As for Lichnowsky, though he had been acting on instructions from Berlin (sent to him on 12 July) to work for a localization of the conflict and to soothe local opinion, he was not lying when he denied detailed knowledge of Austria's intentions. In the days preceding the presentation of the ultimatum, the German Foreign Office itself had difficulty in getting the full picture from Vienna, and was getting irritated as well as impatient as a result.

England was very much the key country in Berlin's calculations. Ideally, the Kaiser and his ministers desired to see Serbia humiliated, or even crushed, by Austria alone. But if other fighters had to enter the ring, they wanted to make sure above all else that England would stay out of it. This was made plain in an analysis of the situation which the German secretary of state, Gottlieb von Jagow, had sent to Lichnowsky:

We must attempt to localise the conflict between Austria and Serbia. Whether we shall succeed in this will depend first on Russia and secondly on the moderating influence of Russia's allies. The more determined Austria shows herself, the more energetically we support her, so much quieter will Russia remain. To be sure, there will be some agitation in St Petersburg, but, on the whole, Russia is not ready to strike now. Nor will France and England be ready for war at present. . . . If we cannot achieve localisation and Russia attacks Austria, a *casus foederis* would arise and we could not discard Austria. I desire no preventive war but if war should come, we cannot hide behind the fence. . . .

I still hope and believe, even today, that the conflict can be localised. In this respect, England's attitude will be of great significance . . . Sir Edward Grey is always talking of the balance of power represented by the two groups [in Europe]. . . . Therefore, if he is sincere and logical he must support us in attempting to localise the conflict.[29]

This was no official telegram to give guidance on deception measures. It was a purely private letter, wound up when the writer realized it was one o'clock in the morning, in which the secretary of state was unburdening himself of what were patently genuine views. If there was a plot already on foot somewhere in Berlin to provoke a European war and plunge Germany joyously into the fray, the man in charge of the Foreign Office had clearly not heard of it.

The final terms of the Austrian ultimatum (or 'note with a time-limit' as it was sanctimoniously styled) were agreed on the morning of Sunday 19 July at a second secret ministerial council held, for greater security, in Berchtold's private Vienna residence. There was some sharp dealing in all directions in the matter of its presentation.

One of those directions led to the All-Highest himself. Like all the Austrian 'hawks' who wrote their account of these days and weeks when the war was over and their own empire destroyed, Berchtold was at pains to present the Emperor as being always in full personal control of events; only thus could the ministerial share of responsibility be diminished. The documented facts tell a different story. Obviously, Berchtold had to secure his royal master's approval to the terms of the ultimatum now agreed with his colleagues. He did this at another audience in Bad Ischl on Tuesday 21 July. In the last of his diary entries to survive, he records that the Emperor had found some of the demands 'very sharp' (even singling out one or two which, in the end, Belgrade could not swallow). But after Berchtold had insisted on the necessity to include these, the Emperor approved the text without alteration.

So far, this would appear to be a straightforward tale of a foreign minister urging a drastic course of action on his sovereign and succeeding with his plea. But what Berchtold does not mention, let alone attempt to explain, either in his diary or in his memoirs, is that the text of the fateful ultimatum had been dispatched by his own office to the Austrian legation in Belgrade already on Monday 20 July, a full day *before* the Emperor's approval was sought and given. Even Berchtold's principal biographer and apologist confessed himself unable to explain this extraordinary state of affairs, and was driven to presume that Berchtold's ministry took the Emperor's approval for granted. One thing is certain. Such an amazing lapse would hardly have happened had the Emperor been where he belonged in Vienna.[30]

It was arranged that Baron Giesl, the Austrian minister in Belgrade, should deliver the ultimatum to the Serbian government at 5 p.m. on the evening of 23 July, by which time the ship bearing the French president and his foreign minister M. Viviani would presumably already be steaming out of St Petersburg on the way home. Originally the intention had been not to show it to any outside power (*including* Germany) until the simultaneous distribution arranged for the morning of the 24th. But for five days the German Foreign Office had been pressing so hard 'to be precisely informed beforehand, not only of the contents of the Note but also as to the day and hour of its publication', that Berchtold was forced into doing what he clearly ought to have done spontaneously – namely, tell all in advance to the ally whose pledge of support had underpinned all his boldness. As a result, Jagow in Berlin was able to read the full text on the evening of Wednesday 22 July; a few hours later it reached Bethmann-Hollweg, still on his Hohenfinow estate.

The reaction of both men was that the note was 'too severe', and Jagow went on to reproach the embarrassed Austrian envoy for only communicating it, under pressure, at the eleventh hour. His irritation did not however prevent him from making the practical suggestion that Giesl should act an hour later than suggested, in order to make quite certain that the French president's ship was clear of Russian waters. As for the German Kaiser, he only learnt about the text on board the *Hohenzollern* a day later still, and then from a Norwegian newspaper report and not from his own chancellor. By the time he had dispatched a peppery telegram of protest to Berlin and turned the royal yacht round to steam for home, half of the time-limit given to Serbia had already expired.

The note which Baron Giesl had handed over to the acting Serbian head of government, finance minister Pacu,* required a general state-

---

* Prime Minister Pašić was out of the capital on an election campaign but returned instantly to Belgrade.

ment of disavowal, followed by ten specific demands. The Germans knew in advance only about the overall proclamation and two of the demands – an investigation, with the participation of 'an Austrian official', into the Sarajevo murders, and proceedings against all members of the Greater Serbia movement. What both the chancellor and the state secretary found 'too severe' was the way Berchtold had both thrust the knife in deeper on these counts and then twisted it in Serbia's flesh. Thus, for example, the immediate dissolution of the 'Narodna Odbrana' and all similar societies was now required, as was a purge of all anti-Austrian teachers and teachings in Serbian schools; the Serbian government was further called upon to dismiss from service 'all officers and functionaries guilty of propaganda against the Austro-Hungarian Monarchy', the list of such persons to be provided by Vienna. As for Austrian participation, that single official to aid the investigation had now become an unstated number of 'representatives of the Austro-Hungarian government', whose task would be 'the suppression of the subversive movement directed against the territorial integrity of the Monarchy'. In other words, Serbia was asked to accept a cultural, administrative and political purge conducted on her own soil by Austrian officials. To agree would have made her, in anything but name, another annexed Habsburg province. It was no wonder that, reading it in London on 24 July, Grey made his oft-quoted remark to the Austrian ambassador that this was 'the most formidable note that was ever addressed by one state to another'. He went on to give a clear warning about the dangers of escalation to Count Mensdorff, who reported to Vienna:

What makes him seriously anxious is the possible effect upon the peace in Europe. . . . He confesses to being most apprehensive that several Great Powers might become involved in a war. Speaking of Russia, Germany and France, he believed that the conditions between France and Russia were very much the same as those between the Powers of the Triple Alliance . . .[31]

That day Grey also called in the German ambassador and gave him the same stern message: 'The danger of a European war, should Russia invade German territory, would become immediate.' Grey was clearly not yet envisaging England being drawn into such a war; but he was ready to do all in his power to stop it. He was ready, he told Prince Lichnowsky, to join Germany in an appeal to Vienna to extend the time-limit. Moreover, ought not the four powers not directly involved – England, France, Germany and Italy – offer to mediate between the two who were – Austria and Russia? Both suggestions were to be spurned in Berlin where the chancellor, at any rate, was determined to

help Austria achieve total subjection of Serbia, and where the general
staff was unrolling the plans which, like all other general staffs, it had
prepared for a war between the rival alliances of Europe.

As Grey had feared, and as Berchtold had planned, it was above all
the lack of time which dashed any hope that joint action could stamp
out these first flames of war. Pašić and his Cabinet deliberated almost
non-stop through Friday 24 July as to how to respond, and met again
the following morning. From St Petersburg, Paris and London the
same advice arrived: yield as much as you can; offer to accept
arbitration; do anything to gain an extra day or two's grace, or even a
few hours. It was a minor tragedy, as well as a strange coincidence, that
at the time there were no regular ministers on hand in Belgrade of any
of the three entente powers to help Pašić. On the evening of 11 July,
Hartwig, the extremely influential Russian envoy, had dropped dead of
a heart attack in, of all places, the study of the Austrian legation, where
he was attempting to clear up with Baron Giesl some points about the
Sarajevo investigation.* There was only a chargé d'affaires in
command at the British legation, while the French minister was out of
action with a nervous breakdown.

Considering that he was on his own, the veteran Pašić did a
magnificent job with Serbia's formal reply. This accepted five of
Berchtold's ten demands either wholly or substantially. It was evasive,
though not outright defiant, on four others. Only Point Six, the
requirement that Austrian bodies of officials should participate on
Serbian soil in the inquiry proceedings, was rejected outright as 'a
violation of Serbia's constitution'. That was more than enough for
Baron Giesl, who was handed the reply by Pašić himself, only a few
minutes before the expiry of the ultimatum at 6 p.m. on the 25th. The
Austrian envoy had already made his arrangements for departure, and
would have taken one misplaced comma as a pretext to break off
relations. After a quick glance he declared the reply to be unsatisfactory. Then, with his entire staff and their personal baggage, he was
at Belgrade's railway station only twenty minutes later to catch the 6.30
sleeper train to Vienna. Rarely in the history of international affairs
have the decks been cleared for war with such speed.

The actual decision to march could only be taken, however, by the
Austrian Emperor in person, and so it is to the villa at Bad Ischl that we
must return. Berchtold had already been there again for two days in the
previous week, to present the final text of the ultimatum for his
sovereign's approval. He arrived with Count Hoyos at 7 a.m. on the

---

* To avoid any suggestion that he had poisoned his diplomatic rival, Giesl gave hasty assurances
that his guest had been offered absolutely nothing to drink.

overnight train from Vienna, and at 9 a.m. was received in the Kaiservilla. The authorized press version of their meeting read:

The Minister of Foreign Affairs, Count Berchtold, was received in audience for one hour. Count Berchtold informed the emperor of the results of the inquiry in Sarajevo [the Wiesner report] and also presented a report on the steps which ought to be taken in Belgrade. The audience thus had the purpose of securing the emperor's approval for the forthcoming diplomatic action.[32]

Berchtold did not see the Emperor again until that evening when he was present at a 'family dinner' at the villa attended by, among others, Princess Gisela of Bavaria, who was visiting Ischl. Politics were never discussed by the Emperor in such a private setting, so we may assume that the matter of the ultimatum had been settled at the relatively brief morning audience. That can only mean that the Emperor raised no objections of such substance as to require re-drafting and a further session. Indeed, it seems probable that he authorized the 'note with a time-limit' just as it stood. Berchtold had departed, well satisfied, for Vienna.

Early on Saturday 25 July, the day the ultimatum was due to expire, he was back at Ischl yet again. Ostensibly his early arrival was to enable him to attend an early dinner which the Emperor was giving that day for the Duke and Duchess of Cumberland (the annual procession of stately visitors to the villa had not been interrupted in any way by the crisis). In fact, of course, the foreign minister wanted to be on hand next to his Emperor when the Serbian reply came through. The Cumberlands left after their monstrously early 'dinner' (the guests were gone by four o'clock) and Berchtold then hung about in an anteroom of the villa impatiently waiting for the message from Belgrade. He stayed till fifteen minutes after the fateful hour of 6 p.m. and then, abruptly, gave it up for the night and returned to his hotel. He could have barely arrived there when Baron Giesl got out of his train at the Austrian frontier station of Semlin to inform Vienna of the diplomatic rupture with the Serbs. Within minutes the news had been passed on to Ischl. Baron Margutti, the aide who took down the telephone message, described what happened when he hurried with it to the villa:

The emperor approached me with a questioning look, I reported what I had just heard from Vienna. His features rigid and his eyes fixed on me, he listened to my words. Then, in a thick choking voice which seemed to struggle to get out and which I have never heard before, he said: 'So, after all!'

I handed over the paper on which I had written down the sinister news. . . . His hands trembled so violently that it took him some time to put on his glasses properly. . . . He put down the note and remained silent for a long while, lost in thought. . . . Then he re-read the message and finally said, as though talking to himself but quite audibly: 'Well, breaking off diplomatic relations does not necessarily mean war.'[33]

Baron Margutti was a loyal courtier who, when writing these post-war memoirs, wanted to put his late imperial master in the best light. His style was somewhat florid and one suspects that, at some points, he tended to put too many eggs in the pudding in an attempt to improve the flavour. But it is inconceivable that his account was pure invention from beginning to end. Even if some of the dramatic trimmings are removed, we are left with the picture of an Emperor devastated at the imminent prospect of war and clutching at last-minute straws to prevent it.

There is another first-hand account of these July days at the Kaiservilla (though not of the 25th itself) which, however, points in exactly the opposite direction. This consists of remarks which the finance minister, Bilinski (who, as stated, was on more or less permanent detachment at Ischl during the period), made in various conversations with Dr Heinrich Kanner, publisher of the Vienna daily, *Die Zeit*, between 1915 and 1917. In these conversations, extracts of which were only made known in 1971 in an Austrian academic paper,[34] Bilinski quotes the Emperor as accepting the fact that the ultimatum to Serbia he had just sanctioned would bring about a wider war: 'Certainly, Russia cannot possibly accept this note.' In other conversations with the journalist, Bilinski went further by asserting that the Emperor was 'always for war' and had been all in favour of it the previous year, when the squabble with Serbia and Montenegro over Scutari reached its height.* If we are trying to assess the role which the European dynasties played in their own catastrophe, we have to decide, as regards the Habsburg monarchy, which of these two contrasting pictures comes closer to the truth.

There are two strong arguments against Bilinski's version. The first he provided himself by failing to repeat these statements in his own memoirs, published after the war, when Franz Josef was dead and his empire had vanished. Had they been intended as a serious contribution to history, it is hard to explain the omission, since to place war guilt on the shoulders of the Emperor would have lessened the share Bilinski himself would have to bear as a supporter of Berchtold's policy. The second argument is even stronger, for it bears the entire weight of Franz Josef's time and tribulations on the throne. Wars had brought him

---

* See *supra*, p. 12.

nothing but disaster. He was under no emotional impulse to start one over the Archduke's murder for, as we have seen, he had no emotional ties with his nephew. At eighty-four, he had no illusions of power or glory left and no other ambition than to die in peace and hand over his empire intact. He was, above all, a weary old man, to whom any strain, anything which interrupted the calm ordering of his calendar, was abhorrent. A man who, at the beginning of July, had been too tired to face the strain of a full-blown state funeral was highly unlikely, by the end of the month, to be rushing joyously into an unpredictable war. Franz Josef was no warmonger, though he could be reproached for not acting decisively enough for peace. However, even on that 25th of July, the Monarchy, and with it Europe, had still to put on its battle armour.

Chapter Sixteen

KING'S MATE

Franz Josef's muttered remark on the evening of 25 July that 'breaking off diplomatic relations does not necessarily mean war' was a futile prayer in the face of the Sarajevo crisis. For between the severance of relations and the declaration of war lay mobilization, and in the Europe of 1914 this came, not as a gap between the two, but as a bridge. Giesl's telephone call from the border station had, in fact, transferred the initiative out of the gloved hands of the diplomats and placed it in the fists of the generals. During the next ten days, the last which old Europe now had left to live, the ambassadors, politicians and even, finally, the sovereigns, scampered after the military to try to hold them back. They always arrived too late, tripped up by that sequence of contingency plans which had long been prepared in all the war offices of the continent for such an emergency.

Thus, only three hours after Margutti had handed over the message from Semlin, Berchtold who had been instantly called back to the villa, had persuaded the old Emperor to agree to partial mobilization. This was under pressure from the chief of staff, General Conrad, who argued that, the moment the break came with Serbia, the Monarchy should prepare at once for hostilities. Berlin joined with Conrad in insisting that any delay would only increase the chances of Russian intervention by giving an impression of weakness. The Austrian chief of staff had long been preparing for his cherished 'preventive war' against Serbia, and the Emperor, as supreme commander, knew and approved of his plans. They involved the mobilization of eight army corps with twenty divisions – about half the total Austrian strength – which, it was reckoned, would be more than enough to overwhelm the twelve Serbian and four Montenegrin divisions they would be facing. The rest of the Monarchy's army, reinforced if need be by divisions switched from this southern strike force, was earmarked for action against Russia in the north. This graver possibility had to be fully provided for in Conrad's plans, though the general himself hoped against hope that it would never arise.[1] His chosen game was in the south and it was for action on that front that he received the Emperor's assent to partial mobilization at 9.53 p.m. on 26 July. The wheels were immediately set in motion, with 28 July fixed as the first day of full implementation. That date was also fixed for the formal declaration of war. The military machine had started to roll with its own momentum.

Seeing this uncomfortable prospect, the peacemakers had been redoubling their efforts; even some of the firebrands were seized with second thoughts. Foremost among the latter was the German Emperor himself, who had now arrived back in a capital which, like Franz Josef, he should never have left. Among the many documents awaiting his perusal on the morning of Tuesday 28 July was the text of Pašić's reply to the Austrian ultimatum. The Kaiser shared the general admiration for its adroitness. But much more than that: he felt it had defused the crisis completely and thus removed the danger of a major explosion. He wrote enthusiastically in the margin:

A brilliant performance for a time-limit of only forty-eight hours. This is more than one could have expected. A great moral victory for Austria, but with it, every reason for war falls away, and Giesl ought to have quietly stayed on in Belgrade! On the strength of this, *I* would never have ordered mobilisation.[2]

Moreover, for once the Kaiser did not content himself with scribbling on margins before tossing the telegram aside. He instantly wrote from his Potsdam palace to state secretary Jagow at the Berlin Foreign Office:

I am convinced that, on the whole, the wishes of the Danubian Monarchy have been acceded to. The few reservations that Serbia makes could be settled by negotiation. [The reply] contains the pronouncement, *orbi et urbi* of the most humiliating kind of capitulation and consequently *every cause for war* falls to the ground.

The Kaiser then agreed to do what the British government had been trying to persuade him to do for ten days past, while he was steaming in and out of Norwegian fjords on his yacht – namely, act as a mediator. Austria, he told Jagow, should be congratulated; informed that a cause for war no longer existed; but should be allowed a 'temporary military occupation of Belgrade' as a pledge ('The Serbians are Orientals, and therefore lying, deceitful and masters at evasion.') On this basis the Kaiser declared himself ready to 'mediate for peace with Austria', and he ordered Jagow to draft a formal proposal for presenting in Vienna along the lines he had sketched out.[3]

That letter was sent at 10 a.m. on the morning of 28 July. Only seventy minutes later, at 11.10 a.m., Berchtold had dispatched to Belgrade his declaration of war, timed to coincide with the mobilization of Austrian forces on the southern front.* Had Austria immediately informed her German ally of the Serbian reply and had the Kaiser been on the spot in Berlin to give his prompt and energetic response, things just might have ended differently. As it was, Bethmann-Hollweg not only took his time about obeying the imperial command but passed it on to the Austrian capital in a totally distorted form. His telegram to the German ambassador in Vienna was not dispatched from Berlin until 10.15 p.m. on the evening of 28 July (and not received until 4.30 a.m. the following morning). It contained no word about the Kaiser's personal offer of mediation and no mention of his express conviction that, now, war could and should be averted. The only point in his sovereign's letter which the chancellor passed on (and that without giving it the force of the imperial recommendation) was the suggestion for a temporary and partial military occupation of Serbia 'in order to secure that the demands for war indemnity are complied with'.

To cap everything, the Berlin telegram ended with general instructions to Tschirschky which contradicted both the spirit and the letter of the Kaiser's instructions:

You will have to avoid very carefully giving rise to the impression that we wish to hold Austria back. It is solely a question of finding a way to realise the objective Austria desires, to cut the vital cord of Greater Serbian propaganda without, at the same time, bringing about a world war; and, if the latter cannot ultimately be avoided, of ensuring as favourable conditions as are possible in which to wage it.

In view of all the other mediation proposals now flying about between the European capitals, Bethmann-Hollweg also expressed nervousness that, by continuing to hold aloof, the German government 'will incur the odium of having been responsible for a world war, even ultimately among the German people themselves'.[4]

The grotesque situation had thus arisen that, on the day the German Emperor had decided to avoid or limit even a localized war, his chancellor was mediating on how decently and effectively Germany might enter a world war. Bethmann-Hollweg's unbelievable obtuseness and folly as late in the day as this (for even he was soon to start changing his tune) should not be allowed to diminish the significance of

---

* The Germans were originally not expecting Austria to declare war for another fourteen days, the period they had been told was necessary to get the Monarchy's army on a proper footing.

the Kaiser's action. It showed – and this is reinforced by what followed – that there never was any preconceived plot for war in his mind in the summer of 1914. His earlier provocative utterances, ranging from remarks like 'the sooner the better' over settling with the Serbs, to the unqualified pledge of support given to the Austrian Emperor, are shown to be typical histrionics on what he imagined would be a confined stage. The moment that stage started to open up, he tried to ring down the curtain, whereas any calculated warmonger would only have welcomed a more violent setting. And if the Kaiser, as autocratic head of state and Supreme War Lord, operating through his own military chancery, had no preconceived war plan for 1914, then it is hard to believe that such a project could have been drawn up, without his knowledge and approval, anywhere else in Berlin, except as a desirable thought in the minds of the general staff.

As for the peace proposals which were now surfacing, these had become so numerous and complex by the last week of July as to almost cancel one another out. The Russian foreign minister, M. Sazanov, firing nervously from the hip, had shot off three different ideas in as many days. On 25 July, the day the Austrian ultimatum to Belgrade was due to expire, he proposed that Russia would stand aside altogether if Serbia was prepared to put her case in the hands of the four so-called non-involved powers – England, France, Germany and Italy. The following day he suggested that perhaps England and Italy by themselves 'might be willing to collaborate with Austria with a view to putting an end to the present tension'.[5] Twenty-four hours later, he came out for direct talks between St Petersburg and Vienna. It was no wonder that Sir Arthur Nicolson, now back at the Foreign Office in London, complained: 'This is confusing. . . . One really does not know where one is with M. Sazanov.'[6]

Sazanov clearly did not know where he was in the maze himself or which path he should tread to reach clear ground. On 26 July, the day he was proposing Anglo-Italian mediation, he found himself in the same railway carriage as the veteran German ambassador in St Petersburg, Count Pourtalès.* The minister promptly asked this well-proven friend of Russia's whether he could come up with any ideas. Pourtalès suggested a compromise whereby Vienna would be persuaded to modify her demands on Serbia who would then 'be advised by Russia to accept'.[7] Quite who was going to persuade Vienna was left unclear. The envoy's own political masters in Berlin were still doing

---

* The two men were returning to St Petersburg after attending military manoeuvres at Krasnoe Selo.

their best to egg Austria on against Serbia, and indeed Pourtalès
stressed twice that he was not speaking in the name of his government.
Though that was the time-honoured formula for putting out a
diplomatic feeler on instructions from home, the ambassador, on this
occasion, seems to have been telling the literal truth. Whatever he
thought at the time, Sazanov gratefully accepted the idea as another
arrow in his quiver of proposals and, after sounding out the Austrian
ambassador on the subject, despatched telegrams to Vienna accordingly. They arrived on the eve of Austria's declaration of war on Serbia,
a step on which Berchtold had made up his mind and from which he
was not to be deterred.

The most realistic chance of averting a catastrophe lay where it had
rested from the start, in London. Despite the fact that, throughout most
of July, the Liberal government of the day had been more preoccupied
with preventing civil war over Ireland than avoiding a European war
over Sarajevo, the Austrian ultimatum on the 26th had, for the first
time, swept the domestic quarrel from the top of the news pages. Sir
Edward Grey, who, twelve months before, had proved himself and
his country the best impartial mediators in an earlier Balkan crisis,
tried to rise again to this far graver challenge. At intervals during the
month he had, as we have seen, warned the German envoy of the
dangers ahead and cautioned him against taking England's detachment from the affair for granted. He had suggested direct talks between
Vienna and St Petersburg as early as 24 July, two days before Count
Pourtalès had aired similar ideas in a Russian railway carriage. Once
the Austrian ultimatum, with all its ugly implications, was on the table,
Grey reverted to his earlier thoughts of mediation by the four powers
not directly involved. On the afternoon of 26 July Germany, France
and Italy were invited to join an ambassadors' conference 'to be held
here at once to endeavour . . . to prevent complications'. All military
operations were to be suspended until the mediators had had time to
report.

It was one of the many ideas that M. Sazanov had flung about in St
Petersburg earlier that week but, as a formal proposal coming from the
most prestigious diplomatist in Europe, it could be expected to carry far
more weight. In the event, the only capital where Grey's proposals
found immediate and total acceptance was the one which mattered
least – Rome. Paris agreed after some initial hesitation, the French
being reluctant to put pressure on their Russian allies at this emotional
high point of their president's state visit to St Petersburg. But it was the
outright rejection which came from Berlin which stopped Grey's peace
move dead in its tracks. Even before he had received the text of the

British proposal, Bethmann-Hollweg turned the idea down flat in an emphatic instruction to Prince Lichnowsky in London: 'We could not take part in such a conference as we would not feel able to summon Austria before a European court of justice in her issue with Serbia.'

The hapless envoy, who had strongly advocated the English proposal, was told to concentrate instead on 'the necessity and possibility of localisation'.[8] In vain did he send back a wail of protest to his chancellor asking how on earth he was expected to argue for localization when the actions of Austria, Germany's closest ally, were so clearly threatening the interests of Russia. The German chancellor's ears were stopped up. Bethmann-Hollweg still clung to the criminally stupid illusion that Austria, riding on Germany's wing, could crush Serbia without having to face the wrath of Russia, and all that entailed. So far from letting Grey's proposals speak for themselves, he even warned Berchtold in advance that he would disassociate Germany from any English mediation plan. This, he announced, he would simply transmit to the German embassy in Vienna but without instructing the ambassador to present it.[9] It was the plainest invitation to Austria to ignore the English peace plan – not that Berchtold, with the bit firmly in his teeth, needed much encouragement in that direction.

Years later the two principal villains of this action, Bethmann-Hollweg and state secretary Jagow, both attempted in their memoirs[10] to justify their behaviour. Austria, they argued, had bitter memories of her treatment at Grey's last London ambassadors' conference, called to sort out the imbroglio of the 1912–13 Balkan Wars. On that occasion, the Dual Monarchy had at least been sitting around the table herself to argue her own case. Now, it was proposed that her two allies, Germany and Italy, would do the arguing for her. This sounded a reasonable proposition were it not for the fact that Italy was already trailing her skirts around the entente camp and would almost certainly place her influence on that side around any mediator's table. This would leave Germany outvoted by three to one and deny her the role she had opted for for three weeks before, namely, to carry her Austrian partner shoulder high to total victory against those treacherous and troublesome Serbs.

Thus, despite Lichnowsky's fresh warning from London that 'the whole Serbian question has developed into a test of strength between the Triple Alliance and the Triple Entente' and that, 'if it comes to war under these circumstances, we shall have England against us'[11] the chancellor was not to be moved. This was the high point both of German folly in the crisis and, therefore, of German responsibility for the ultimate disaster. The Kaiser's ministers on that 27–28 July were like men who, despite warnings about strong tides, were still wading doggedly out to sea, with the water, by now, up to their armpits. It was only two days later, when they felt their feet going under them, that they realized the danger, turned, and struck out in panic to regain the shore. By then it was too late; the undertow had got hold of them all.

Though we have taken our eyes off the monarchs for a while, they were never far from the centre of the stage and were soon to be brought right back to the centre of it, in one last frantic display of dynastic diplomacy. Even George v was becoming increasingly involved from London, despite that ingrained distaste of his, already described, for European politics. Moreover, as his is the only personal diary of any European monarch to have been kept and to have survived, he provides – albeit in regrettably brief and matter-of-fact style – a unique royal record of these traumatic days.

There was certainly nothing wrong with his basic judgement. As early as Saturday 25 July, the day the London newspapers were bursting with the news of the Austrian ultimatum, he writes, after a long talk with Sir Edward Grey at Buckingham Palace: 'It looks as though we were on the verge of a European war'. The following day he repeats the verdict and notes: 'Henry of Prussia came to see me early, he returns at once to Germany.' The bald statement conceals an interesting exercise on the German Emperor's part to deploy members of his own family as envoys extraordinary. As the Crown Prince seemed such a palpable disaster for this, or indeed any other delicate role, the Kaiser's favourite emissary was his eldest brother, Prince Henry of Prussia. The Prince knew King George well and had attempted in previous years to make political capital for Germany out of their friendship.

His mission, over breakfast at Buckingham Palace this Sunday, was to persuade England, through her monarch, to keep out of any wider war which might develop from the Serbian crisis. According to Prince Henry's report to his brother after returning to Germany, King George had promised that in London they 'would try all we can' to remain neutral, though the Prince himself doubted whether any such stance would be permanent 'in view of England's relations with France'.[12]* Both Prince Henry and the King were to return to the charge soon,

---

* A note on a separate half-sheet of paper which the King made later presents the conversation in a somewhat different light. According to this, on being asked by Prince Henry how England would act if there were a European war, King George had replied: 'I don't know what we shall do, we have no quarrel with anyone and I hope we shall remain neutral. But if Germany declared war on Russia and France joins Russia, then I am afraid we shall be dragged into it.'[12]

when the pace hotted up, with the Kaiser and the Tsar riding in the final mêlée beside them.

In every major continental capital it was the generals who now hotted that pace up beyond containment. Each step they urged upon their sovereigns was intended to place their armies in the best position to fight that European war which, by 28 July, had appeared on the horizon. But as one German ambassador in the thick of it all bemoaned, 'The danger of every preparatory military measure lies in the counter-measures of the other side.'[13] And so, by a remorseless process of escalation, the preparations for that wider war which, at first, had seemed only likely, made such a conflict highly probable and, at the end, unavoidable. The decisive rung up this ladder lay in St Petersburg. That was also the only continental capital where the ruler tried, even if briefly and unavailingly, to hold back his generals from climbing higher.

On the morning of 28 July, the day of Berchtold's declaration of war against Serbia,* the only formal military preparation under way on the continent (there were plenty of unannounced contingency steps) was Austria's partial mobilization on her southern front, and, of course, the Serbian mobilization against her. Whether this Balkan conflict would turn into a European one would depend on if, and how, the Tsar would respond to the frantic appeal for succour which he had received from his 'Little Slav' brothers in Belgrade. Already on 25 July, at a ministerial council held at Krasnoe Selo, certain military precautions had been taken. A million Russian soldiers who were completing their midsummer manoeuvres were ordered to return on immediate standby to their barracks or home stations. More ominously, the decision was taken 'in principle' to respond to the massing of Austrian troops against Serbia by mobilizing in the four military districts – Odessa, Kiev, Moscow and Kazan – from which any Russian action against the Habsburg monarchy would have to be mounted.

On the afternoon of 28 July this partial mobilization was officially notified to the other European powers. The Russian foreign minister, Sazanov, was at pains to emphasize in Berlin that Russia had no intention of attacking Germany and did not even intend to recall her ambassador in Vienna from his post 'for the time being'.[14] Russia – and with her Europe – might just have escaped the furnace had this position

---

* It is worth noting that, even here, the Foreign Minister took it upon himself to alter, when back in Vienna, the form of words approved by his sovereign in Bad Ischl. A reference to a skirmish between Austrian and Serbian troops, with the latter cast as the aggressors, was omitted altogether, without clearance.

been held. The crucial struggle, over the next forty-eight hours, was the struggle for the Tsar's kindly but feeble will. One scale was weighed down heavily by his generals and armed service ministers who argued to a man that, for a variety of technical reasons, he must proceed to general mobilization at once; only thus, they dinned in on him, could Russia's cumbrous military machine, operating over such enormous distances, be got into motion to fulfil any demands that France might now make upon them in accordance with the military convention of 1894. It was an argument calculated to appeal to a sovereign who had only just bid an emotional farewell to his distinguished guest, the French president. It also stirred old resentments in the Tsar's mind: the military defeat in the Far East in 1905 and the political defeat in the Balkans over the annexation crisis of 1908–9 still rankled. Whether this new challenge was to be fought out on the battlefield or around the conference table, further humiliation was not to be contemplated.

On the other scale of the balance lay the Tsar's instinctive dread and loathing of war: dread for what it might well do to his shaky empire; and loathing for the suffering which he knew it would bring – not least on his own armies, whose heaviest weapon was their sheer numbers. If the Europe of 1914 were to be divided into what a later generation would characterize as 'hawks' and 'doves', Nicholas II was, at heart, the whitest royal dove of them all. It was this which made so ironic the role he was to play in setting all the hawks on the continent free.

The first round went to the military. Already on the morning of 29 July they had got the Tsar's signature to separate orders for general as well as partial mobilization, though under Russian law the former could only come into force when counter-signed by the ministers of war, the navy, and the interior. After a hectic and confused day, during which the military case was greatly aided by the news that Austrian guns had started to bombard Belgrade, these formalities were completed and the ukase was formally issued at 6 p.m. But at this point the Kaiser jumped into the scales for peace.

At the suggestion of his chancellor (though altering the text submitted to him), the German emperor had embarked on the last of those 'Willy–Nicky' exchanges which – so it was imagined in Potsdam – had achieved so much in the past. As we have seen, once away from the dream world of his yacht and back in his capital, with the war drums sounding all around him, the Kaiser had belatedly started to urge restraint on his ministers. He now began to back this up with some dynastic diplomacy. King Nikita had been the first target. In a personal telegram to the Montenegrin ruler, the Kaiser accepted that, as fellow-sovereigns, they both had the right to expect that the murderers of

Franz Ferdinand would get their just desserts. He none the less appealed to Nikita to join him in his efforts to reach a peaceful end to the crisis with Austria. It was, of course, a vain hope, for the King had already resolved to throw his hand in with Serbia, confident of Russian support.

It is worth noting that Nikita's two grand-duchess daughters, who were among the shrillest voices in St Petersburg clamouring for war, had been asserting, the week before, that their father's mind was already made up on the subject. In his indispensable if heavily embroidered memoirs, M. Paléologue, the French ambassador to the Tsar, describes how they had chattered away quite openly to him at a reception for the French president, speaking so rapidly together that he was never certain which voice was Militza's and which Anastasia's: 'I had a telegram from my father today in an agreed code; he tells me that we shall have war before the month is out. . . . What a hero my father is! He's worthy of the Iliad.' And then, later, the Grand Duchess Anastasia by herself at dinner: 'War is going to break out. . . . There will be nothing left of Austria. . . . Our armies will join up in Berlin. . . . Germany will be destroyed.' At that moment, according to the ambassador, the chatterbox caught the Tsar's disapproving eye, resting on her from the head of the table, and fell silent.[15]

If the Kaiser hoped for little in the way of an encouraging echo from the King of the Black Mountains, he could expect a better response from St Petersburg, despite the likes of the Montenegrin grand duchesses. His first telegram to the Tsar, dispatched in the early hours of 29 July, repeated the theme of the sacred brotherhood of monarchs. After deploring the Sarajevo crimes he wrote:

The spirit which led the Serbians to murder their own king and his wife* still dominates the country. You will doubtless agree with me that both of us, you and me and indeed all Sovereigns, have a common interest in insisting that everyone morally responsible for the dastardly murder should receive the punishment they deserve.

None the less, he went on, he was now 'exerting his utmost influence' with Austria to arrive at 'a satisfactory understanding' with Russia. He accepted that it was difficult for the Tsar 'to face the drift of . . . public opinion' over the crisis but ended: 'I confidently hope that you will help me in my efforts to smooth over any difficulties which may still arise.'[16]

It is not recorded when this telegram was received in St Petersburg

---

* Even eleven years later, the Kaiser evidently could not bring himself to refer to Draga as 'queen'.

but in any case it had crossed with another telegram sent by the Tsar to the German emperor in these same early hours of 29 July. In this (written, like all their exchanges, in English), the Tsar poured out his heart, with much underlining, in a message which clearly expressed his personal anguish and owed nothing to any drafting by his ministers:

Am glad you are back. In this gravest moment I appeal for your help. An *ignoble* war has been declared against a *weak* country. The *indignation* in Russia, *shared fully by me*, is *enormous*. I foresee that very soon I shall be *overwhelmed* by the *pressure* brought upon me, and be *forced* to take extreme measures which will *lead to war*. To try and avert the calamity of a European war, I beg you in the name of our old friendship to do what you can to *stop* your *allies* from *going too far*.[17]

It was a pity that these first two messages had crossed, more especially as the Tsar's telegram countered with such emotion some of the arguments put forward by William II. The mere sight of any message coming from any quarter with such copious personal emphasis brought out, almost automatically, the exclamation marks and under-linings from the Kaiser's side. This telegram, he minuted, was a confession of the Tsar's 'own weakness and an attempt to put the responsibility on my own shoulders'. Why, he went on, had the Tsar not addressed the Emperor Franz Josef instead of him (a very pertinent question!); and why had not copies of all such messages been sent to 'His Majesty the King in London for his information'?[18]

Nicholas was never, of course, to see those marginal comments. He was content enough with the telegram he had received from Potsdam but only curious that it sounded very different in tone from the noises being made that day by the German chancellor in nearby Berlin. That afternoon, in what was to prove one of his last assertive moves before the great volte-face, Bethmann-Hollweg had sent the following curt instruction to his ambassador in St Petersburg: 'Kindly draw M. Sazanov's serious attention to the fact that, if Russia continues with her mobilisation measures, we would be forced to mobilise and, in that case, a European war could hardly be prevented.'[19]

The wretched Tsar did not know whom to listen to, the Kaiser or his chancellor. In a puzzled telegram sent that evening to Potsdam, he begged his German cousin 'to explain this divergency'. He then put forward the sincerely felt but totally futile suggestion of handing the whole Austro-Serbian crisis over to the standing International Tribunal at The Hague for a solution.

From this point onward, quite apart from the steadily worsening crisis which enveloped them, the two monarchs got their own personal lines more and more crossed. Later that night the Kaiser sent back a somewhat austere reply, denying that Austria's action against Serbia was 'ignoble' and urging Russia to stand aside from the conflict while he, as promised, acted as mediator between St Petersburg and Vienna. There was no mention of those German threats to mobilize which his chancellor had issued in the afternoon. Poor Nicholas seems to have taken this omission as a sign that the threats were not so serious after all and, in another typically open-hearted effusion, blurted out the truth about Russia's state of readiness, again with much underlining:

The *military measures which have now come into force were decided five days ago* for defence reasons because of Austria's preparations. I hope from all my heart that these measures *won't in any way interfere* with your part as mediator which I greatly value. *We need your strong pressure on Austria* to come to an understanding with us.

This was a deadly indiscretion to drop in front of someone of the Kaiser's temperament. He snorted in a comment that the Tsar had clearly been playing him along, in order to get 'almost a week ahead of us' in the mobilization process. 'I cannot agree to any more mediation. . . . It is only a manoeuvre, in order to hold us back and increase the start they have already got. My work is at an end!'[20]

The irony of this theatrical gesture of despair was that, had he but known it at the time, the Kaiser's telegram urging restraint and repeating his offer to mediate had had a profound, if only transitory, effect on his cousin. On receiving it at 9.40 p.m. at the Peterhof, Nicholas resolved, without consulting anyone, to cancel the ukase for general mobilization which he had signed that morning and replace it with the less deadly partial measures. An extraordinary tussle by telephone with his key military advisers followed. General Dobrovolski, who was in charge of war preparation measures, was actually at the central telegraph office and about to dispatch the general mobilization order to all corners of the Russian empire when General Ianushkevich, the chief of the general staff, recalled him at the Tsar's command. Neither they nor the minister of war, General Sukhomlinov, could persuade the Tsar to back down and so, at around midnight on 29 July, the order for partial mobilization, to match that of Austria, was passed down instead.

Had the Tsar continued to stand his ground, peace in Europe might still have been saved. But throughout the next day, Thursday 30 July, his war minister, his chief of staff and his foreign minister, Sazanov, hammered away at him to step up the military preparations. First the generals tried by telephone, only to have their royal master hang up on them in irritation. It was Sazanov who secured an audience at the Peterhof just after lunch – who worked the fateful change of mind. Diplomacy, he said, had run its course.* Therefore the empire must now be made ready for war if its own military arm was not to be weakened and its allies disconcerted. (France had assured Russia of her support in the crisis that same day.)

In torment, the Tsar protested: 'But think of the responsibility you are asking me to take on! Think that this means sending thousands and thousands of men to their deaths.'[21]

Both their consciences, the foreign minister assured his sovereign, would be clear. It was a question of safeguarding the Tsar's vital interests. For another hour the Tsar wrestled with the dilemma. Then, abruptly, at the stroke of four in the afternoon, he gave way to Sazanov's pleading and authorized the immediate reinstatement of full mobilization. A relieved Sazanov left the imperial presence and telephoned the news from the ground floor of the palace to the chief of staff: 'Give your orders', he told General Ianushkevic, 'and then disappear for the rest of the day.'[22]

This time no countermanding instruction was sent to the central telegraph office, from where, at 6 p.m. Dobrovoloski started sending out his general mobilization orders. During the night the red call-up placards were posted up in towns and villages throughout the empire. When Friday 31 July dawned, there was no way back for the Tsar, nor for Europe.

It was the first time in the month-old crisis that the ordinary citizen of that continent really felt the hot breath of war on his neck. Up until then, despite the newspaper editorials, which had grown steadily graver and the news headlines which had become ever more alarming, the peaceful routine of life had stumbled forward in the same mechanical fashion as the military juggernaut which was coming up fast beside it. In England the great four-day race meeting at Goodwood, which marked the end of the London season, had gone on in scorching weather, though the absence of the King had caused much comment. It was reported, however, that he was still hoping to attend the Cowes Regatta the following week, and then go up north for the grouse-shooting. In Bavaria the annual Wagner Festival at Bayreuth had been launched as usual, and was fully attended. Thousands of language enthusiasts had set out for Paris from all over the continent to

---

* The talks he had held with the German ambassador that day to try to break the deadlock on a bilateral basis had indeed got nowhere, but that was a far cry from Sazanov's despairing verdict.

attend an Esperanto conference which was due to last until 2 August. The court calendars also continued on their serene course. In Berlin, for example, the betrothal was announced of Prince Adalbert of Prussia, the Kaiser's third son, to Princess Adelheid of Saxe-Meiningen.

It was to the German capital that the focus now shifted, once the Tsar had called up his millions and set the final act of the tragedy in motion.

To the present-day generation, so used to receiving teleprinter flashes of important announcements within minutes of their being made anywhere on the globe and viewing actual happenings, within hours, by satellite television, the idea that desperately vital news could be slow in travelling must seem strange. Yet in the summer of 1914 not the least of the barriers faced by the would-be peacemakers was the snail-like pace in transmission of an overloaded telegraphic service, which was compounded by the lack of swift and reliable telephone communications (let alone the absence of any top-level 'hot line'). Thus it was that, in St Petersburg, the German military attaché, Major Eggeling, only heard after breakfast on the Friday that Russia had finally and irrevocably ordered general mobilization some fifteen hours before. (Today, a radio set would have given him the news by interrupting all programmes throughout the night before.) The major set off at once for his embassy, but it was not until 10.20 a.m. that morning that his ambassador, the nerve-racked Count Pourtalès, got his message off to his chancellor.[23]

This, in turn, was not received by Bethmann-Hollweg for another hour and twenty minutes, so that it was not until after midday that a meeting could be held with the Kaiser, who had motored in immediately from Potsdam. They decided to proclaim a state of so-called 'drohende Kriegsgefahr' ('Threatening danger of war)', a form of martial law which caused the basic preparatory military measures to be set in motion. Technically this was only an amber light. In practice, like the amber on a modern traffic signal, it automatically turned to red. As Bethmann telegraphed to his ambassador in Vienna immediately after the meeting (the message took two and a half hours to get there): 'After the Russian total mobilisation, we have proclaimed a state of threatened danger, which will presumably be followed within forty-eight hours by general mobilisation. The latter inevitably means war.'[24]

The chancellor was thus brought up sharply to face the edge of the abyss which until now he had foolishly expected Austria to vault over, unharmed, on Germany's back. He had already seen the abyss opening up before him the day before, when it became clear both that Russian mobilization was imminent and that all hopes of a direct settlement between Vienna and St Petersburg had gone, partly through Austrian intransigence. His bombast had subsided like a punctured balloon. In the early hours of 30 July he had telegraphed this stern message to his ambassador in Vienna:

We cannot expect Austria to deal with Serbia, with whom she is at war. However, the refusal to hold any exchange of views with St Petersburg would be a serious error as it would directly provoke armed interference by Russia, which it is in Austria's interests, beyond anything else, to prevent.

We are, of course, ready to fulfil the obligations of our alliance, but we must decline to be drawn wantonly into a world conflagration by Vienna, without having any regard paid to our counsel. . . . Please talk to Count Berchtold at once, with great emphasis and gravity.[25]

This extraordinary message deserves reading a second time. Had it been sent forty-eight hours earlier (let alone a week earlier, before the Austrians had launched their ferocious ultimatum in Belgrade) a European war might well have been averted. It represented a complete change of instructions, both in substance and in tone. The wretched ambassador in Vienna, Tschirschky, was now being told to do what he had been sharply rebuked by the Kaiser for doing at the beginning of the crisis: namely, to urge moderation and restraint on their Austrian ally.

That this was no tactical zigzag on the chancellor's part but a complete change of course is shown by his further telegram to Tschirschky sent off at 9 p.m. that evening, a message which took a full six hours to reach Vienna. As Russia's military preparations had caused the Kaiser to drop out as referee, and as the Austrians were dodging direct talks with St Petersburg, the only hope now left for peace was to fall back again on England and Sir Edward Grey to lead a last-minute European mediation effort.* Tschirschky was told to speak 'most emphatically . . . to Count Berchtold and perhaps also to Count Tisza', and 'urgently press' on them to accept the British proposals which, they were assured, would 'preserve Austria's status in every way'.[26]

As he saw disaster approaching, Bethmann-Hollweg tried to keep England out of it, as well as pull Austria back from it. But his approach

---

* Grey's final proposal, which was a variant on the four non-committed powers theme, was presented in Berlin on the evening of 31 July. It called for Germany to take soundings in Vienna while he would approach St Petersburg to try to find a solution in parallel. But by then Russia had mobilized; the German reply was that no further mediation was possible until that mobilization order was withdrawn.

to London was as clumsy as his move in Vienna had been tardy. On the
evening of 29 July, Sir Edward Goschen, the British ambassador in
Berlin (who had only seen fit to return from his holiday in England two
days before) was summoned by the chancellor who then, without ado,
made 'a strong bid for British neutrality'. It was a shifty and tortuous
bribe which was offered in return. The chancellor knew full well that
German war plans called for an attack on France, England's ally in all
but name, through Belgium, England's strategic cross-Channel
rampart. As he could hardly promise that this, a modification of the
famous 'Schlieffen Plan', would never be carried out, he offered only
political reassurances instead. Germany was not aiming to crush
France and, even if victorious against her in war, would seek no French
territory, provided England had kept out of the fight. (The same
assurance was not forthcoming for the French colonies.) Germany
would leave Holland alone if everyone else did. The envoy's report then
continued with the ominous words:

As regards Belgium, his Excellency could not tell to what operations Germany
might be forced by the action of France but he could state that, provided
Belgium did not take sides against Germany, her integrity would be respected
after the conclusion of the war.[27]

It was a clear admission that, even while trying belatedly to preserve
a European peace of sorts, Bethmann-Hollweg, with the chief of staff,
General von Moltke, breathing down his neck, was making political
provisions for an all-out war. His offer, suggesting, in effect, that
England should save her own skin by throwing both France and
Belgium to the German dogs was dismissed in London with the
contempt it merited. Sir Eyre Crowe, the prestigious Foreign Office
under-secretary of the day, wrote under Goschen's dispatch before
even submitting it to Grey: 'The only comment that need be made on
these astounding proposals is that they reflect discredit on the
statesman who makes them.'[28] Grey duly informed the German
chancellor that his proposals 'cannot for a moment be entertained',
adding that the proposed bargain would be 'a disgrace from which the
good name of this country would never recover'.[29]

What, meanwhile, of Germany's Supreme War Lord? By the end of
July another change of colour had transmuted the Kaiser's chameleon
soul. Once obliged to retire as Europe's arbiter, he had lost the only role
which appealed to him. Moreover, he was becoming increasingly irked
with his Austrian ally, who was now proving as difficult to rein in as she
had earlier been eager, with German spurs dug in her flanks, to charge
forward. On the evening of 30 July the Kaiser had therefore backed up

his chancellor's restraining moves in Vienna with a personal telegram to Franz Josef – almost the only occasion on which the old Habsburg monarch was approached directly in the final crisis. In his message the Kaiser had pressed for 'a decision as soon as possible' on his earlier proposal that, whatever happened, Austria should halt her armies at Belgrade to ensure Serbian compliance. He was never to receive this assurance.

Sir Edward Grey's last offer for mediation had also run up against a stone wall in Vienna, though, characteristically, the wall had some very baroque mouldings on it. Count Berchtold reported his sovereign's views, which doubtless echoed his own, to a Cabinet Council the following morning:

His Majesty had instantly declared that the cessation of hostilities against Serbia was impossible and had approved the proposal of carefully avoiding acceptance of the English offer on its merits, but agreed that, in the form of our reply, we should show that we desired to meet England's wishes and thus not offend the German Government by also meeting the wishes of the German Chancellor.[30]

All that Berchtold was now concerned with was gaining time until his empire, and Europe with it, was well and truly over the abyss. Franz Josef, still holding aloof from any joint meeting with his responsible ministers, was being dragged along with him, a nodding coachman unable to steer his own carriage.

In Berlin the Kaiser probably realized, in his heart of hearts, that it was his own bombastic encouragement of his ally a month before which was largely responsible for the disaster now looming. But, like all people, royal and non-royal alike, who refuse to admit, let alone face up to, their own blunders, he sought a scapegoat instead. For this there could only be one candidate: his uncle, King Edward VII of England. Dead these four years or more, His late Majesty is now reintroduced on to that European scene he had known and loved so well as its arch-villain, who had deliberately engineered the tragedy about to engulf it.

On the morning of 30 July the Kaiser was reading a despach just received from Count Pourtalès in St Petersburg in which the envoy reported on the diplomatic deadlock over direct mediation and the grave consequences of Russian mobilization. At this, the German Emperor unburdened himself of a diatribe longer than the despatch itself and remarkable, even by the writer's own impulsive, soul-baring standards, for what it betrayed:

Frivolity and weakness are to plunge the world into the most dreadful war, whose ultimate aim is the destruction of Germany. For I have no doubt left:

England, France and Russia have *agreed* among themselves – after laying the foundation of a *casus foederis* for us through Austria – to use the Austro-Serbian conflict as an excuse for waging a '*war of extermination*' against us. . . . That is the naked truth of the situation which, slowly and subtly set in motion by Edward VII, had been systematically developed by concealed deliberations between England, Paris and St Petersburg. And so the stupidity and ineptitude of our ally is turned into a snare for us, and the famous 'encirclement' of Germany has finally become an accomplished fact, despite all the efforts of our politicians and diplomats to prevent it. The net has been suddenly thrown over our head and England sneeringly reaps the most brilliant success . . . while she twists the noose of our political and economic destruction, brought about by our fidelity to Austria, and we squirm *isolated* in the net. . . . A great achievement, which provokes admiration even from him whose destruction will result! Edward VII is stronger after his death, than I, who am still alive . . .

The diatribe ended:

Our consuls and agents etc. in Turkey and India must set the whole Mohammedan world ablaze in fierce rebellion against this hated, lying and ruthless nation of shopkeepers, for if we are bled to death, England shall at least lose India.[31]

This outburst disposes once again (and this time comprehensively), of the notion that the Kaiser had set out, from the very start of the 1914 crisis, to convert it into a European war for which Germany was only longing. He is horrified, not exulted, by the catastrophe now facing him and seeking only to bury, from his own conscience, the part he had personally played at the beginning to bring it about. It was he and his chancellor, and not the Entente powers who, after Sarajevo, had established the *casus foederis* with the Habsburg monarchy – indeed, proclaimed it loudly in their messages of encouragement to Vienna. And if there was one country in Europe still hoping against hope that the net of war was not going to close over it – and still uncertain even as to how to behave if it did begin to descend – that country was England. To illustrate that, we only have to move back to London to view the situation from Westminster and Buckingham Palace in these last days and hours of peace.

It was only on Thursday, 30 July, that the crisis on the continent finally supplanted the crisis at home in the British government's mind, when the debate scheduled in the House of Commons that day on the Irish question was postponed because of the gravity of the European situation. The Prime Minister, Mr Asquith, and the leader of the Unionist Opposition, Mr Bonar Law, felt obliged to announce that, whatever divided them on domestic issues, they stood united in the face of this gathering storm across the Channel. But Mr Asquith still held back from any public comment, let alone commitment over the crisis. The following day, Friday, he told Parliament 'I shall prefer not to answer any questions until Monday.' This reassuring English faith in the weekend to solve all mankind's problems was greeted with approving mutterings of 'Hear, Hear', from both sides of the House.

Early that same Friday morning (to be precise at 12.45 a.m.) Rear-Admiral Sir Colin Keppel, equerry to King George, woke up his royal master, who had just retired to bed after a long and tiring day of meetings and discussions over the crisis. The King's diary notes: 'I got up and saw him in the audience room and he showed me a draft of a telegram he wanted me to send to Nicky as a last resort to try and prevent war, which of course I did.'[32]

In this telegram the King pointed out to his cousin the paralysing effects which – so the Germans were claiming – Russian mobilization was having on all mediation efforts. He continued:

I cannot help thinking that some misunderstanding has produced this deadlock. I am most anxious not to miss any possibility of avoiding the terrible calamity which at present threatens the whole world. I therefore make a personal appeal to you to remove the misapprehension which I feel must have occurred, and to leave still open grounds for negotiation and possible peace. If you think I can in any way contribute to that all-important purpose, I will do everything in my power to assist in re-opening the conversations between the powers concerned . . .[33]

The situation would have been droll had it not been so desperate. The King's father, Edward VII, would have been busy long ago trying to knock some sense into the heads of his two nephews in Berlin and St Petersburg – as well as appealing, as nobody in London seems to have thought of doing throughout – to that remote dynast in the Vienna Hofburg. King George was being wheeled into action to offer himself as a European arbiter only at the instigation of his Prime Minister, and then only in the early hours of Friday 31 July, when the general mobilization placards were being posted up all over Russia.

It was somewhat too little and much too late, for those placards were now opening up all the arsenals of Europe. The next day, Saturday 1 August, saw general mobilization ordered almost simultaneously in Germany and France. General Joffre, the French commander-in-chief, had forced the decision on his Cabinet by warning the French ministers that, if the decision were further delayed, he would no longer assume his responsibilities. Mobilization was accordingly ordered shortly before 4 p.m. In Germany, Joffre's protagonist, General von Moltke, already had his divisions deploying for the invasion of Belgium and Luxembourg. However, he could only set them marching once the Supreme War Lord had given the command. This the Kaiser did, also on the afternoon of 31 July, but there was one last semi-farcical episode at Potsdam which revealed, among other things, what a reluctant war lord he really was. He had barely signed the order than the text of a telegram was rushed to him which had just been received from Prince Lichnowsky in London. (This, too, had been more than five hours in transmission.) The behaviour of William II on reading it suggests that, had he received it earlier, the German mobilization order might never have been dispatched at all that afternoon, though the respite, admittedly, could have been only temporary. What the fanatically anglophile German envoy had to report was a message just passed to him from Sir Edward Grey which seemed to suggest that 'in case we did not attack France, England would remain neutral and would guarantee France's neutrality'.[34]

This seemed almost too good to be true, opening up the lush prospect of Germany joining Austria in a war against Russia with no fear of threat on the whole of her western flank. The Kaiser, though almost unable to believe in such providence, decided none the less that it might as well be true. He ordered a halt in the German advance towards Luxembourg (for a few hours, the Second Infantry Division at Trier did indeed cancel its projected march into the Grand Duchy) and a general redeployment instead against Russia. The Kaiser even called for champagne to celebrate this stroke of fortune, whereas Moltke, his cherished invasion plan seemingly threatened, withdrew to his study in tears, perhaps more inclined at that moment to swallow cyanide. The chief of staff did not have to suffer for long. Before midnight another telegram came in from the hapless Lichnowsky saying that he had unfortunately been given a false impression and that there was no question of the Western powers remaining neutral.[35]

This dashed such hopes as the Kaiser had been entertaining of leaning once more on King George to secure British neutrality. (One of the many allusions under which the German emperor suffered was to imagine that the Crown of England continued to have the same influence over the country's diplomacy as it had exerted during a quite exceptional decade under Edward VII.) Thus, for the past forty-eight hours, Prince Henry of Prussia, now back in Berlin, had been trying to exploit by telegram that opening which he imagined the King had given him over breakfast at Buckingham Palace the previous Sunday. On 30 July, after consulting with his imperial brother, the Prince had

telegraphed the King about the danger posed by the military preparations on Germany's flanks:

If you really and earnestly wish to prevent this terrible disaster, may I suggest
you using your influence on France and also Russia to keep neutral. . . .
Believe me that William is most sincere in his endeavours to maintain peace
but the military preparations of his two neighbours may at last force him to
follow their example for the safety of his own country . . .[36]

To this, the King could only reply that he was doing all he could but
repeated that the last chance of getting Russia to hold her hand was for
Germany to persuade her Austrian ally 'to be satisfied with the
occupation of Belgrade and neighbouring Serbian territory as a hostage
for the satisfactory settlement of her demands'. As we have seen, this
'Halt in Belgrade' formula had failed to halt anything, thanks largely to
the war party around Franz Josef in Vienna. Again, one is struck by the
isolation of the aged Habsburg ruler. George V and his Prime Minister
never seem to have thought it worth while to address this personal
appeal – which, after all, concerned the operation of Austrian troops –
to the sovereign who, in the last analysis, controlled those troops.*

On the evening of 1 August, before Lichnowsky's second and more
sobering message about England's intentions had reached Berlin, the
Kaiser tried to follow up Prince Henry's efforts with another appeal of
his own to King George. There were several remarkable things about
this telegram. The first was the speed at which, compared with most
other royal and ministerial messages exchanged that week, it reached
its target. The Royal Archives copy shows that it was dispatched from
Potsdam at 7.05 p.m., and was already being sent out for delivery to the
King in Buckingham Palace ten minutes later. It would have helped
matters had all high-level dispatches sent off during the crisis been
received so promptly, instead of being delayed for hours on end during
transmission.

The other remarkable aspect of the Kaiser's telegram is the perfectly
frank picture it gives of what his army was already about – namely
invasion. After expressing regret that what he erroneously describes as
'the telegram of your Cabinet' had arrived so late in the proceedings he
went on:

---

* Franz Josef's personal role in this last flurry of dynastic diplomacy seems to have been confined
mainly to an appeal to King Victor Emmanuel of Italy to honour his obligations in any
forthcoming European clash as a partner in the Triple Alliance. The little King sent back
replies to both Vienna and Berlin saying that he proposed only to maintain a 'cordial attitude'
towards them. On 3 August he declared his neutrality and, nine months later, came in on the
side of the entente.

But if France offers me neutrality, which must be guaranteed by the British fleet and army, I shall of course, refrain from attacking France and employ my troops elsewhere. I hope that France will not become nervous. The troops on my frontiers are in the act of being stopped by telegraph and telephone from crossing into France.[37]

By the time the Kaiser sent that telegram to Buckingham Palace, not the slightest doubt remained about his troops being 'employed elsewhere'. An hour before in St Petersburg, at six in the evening, Count Pourtalès made the last of his many calls on Foreign Minister Sazanov. The day before, the envoy had been instructed to hand over an ultimatum demanding that Russia must either cancel her mobilization or face the consequences. Now he had come to announce those consequences. Three times, almost choking with emotion, Pourtalès asked the minister whether Russia was prepared to stand her forces down. Three times Sazanov replied that she was not.

'In that case, I am instructed to hand you this note,' replied the ambassador, drawing Germany's declaration of war from his pocket. At this, the veteran ambassador, who had striven at his post for seven years to hook up again Bismarck's broken line to St Petersburg, turned away to the window and wept openly. He was not the only heart-broken envoy between the rival alliances to be in tears that week.

From now on, the escalation was unstoppable as what Bethmann-Hollweg called the 'iron dice' (it was the only striking phrase this tedious, disastrous figure ever coined) started to roll. In this final act, the monarchs had only what, in stage parlance, would be called 'walk-on' parts to play. Declarations of war between every continental member of the two power blocs – with the exception of maverick Italy – became automatic after Pourtalès had handed over his note. Only over London did an anguished question mark hang for another forty-eight hours. The anguish was not confined to that capital. The French, who had been pressing hard for assurances of British help, were still, at the beginning of August, left without a firm answer. In St Petersburg the British ambassador, Sir George Buchanan, felt it prudent not even to turn up alongside his French colleague at a special service held in the Winter Palace on Sunday 2 August to pray for the success of the Russian army. Though invited, he had decided to stay away, 'having no information as to the attitude of His Majesty's Government in war'.[38]*

That same Sunday was also the day of decision in London, where the

---

* His telegram reporting this had to be sent to London via Aden as normal channels were already disrupted.

Cabinet sat, almost without a break, to determine England's course. Asquith knew that some of his ministers, for pacifist or other reasons, were for non-intervention.* He was still uncertain of public opinion despite the news, which had reached London around noon, that the German army had now entered Luxembourg.

Two factors proved decisive. The first was a written assurance of support given by the Unionist Opposition leaders. Indeed, in his letter, Mr Bonar Law had actually urged the Prime Minister on: 'It would be fatal to the honour and security of the United Kingdom to hesitate in supporting France and Russia at the present juncture.'[39]

The second and really crucial factor was the German invasion of Belgium, a pre-essential for the execution of German war plans in the west. Belgium, seat of the cross-Channel ports, was a very different case, both to the man in the Clapham omnibus and the staff officer in Whitehall, from tiny, land-locked Luxembourg. That evening, as a somewhat pharisaical preliminary to invasion, Germany had informed Belgium that, though she would be regrettably obliged to enter Belgian soil, she would leave again after victory, having paid all her war dues and debts, provided the country stayed 'benevolently neutral'.[40] Belgium was given twelve hours to reply. At 7 a.m. the following morning she threw the giant's challenge back in his teeth and announced that she would fight to repel all invaders.

The young King Albert sent 'a supreme appeal' to King George asking for his personal intervention 'for the safeguarding of Belgian neutrality'.[41] The King was able to reply that Sir Edward Grey's statement in Parliament that same afternoon, Monday 3 August, would prove England's 'desire and intention' in this respect.[42]

Indeed it did. In a skilful speech, the foreign secretary did not yet announce war against Germany but left no doubt that this was now the only choice. If Belgium fell, Holland and Denmark would follow and if France were then crushed and eliminated as a great power, England would be faced by the 'unmeasured aggrandizement' of Germany. There was thunderous approval, inside and outside the House of Commons. The following day, 4 August, German troops decided the issue once and for all by crossing the Belgian frontier at Gemmenich. At 2 p.m. Grey issued a ten-hour ultimatum to Berlin to withdraw. The British ambassador took the ultimatum to Bethmann-Hollweg early that evening. Goschen found him agitated, maudlin, resentful, yet still unrepentant. What was the mere word 'neutrality' worth, the

---

* Two members, Lord Morley and Mr John Burns, resigned the following day when war, though seemingly inescapable, had still not been declared.

chancellor demanded. He went on to utter the famous words: 'Just for a scrap of paper, Great Britain was going to make war on a kindred nation who desired nothing better than to be friends with her'. When Goschen reminded him that honour was indeed at stake, all the chancellor could reply was: 'But at what price!'[43]

So it was the soldiers who, predictably, had finally set the 'iron dice' rolling: General Conrad against Serbia and General Moltke against Belgium and France. Nothing is more typical of the role which the mighty continental emperors were reduced to in these last days of peace than the fate which befell their final messages. The telegram from St Petersburg in which the Tsar pleaded to King George V to 'support France and Russia in fighting to maintain the balance of power in Europe' petered out before it was finished in transmission via Aden. The Kaiser's last appeal to Nicholas to stand his army down is marked in the Russian archives: 'Received after war had been declared.'[44]

The process by which the conflict had spread, within six weeks, from the Bosnian mountains to the Channel ports and escalated from a Balkan clash into a European war was as logical in one way as it was ludicrous in another. The matrix of rival defensive pacts and under-standings which crisscrossed the continent served not as the insulator of a mounting tension but as the conductor and magnifier of the current. Yet it is of little use to blame the system entirely, as though human beings were not also at work. It was human beings who brought about the initial crisis at Sarajevo and who then provoked or allowed that crisis to end in catastrophe. The lines along which the escalation sped may have been fixed in advance, but they still could have been blocked, had the wit and will been there.

The so-called 'war guilt' of individual governments and statesmen has been endlessly rehearsed, and the woeful egotism or blindness of a Berchtold or a Bethmann-Hollweg emerges clearly enough again in this narrative. As for the monarchs of old Europe, who have been our prime concern in this study, almost every one of them also shares some portion of responsibility. In the Balkans, it was the intensified Greater Serbia agitation launched under the bloodstained Karageorgević dynasty in Belgrade and echoed, comically but dangerously, by the fellow-Slav neighbour King Nikita of Montenegro, which prepared the soil from which a Gavrilo Princip was to spring. Each of the Balkan rulers and, above all, the preposterous Ferdinand of Bulgaria, contrib-uted with their sporadic fighting and incessant bickering to what these days would be termed progressive destabilization of the region, creating a chaos in which violence and terrorism could prosper. Only that austere Hohenzollern, King Carol of Rumania, can be called well-intentioned throughout and relatively guiltless.

As for the great emperors of the continent, the German Kaiser is clearly branded by the bombast which marked his whole reign and which reached a fateful climax in 1914 by the rash encouragement which he fed to the war party in Vienna. His ally, the aged Austrian emperor Franz Josef can be reproached for remaining aloof, in the style of *his* whole reign, from a crisis which he ought to have bent down and controlled in person from his own capital, instead of surveying from afar in that deceptively tranquil summer retreat of his. The Tsar's personal contribution to the disaster was also a certain remoteness, shut off from reality in his wife's dream world of Tsarkoe Selo, a remoteness compounded in his case by a tragic feebleness of will. The most powerful of all three autocrats, he proved, when the test came, the weakest.

In England, Edward VII, though accused by his imperial nephew in Berlin of being a warmonger had, in fact, both preached and practised the doctrine of European peace all his life. What the Kaiser called the encirclement of a benign Germany was envisaged by his uncle as the containment of a lethal Germany.

That leaves the honest, uninspired George V, of whom not even the Kaiser could find a harsh word to say. Indeed, the only cause for regret about King George in the summer of 1914 was that he was not his own father; but that can hardly be raised up into a rebuke. Just as his father would have done, George V strove to the end to keep his own crown and country away from the maelstrom towards which – witlessly or wilfully – his fellow-sovereigns across the Channel were steering. Four years later, when the storm was exhausted, he at least had the lugubrious satisfaction of seeing his own throne intact under him, whereas so many of theirs had been swept away, by their own folly or laxity, for ever.

NOTES

ABBREVIATIONS

ARB   AUSTRIAN RED BOOK
BD   BRITISH DOCUMENTS ON THE ORIGINS OF THE WAR
DDF   DOCUMENTS DIPLOMATIQUES FRANÇAIS
FO   FOREIGN OFFICE RECORDS
FYB   FRENCH YELLOW BOOK
GP   DIE GROSSE POLITIK DER EUROPÄISCHEN KABINETTE, 1870–1914
KD   KAUTSKY DOCUMENTS
OUA   OESTERREICH-UNGARNS AUSSENPOLITIK
RA   ROYAL ARCHIVES WINDSOR

INTRODUCTION: WEDDING IN BERLIN

1 *The Times*, 22 May 1914.
2 *The Kaiser's Daughter, Memoirs of Princess Victoria Louise*, London 1977, p. 72.
3 Ibid., p. 79.
4 Royal Archives Windsor (henceforth cited as RA), G.V p. 586, from which dispatch this and the following details are taken.

Chapter 1   MONTENEGRO: KING OF THE BLACK MOUNTAINS

1 Quoted in W. Denton, *Montenegro, Its People and their History*, London 1877, p. 26.
2 Lady Strangford, *The Eastern Shores of the Adriatic*, London, 1864, pp. 145–7.
3 Ibid., p. 150.
4 The Misses Muir Mackenzie and A.P. Irby, *Travels in the Slavonic Provinces of Turkey in Europe*, London 1867, p. 61.
5 There are useful genealogical tables in Tiri Louda and Michael MacLagan, *Lines of Succession*, London 1981, and an excellent selection of contemporary photographs in Geoffrey Finestone, *The Last Courts of Europe*, also London 1981.
6 *Die Grosse Politik der Europäischen Kabinette 1870–1914*, (henceforth cited as GP), Vol. 33, No. 12152.
7 Grey of Falloden, *Twenty-Five Years*, Vol. I, London 1925, pp. 264–72.
8 GP Vol. 34/II, No. 13067.
9 Ibid., No. 13190.
10 *Documents Diplomatiques Français* (henceforth cited as DDF), Sér. 3, Vol. 5, No. 179.
11 Ibid., No. 195.

12 GP Vol. 34/I, No. 12787.
13 Denton, p. 64
14 GP Vol. 6, No. 1356.
15 DDF Sér. 3, Vol. 9, No. 99.
16 DDF Sér. 3, Vol. 1, No. 630.
17 DDF Sér. 3, Vol. 10, No. 43.
18 M. Bogičević, *Die Auswärtige Politik Serbiens, 1903–1914*, Berlin 1928, Document No. 904.
19 *British Documents on the Origins of the War* (henceforth cited as BD), Vol. 10, Part 1, No. 310.

Chapter 2   SERBIA: MANY PRINCES, ONE CROWN

1 The best recent work in English on Serbia in the nineteenth and early twentieth century is the two-volume study by Michael Boro Petrovich, *A History of Modern Serbia*, New York 1976.
2 Petrovich, Vol. II, p. 369.
3 H. Vivian, *Serbian Tragedy*, London 1904, and Chadomille Mijatovich, *A Royal Tragedy*, London 1906, give detailed contemporary accounts of the scandal.
4 Vivian, p. 42.
5 R. R. Rosen, *Forty Years of Diplomacy*, London 1922, Vol. I, pp. 111–18.
6 Mijatovich, pp. 80–91 and 120–49 gives an inside account of the marriage crisis in the Belgrade court and government.
7 Foreign Office Records (henceforth cited as FO), 105, Piece H9, 157 (Serbia).
8 Vivian, p. 94.
9 FO 105, H9.

Chapter 3   SERBIA: THE FATAL CRUSADE

1 FO 105, Piece H9, dispatch of 22 June 1903.
2 Petrovich, p. 534.
3 An account of their arrival is given in the *Journal de Génève* of 22 June 1903.
4 FO 105, H9, dispatch of 27 June 1903.
5 BD Vol. 5, No. 99.
6 M. Bogičević Document No. 1.
7 FO 105, H9, message of 30 June 1903.
8 Ibid., dispatch of 19 June 1903.
9 BD Vol. 5, Nos. 109 and 110.
10 Ibid., No. 118.
11 Ibid., Nos. 122 and 123.
12 Petrovich, p. 564.
13 Ibid., p. 583.
14 GP Vol. 26 (II), No. 8919.
15 Petrovich, p. 561.
16 BD Vol. 9, No. 545.
17 Petrovich, p. 603.
18 GP Vol. 38, No. 15533.
19 Bogičević, No. 399.
20 Ibid.

21 DDF Sér. 3, Vol. 10, No. 207.
22 Ibid., No. 285.
23 Ibid., No. 437.
24 Ibid.

Chapter 5 BULGARIA: THE BALKAN FOX

1 Egon Cesar Conte Corti, *Alexander von Battenberg*, London 1954, p. 241.
2 Stephen Constant, *Foxy Ferdinand, Tsar of Bulgaria*, London 1979, pp. 13–14.
   Constant drew on family papers for his account of the episode which can be
   taken as more authentic than various earlier versions.
3 *The Letters of Queen Victoria*, London 1930, Third Series 1866–1901, Vol. I,
   p. 229.
4 Meriel Buchanan, *Diplomacy and Foreign Courts*, London 1928, p. 65.
5 Queen Marie of Rumania, *The Story of my Life*, London 1934, p. 251.
6 For accounts of Ferdinand's court life and private life in these early years *see,
   inter alia*, Constant op. cit., pp. 76–102; Buchanan, op. cit., pp. 71–81; B. von
   Sydacoff, *Bulgarien und der Bulgarische Fürstenhof*, Berlin 1896, pp. 42 *et seq.*; Hans
   Madol, *Ferdinand von Bulgarien*, Berlin 1931, pp. 69 *et seq.*, J. Macdonald, *Czar
   Ferdinand and his People*, London 1913, pp. 288 *et seq.*
7 Constant, p. 96.
8 Louise of Tuscany, *My own Story*, London 1911, pp. 65 *et seq.*
9 *Letters of Queen Victoria*, pp. 123–4.
10 Constant, p. 143.
11 Idem, p. 159.
12 Harold Nicolson's *First Lord Carnock*, London 1930, pp. 106 *et seq.* gives details of
   Stamboloff's last hours and funeral.
13 Gordon Brook-Shepherd, *Uncle of Europe*, London 1975, pp. 224–5.
14 RA E.VII W52.
15 BD, Vol. 5, No. 2617.
16 *Oesterreich-Ungarns Aussenpolitik*(henceforth cited as OUA), Vol. 1, No. 1.
17 BD Vol. 5, No. 584.
18 GP Vol. 26, No. 9338.
19 Idem.
20 BD Vol. 5, No. 625.
21 Constant, p. 188.
22 Buchanan, p. 68.
23 BD Vol. 5 No. 436.
24 M. Bogičević, pp. 124–5.
25 Madol, pp. 126–8.
26 BD Vol. X, Part 2, No. 476.
27 R. R. Rosen, Vol. I, p. 64.
28 Bogičević, Document No. 924.
29 Baedeker 1905.
30 GP Vol. 26(2), No. 9285.
31 RA G.V p. 513, Bax-Ironside to Lord Stamfordham, 22 May 1911.
32 Constant, p. 258.
33 Maurice Paléologue, *Journal 1913*, Paris 1947, p. 152.
34 RA G.V p. 513, Bax-Ironside to Lord Stamfordham, 9 April 1913.
35 Idem.
36 Constant, p. 284.

Chapter 5   RUMANIA: PRUSSIAN IRON

1 Maude Parkinson, *Twenty Years in Rumania*, London 1921, pp. 61–2.
2 Ibid., p. 63.
3 These and the following impressions of court life under Carol and his queen are based mainly on the memoirs of their niece (Marie of Rumania, *The Story of my Life*, London 1934, Vol. 2, especially pp. 55–5, 85–95, 268–71; Parkinson, pp. 167–79 and 199–205; and Bernhard Prince von Bülow, *Memoirs*, London 1931, Vol. I, pp. 619 *et seq*. References are only given for direct quotes.
4 Marie of Rumania, p. 85.
5 Ibid., p. 52.
6 Bülow, pp. 647–8, gives a racy account of the episode.
7 Marie of Rumania, pp. 42–3.
8 DDF Sér. 3, Vol. 7, No. 56.
9 Ibid., No. 165.
10 Ibid., No. 220.
11 BD Vol. 9, Part II, No. 1229.
12 Ibid.
13 DDF Sér. 3, Vol. 10, No. 397.

Chapter 6   GERMANY: THE VOLCANO OF EUROPE

1 Roger Fulford (ed.), *Dearest Mama, Letters between Queen Victoria and the Crown Princess of Prussia*, London 1968, Vol. II, pp. 203.
2 Alexander Reissner, *Berlin 1675–1945*, London 1984, p. 57.
3 A. J. Ryder, *Twentieth Century Germany from Bismarck to Brandt*, London 1972, pp. 24 *et seq*. gives an excellent summary of the cultural scene.
4 Bernhard Prince von Bülow, *Memoirs*, London 1931, Vol. I, p. 259.
5 Queen Marie of Rumania, p. 221.
6 The classic examples are the ghost-written *Secrets of Potsdam* and *More Secrets of Potsdam* by Count Ernst von Heltzendorff, London and New York, 1917.
7 Heinrich Graf von Lützow, *Im diplomatischen Dienst der K. und K. Monarchie*, Vienna 1971, p. 125.
8 Isabel V. Hull, *The Entourage of Kaiser Wilhelm II*, Cambridge 1982, p. 33.
9 Admiral Alexander von Müller, quoted in Hull, p. 34.
10 Field Marshal Graf Alfred von Waldersee, *Denkwürdigkeiten*, Berlin 1923, Vol. II, p. 34.
11 Hull, p. 21.
12 Waldersee, p. 154.
13 Count Axel von Schwerin, *The Berlin Court under William II*, London 1915, p. 25.
14 GP Vol. VII, No. 21.
15 *Hamburger Nachrichten*, 24 January 1892.

Chapter 7   GERMANY: IMPERIAL FANTASY

1 Bülow, Vol. I, p. 81.
2 Ibid., p. 356.
3 GP Vol. 19, pp. 458 *et seq*.
4 Ibid., 'Nicky' to 'Willy', 7 October 1905.

5 Bülow, Vol. I, p. 137.

6 Ibid., p. 140.

7 *The Letters of Queen Victoria*, London 1930, Third Series 1866–1901, Vol. I, pp. 440–41.

8 Reproduced in GP Vol. 17, No. 5029.

9 RA G. V, W.42, No. 136, Sir Frank Lascelles to Lord Knollys, 11 October 1902.

10 GP Vol. 21 (I), No. 7082.

11 Ibid., (II), No. 7205.

12 GP Vol. 27 (II), No. 9910.

13 GP Vol. 21 (II), No. 7617.

14 Ibid., No. 7208.

15 Ibid., No. 7180.

16 GP Vol. 21 (I), No. 6961.

17 BD Vol. 10, Part 2, pp. 700–701.

18 GP Vol. 26 (I), No. 8939.

19 Ibid., Comment of William II.

20 GP Vol. 26 (II), No. 9188.

21 Quoted in Sir Philip Magnus, *King Edward VII*, London 1964, p. 400.

22 Müller, quoted in Isabel V. Hull, *The Entourage of Kaiser Wilhelm II*, Cambridge 1982, pp. 261–2.

23 Private diary of Luis de Soveral, quoted in Gordon Brook-Shepherd, *The Uncle of Europe*, London 1975, p. 255.

Chapter 8 AUSTRIA: THE GOLDEN PRINCE

1 Letters of Queen Caroline, quoted in Franz Herre, *Kaiser Franz Joseph von Oesterreich*, Cologne 1978.

2 C. A. Macartney, *The Habsburg Empire*, London 1968, pp. 322–408, is especially strong on the course of events in Hungary, the author's life-long speciality.

3 Franz Josef to Elisabeth, Verona 26 June 1859, quoted in Conte Corti *Kaiser Franz Joseph*, Vienna 1965, pp. 153–4.

4 Quoted in Conte Corti, p. 205.

Chapter 9 AUSTRIA: THE STONE IDOL

1 Letter from Franz Josef to Elisabeth, 1 November 1887, quoted in Conte Corti, *Kaiser Franz Joseph*, p. 384.

2 Albert von Margutti, *The Emperor Franz Josef and his Times*, London 1921, pp. 45 et seq.

3 Nora Fugger, *Im Glanz der Kaiserzeit*, Vienna 1930, pp. 323–4.

4 Conte Corti, *Elisabeth*, Salzburg 1934, p. 509.

5 Franz Ferdinand papers (Nachlass FF). Draft Letter to Franz Josef of 19 May 1900.

6 Hugo Hantsch, *Leopold Graf Berchtold*, Vienna 1963, Vol. I, p. 168.

7 GP Vol. 26, No. 731.

8 Report of Kosutić, 3 March 1909, quoted in Sidney Fay, *The Origins of the World War*, New York 1935, Vol. I, p. 385.

9 M. Bogičević, Document No. 428.

10 Ibid., No. 441.

11 Ibid., No. 446.
12 RA W.44, No. 91.
13 RA X.22, No. 43.
14 Empress Zita to author, first quoted in Gordon Brook-Shepherd, *The Last Habsburg*, London 1968, pp. 26–27.

Chapter 10   ITALY: THE MAKE-WEIGHT KINGDOM

1 F. Cognasso, 'I Savoia nella politica europea', quoted in Robert Katz, *The Fall of the House of Savoy*, London 1972, p. 10.
2 Maude Parkinson, *Twenty Years in Rumania*, London 1921, p. 180.
3 Walburga Lady Paget, *Scenes and Memories*, London 1912, pp. 154–6.
4 Ibid., p. 200.
5 Bülow, Vol. I, p. 660.
6 Private letter of Crispi to Depretis, quoted in Katz, p. 67.
7 GP Vol. 3, 224–5.
8 Ibid., p. 185.
9 Denis Mack Smith, *Italy, A Modern History*, Ann Arbor 1969, p. 185.
10 Lützow, p. 124.
11 Ibid., p. 123.
12 Katz, p. 176.
13 DDF Sér. 2, Vol. 14, No. 348.
14 Richard Bosworth, *Italy, the least of the Great Powers*, London 1979, p. 161.
15 GP Vol. 30, Part I, No. 10916.
16 A. Albertini, *La Dinastia di Savoia*, Perugia 1895, p. 155.
17 DDP Sér. 3, Vol. 2, No. 283.
18 GP Vol. 39, No. 15721.

Chapter 11   RUSSIA: THE ALIEN GIANT

1 *Letters of Queen Victoria*, London 1907, Vol. 5, Queen to Princess Vicky, 22 September 1858.
2 Joseph Conrad, *Notes on Life and Letters*, London 1921, pp. 130–31.
3 Quoted in Edward Crankshaw, *The Shadow of the Winter Palace*, London 1976, p. 91.
4 Manifesto text in Hugh Seton-Watson, *The Russian Empire 1801–1917*, Oxford 1967, p. 463.
5 George F. Kennan, *The Fateful Alliance: France, Russia and the Coming of the Great War*, Manchester 1984, p. 68.
6 GP Vol. 7, No. 1514 gives Giers's own account of the ceremony, possibly coloured up especially for the Germans.
7 Georges Michon, *L'Alliance Franco-Russe*, Paris 1927, p. 92.
8 DDF Sér. 2, Vol. 9, No. 134.
9 Quoted in Robert K. Massie, *Nicholas and Alexandra*, London 1968, p. 65.

Chapter 12   RUSSIA: END OF THE LINE

1 R. R. Rosen, p. 59.

2 BD Vol. 4, no. 243, 2 January 1907.

3 GP Vol. 22, No. 7877.

4 *Letters of the Tsaritsa to the Tsar, 1914–1916*, London 1923, pp. 455.

5 *Letters of the Tsar Nicholas and Empress Marie*, edited by J. Bing, London 1937, pp. 116–7.

6 *The Letters of Tsar Nicholas*, p. 179.

7 RA, W.45, No. 105, Hardinge to Knollys, 1 February 1905.

8 RA, X.20, Spring-Rice to Knollys, 31 October 1905.

9 *Letters of Tsar Nicholas*, pp. 185–9.

10 Harold Nicolson, *First Lord Carnock*, London 1930, pp. 222–3.

11 Marie, Grand Duchess of Russia, *Memories of a Princess*, New York 1930, pp. 88–9.

12 Maurice Paléologue, *Alexandra-Feodorovna, Impératrice de Russie*, Paris 1932, p. 78.

13 RA E.VII, Hardinge to Knollys, 26 August 1904.

14 William II, *Letters to the Tsar*, London 1920, pp. 104–5.

15 Ibid., pp. 188–9.

16 *Letters of Tsar Nicholas*, p. 236.

17 GP Vol. 26, I, No. 9112, Pourtalès to Bülow.

18 GP Vol. 26, II, No. 9187, Emperor Nicholas to Emperor William.

19 *Letters of Tsar Nicholas*, p. 240.

20 Ibid., p. 279.

21 BD Vol. 9, I, No. 553.

22 GP Vol. 33, No. 12258 (footnote, letter of Izvolski to Sazanov).

23 Original French text of telegram in BD Vol. 9, II, No. 1055 (enclosure).

24 Quoted in GP Vol. 33, No. 15535 (footnote).

25 BD Vol. 10, No. 537.

26 *Letters of Tsar Nicholas*, pp. 271–2.

27 Princess Catherine Radziwill, *The Intimate Life of the Last Tsarina*, London 1929, pp. 75–6.

28 RA, G.V p. 254 A/6.

29 DDF Sér. 2, Vol. 10, No. 267.

Chapter 13 ENGLAND: THE WIDOW'S HERITAGE

1 Roger Fulford (ed.) *Dearest Child (Letters between Queen Victoria and the Princess Royal) 1858–1861*, London 1964, p. 337–8.

2 Roger Fulford (ed.), *Dearest Mama (Letters between Queen Victoria and the Crown Princess of Prussia)*, London 1968, p. 294.

3 Ibid., 15 April 1864, p. 320.

4 Ibid., 3 July 1863, p. 242.

5 *Letters of Queen Victoria*, Vol. IV, p. 190. Queen to Lord Clarendon.

6 Ibid., p. 120, Lord Russell to Queen, 23 September 1863.

7 Ibid., p. 145, Lord Palmerston to Queen, 8 January 1864.

8 Ibid., p. 185, Lord Palmerston to Queen, 10 May 1864.

9 Ibid., p. 187, Queen to King Leopold, 12 May 1864.

10 *Letters*, Vol. V, p. 80, Vicky to Queen, 7 November 1870.

11 *Dearest Child*, p. 212.

12 Ibid., pp 212–3.

13 Ibid., pp. 227–8, Vicky to Queen, 25 October 1876.

14 Ibid., p. 39, Queen to Vicky, 10 February 1858.
15 Ibid., Queen to Vicky, 22 September 1858.
16 *Letters*, Vol. V, p. 625.
17 *Letters*, Vol. IX, p. 301.
18 *Letters*, Vol. IV, Queen's Journal, 27 January 1866.
19 *Letters*, Vol. IX, William II to Queen, 18 December 1896.
20 *Briefe Wilhelm II an den Zaren 1894–1914*, Berlin 1920, p. 309.
21 *Letters*, Vol. IX, pp. 343–4.
22 *Letters*, Vol. IV, Queen to King of Prussia, 10 April 1866.
23 *Letters*, Vol. V, p. 33.
24 Ibid., pp. 495–7.
25 See F. Hardie, *The Political Influence of Queen Victoria*, London 1935, p. 175.
26 *Letters*, Vol. VI, p. 485. Queen to Lord Hartington, 25 Marh 1884.
27 Ibid., p. 597.
28 *Letters*, Vol. IV, p. 210, Queen to Lord Clarendon, 4 June 1864.
29 Ibid., p. 190.
30 Bishop Magee's letter quoted in Sidney Lee, *Life of King Edward VII*, 2 vols, New York 1925, p. 179.
31 Quoted, without source, in Giles St Aubyn, *Edward, Prince and King*, London 1979, p. 245.
32 Lee, I, p. 451.
33 Ibid., p. 360.
34 GP Vol. VI, No. 5029.
35 Lee, II, p. 428.

Chapter 14   ENGLAND: THE UNCLE OF EUROPE

1 BD Vol. II, No. 81.
2 Ibid., No. 92.
3 Letter of Lansdowne to Balfour, January 1903, quoted in George Monger, *The End of Isolation*, London 1963, p. 113.
4 Lee, Vol. I, p. 360.
5 DDF Sér. 2, Vol. II, No. 450.
6 Hermann von Eckardstein, *Ten Years at the Court of St James*, London 1921, p. 245.
7 DDF Sér. 2, Vol. II, No. 135.
8 Gordon Brook-Shepherd, *Uncle of Europe*, London 1975, pp. 156–7.
9 *Le Figaro*, 3 May 1903.
10 Brook-Shepherd, p. 204.
11 *See*, for example, Monger, p. 127.
12 Full drafts and final text in BD Vol. 2, pp. 374 *et seq*.
13 Letter quoted in Lee, II, p. 34.
14 DDF Sér. 2, Vol. VI, Delcassé to Bompard, 25 April 1905.
15 Lansdowne MSS: Lord Lansdowne to Mr Lister, 10 July 1905.
16 DDF Sér. 2, Vol. IX, No. 106.
17 Hardinge to Bertie, 22 April 1904, quoted in Monger, p. 160.
18 Quoted in Lee, II, p. 565.
19 FO 800/103/4367. See E. Grey to Lord Knollys.
20 Lord John Fisher, *Memories*, London 1919, p. 187.

21 Fisher, p. 134.
22 Brook-Shepherd, pp. 310–11.
23 GP Vol. 24, Nos. 8224–6 gives the Kaiser's own running account of the talks.
24 Henry Wickham Steed, *Through Thirty Years*, London 1924, Vol. I, p. 282.
25 DDF Sér. 2, Vol. XI, No. 558 and Annexe.
26 Daisy Pless *From my Private Diary*, London 1931, pp. 176–7.
27 GP Vol. 28, No. 10260.
28 Brook-Shepherd, pp. 211–12.
29 Frederick Ponsonby, *Recollections of Three Reigns*, London 1952. The second work is Siegmund Munz's *King Edward VII at Marienbad*, one of the worst but most indispensable books ever written.
30 Lord Thomas Newton, *Lord Lansdowne*, London 1929. Quoted in Giles St Aubyn, *Edward, Prince and King*, London 1979, p. 328.
31 Ponsonby, p. 173.
32 For a detailed account of the visit, based on the Royal Archives, Windsor, and Count Mensdorff's private diary, *see* Gordon Brook-Shepherd, *Victims at Sarajevo*, London 1984, pp. 205–10.
33 RA, G.V, Queen Mary to the Grand Duchess Augusta of Mecklenburg–Strelitz, 27 November 1913.

Chapter 15 FATAL GAMBITS

1 *See* Vladimir Dedijer, *The Road to Sarajevo*, London 1966, pp. 388 *et seq*.
2 Gordon Brook-Shepherd, *The Last Habsburg*, London 1968, p. 26–77.
3 DDF Sér. 2, Vol. 10, No. 474.
4 Bogičević, Document No. 977.
5 DDF Sér. 2, Vol. 10, No. 460.
6 Parliamentary report in *Daily Telegraph*, 1 July 1914.
7 *See* Gordon Brook-Shepherd, *Victims at Sarajevo*, London 1984, pp. 229–30, for Baron von Morsey's Konopischt diary.
8 Quoted in Robert A. Kann's academic paper, 'Kaiser Franz Josef und der Ausbruch des Weltkrieges', Vienna 1971, p. 16.
9 Conrad von Hötzendorf, *Aus meiner Dienstzeit*, Vol. IV, pp. 33 *et seq*.
10 *Austrian Red Book*, (henceforth cited as ARB), Vienna 1919, Vol. 1, No. 1.
11 Ibid., No. 2.
12 Interview reprinted in *Neue Freie Presse*, Vienna, 1 July 1914.
13 Karl Kautsky (ed.), German Documents on the Outbreak of the War, No. 7, English translation, 1924. (Referred to as KD/N/Kautsky Documents.)
14 Emmanuel Geiss, *July 1914*, London 1967, p. 62.
15 KD No. 5.
16 Ibid., No. 14.
17 Ibid., No. 26.
18 Quoted in Alfred von Wegerer, *Kritische Bemerkungen*, Berlin 1923, Appendix 2.
19 Quoted in Fay, Vol. II, p. 211 (footnote).
20 Conrad, Vol. III, pp. 667–74.
21 KD No. 74.
22 This and the following extracts are translated from the record of the meeting given in the ARB (Vol. I, No. 8). The same Count Hoyos who had just been on the mission to Berlin kept the minutes which were edited somewhat by Berchtold afterwards.

23 For the extracts from Berchtold's diary and his post-war memoirs *see* Hugo Hantsch, *Leopold Graf Berchtold*, Vienna 1963, Vol. II, p. 570 and pp. 588–9.
24 Freiherr von Musulin *Das Haus am Ballplatz*, Munich 1924, pp. 223–7.
25 *French Yellow Book* (henceforth cited as FYB), Paris 1914, No. 18.
26 BD Vol. XI, No. 56.
27 FYB Nos. 13 and 14.
28 BD Vol. XI, No. 68.
29 KD No. 72.
30 Hantsch, pp. 602–5 gives full details of the events on 20–21 July.
31 BD Vol. XI, No. 91.
32 ARB No. 10600.
33 Albert von Margutti, *Vom Alten Kaiser*, Vienna 1921, pp. 403–4.
34 Robert A. Kann, *Kaiser Franz Josef und der Ausbruch des Krieges*, Austrian Academy of Sciences, Vienna 1971.

Chapter 16 KING'S MATE

1 Conrad von Hötzendorf, Vol. IV, pp. 110–24, gives his thoughts on the situation.
2 KD No. 271.
3 Ibid., No. 323.
4 KD No. 323.
5 BD Vol. XI, No. 179.
6 BD Vol. XI, No. 179 (footnote).
7 Ibid., No. 248.
8 ARB No. 10793.
9 KD No. 99.
10 Bethmann-Hollweg, *Betrachtungen zum Weltkrieg*, Berlin 1921.
11 KD No. 374.
12 Harold Nicolson, *King George V*, London 1952, pp. 245–6.
13 KD No. 124a.
14 Telegram quoted in Emmanuel Geiss, *July 1914*, London 1967, p. 262.
15 Documents from the Tsarist Archives, *Internationale Beziehungen*, (German translation, Berlin 1934) No. 184.
16 Maurice Paléologue, *La Russie des Tsars*, Paris 1921, pp. 14–15.
17 KD No. 335.
18 KD No. 322.
19 Ibid.
20 KD No. 127.
21 KD No. 390.
22 Paléologue, p. 39.
23 Quoted in Fay, II, p. 472.
24 KD No. 473.
25 KD No. 396.
26 KD No. 441.
27 BD Vol. XI. No. 293.
28 Ibid., separate minute.
29 BD Vol. XI, No. 303.
30 ARB No. 11203.

31 KD No. 401.
32 RA private diary of King George V, entry for 31 July 1914.
33 BD Vol. XI, No. 384.
34 KD No. 562.
35 KD No. 603.
36 RA G.V Q 1549/5.
37 RA G.V Q 1549/12.
38 BD Vol. XI, No. 560.
39 Letter published in the London *Times*, 15 December 1914.
40 KD Nos. 376 and 648.
41 RA G.V. Q 1549/19.
42 RA G.V Q 1549/20.
43 BD Vol. XI, No. 594.
44 *Int. Bez.* (Tsarist Archives), No. 416.

INDEX

Aarenau, Major Alexander Brosch von, 153

Abdul Hamid, Sultan of Turkey, 58

Abruzzi, Duke degli, 177

Adalbert, Prince of Prussia, 319

Adelhaid, Archduchess of Austria, 160

Adelheid, Princess of Saxe-Meiningen, 319

Adowa, Battle of (1896), 170, 175

Adrianople, 66–8

Aehrenthal, Baron Alois von, 60; and Bosnia/Herzegovina, 148–51, 213; replaced, 153; and Hardinge, 260; at Marienbad, 267

Afghanistan, 258, 259n

Africa: European expansion into, 167–8, 170, 175–6

Agadir crisis (1911), 113, 176

Albania, 12–14, 43–4, 167, 178

Albert, Prince Consort of Victoria, 221–2, 226; and Edward VII, 232; death, 233

Albert I, King of the Belgians, 328

Alexander II, Tsar of Russia, 21, 48, 186–7, 213–14

Alexander III, Tsar of Russia, 15; antipathy to Germans, 48, 188–9; and Bulgaria, 48–9; death, 55, 194, 238; alliance with France, 102, 189–91; character and reign, 187–9, 197, 238; marriage, 188, 237; and Tsarevich, 192–3; given Garter, 238

Alexander, Grand Duke of Russia, 194

Alexander, King of Serbia, 24; proclaimed King, 25; assumes power, 27n; and mother, 27–8; marriage, 28–9, 34; scandal over heir, 29–30; assassinated, 32–3, 35

Alexander, Crown Prince of Serbia, 40, 43, 46, 282

Alexander Battenberg, Prince ('Sandro'), ruler of Bulgaria (later Count of Hartenau), 47–9, 56, 188, 229

Alexander, Prince of Hesse, 48n

Alexander Cuza, Prince, ruler of Wallachia & Moldavia (and Rumania), 20, 70, 72

Alexandra, Queen of Edward VII of England, 103, 188; Marie Feodorovna visits, 213; marriage, 223; and Bismarck's war with Denmark, 223–4, 263; social life, 234; relations with husband, 246–7; visits Germany, 262–4; and husband's infidelities, 267, 269

Alexandra Feodorovna, Tsarina of Nicholas II: marriage, xviii, 193–4; unpopularity, 194, 199, 211; character, 195; relations with husband, 198–9; children, 210; and Rasputin, 211; appearance and style, 219; heart complaint, 219–20; visits Balmoral, 258

Alexeyev, Admiral Eugene, 201–2

Alexis, Grand Duke of Russia, 192n

Alexis Nicolaievich, Tsarevich (son of Nicholas II), 210–11, 216

Alfonso XIII, King of Spain, 107, 270–1

Algecira conference (1906), 116

Alsace and Lorraine, 189

Anastasia, Grand Duchess of Russia, 8, 16–17, 211, 315

Andrássy, Count Gyula, 141n, 142–3

Anna, Princess of Battenberg, 9

Anna, Princess of Prussia, 123

Annunzio, Gabriele d', 175–6, 178

Antoinette Murat, Princess, 73

Antonia Koháry, Princess, 50

Aosta, Duke, 172

Aosta, Princess Hélène (of Orleans), Duchess of, 172

Arthur, Prince, Duke of Connaught, 104, 283, 285

Asquith, Herbert Henry, 13, 263, 272n, 283, 323–4, 326, 328

Assembly of Russian Factory and Mill Workers, 203

August Wilhelm, Prince (son of Kaiser), 91

Augusta Victoria, Empress of William II ('Dona'): marriage, 88, 91; character, 88–9, 94; friendship with Marie Esther Waldersee, 93; and William's threatened abdication, 112; military retinue, 114; visits England, 229, 262

Augustus, Prince of Saxe-Coburg-Gotha, 49

Augustus, Prince of Saxe-Coburg-Gotha (son of preceding), 50n, 59

Austria and Austro-Hungarian Empire: 1879 pact with Germany (Dual Alliance), xviii, 143, 187; annexes Bosnia and Herzegovina, 10–11, 22, 41–3, 59–60, 77, 108–10, 142, 147–52, 167, 213–15; and Balkan Wars, 13, 191, 311; and Serbia, 22–3, 40; development as power, 69; relations with Rumania, 77; constitution and government, 121–2, 127–8, 141–2; Piedmont war, 125–7; defence quadrilateral, 125–6; 1866 French treaty, 128; 1866 Prussian defeat, 129, 142, 225, 230; and 1867 Compromise with Hungary, 130–3, 141; racial composition, 131n; relations with Italy, 178–9; and Russo-French alliance, 191; supports Germany in war with Denmark, 224; relations with England, 260; 1914 ultimatum to Serbia and war danger, 287–90, 292, 294–7, 299–303, 309; partial mobilization, 306–7, 313; declares war, 308, 310, 313; bombards Belgrade, 314; and Russian involvement, 320; William urges restraint on, 322, 326; see also Franz Josef

Averescu, General Alexander, 72

Baccarat Case (1891), 236

Bach, Alexander von, 127

Bad Ischl, 137, 260–1, 286–7

Baillet-Latour, Count, 117

Balfour, Arthur James, 248, 252, 273

Balkans: opposition to Turks, 10, 216; Wars of 1912–13, 11–12, 15, 43, 65, 78, 115, 177, 216, 311; Ferdinand seeks alliance in, 65; Nicholas II and, 67, 213–16; Franz Ferdinand on, 154; Tisza on, 288; see also individual countries

Baratieri, General Oreste, 170

Barucci, Giulia, 235

Beatty, Admiral Sir David (later Earl), 218

Belcheff, Madame, 53

Belgium: and German war plans, 321, 325; invaded, 328

Belgrade: character, 27, 73; rebuilt, 39–40; Austrians bombard, 314

Benckendorff, Count Alexander, 13n, 242

Benedek, General Ludwig von, 129

Berchtold, Count Leopold: on Izvolski, 148–9; appointed Austrian foreign minister, 153; and start of 1914 war, 286–7, 290, 294–303, 329; declaration of war, 308, 311, 313; and German support, 320; rejects English mediation offer, 322

Berchtold, Countess Nandine, 149–51

Berlin: developed, 86–7

Berlin, Congress and Treaty of (1878), 10, 22, 47–8, 56, 142, 167, 187, 225

Bertie of Thame, Francis Leveson, 1st Viscount, 242

Bertrab, Lieut.-General, 292

Bethmann-Hollweg, Theobald von: supports Austrians, 115; character and dress, 115n; and Italian annexation of Libya, 177; and start of 1914 war, 289, 293n, 300, 327, 329; hinders Kaiser's mediation proposal, 308–9; rejects Grey's peace proposals, 310–11, 320–1; and Russian involvement, 316, 319; message of restraint to Tschirschky, 320; and German war plans, 321; on 'iron dice', 327; and English ultimatum, 328

Biarritz: Edward VII in, 268–72

Bilinski, Leon von, 287, 294n, 304

Bismarck, Prince Otto von: abolishes
Cumberland's kingdom, xvii; forms
German empire, xviii, 85–6, 222, 225;
and Prince Alexander of Serbia, 24;
on Coburgs, 50; deposed, 56, 94–5;
and Russian 'Re-insurance' Treaty,
96, 101, 143, 187; death, 97;
challenges Habsburgs for supremacy,
128, 130, 225; and Austrian
constitutional changes, 142; and
Hungary, 142; pact with Austria, 143;
and Italy, 166–9, 179; Tsar Alexander
III resents, 188; war with Denmark,
223–4, 263, 273; and Queen Victoria,
225, 230; see also Prussia

Björkö (Gulf of Finland), 101–3, 212,
260

'Black Hand' ('Crna Ruka'), 42, 155,
279–80

Blondel, Jean Camille, 78

Boer War, 106, 111, 231, 244–5

Bohemia, 141

Boisdeffre, General Raoul de, 189–91

Bojana, Lake, 13

Bonham, Sir George, 30, 37

Boris, Prince of Tirnovo, later King of
Bulgaria, 55–6, 172n

Borodino, Battle of (1812), 218

Bosnia: annexed by Austria, 10–11, 22,
41, 43, 59–60, 77, 108, 142, 147–52,
167, 213; and Turkey, 21, 148;
revolutionaries, 279–80

Boxer Rebellion (China, 1900), 99, 201

Brahm, Otto, 87

Brandon, Lieut., xix

Bresci, Gaetano, 171

Brindle, Monsignor, Bishop of
Nottingham, 271

Britain see England

Brodrick, St John, 248

Buchanan, Sir George, 59, 218, 327

Buchanan, James, 236

Bucharest, 69, 72–3

Bucharest, Treaty of (1913), 43, 78–9

Buchlau agreemen(1908), 149, 151, 267

Bulgaria: power ambitions, 7; freedom
from Turks, 11, 21, 46, 60; 'Greater',
22, 48, 66; 1884 Serbian war with, 23,

48; in Balkan Wars, 43, 65–7; Russia
rearms, 44; rulers appointed, 47, 49,
51–2; Turkish atrocities in, 47n;
relations with Russia, 48; supports
Central Powers, 68; and Rumania,
78; relations with Serbia, 151, 217; see
also Ferdinand

Bülow, Count Bernhard von: on 'Dona',
88; status, 95; on Kaiser, 98–9; and
Morocco, 100; and Björkö agreement,
101–3; threatens resignation, 103; and
Austrian annexation of Bosnia &
Herzegovina, 108–9, 214; and
Eulenberg scandal, 110; and Kaiser's
Daily Telegraph interview, 111; and
Kaiser's proposed abdication, 112;
dismissed, 114; on Queen Margherita
of Italy, 165–6; on Italy, 179; and
Empress Victoria's funeral, 246;
opposes Anglo-French entente, 255–6

Bunsen, Sir Maurice de, 297–8

Burns, John, 328n

Cabrinović, Nedeljko, 155, 279–82

Cairoli, Benedetto, 164

Cambon, Paul, 242, 245, 248–9, 256,
263

Cambon, Pierre Paul, 39

Campbell-Bannerman, Sir Henry, 256,
258, 267

Caneva, General, 177

Capelle, Admiral Eduard von, 292

Caprivi, Leo von, 95, 189

Carlos I, King of Portugal, 62, 250

Carnot, Marie François Sadi, 171, 191n

Carol I, King of Rumania: accession and
reign, 69–72, 222; treaty with Central
Powers, 70, 77, 80; character, 73, 75–
6, 330; marriage, 73, 75; and Nando's
infatuation, 75–6; international
relations, 77–8; death, 80; and
assassination of Franz Ferdinand,
283, 285; and start of war, 330; see also
Rumania

Caroline, Queen of Bavaria, 118

Carrington, Charles, 232

Carson, Sir Edward, 298

Caserio, Ieronimo, 171

Cassel, Sir Ernest, 235, 260, 269

Cavour, Count Camillo, 125, 157–8,
161, 166

Cetinje (Montenegro), 5–6, 15
Chaadayev, Peter, 185–7
Chamberlain, Joseph, 229
Charikov, 33, 213
Charles, Emperor of Austria, 154, 280
Charles I, King of Portugal see Carlos I
Charles Albert, Duke of Savoy, 178
Charles Anthony, Prince of
    Hohenzollern, 70
Charlotte, Empress of Mexico, 133, 134n
Charlotte, Princess of Brunswick-
    Wolfenbüttel, 184
Chaulet, Professor, 29–30
Cherniaev, General Mikhail, 21, 49n
Chlodwig, Prince of Hohenlohe-
    Schillingfürst, 95
Churchill, Winston L. S., 263
Clarendon, Edward Hyde Villiers, 5th
    Earl of, 224
Clemenceau, Georges, 267
Clementine, Princess (mother of
    Ferdinand of Bulgaria), 50, 53
Compromise of 1867 (Austria-
    Hungary), 130–2, 141
Connaught, Duke of see Arthur, Prince
Conrad von Hötzendorff, General
    Franz, 148, 151–5, 179, 287–8, 293,
    294n, 306, 329
Conrad Hohenlohe, Prince, 178
Conrad, Joseph, 185
Constantine, Grand Duke of Russia, 44,
    81, 188
Corfu, 90–1
Cornwallis-West, Daisy (Princess Mary
    Pless), 264
Corti, Count Egon Cesar, 167
Crimean War (1853–6), 125n, 187
Crispi, Francesco, 164, 166–70, 173–4
Crowe, Sir Eyre, 321
Cumberland, Duke and Duchess of, 303
Custozza, Battle of (1849), 120
Cyprus, 167, 226
Czechoslovaks, 141
Czernin, Count Otto, 79, 141n
Czuber, Bertha, 138

Dagmar, Princess of Denmark see Marie
    Feodorovna
Daily Telegraph: interview with Kaiser,
    110–11, 262

Danilo, Crown Prince of Montenegro, 3,
    9, 285
Danilo, Prince (uncle of King Nicholas
    of Montenegro), 6
Danilo Petrovich of Njegosh, ruler of
    Montenegro, 7, 14
Deák, Ferenc, 130
Dedeagach (Aegean port), 68
Delbrück, Clemens von, 293n
Delcassé, Theophile, 101, 256
Denmark: Prussian war with, 188, 224,
    263, 273
Depretis, Agostino, 173
Descos, Leon Coullara-, 45
Deville (mayor of Paris), 254
Dimitrievic, Captain Dragutin ('Apis'),
    31, 43–5, 155, 279–80
Disraeli, Benjamin, Earl of Beaconsfield,
    167, 226–7, 230, 237
Dobrovolski, General, 317–18
Dodecanese islands, 177
Dogali, Battle of (1887), 170, 175
Dogger Bank incident (1904), 212, 257,
    259
Draga (Mashin), Queen of Alexander of
    Serbia, 28–33, 35, 315n
Drouyn de Lhuys, Edouard, 245
Dual Alliance (Austro-Hungary and
    Germany), 143, 168, 187; see also
    Triple Alliance
Duma (Russian parliament), 207, 209–
    10
Dumaine, Alfred, 297–8
Dumba, Constantin von, 38

Eckhardstein, Baron Hermann von, 245
Edmonstone, Admiral Sir William, 268
Edward VII, King of England: relations
    with Kaiser, xxi, 103–8, 188, 201,
    228, 245–9, 261–2, 330; funeral, xxi,
    272–3; leadership of European
    society, 37, 232–3, 236; and Peter
    Karageorgević, 37–8; and Ferdinand
    of Bulgaria, 55, 58–9, 63; mistresses
    and affairs, 89, 235, 267–9; accession,
    104–5, 239–40; relations with
    Nicholas II, 108, 258–9; and German
    naval expansion, 113, 265; at spas
    (and 'spa diplomacy'), 149, 246–7,
    265–72; and Austrian annexation of

Bosnia & Herzegovina, 150; visits
Rome, 164; hostility to Prussia, 188,
228; and Russo-Japanese war, 212,
attitude to European powers, 221,
237–9, 273–4; marriage, 222–3; and
Prussian war with Denmark, 224;
restricted by Victoria, 231–2;
Rosebery gives access to secrets, 232;
upbringing, 232–3; life-style, 233–6,
260; visits USA, 236–7; visits India,
237; indifference to imperial title, 237,
241; attachment to France, 239;
cosmopolitanism, 241; advisers and
appointees, 241–3; and entente with
France, 245–6, 254–6, 273; secret
1903 European tour, 250–5; and
Russian alliance, 257–60; relations
with Franz Josef, 260–1; negotiations
with Germany, 261–2; 1909 visit to
Kaiser, 262–4; bronchitis, 265, 272;
and marriage of Alfonso XIII and Ena,
270–1; death, 272–3; influence, 273–4;
Kaiser blames for war, 322–3; and
start of war, 324; preaches peace, 330
Eggeling, Major Bernard von, 319
Egypt, 100, 255
Eitel Friedrich, Prince (Kaiser's second
son), xx, 112n
Elena, Queen of Victor Emmanuel III of
Italy: marriage, 8, 171–2; and Balkan
Wars, 14; as Queen, 171–2; children,
172; and Italian foreign affairs, 178;
and Sarajevo assassination, 283
Eleonore (of Reuss), Queen of
Ferdinand of Bulgaria, 62–3
Elisabeth, Empress of Austria ('Sisi'): in
Corfu, 90; marriage, 124, 287; and
Hungarian Compromise, 133;
declining marriage relations and
travels, 134–5, 139; and death of
Rudolph, 140; stabbed to death, 140,
171; greets Italian king and queen,
168n
Elisabeth, Princess of Hesse (later Grand
Duchess of Russia), 88
Elisabeth, Princess (daughter of
Rudolph), 138
Elisabeth (of Wied), Queen of Rumania
('Carmen Sylva'), 63, 73–7, 222
Elisabeth, Princess of Saxony, Duchess
of Genoa, 163

Elise, Queen of Prussia, 123
Ellenborough, Lady, 121
Emmanuel II, King of Portugal, 62
Ena, Queen of Alfonso XIII of Spain
(Victoria Eugenie), 107, 270–1
England (Great Britain): suspends
relations with Serbia, 37–8; relations
with Germany, 103–8, 112, 221–8,
244–5; agreements with Russia, 108,
217–18, 257–9; and German naval
expansion, 115, 265; Russian
suspicion of, 190; entente with
France, 245–6, 254–8; and naval
standard, 263; and start of 1914 War,
298–9, 310–11, 323–4; attempted
peace mediation, 320, 323; and
German war plans, 321; hesitates
over declaring war, 327–8
Entente Cordiale (France & England),
245–6, 254–8
Ernescu, Georges, 74
Ernest, Duke of Saxe-Coburg-Gotha,
243n
Ernst August, Prince, Duke of
Brunswick and Lüneburg: marriage,
xvii–xx; and Hanoverian throne, xviii;
son, xx
Esher, Reginald Baliol Brett, 2nd
Viscount, 241, 263
Ethiopia: Italy and, 170
Eugénie, Empress of Napoleon III of
France, 226, 239
Eulenburg, Count Philipp zu, 93, 96,
106; disgraced, 110, 114

Falk, General von, xix
Falkenhayn, General Erich von, 292
Fashoda incident (1898), 227–8, 252
Faure, Felix, 58
'February Patent' (Austria), 128
Ferdinand I, Emperor of Austria, 118–
19
Ferdinand, King of Bulgaria: described,
49–51, 62–3; accepts crown of
Bulgaria, 49, 51, 229; court, 52; first
marriage, 52–5; mistresses, 53; son's
religion, 55–6; recognized, 56, 59;
deposes Stamboloff, 56–7; relations
with European monarchs, 58–9, 63–4;
relations with Austria, 60; declares

himself Tsar, 60, 62, 213, 217;
homosexuality, 62; remarries, 62–3;
international political manoeuvres,
63–6; awarded Golden Fleece, 64;
borrowings, 64; extravagance, 65;
attacks Macedonia, 67, 78; supports
Central Powers, 68; threatened by
Nicholas II, 217; at Marienbad, 268;
Tisza lures, 288; and start of 1914
War, 329

Ferdinand I, King of Rumania
('Nando'), 74–7, 80

Ferdinand Karl, Archduke of Austria,
138

Fisher, Admiral John Arbuthnot, 1st
Baron, 241, 259

Flahault, General Auguste, Count de,
244

Flotow, Baron Hans von, 296

France: alliance with Russia, xix, 189–
91, 217–18, 227, 245, 257; aid and
influence in Serbia, 39, 73; influence
in Rumania, 73; aid for Rumania, 79;
1870 defeat by Prussians, 85–6, 142,
161, 189, 227, 230; primacy in
Morocco, 100–1; expansion in Africa,
167; relations with Italy, 167–9; and
Nicholas II, 215–16; and German-
Austrian mobilization, 191; 1870
republic, 227; Edward VII's affection
for, 239; entente with England, 245–6,
254–8; Edward visits (1903), 252–5;
German hostility to, 256–7; English
military support for, 262–3; and start
of 1914 War, 297–9, 301, 310;
promises support for Russia, 318; and
German war strategy, 321;
mobilization, 324; and English
hesitation, 327–8

Franz Ferdinand, Archduke of Austria:
assassinated, 46, 79, 154, 156, 275,
279–82; visits Rumania, 77; antipathy
to Hungary, 77–8, 146–7; as successor
to throne, 139; courtship and
marriage, 143–6, 262, 274; political
aims, 146–7; and Balkans, 154;
foresees death, 154–5, 280; burial,
154, 285–6; despises Italy, 179;
Kaiser invites to 1914 naval exercises,
180; visit to Windsor, 274;

international reactions to death, 282–
4

Franz Josef, Emperor of Austro-
Hungary: as godfather to Ernst's son,
xx; recognizes Peter Karageorgević,
36–7; and Bulgarian religious
problems, 55; and Ferdinand of
Bulgaria, 58–60, 64; gives precedence
to Kaiser over Edward, 104; and
annexation of Bosnia & Herzegovina,
109, 147, 150–2, 213–14; reign, 117,
119–23; accession, 119; appearance,
119; relations with army, 120–1;
constitutional changes, 121–2, 127–8,
141–2; marriage, 123–4; stabbed, 122;
Piedmont defeat, 126–8; Königgratz
defeat, 129–30, 142; and 1867
Hungarian Compromise, 131–3, 147;
declining marriage relations, 134–5,
138–40; and Katharina Schratt, 135,
137; life style and work, 135–8, 153;
image, 136–7, 141; family scandals
and tragedies, 138–41; meets Nicholas
II, 143, 147; and Franz Ferdinand's
marriage, 145–6; decline and fatigue,
152; 60th anniversary of reign, 152–3;
and Franz Ferdinand's Sarajevo visit,
155–6, 280; greets Italian king, 168n;
Queen Victoria's attitude to, 226; and
Boer War, 231; on Mensdorff's
anglophilia, 242; relations with
Edward, 260–1, 267; visits
Marienbad, 268; and assassination of
Franz Ferdinand, 282, 286, 305;
bronchitis, 286; and start of 1914 War,
286–8, 290–1, 295–7, 299–300, 302–5,
322; reaction to prospect of war,
304–6; agrees to mobilization, 306–7;
Kaiser urges restraint on, 322; and
control of troops, 326; responsibility
for war, 330

Franz Karl, Prince of Austria, 118–19

Frederica, Princess of Hanover, 270

Frederick III, Emperor of Germany, 83,
85, 105, 229

Frederick, Duke of Holstein-Gottorp,
184

Frederick Augustus, Crown Prince of
Saxony, 54

Frederick William IV, King of Prussia,
123

Frederick, Archduke of Austria, 144
Freycinet, Charles de, 189, 191
Fullon, General, 203
Fürstenberg, Karl Egon IV, Fürst zu, 94
Fürstenberg, Irma, Fürstin (née Schönborn), 94
Fürstenberg, Maximilian Egon, Fürst zu, 93–4, 96, 111

Gapon, Father George, 203, 205
Garibaldi, General Giuseppe, 157
Gavrilović, Mihajlo, 282
Genchich, George, 32
George V, King of England: at Ernst-Victoria wedding, xvii, xix–xx, 64; as godfather to Ernst-Victoria's son, xx; 1913 official birthday, xx–xxi; coronation, 62; and Ferdinand, 65, 67–8; and foreign affairs, 221, 274; and Kaiser, 274; entertains Franz Ferdinand, 274; and Sarajevo assassination, 283; and start of 1914 war, 312; telegrams to and from Nicholas II, 324, 329; Kaiser negotiates with for peace, 325–7; Belgian appeal to, 328; strives for peace, 330
George VI, King of England: speech impediment, 84
George, Crown Prince of Serbia, 40, 43, 214
George Petrovich (Karageorge), Prince of Serbia, 18–19, 22, 36
German League, 130
Germany: 1879 pact with Austria (Dual Alliance), xviii, 143, 187; and Serbia, 41; provides rulers for Turkish ex-provinces, 47; relations with Rumania, 77, 79; empire formed, 85–6, 222; growth and power, 86; 1887 treaty with Russia, 96; 1905 attempted treaty with Russia, 101; relations with Britain, 103–8, 112, 221–8, 244–5; and Austrian annexation of Bosnia & Herzegovina, 109–10, 214-15; naval expansion, 111–13, 115, 248, 261–3, 265; prepares for war, 115–16; challenges Austria, 130, 142; opposes Russia and Slavs, 142–3; and Italy's membership

of Triple Alliance, 179; and Russo-French alliance, 191, 217; opposes Anglo-French alliance, 255–7; influence in Russia, 258; and start of 1914 War, 228–91, 293–4, 296, 299–301; rejects Grey's mediation proposals, 301, 310–12; attempts to mediate for Austria, 307–8; war strategy, 321, 325; mobilization, 324; invades Luxembourg and Belgium, 328; see also Prussia; William II
Giers, Nikolai, 189–91
Giesl von Gieslingen, Baron Wladimir von, 13, 300, 302–3, 306
Giolitti, Giovanni, 173–7
Giron, Monsieur, 54
Gisela, Princess of Bavaria, 303
Gladstone, William Ewart, 230, 244
Goluchowski, Count Agenor, 89, 141n, 148
Gordon, General Charles George, 230–1
Gordon-Cumming, Sir William, 236
Goremykin, Ivan Logginovich, 209
Goschen, Sir Edward, xx–xxi, 262, 321, 328–9
Granier, Jeanne, 253
Granville, Granville George Leveson-Gower, 2nd Earl, 230, 238
Greece, 11, 229
Grenaud, Comte de, 52
Grey, Sir Edward: and Balkan Wars, 13; and Serbian regicides, 38; and German naval expansion, 113; and Cassel, 235; and Anglo-French alliance, 256, 263; on Edward's proposed meeting with Nicholas II, 258; meets Franz Ferdinand, 274; attempted mediation before 1914 War, 298–9, 310–11, 320–2; on Austrian ultimatum to Serbia, 301–2; talks with George V, 312; offers to guarantee French neutrality, 325; and invasion of Belgium, 328
Grillparzer, Franz, 121
Gyulai, Count Ferencz, 125

Habsburg monarchy: fortunes, 117–19, 121, 128, 130; scandals and tragedies, 138–40; pedigree, 183; see also Franz Josef

Haldane, Richard Burdon, Viscount, 263, 268
Harden, Maximilian, 87
Hardinge, Sir Charles (*later* 1st Baron): on 1905 Russian revolution, 204–5; as Edward's adviser, 241–2; accompanies Edward to France, 251; and alliance with Russia, 257; and Austria, 260; negotiations with Germany, 261
Hartwig, Nikola Hendrikovich, 302
Hauptmann, Gerhart, 87
Heeringen, Admiral von, 115
Helena, Duchess of Bavaria, 123–4
Hélène, Princess, Grand Duchess of Russia, 44
Henry, Prince of Prussia (Kaiser's brother), 98, 312, 325–6
Hermann, Prince of Wied, 75
Herzegovina: annexed by Austria, 10–11, 22, 41, 43, 59–60, 77, 108, 142, 147–52, 167, 213; and Turkey, 148
Hilde, Princess of Dessau, 222
Hohenwart, Count Karl Sigmund, 141–2
Holstein, Baron Frederick von, 96, 100
Homburg (Germany), 246–7
Horowitz, Emil von, 134
Hoyos, Count Alexander von, 291, 296, 302
Hristić, Artemisia, 24, 26
Huguet, Colonel Auguste, 263
Hülsen-Haeseler, Count Dietrich, 111
Humbert of the White Hands, 158–9
Humbert I (Umberto), King of Italy: accession and reign, 163–6; and Rome feuds, 164; attempted assassination, 164; mistresses, 165; meets Franz Josef, 168n; and Sicilian unrest, 169; and Ethiopia, 170; assassinated, 171, 173
Humbert II (Umberto), King of Italy, 172
Hungary: Franz Ferdinand's antipathy to, 77–8, 146–7; and Rumania, 78; 1848 revolution, 118, 120; and Austrian constitutional changes, 128, 141; 'Compromise of 1867' with Austria, 130–3, 141, 147; and Bismarck, 142; Compromise

decennial reviews, 147; pro-English, 226; *see also* Austria and Austro-Hungarian Empire

Ianushkevic, General, 317–18
India, 230, 237
Isabella, Archduchess of Austria, 144, 146
Ischl *see* Bad Ischl
Italy: in Triple Alliance, xviii, 168, 178–9; unification, 128, 157, 164; territorial claims, 167, 178; colonial expansion in Africa, 168, 170, 175–7; political democratization and reforms, 173–5; population, 174; industrial economy, 174–5; relations with Austria, 178–9; supports mediation to prevent 1914 war, 310; position in War, 326n, 327
Izvolski, Alexander Petrovich: and Serbia, 41; and Ferdinand, 61; character, 148–9; and Bosnia/Herzegovina annexation, 149–51, 213; and Racconigi Bargain with Italy, 179; transferred to Paris, 216; and Edward VII, 257, 267; at Marienbad, 267

Jagow, Gottlieb von, 298, 300, 307
Japan: defeats Russia (1904), 200–2, 212–13, 257; 1902 pact with England, 257
Jews: in Rumania, 71; and Russian pogroms, 203, 209; Edward VII's friendship with, 233, 235
Joanna, Queen of Bulgaria, 172n
Joffre, General Joseph Jacques Césaire, 324–5
Johann Salvator, Archduke (*later* Johan Orth), 138
John, King of Saxony, 129
John VIII Paleologus, Emperor of Constantinople, 184
Joseph II, Emperor of Austria, 14, 119
Julia (Hauke), Princess of Hesse, 48n
Junkers (of Prussia), 113–14
Jutta, Princess (wife of Prince Danilo), 9

Kailer, Rear-Admiral von, 294n
Kalcheff, Konstantin, 49

Kanner, Heinrich, 304
Karageorgević clan and dynasty
    (Serbia), 18–20, 23, 34, 329
Karl Ludwig, Archduke of Austria, 139,
    141, 143n, 145
Kaulbars, General Nikolai, 49
Kchessinska, Mathilde, 193
Kechko family, 23
Keppel, Alice Frederica, 89, 268–9,
    271–2
Keppel, Rear-Admiral Sir Colin, 324
Keppel, Hon. George, 268–9
Kerzl, Dr (Franz Josef's physician),
    286
Ketteler, Baron von, 99
Khartoum, 230–1
Khodynka meadow disaster, 195, 197,
    205
Kinsky family, 144
Knollys, Sir Francis (later 1st Viscount),
    59, 204, 241, 250
Königgratz, Battle of (1866), 129, 142,
    161
Konopischt (Bohemia), 284
'Köpenick, Captain of', 114
Kossuth, Lajos, 120, 130, 132
Kostić, Major Ljuba, 38
Kostroma (Russia), 220
Kotor (Dalmatia), 4
Krobatin, Alexander von, 294n
Kruger, Paul, 106n
Kühlmann, Richard von, 100
Kuropatkin, General Aleksei
    Nikolaevich, 202
Kutuzov, General, 56
Kyrill, Prince of Preslav, 56

Lamsdorff, Count Vladimir N., 102
Land and Freedom Party (Russia), 186
Langtry, Lillie, 266–8
Lansdowne, Henry Charles Keith
    Petty-Fitzmaurice, 5th Marquess of,
    107, 244–5, 247–9, 251, 255–6, 274
Lanza, Giovanni, 161
Lascelles, Sir Frank, 106, 262
Lausanne, Treaty of (1912), 177
Law, Andrew Bonar, 323, 328
Lazarević, Colonel Luka, 38
Léger (architect), 39
Léhar, Franz: 'The Merry Widow', 3

Lenin, Vladimir Ilyich, 207
Leo XIII, Pope, 55, 251–2
Leopold II, King of the Belgians, 50n,
    222
Leopold, Prince, Duke of Albany, 104
Leopold Ferdinand, Duke of Tuscany,
    138
Leopoldine, Princess (daughter of Pedro
    II of Brazil), 50n
Libenyi, Janos, 122
Libya, 168, 175–7, 179
Lichnowsky, Prince Karl Max, 13n, 298,
    301, 311, 325–6
Lipton, Sir Thomas, 234
Litta, Duchess, 165, 171
Lloyd George, David, 268
Loisinger, Joanna (wife of Alexander of
    Bulgaria), 49
London, Treaty of (1913), 43
Lonsdale, William Lowther, 2nd Earl
    of, 249
Loubet, Emile, 249, 251
Louis Philippe, Emperor of France, 50
Louis Philippe, Crown Prince of
    Portugal, 62
Louise, Princess of Saxony, 54, 138
Louise, Princess (daughter of Leopold II
    of Belgium), 50n
Luccheni, Luigi, 140, 171
Lunyeritsa family (Serbia), 29
Lützow, Count Heinrich von, 89
Luxembourg, 325, 328

Macedonia, 43, 66–8
Mafalda, Princess of Italy, 172
Magee, William Connor, Bishop of
    Peterborough, 233
Magyars see Hungary
Mahdi, 230
Marchand, Captain Jean-Baptiste, 252
Margherita, Queen of Humbert I of
    Italy, 163–6, 168n, 170–1, 174
Margutti, Baron Albert von, 303–4, 306
Maria Christina, Princess (daughter of
    Archduchess Isabella), 145
Maria Theresa, Archduchess of Austria,
    145
Marie, Princess of Altenburg, 222
Marie, Princess of Hohenzollern-
    Sigmaringen, 222

Marie, Princess of the Netherlands, 222

Marie, Princess (wife of Ferdinand of Rumania), 75–7

Marie Feodorovna, Empress of Alexander III of Russia (Princess Dagmar): marriage, 188, 194–5, 237; children, 192; popularity, 194; relations with Alexandra, 195; letters from Nicholas II, 200, 208, 213, 215, 216

Marie-Louise, Queen of Ferdinand of Bulgaria, 54–6

Marie Paulovna, Grand Duchess of Russia, 62

Marie Valerie, Princess of Austro-Hungary, 133

Marienbad (Bohemia), 265–8

Marlborough House set, 234

Mary, Queen of George V of England, xviii, xix, 274

Mashin, Colonel Alexander, 32, 38

Mashin, Nikodem, 29, 31

Massimo, Princess, 162

Mathilde, Archduchess of Austria, 163

Maximilian I, Emperor of Austria, 137

Maximilian (Ferdinand Max), Emperor of Mexico, 133–4, 161

Mayerling tragedy (1889), 139

Mazzani, Giuseppe, 157–8

Menabrea, General Luigi Federico, 163

Menelik, Emperor of Ethiopia, 170

Mensdorff-Pouilly, Count Albert, 13n, 68, 242, 269, 301

Messel, Alfred, 86

Metternich, Prince Klemens Wenzel, 117, 119, 122, 127

Metternich, Count Paul, 108, 243, 298

Mexico, 133–4, 161

Michael (Romanov), Tsar of Russia, 183, 220

Michael, Grand Duke of Russia (brother of Tsar Nicholas II), 210

Michael Obrenović, Prince of Serbia, 19, 31

Mihai the Brave, Prince of Wallachia, 69

Milan Obrenović, King of Serbia (later Count of Takovo): reign, 20–2; marriage, 23–5; abdicates, 25, 29; settlement, 26–7

Milena, Queen of Nicholas of Montenegro, 8

Militza, Grand Duchess of Russia, 8, 14–17, 211, 315

Miloš Obrenović, Prince of Serbia, 19

Mirko, Prince of Montenegro, 9

Mišić, Colonel Živojin, 38

Mlada Bosna movement, 279n

Moldavia, 69, 71

Moltke, General Helmuth von, 115, 292–3, 321, 325

Monson, Sir Edmund, 249, 251

Montagu-Stuart-Wortley, Colonel, 111n

Montebello, Marquis de, 195

Montenegro: described, 3–5; status, 5–6; power ambitions, 7, 9; wins freedom from Turks, 10–14, 21, 43, 177, 216; relations with Serbia, 16, 44, 304; Italy and, 178; and Sarajevo assassination, 283

Montenuovo, Prince Alfred, 146, 285

Mordaunt, Lady Harriet, 235

Morley, John, Viscount, 328n

Morocco, 100–1, 176, 245, 255–6

Morosini, Countess Anna, 89

Morsey, Baron Andreas von, 284

Mountbatten, Edwina, Countess of (née Ashley), 235n

Müller, Admiral Georg Alexander von, 115

Muraviev, Count Mikhail Nikolaevich, 148

Mussolini, Benito, 178n

Musulin, Baron Alfred von, 296

Napoleon III, Emperor of the French: and Piedmont, 125–6, 158; 1866 treaty with Austria, 128; and Mexican Emperor, 133, 160–1; and Italy, 160; defeat by Prussians, 161, 227; Queen Victoria's relations with, 227; flight to England, 227; Edward and, 239

Narodna Odbrana (National Defence), 42, 301

Natalie, Princess (wife of Prince Mirko), 9

Nathalie (Kechko), Queen of Milan of Serbia, 23–4, 26–8

Neue Freie Presse, 16

Nicholas ('Nikita'), King of
Montenegro: character and
appearance, 5–7; children's
marriages, 8–10, 34, 36; in Balkan
Wars, 10–14, 65; and Serbian threat,
11; yields Scutari, 14, 154; revenues,
14–16; connections with Austria, 15–
16; and Peter Karageorgević, 36; and
Sarajevo assassination, 282; and start
of 1914 War, 315, 329
Nicholas I, Tsar of Russia, 186
Nicholas II, Tsar of Russia: at Ernst-
Victoria wedding, xviii, xx, 64; as
godfather to Ernst-Victoria's son, xx;
and Montenegro, 16; recognizes Peter
Karageorgević, 36; and Serbian
appeal for help, 41, 44–5, 115; and
Bulgaria, 55; and Ferdinand, 58, 60–
1, 64, 67; and Balkans, 67, 213–17;
visits Carol of Rumania, 79; Kaiser
meets at Björkö, 101–3, 212, 260;
meets Edward VII, 108, 258; and
Austrian annexation of Bosnia &
Herzegovina, 109, 150–2, 214–16;
meets Franz Josef, 143, 147; Victor
Emmanuel supports, 178–9; character
and upbringing, 192–3, 198–200, 211;
marriage, 193–4; coronation, 195,
198; separation from people, 196–7,
205, 209–11; reign, 197–8, 200; and
Russo-Japanese war, 200–2, 212–13;
and 1905 revolution, 203–5, 208;
establishes parliament and
constitutional reforms, 207–9; and
English alliance, 217–18, 259–60; and
Russian readiness for war, 220;
relations with Edward, 238, 258–60;
hears of Sarajevo assassination, 285;
and war threat, 292; and Russian
mobilization, 313–14, 317–18, 324;
Kaiser negotiates with, 314–17, 329;
telegrams to and from George V, 324,
329; responsibility for war, 330
Nicholas Nicolaievich, Grand Duke of
Russia, 8, 206
Nicolson, Sir Arthur (later 1st Baron
Carnock), 57, 209, 309

Obolensky, Prince Alexei, 208
Obrenović clan (Serbia), 18–20, 25, 29,
33

Obruchev, General, 190
'October Diploma' (Austria), 127
Odessa (Russia), 206
Olga, Grand Duchess of Russia, 258
Orient Express (railway train), 64–5
Orloff, Prince, 259
Otto, Archduke of Austria, 138
Ottoman Empire (Turkey): Montenegro
wins freedom from, 10; and Balkan
Wars (1912–13), 11–14, 43, 65–6,
177, 216; occupies Serbia, 18; Serbia
resists, 20–2; Tsar divides, 22; bought
off over Bosnia and Herzegovina, 41;
Bulgarian independence from, 60;
regains territory, 68; Rumanian
independence from, 70; 'Young
Turks' in, 148; and Italians in Libya,
176–8; Russian war with, 225

Pacu, Laza, 300
Paléologue, Maurice, 211, 220, 315
Palmerston, Henry John Temple, 3rd
Viscount, 224–5, 237
pan-Slavism, 41–3, 148, 186, 214
Panitza, Major, 53, 56–7
Panther (German gunboat), 113, 176
Paris: Edward VII's 1903 visit to, 253–5
Paris Exhibition (1878), 239
Parma, 126n
Pasic, Nikola, 38–9, 41–2, 44–5, 214,
217, 280; and start of war, 300n; reply
to Austrian ultimatum, 302, 307
Passanante, Giovanni, 164
Paul, Grand Duke of Russia, 192n
Pedro II, Emperor of Brazil, 50n
Peleş Castle (Rumania), 76
Peleşor (palace, Rumania), 77
'People's Will' (Russia), 186
Persia, 258, 259n
Peter I (the Great), Tsar of Russia, 14,
184–6
Peter, Grand Duke of Russia, 8, 15
Peter, Prince of Montenegro, 9
Peter Karageorgević, King of Serbia:
marriage, 8, 36; accession, 16, 34–7;
described, 35–6; recognition, 36–9;
and Serbian national prosperity, 40;
and 'Greater Serbia', 43; seeks
Russian alliance, 44–5, 214;
abdicates, 45, 282; Nicholas II and,

150; and 1909 Austrian ultimatum, 215; threatened by Nicholas II, 217
Petroff, Colonel and Madame, 53
Petrovich family (Montenegro), 7–10
Petrovich, General, 32
Philip, Prince of Saxe-Coburg-Gotha, 50n, 59
Philip of Lyons (French mystic), 211
Piedmont, 125, 157, 163
'pig war' (1913), 43
Pius IX, Pope, 123, 163
Plehve, Vyacheslav, 202–3
Pless, Princess Mary see Cornwallis-West, Daisy
Plevna, Battle of (1878), 70
Plunkett, Sir Francis, 152
Pobedonostsev, Constantin, 187, 192–3
Poincaré, Raymond, 217, 297, 314
Ponsonby, Frederick ('Fritz'), 253–4, 259, 266
Popović, Colonel Damjan, 38
Popović, General, 45
Port Arthur, 200–2
Potapov, General, 15
Potemkin (Russian battle-cruiser), 206
Pourtalès, Count Friedrich von, 214, 309–10, 319, 327
Prague, Treaty of (1866), 130
Princip, Gavrilo: assassinates Franz Ferdinand, 79, 155–6, 275, 279–83, 286, 329; death in prison, 282n
Prussia: 1870 war with France, 85–6, 142, 189, 230; 1866 defeat of Austria, 128–9, 142, 225, 230; invades Schleswig-Holstein, 188, 224; see also Bismarck, Prince Otto von; Germany
Punch (magazine), 95

Racconigi Bargain (1909), 178–9
Radetzky, General Johann, 118, 120, 125, 127
Rasputin, Gregory Efimovich, 211–12, 216n, 219
Reed, Sir James, 265
Reid, Whitelaw, 242
Reval (now Tallinn), 259
Revolutions of 1848–9, 119–21
Ribot, Alexandre, 189–91
Risler, Edouard, 151
Risorgimento (1861), 157–8, 160–1

Ristić, Jovan, 26
Robert, Duke of Bourbon-Parma, 54–5
Rodzianko, Michael, 219
Romanov dynasty, 183–4; 300th anniversary, 219; see also individual rulers
Rome: as Italian capital, 161–3; royal court, 164–6, 173
Roosevelt, Franklin Delano, 84
Roosevelt, Theodore, 202
Rosa, Queen of Emmanuel II of Italy ('La Rosina'; Countess Mirafiore; née Vercellana), 160, 162, 165
Rosebery, Archibald Primrose, 5th Earl of, 232, 274
Rothschild, Sir Anthony de, 233
Rothschild, Leopold de, 233
Rozhdestvenski, Admiral Zinovi Petrovich, 202, 257n
Rudolph, Crown Prince of Austria, 124, 138–9; death, 139, 284
Rumania: in Balkan Wars, 67–8, 70, 78; stability, 69, 71–2; independence, 70; treaty with Central Powers, 70, 77, 80; economy, 71; peasant unrest in, 71–2; international relations, 77–9; in war against Germany, 80; and Franz Ferdinand, 283; see also Carol I
Rumelia, Eastern, 48
Rumerskirch, Baron Carl, 285
Russia: alliance with France, xix, 189–91, 217–18, 227, 245, 257; and Balkan Wars, 11, 14; aids Montenegro, 14–16; relations with Serbia, 40–1, 44, 115; and Bulgaria, 48–9, 66; seeks gateway in Balkans, 69–70; relations with Rumania, 77–9; Bismarck's 're-insurance' treaty with, 96, 101, 143, 187; attempted 1905 treaty with Germany, 101; 1907 agreement with England, 108, 257–9; German-Austrian resistance to, 142–3; Franz Ferdinand's policy on, 147; isolation and westernization, 184–7; reforms, 186; revolutionaries in, 186–7, 189; under Alexander III, 187–9; 1904 defeat by Japan, 200–2, 212–13, 257; 1905 revolution, 202–8; pogroms, 203, 209; Duma established, 207, 209–10; and Austrian annexation of Bosnia &

Herzegovina, 213–14; rearms, 217; alliance with England, 217–18, 245, 257–8; readiness for war, 220; war with Turkey, 225; Victoria's antipathy to, 226–7, 230; Edward's sympathy for, 237–9; and Austrian 1914 war threats, 291, 294, 297, 299, 301, 309, 311; peace proposals, 309; mobilization for war, 313–14, 317–19, 320n, 324; and German war plans, 325; and English hesitation over war, 328; declares war, 329; *see also* Nicholas II

Sadowa, Battle of (1866), 225
St Petersburg, 184, 203–6
Salisbury, Robert Arthur Talbot Gascoigne-Cecil, 3rd Marquess of, 50, 54, 104, 227, 244–5, 274
San Giuliano, Marquis Antonio di, 107, 176
San Stefano, Treaty of (1878), 21
Sanjak of Novi Pazar, 11–12, 142
Santa Fiore, Vincenza, Countess of, 165
Sarajevo: assassination of Franz Ferdinand at, 46, 79, 116, 154–6, 275; described, 279–83; and start of 1914 War, 191; report on, 302–3
Sardinia, 157, 159
Savoff, Colonel and Madame, 56–7
Savoy, House of, 157–60, 168; *see also* Italy
Sazanov, Sergei Dimitrievich, 14, 309–10, 313, 317–18, 327
'Scala' (road, Montenegro), 4
Schleswig-Holstein, 223–4
Schlieffen Plan, 321
Schratt, Katharina, 135, 137, 139, 145
Schwarzenberg, Prince Felix, 121–2, 127, 129
Scutari (Shkoder), 12–14, 16, 154, 304
Sedan, Battle of (1870), 161
Serbia: and Montenegro, 5, 11, 16, 304; power ambitions, 7; opposition to Turkey and Balkan Wars, 11, 13, 20–2, 43, 216; rulers, 18–20, 26–7, 35; relations with Austria, 22–3; government, 22–3, 26–7; war with Bulgaria, 23, 48; 1888 constitution, 25, 29; army revolt, 31; England

suspends relations with, 37; French influence in, 39; Ferdinand and, 67–8; national resurgence, 40; relations with Russia, 40–1, 44, 115, 214, 217; and pan-Slavism ('Greater Serbia'), 41–5, 148, 329; and Austrian annexation of Bosnia & Herzegovina, 41–2, 60, 150–1, 215; acquires Macedonia, 43; Carol of Rumania supports, 79; army, 217; and Sarajevo assassination, 280, 282, 297; Austrian ultimatum and start of 1914 War, 288–91, 293–302, 309; reply to Austria, 302–3; and Austrian mobilization, 306; and Austrian declaration of war, 308, 310, 313; Austrian occupation of, 326, 329
Serbian Literary Herald, 39
Serge, Grand Duke of Russia, 88, 192n, 205
Sermoneta, Duke of, 164
Shebeko, Count Nikolai Nikolaievich, 297
Sherman, General William Tecumseh, 49
Sicily, 169
Sidonie, Princess of Saxony, 123
Simplicissimus (journal), 87
Slavs: German-Austrian resistance to, 142–3; *see also* pan-Slavism
Slivnitsa, Battle of (1885), 23
Socialist Revolutionary Party (Russia), 205
Sofia, 53
Solferino, Battle of (1859), 125, 127
Sophie, Archduchess (mother of Franz Josef), 118–19, 123, 135n
Sophie, Duchess of Hohenberg (wife of Franz Ferdinand): assassinated, 77, 279, 281; marriage, 144–5, 156, 274; status, 146; visit to Sarajevo arranged, 155, 280; funeral, 285n
Sophie, Princess of Saxe-Coburg-Saalfeld, 243n
Soveral, Marquis Luis Augusto Pinto de, 116, 249–50, 251n, 272–3
Spain, 271
Spring-Rice, Sir Cecil, 242
Stamboloff, Stefan, 51, 54–7; assassinated, 57
Stamfordham, Arthur John Bigge, Baron, xxi

Stefan Dušan, Tsar of Serbia, 18
Stephanie, Princess (wife of Rudolph), 138
Stewart, Bertrand, xix
Stoiloff, Constantin, 57
Stolypin, Peter Arkadyevich, 211, 259
Stolzing, Colonel von, xxi
Strangford, Emily Anne Smyth, Viscountess, 6–7, 10
Strauss, Johann, the elder, 120
Strauss, Oscar: *The Chocolate Soldier*, 52
Stubel, Milli, 138
Stürgkh, Count Karl, 294n
Sudan, 230
Suez Canal, 225
Sukhomlinov, General Vladimir Alexandrovich, 44, 317
Süsskind, General von, xix
'Sylvester Patent' (1851: 'New Year's Decree'), 121
Szögenyi-Marich, Count Ladislaus, 291

Taft, Robert, 242
Talleyrand, Charles Maurice, 292
Tangier, 100, 176, 255–6
Tenniel, Sir John, 95
Theodosius, Metropolitan, 25
Thesiger, Wilfred, 37
Thrace, 65–6, 68
Three Emperors' League (or Alliance), 143, 147, 187–8
Timok rebellion, Serbia (1883), 23
Tirpitz, Grand Admiral Alfred von, 115, 284, 293
Tisza de Boros-Jenö, Count Stephen, 287–8, 290, 294–7, 320
Tittoni, Tommaso, 179
Togo, Admiral Heihachiro, 202
Toselli, Enrico, 54
Transylvania, 69, 77
Trench, Captain, xix
Trentino, 167
Trieste, 167, 178
Triple Alliance (Germany/Austria/Italy), xviii–xix, 107, 168, 178–9, 190–1
Triple Entente (France/Russia/England), xix, 101
Tsarskoe Selo (Russia), 199
Tschirschky, Count Heinrich von, 101, 261, 288–9, 308, 320

Tsushima, Battle of (1904), 202
Tunisia, 167
Turkey *see* Ottoman Empire
Tweedmouth, Edward Marjoribanks, 2nd Baron, 113
Tyrol, South, 168

United States of America: Edward VII visits (as Prince of Wales), 236–7

Vacarescu, Helen, 75–6
Vaglia, General Ponzio, 166
Varesanin, General Marian, 279n
Vassiltchikov, Prince, 205n
Vatican (Holy See): and *Risorgimento*, 161–2; Edward VII visits, 251–2
Venetia, 128
Venice, 161
Vera, Princess of Montenegro, 9–10
Vetsera, Marie, 139
Victor Emmanuel II, King of Italy: accession and reign, 157, 159, 161–2, 165; death, 163; foreign policy, 166–7; monument to, 176
Victor Emmanuel III, King of Italy: marriage, 8, 171; and Montenegrin demands, 13–14, 178; birth, 163–4; appearance and character, 171–2; accession and reign, 171–2; democratic style, 173; and occupation of Libya, 176–7; foreign affairs, 178–9; and Kaiser, 179–80; and Edward VII's visit, 252; and Sarajevo assassination, 283; position in 1914 War, 326n
Victor Emmanuel, Duke of Savoy, 178
Victoria, Queen of England: dynastic connections, xviii; and Alexander of Bulgaria, 49; and Ferdinand of Bulgaria, 50, 54; and Kaiser's arm treatment, 84; on Germany, 86; on Kaiser, 104, 228–9; on Romanovs, 183; pro-German policy, 221, 223–6, 229–30; and Edward's marriage, 222; and Prussian war with Denmark, 223–5; and Franco-Russian alliance, 227; death and funeral, 229, 239–40; and Balkans, 230; proclaimed Empress of India, 230, 237; and Gordon's death, 230–1; restricts Edward, 231–2, 236; remoteness, 234

Victoria, Empress of Germany (Empress Frederick: Princess 'Vicky'), 83–5, 183; and Edward's marriage, 222–3; and England's relations with Prussia, 225–6; as Empress, 230; Kaiser and, 238; Edward visits, 246; illness and death, 246

Victoria Louise, Princess, Duchess of Brunswick and Lüneburg, xvii–xx, 64, 91

Vidov-Dan, Battle of (1389), 281

Viviani, René, 300

Vladikas (Montenegrin bishops), 7

Vladimir, Grand Duke of Russia, 61, 192n, 205n

Vladivostok, 200n

Voigt, William, 114n

Votiniuk, Sergeant Major, 219

Waddington, Mary Alsop King, 173

Wagner, Richard, 87

Waldersee, General Count Alfred von, 91–2, 94–6, 99, 293

Waldersee, Countess Marie Esther, 92–3

Wallachia, 69

Warwick, Frances Evelyn ('Daisy'), Countess of, 268

Wedel-Piesdorf, Baron Georg von, 90

Wiesner, Friedrich von, 296

Wilhelmina, Queen of the Netherlands, 39

William I, Emperor of Germany, 85, 230

William II, Emperor of Germany ('the Kaiser'): daughter's wedding, xvii–xx, 64; on British suffragettes, xxi; deposes Bismarck, 56, 94–5; Ferdinand visits, 58; congratulates Carol of Rumania, 79; power and character, 83, 85, 87–8, 98–100; disabled arm, 83–5, 211; accession, 85, 87; marriage, 88–91; distractions and travels, 89–91; advisers and confidants, 91–4, 114; and Russian treaty, 96; rhetoric, 98–9; 1905 Tangier episode, 101, 176, 255–6; Björkö meeting with Nicholas II,

101–3, 212, 260; strained relations with Edward VII, 103–8, 188, 228, 236, 238, 240, 246–9, 261–2; Queen Victoria on, 104, 228–9; and Boer War, 106, 111, 231; and Alfonso XIII's marriage, 107, 270; and Austrian annexation of Bosnia & Herzegovina, 109–10, 150, 214–15; *Daily Telegraph* interview, 110–11, 262; threatens abdication, 112; and German naval build-up, 113, 248, 261–2, 265; and Junker influence, 113–14; cabinet government, 114–15; preparation for war, 115–16; visits Franz Josef on 60th anniversary of coronation, 152; relations with Italy, 179–80; Alexander III's antipathy to, 188; on Nicholas II's weakness, 198; and Russo-Japanese war, 200–1, 212; Nicholas II dislikes, 201; and death of Queen Victoria, 229; and Edward's accession and title, 240–1; and mother's funeral, 246; and Edward's 1903 tour, 252; attacks Anglo-Japanese pact, 258; fêted at Windsor, 262; entertains Edward and Alexandra (1909), 263–5; alarms George V, 274; and Sarajevo assassination, 284–5, 289; and start of 1914 War, 288–92, 294, 300, 330; Norwegian cruise, 294; praises Pašić's reply to Austria, 307; offers to mediate for Austria, 307–9, 317; and English position at start of war, 312; attempts restraint over war threat, 314–16, 321–2; correspondence with Nicholas II, 314–17, 329; blames Edward for war, 322–3; orders mobilization, 325; telegram to George V, 326–7

William, Crown Prince of Germany, 112

William, Prince of Denmark, 229

Windisch-Graetz, Field-Marshal Albert, 118–20

Witte, Count Sergei Yulievich, 102, 206–9

Wölfling, Leopold *see* Leopold Ferdinand, Duke of Tuscany

Wren Sir Cristopher, 234n

Xenia, Princess of Montenegro, 9–10

Yolanda, Princess of Italy, 172
Young Turks, 148, 261

Zerajić, Bogdan, 279n

Zita, Empress of Austria, 154
Zorka, Queen of Peter Karageorgević of
   Serbia, 8–9, 34, 36
Zuckmayer, Carl, 114n
Zukunft, Die (journal), 87